Counselling for Managers:

an Introductory Guide

by

John Michael Hughes

Published by

BACIE

16 Park Crescent, London W1N 4AP
Tel: 071 636 5351   Fax: 071 436 2624

© John Michael Hughes 1991

British Library Cataloguing in Publication Data
Hughes, John Michael
  Counselling for managers: an introductory
  guide. – (Training books for managers)
  I. Title   II. Series
  658.385

  ISBN 0-85171-094-8

Cover design by Karen Greville-Smith

Printed by Gwynne Printers, Hurstpierpoint, Sussex

Contents

To

Ken Swann

Acknowledgements

In preparing this short book I have been enormously encouraged and assisted by the generous feedback and critical comment I have received from many friends and colleagues, including Frank Ashton, Wendy Bannon , David Charles-Edwards, Carol Christian, Elisabeth Davies, Wendy English, Judith Horsfield, Carol Lomax, Pat Lockley, Fokkina McDonnell, Jim Mercer, Norman Prescott, Vivien Whitaker and Tony Milne. I also wish to thank the following persons for permission to quote from their published work: John Burgoyne, Michael Megranahan, Michael Reddy, Lewis Rushbrook and Derek Torrington.

In particular, the original basis for this booklet was first published in August/September 1989, as a two-part article entitled 'The Case for Counselling' in the 'Gazette' of the Institute of Medical Laboratory Sciences. I am grateful to the Institute and to Roy Owen, Editor of the 'Gazette', for permission to use it.

I should especially like to thank the contributors of the cartoons and diagrams: Gordon Cowan of Manchester Polytechnic, Barry Hutchinson and Bartholomew Leung of Hong Kong Polytechnic, and Philip Pye. The illustrations they have provided go a long way towards relieving the seriousness of the text, and to illuminate many of the main points made.

I owe a special word of thanks to Vera Sorensen and Caroline Berresford, who did the typing.

Finally, I wish to acknowledge all the help and encouragement I have received from my Editor at BACIE, Jill Darling.

As always, final responsibility for the book and any shortcomings it contains rests with me.

A Note on Terminology

In a pure 'counselling' context it is usual to employ the terms 'counsellor' and 'client' to refer to the two persons engaged in the process. In a 'managerial' situation it is more usual to speak of 'manager' and 'subordinate' (or 'colleague', as the case may be). This book follows the precedent established by David Megginson and Tom Boydell in *A Manager's Guide to Coaching* (BACIE, 1979), by using the terms 'manager' and 'colleague' to refer to the two persons meeting in a counselling interview.

Introduction

The Concept of Counselling

My purpose in this brief book is to introduce you to the concept of counselling, and to inform you about its potential and possibilities, problems and pitfalls. I am not attempting to instruct you in how to do it, though I do offer some guidelines for beginners.

Counselling in practice cannot be learned from books, but some initial understanding of what it involves can be a great help in making a start. Just as a working knowledge of accountancy does not make a manager an accountant, neither will reading this book turn you into a counsellor. Both kinds of knowledge simply help a manager to manage better. When specialised assistance is required, the good manager knows when and where to get it.

If you wish to take the topic further, I offer a brief bibliography for follow-up reading and reference at the back of the book.

Communication, Conversation and Management

The essence of counselling is person-to-person communication, in the context of a controlled conversation. American research has demonstrated that the main burden of managerial work is communicational, within a complex network of human relationships (interpersonal and inter-role) which go to make up a working organisation.[1] Likewise, British research confirms that as much as 80% of many managers' time can be spent in oral communication with others.[2]

Managers use communication skills constantly, and you will frequently find yourself in implicit counselling situations with colleagues, whether or not you use the term itself. For you to have some elementary understanding of the counselling process therefore seems quite sensible. You may also wish to develop further the

9

skills of conversational control, which you will find equally useful in other settings, such as the leadership of groups and the chairing of meetings.

Investing in People

A 'counselling' approach to the management of people at work is entirely consistent with the national standard for 'Investors in People', which recognises that it is people who make profits. Time spent counselling colleagues is time invested in *people*, often claimed to be an organisation's most valuable asset.

When approached by colleagues to help with particular problems or opportunities, an informed and skilled response is likely to be much more effective than one based simply on unexamined experience. All of us assume too readily that what 'works' for one person will work equally well for another, and fail to recognise that individual differences are important.

The Need for Training

I cannot emphasise too strongly that to do counselling effectively requires proper training. This of course applies equally to any other occupational practice, including such obviously managerial ones as budgeting, delegation and running a meeting.

However, since the skills employed in counselling are essentially extensions of the social skills which we generally acquire during our upbringing, education and experience, it is all too easy to suppose that these will be sufficient in themselves.

Both experience and research show that this is patently not so, and that indeed great harm can *sometimes* be done by well-meaning but 'amateur' efforts. The wise manager, then, who wishes to add counselling skills to an existing repertoire of 'core competencies', would be well advised to seek specialised training (not necessarily long) in pursuing further development, both personal and professional. I give sources of further information and training at the back of this book.

. . . indeed great harm can sometimes be done by well-meaning but 'amateur' efforts.

Chapter 1

Counselling Considered

The term 'counselling' is commonly misused, much misunderstood, and sometimes shrouded in professional mystique. I shall make an attempt here to 'de-mystify' the concept and to offer you a description of counselling as a process which is accessible to managers, and which you can use effectively in your day-to-day duties.

Sometimes it helps to approach the problem of definition in a round-about way, by saying first what something is *not*, before stating in more positive terms what it actually is. Michael Megranahan writes that: *'Counselling:*

- *is not thinking or acting for another person, nor is it directing them towards a decision*
- *is not repeating cliches about what someone else might do*
- *is more than being sympathetic towards another person's feelings, talking something over or merely the application of techniques*
- *does not impose solutions, opinions, values or judgements*
- *does not minimise, reject or question the worth of what the person wishes to discuss*
- *is not about criticising or manipulating the person.'* [3]

It follows that counselling is *not* primarily about giving advice, telling others what to do, or doing things for them. Nor does it involve boring them with stories about what happened to you in similar circumstances, nor suggesting solutions to their problems based on your own experience – prefaced perhaps by that fateful phrase: 'If I were you . . .'!

Equally, counselling is *not* about delving deeply into people's personalities to discover what happened to them in early childhood, or to lay bare the trials and traumas which have beset them from time to time along life's journey. Such issues will sometimes emerge during the counselling process and may impinge on its outcome, but they are not its primary focus.

Counselling cannot be prescribed for people. It is not a treatment or a technique, to be applied in a 'medical' manner as if someone were sick. Sometimes colleagues who come for counselling *are* sick, a fact which needs to be recognised and dealt with appropriately. But you are not a doctor, and you should refrain from making amateur diagnoses.

Nor should you use counselling for disciplinary purposes, when the aim of the exercise is to correct unacceptable behaviour and perhaps administer a reprimand. In both instances, counselling *skills* may be used quite legitimately to help uncover underlying problems and difficulties; and colleagues may quite properly be *referred* for counselling help, at their own request or at your suggestion, if such action seems warranted.

What is Counselling?

So what *is* counselling? What is this process which sometimes seems so elusive, and so difficult to describe? I take the view that counselling is one of a number of approaches to helping people which have at their core a 'HOT' relationship of *h*onesty, *o*penness and *t*rust, and which have as their central process the practice of 'paying positive attention to people'. This is illustrated in the diagram overleaf (Figure 1) in which *four* such approaches are shown:

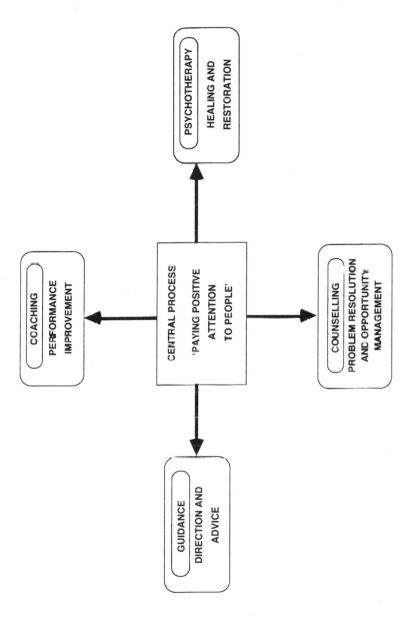

Figure 1: The relationship between counselling and some other helping strategies.

In this book I suggest that the 'vertical' dimension in the diagram, that of coaching and counselling, will be of more immediate relevance for you than the 'horizontal' dimension of guidance and therapy, which you may rightly see as the province of staff specialists, either inside or outside your organisation.

Nevertheless, it is worth pausing for a moment to consider the 'horizontal' dimension, in order to appreciate and understand the practice of counselling more fully.

The British Background

The British tradition in the past has approached counselling from the standpoint of advice-giving, so that the terms 'guidance and counselling' have often been linked in the same phrase. This tradition has developed strongly in an educational setting, giving emphasis, quite properly, to such matters as career choice and occupational selection.

Thus the specialist 'careers counsellor' is to be found in many schools and colleges, undertaking the task as an additional role or as a full-time post; and careers guidance itself constitutes a well-established occupation, with its own extensive literature.

In this and in many other specific situations* the specialised counsellor is likely to be expert in some particular field, and *does* have a very great deal of knowledge which it would be improper to withhold from clients. Offering advice and supplying information therefore do have a proper place here.

The American Approach

The transatlantic tradition is very different. In America, the two terms 'counselling and psychotherapy' are very often linked together and spoken of in the same breath, as if inseparable. To some extent

*eg debt, drug addiction, AIDS, etc: see Megranahan [op cit] for a fuller treatment.

this may be true, in that effective counselling will usually be therapeutic.

Yet an important distinction does need to be drawn between the two, on the dimensions of *time* and *depth*. To take a crude analogy from motor mechanics, counselling may be likened to dealing with daily running problems, and psychotherapy to a 'garage job', requiring major overhaul or even a complete re-build.

Psychotherapy *is* about exploring the depths of someone's personality, if necessary, and confronting the pains and traumas of life, past and present, in such a way that healing can happen. This is highly skilled work, for which extensive training is required. It lies well beyond the scope and competency of most managers, since it takes a lot longer and goes much deeper than everyday counselling can afford.

Conclusion

Counselling as I see it comes somewhere between these two traditions. It contributes via its skills to both guidance and therapy, and has strong connections with coaching in the context of management.

Simply put, it consists of *helping others to help themselves*, in managing their own problems and opportunities. It may be defined more broadly as '*an opportunity to explore, discover and clarify ways of living more resourcefully and towards greater well being*' (British Association for Counselling); or more specifically, to quote Michael Reddy, as a set of personal competencies: '*to help people manage their own problems, using their own resources.*'[4]

Therefore the emphasis lies not on doing things *to* or *for* other people, but on working *with* them, in ways which help them to make constructive changes in their own lives.

Drawing upon both the educational and the medical traditions, I see counselling as essentially an educative process, which offers others an opportunity to reconstruct reality for themselves on better terms for the future than in the present or in the past. It achieves this by entering into supportive relationships of mutual respect which enable others to take full responsibility for their own

'to help people manage their own problems, using their own resources.'

situations, and empowers them to take action in attempting to resolve their own difficulties and exploit their opportunities.

What is a 'Problem'?

I have been told that the Chinese often use two characters together to symbolise a crisis — a combination of challenge and opportunity. So it is with problems, which, as Peter Honey points out,[5] 'come in all sorts of shapes and sizes', and may just as often represent positive challenges to be seized as negative difficulties to be overcome. It is the same with *stress*, which in itself is neutral, but which can be either scourge or stimulant, depending upon how you perceive it.[6]

Counselling can sometimes convey a negative image because the personal problems which colleagues bring to discuss are too easily presumed to be 'deep difficulties', which somehow stigmatise people as being weak, inadequate, or lacking in something. On the contrary, so-called 'problems' often prove to be real opportunities for personal growth and career development. This represents the creative use of counselling as a managerial skill, in contrast to its compensatory function as a remedial therapy.

Examples of 'problematic' issues which colleagues may bring for counselling

(1) Feelings of 'stress' generated at work by various factors (eg work overload or underload, working conditions, responsibilities and relationships).
(2) Fears about personal health, 'burn-out' or breakdown.
(3) Doubts concerning career prospects and promotion possibilities.
(4) 'Personality clashes' with colleagues.
(5) Feelings of being excluded or alienated from particular groups.
(6) Difficulties in coping with critical evaluation from others.
(7) Inability to confront or challenge colleagues in a realistic, constructive way, for fear of unpopularity or social disapproval.
(8) Perfectionist tendencies, leading to unrealistic expectations.
(9) Fear of failure/lack of success.
(10) Taking on too much (or too little) responsibility for others.
(11) A sudden crisis of confidence, following apparent success.
(12) Delayed or resumed grieving, after some significant loss.
(13) Feeling the strains of transition (including loss of relationships).
(14) 'Existential loneliness' (or loss of meaning of life) in someone with 'normal' friends and family.
(15) Retreat into a fantasy world of imagination, as a way of coping with pressure.
(16) Fear that personal losses and private anxieties are becoming more evident to others.
(17) Doubts about continuing competence and ability.
(18) Substance abuse (smoking, drinking, drug addiction).
(19) Financial problems.
(20) Domestic difficulties.

(Adapted from a list compiled by Carol Lomax)

. . . it is imperative that colleagues 'own' their problems

Certainly most problems require some constructive resolution. As distinct from *puzzles* (which have unique solutions), *problems* can often be resolved in a variety of ways, which need to be weighed and carefully considered before a choice is made. It is here that you must exercise the greatest self-discipline, *not* to 'manage' a colleague, or impose a solution of your own. As Peter Honey stresses, it is imperative that colleagues 'own' their problems and take full responsibility for reaching their own solutions in their own way, with their manager's assistance, if it helps.[7]

This is where the skills of counselling are so very different from the usual 'proactive' skills commonly associated with managing, especially the use of 'managerial authority', which in most instances is out of place in a counselling context.

Chapter 2
Counselling in Context

Counselling or Counsellor?

Is Counselling for me?

From this description I imagine that you may perhaps have come to the conclusion that counselling is not for you! You may feel that you have neither the time nor the training for it; that your organisational position prevents you from doing it properly; that the internal culture of your enterprise is not conducive to counselling; and that you lack any personal inclination to engage in it. Michael Reddy gives five reasons why managers may be reluctant to undertake counselling activities:

- *they fear that their assessing/controlling role will be undermined*
- *they believe that a show of sympathy on their part will be exploited by subordinates*
- *they think that being sympathetic with a person means they cannot make any further demands on him or her*
- *they say that their job description does not involve 'social work'*
- *they say they simply don't have the time'*

He then makes the important point that for those managers who really are resistant to counselling as part of the job, the best advice is 'Don't'.[8]

Opportunities for Counselling

Yet within many employment organisations, daily life is full of opportunities for you to make use of counselling skills, without regarding yourself as a 'counsellor' in the specialised sense of that term.

Indeed, there is good reason for you to develop such skills as part of your managerial repertoire, not simply for helping colleagues with personal or professional problems, but also for appropriate use in everyday managerial encounters, such as in face-to-face

conversations, team briefings, committee meetings, formal interviews for staff selection and appraisal, and not least in telephone calls!

Furthermore, a secondary spin-off from counselling can be much personal growth and development for you. Lewis Rushbrook writes:

'Counselling can be undertaken for the very reason that it is such a powerful instrument for personal growth. Its 'plusses' include factors such as:

- *it is a face-to-face relationship – more typical of most management situations than much classroom learning*
- *it is confidential, encouraging greater openness and honesty*
- *it includes and values the manager's feelings*

- *it embraces the 'irrational' dimensions of management, such as culture and style, a 'feel' for which is so essential for success.*[9]

You need not therefore regard counselling with suspicion, or see it as a 'soft option' for which you haven't time.

In fact, counselling another person can be hard work. It is both intellectually challenging and emotionally demanding, and can leave both of you feeling exhausted as well as exhilarated if some progress has been made. 'Emotional and spiritual labour' is not so well recognised or rewarded as other forms of work, physical and intellectual; nor is it generally to be found in most descriptions of managerial work, though it is there by implication.

So do not fight shy of counselling, or of developing the skills which good counselling requires, since its potential rewards to you and your colleagues are considerable, particularly in terms of improved working relationships and 'unblocked' communication channels.

Counselling and Role. Conflict

Managerial Work

I am well aware that you are not employed to be a counsellor, but to occupy a role within the executive structure of an enterprise, to which attach certain attributes of authority, accountability, responsibility and power.[10] Your primary purpose is to achieve the controlled performance of work in the pursuit of corporate goals, be they sectional targets or overall organisational objectives. A good manager is held accountable for the performance of that work to acceptable standards, and is accorded commensurate authority to do it, whilst remaining responsible for the work delegated to or shared with others.

It follows that relationships with other people – including superiors, subordinates, colleagues, clients and customers – are an inescapable part of the job. It is I believe, the *quality* of these relationships which will very largely determine the success of your enterprise, and its effectiveness as a working organisation.

Role Conflict

How then can you resolve the inherent role-conflict posed by the

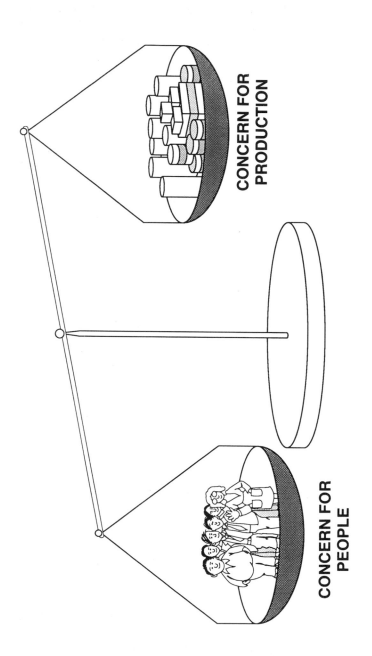

Figure 2: Keeping people and production in balance

need to pursue performance on the one hand, and to care for colleagues on the other? How can you demonstrate both 'concern for people' *and* 'concern for production', to use the terms of the 'Managerial Grid'[11]?

The reality is that inherently this is what you are paid for, what management is 'all about', and what makes managerial work different and difficult. John Burgoyne puts it well:

'One of the special features of managing is that it has to create and define its own task, rather than tackle one that is pre-structured for it, which is the case with non-managerial work.'

He goes on to say that:

'Managerial work is always at the boundary between order and chaos, between what has not been done and what has already been done. Managing is literally a creative activity . . .[12]

Managers are usually well aware of the inherent tensions in their roles, the creative conflicts which they are called upon to manage, between process and task, production and people. They are conscious of this in-built dichotomy to their work and are often able to contain it. They recognise that being available for people does not mean neglecting the task; nor does focusing on the problem mean ignoring the person. Good managers can do both. They can balance these two competing claims, and from the creative tensions between them can often assist colleagues to reach reasoned and responsible resolutions to their difficulties and to exploit their opportunities constructively.

Position Power

It is important here to recognise the *power* dimension which is present in all human relationships, and which in the case of managing is usually institutionalised as *authority*. You will always be in a position to instruct a subordinate, inform a superior, or advise a colleague, and you cannot set aside this authority without acting out of role. Clearly this has implications for such issues as confidentiality and trust (to be taken up again in Chapter 3).

Nevertheless, it is your *availability* to colleagues which matters most. People with problems usually seek help from those whom they perceive intuitively to be open, available and discreet, often demonstrated by a willingness to offer help on other occasions.

For some people, going to see a counsellor still carries some social stigma . . .

Hence your position as a manager can be a distinct advantage. To see one's manager about something is no shame, and can cover a multitude of eventualities.

For some people, going to see a counsellor still carries a social stigma, with assumed implications of inadmissible weakness or personal incompetence. It may still be easier for someone to see their manager (or their doctor, for that matter) about a personal problem rather than admit to a need for counselling.

Taking the Initiative

Indeed, you may well be the one to make the first move. Traditionally, it is the client who approaches the counsellor for help, either self-initiated or by referral. I believe that you can be more proactive than the counsellor, in being on the look-out for signs of ill-health, distress, under-performance or poor working relationships amongst colleagues, which may suggest some appropriate action on your part.

This could be simply an invitation to a colleague to talk, 'without strings', in a way which brings difficulties out into the open, for further discussion if necessary, and without threat of sanctions. Such timely interventions can often defuse potentially explosive situations, or bring to light festering feelings which only get worse if left alone.

Counselling and Culture

Formal or Informal?

It is not necessary for the counselling process to be formalised for it to happen. Indeed, a lot of effective listening and expression of feelings happens quite haphazardly, informally and spontaneously, 'on the hoof', as someone has said, in clubs, pubs, cafes and in the 'corridors of power'.

Any place where people meet, for whatever reason, offers an opportunity for interpersonal exchanges to occur. As Michael Reddy points out:

'a lot of good counselling and helping is done in passing, does not need to take long, does not have to be in a formal setting and does not require a degree to do it.'[13]

Affirming Individuals

Yet for counselling to be recognised and accepted in an organisation as a reputable activity, contributing both to the welfare of its participants and to the enhancement of its performance, then as David Charles-Edwards suggests, a *congruent culture* is needed to support it.[14] By this is meant an internal attitude and approach to organisational participants which values them as people and affirms them as individuals, each with a unique combination of contributions to make and difficulties to deal with.

Such an approach to what is currently called human resource management regards people primarily as assets to be invested in and developed, not as costs to be minimised or cut. Managers too are included here, along with non-managerial employees. Harsh economic realities may dictate unpleasant decisions at times, but that is no reason to treat employees as less than what they truly are: human beings, an organisation's ultimate asset.

Organisational Counselling

An organisational culture which embraces such core values as respect for individuals, the acceptance of feelings as facts (just as much as figures), and the recognition of right relationships as the key to organisational success, is one in which counselling can flourish.

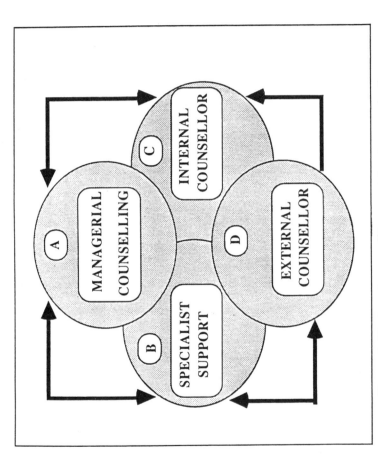

Figure 3: Modes of counselling provision in organisations.
(Adapted from: 'Counselling as a Training Resource', by David Charles-Edwards,.1989[15])

This may find provision in one or more of *four* main modes, as indicated in the diagram on p.28:

A   *Managerial counselling.* Managers use counselling skills in an informed and responsible way, to help colleagues as much as they can, both reactively and proactively, within the constraints of their managerial roles.

B   *Specialist support.* Personnel and other support staff (eg welfare and occupational health workers) in the specialised field of human resource management may have had some basic counselling training and may be able to take up the explicit role of counsellor from time to time, in what Charles-Edwards calls a 'sometimes a counsellor' capacity. [15]

C   *Internal counsellor.* Organisations large enough to do so, and committed to the welfare of their employees, create posts for full-time fully trained counsellors, in much the same way as colleges and universities have done for many years.

D   *External counsellor.* Specialised needs (eg debt, drink, drugs, divorce, etc) are referred to and rely upon external agencies when necessary, in support of internal provision which usually comes first.

These four modes of provision are not alternatives, but complementary, and they help to put the specific contribution which managers can make within a wider perspective.

Counselling and Coaching

Complementary Competencies
In Figure 1, I suggested that coaching is the natural counterpart to counselling in a managerial context. Tony Milne has drawn attention to the considerable degree of overlap between these two activities, and the commonality of skills which they employ. [16]

The main difference is in their primary purposes. *Coaching* is essentially skills-centred and performance-orientated, concerned with reaching required standards of performance at work and with making improvements. *Counselling* is fundamentally person-centred and process-orientated, concerned with the management

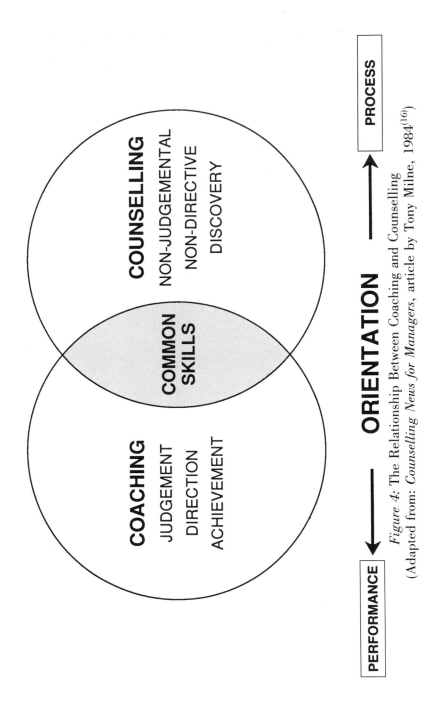

Figure 4: The Relationship Between Coaching and Counselling
(Adapted from: *Counselling News for Managers*, article by Tony Milne, 1984[16])

of problems and opportunities and their potential resolution. *Both* are to do with helping others to help themselves, and are clearly complementary, employing common skills of communication and feedback. This complementarity is expressed in diagrammatic form in Figure 4, which indicates that coaching is likely to involve more judgement and direction than is common in counselling, in which a non-judgemental approach is usually recommended.

A more detailed description of coaching can be found in '*A Manager's Guide to Coaching*' referred to previously.

Chapter 3
Counselling in Process

Types of Interaction

Derek Torrington[17] suggests that most managerial interactions in an organisation fall into one or more of *four* main categories, which he depicts as follows:

- *exposition*, in which the main aim is to impart information to other people, as for example in informing, instructing, briefing and delegating;

- *enquiry*, in which the objective is to elicit information from other people in various ways, such as direct questioning, surveys and searches;

- *joint problem-solving*, in which 'the answer' may not be known in advance by either party, and the aim is to reach a resolution by a process of collaborative exploration and discovery;

- *conflict resolution/accommodation*, in which there is some fundamental opposition of interests between those concerned, calling for negotiation and bargaining, and sometimes for mediation and arbitration.

Counselling clearly comes into the third of these categories. It involves making time and space for people to talk, in confidence, about whatever may be troubling or exciting them, to a colleague who cares. Invariably this will involve more listening than talking on your part, offering feedback rather than advice, and refusing to be judgemental.

Responsibility for disclosure will rest with the person seeking help, whilst responsibility for receiving a colleague's revelations will rest with you, usually in strict confidence. Discretion is required here, since a manager must consider the legitimate interests of the organisation as a whole as well as those of the individual, a point to be taken up again shortly.

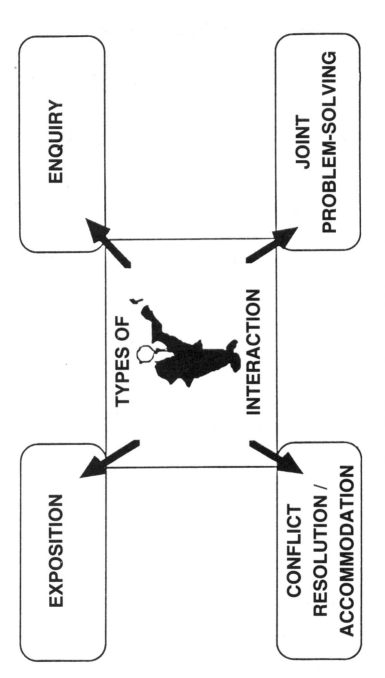

Figure 5: Types of managerial interaction.

Approaching the Encounter

Whilst there is no 'correct' way to conduct a counselling interview, I believe that certain general guidelines can be suggested to facilitate the encounter, based on detailed research findings of what actually works in practice.

Before examining these, it will be useful to consider what I will call 'optimal conditions', which can help a great deal to create a climate conducive to effective counselling.

Creating the Conditions

Ideal conditions for counselling may, perhaps, be a luxury. Nevertheless, you can do much to approximate the environment which full-time counsellors would hope to provide, by paying attention to the following points:

Time and Pace

To do counselling properly requires *time*. It is not something which can just be 'fitted in' between meetings or other hectic activities in your normally busy day. Though much *can* be done 'on the hoof' in mini-counselling sessions of an informal, spontaneous nature, counselling usually works best when it has been planned and properly prepared for.

Appointments are a good basis, made well in advance at a time mutually convenient to you both, and booked in each other's diaries. If this is not possible, you may be able to reschedule your work plans to accommodate a colleague's need, especially in an emergency.

Counselling takes as long as it takes, which cannot be predicted. Yet managerial time is not normally so elastic, and for your own peace of mind you will probably want to work within fairly secure time boundaries so as not to neglect your other duties. It can be very useful therefore to have a clock clearly visible in the place where you meet. Then you can both be aware of the time-space available, agree about when the encounter is likely to finish, and whether or not it can be extended.

I would recommend counselling sessions of no longer than an hour (or less), with the opportunity to make further appointments if necessary. Counselling cannot be rushed, and you will do well to remove all time pressures from yourself and your colleague, if you can, for the duration of each encounter. As Derek Torrington has suggested, your aim should be to create 'an atmosphere of timeless calm'.

Space and Place

Counselling should not be a furtive 'hole-in-the-corner' kind of activity. To work well it needs to create a sense of *spaciousness* for a colleague – sometimes achieved most easily out of doors!

Counselling is also a confidential matter, and requires privacy, free if at all possible from observation and interruption. Your office can often provide a suitable haven – especially if screened by someone who can forestall interruptions and deflect telephone calls.

However, a manager's office is not 'neutral territory', and cannot fail to send signals to colleagues concerning your status, position and power. Things like room layout, size of desk or carpet, privileged furniture and fittings, family photographs and personal memorabilia, all legitimate in themselves, can sometimes detract from the sense of security which you will wish to create for colleagues who come to you for counselling.

Consequently, you may decide occasionally to use some other quiet and convenient location, or seize the opportunity offered by a drink together, a meal in a restaurant, a railway journey, or even a game of golf!

Seating and Signing

Counselling can sometimes be an interpersonal encounter of great delicacy and intimacy. If you remain seated behind a large desk whilst a colleague stands on the other side, or sits in a chair at a lower level, then the confidence and trust which the relationship requires are unlikely to be established.

If the room is big enough, it is very advantageous to set aside some part of it for this kind of personal encounter, equipped with a couple of easy chairs of the same height. In addition, a low coffee table placed alongside (or in between) can serve as a small 'protective shield', so that neither of you feels threatened by the risk of too much intimacy.

If you move from behind your desk to this area, inviting a colleague to follow, this indicates very clearly that you are putting aside other considerations for the time being, to focus fully on your colleague's problem.

The two chairs are probably best arranged facing across each other at an angle of 45° or thereabouts, so that you and your colleague are not confronting each other head-on, which can be quite intimidating. By this arrangement, each of you is left with an 'escape route' directly in front, so that eye-contact need not be maintained indefinitely, and painful emotions can perhaps be contained more easily.

It also helps if both of you can see each other clearly, without one or the other being hidden by shadow or blinded by the glare from a window. Needless to say, the temperature of the room should be comfortable for you both.

All of these 'signs' help to establish a favourable climate in which a positive, helping relationship can flourish.

Contract and Confidentiality

At the outset of the encounter, neither you nor your colleague may know for sure what the problem really is – though both of you may imagine you do. It is important therefore to set aside any preconceptions, and for you especially to approach the issue with an open mind.

I find it helps if a firm framework of agreement can be established, to work on a problem together for as long as it takes to reach a resolution, or until either of you feels that as much as possible has been done, within the constraints of the situation.

This is called *making a contract*, and it is simply an overt way of acknowledging the importance of agreeing terms, somewhere near the start of the encounter, concerning what each of you expects of the other, and what it may be reasonable to hope for.

Here, I should like to repeat the point that in counselling colleagues you do not undertake to solve their problems, or to take responsibility for anything that they may be feeling.

What you are offering is *help*: a listening ear, a reflective suggestion, a probing question, a ventured interpretation. It remains your colleagues' responsibility to receive these responses, and to act upon them accordingly by personal choice in the matter.

Likewise, you cannot abdicate responsibility for the performance-related aspects of your role, and its accountability within the wider organisation, which may occasionally demand some action on your part.

Nevertheless, some of the issues which arise in counselling can be of a highly confidential nature. Indeed, a 'ring of confidentiality' should surround the whole encounter, made plain and explicit from the start. This also applies to any notes or records you may keep, which should always be stored securely, and available to no-one else.

Only in the case of suspected criminal offence or intent, or if the lives of others are seriously endangered, should you consider breaking this rule; and only then to a responsible person (eg senior manager, doctor, police) after informing your colleague accordingly. It is probably wise to indicate at the outset if necessary that implied or intended threats to life, health or safety may constitute an exception clause to this general 'contract of confidentiality'.

Confidentiality will always be a critical issue for the manager, since the other dimensions of the job do not go away whilst you are engaged in counselling. In every instance, discretion will be the key to judgment, since confidence, once betrayed, is broken forever. A colleague has only to hear once, from another colleague, a 'confession' made to you in confidence, for trust in you to be destroyed completely.

If you judge it necessary to disclose elsewhere matters revealed in a counselling interview, then at the very least you should inform your colleague of your intention and obtain his or her agreement, if possible.

Conducting the Conversation

A Model of the Counselling Process

A counselling interview is really a creative conversation, conducted by you and controlled by your colleague. Though differences of status, power and position will inevitably be present and cannot be ignored, you should aim for a non-manipulative relationship based on mutual respect and equality as persons if counselling is to succeed.

Though there is no universally correct way of conducting a counselling interview, rigorous research has shown that effective counselling tends to pass in sequence through certain identifiable *stages*, and to require certain specific *skills*,[18] as indicated in the diagram (Figure 6) overleaf. An understanding of this model may help you to manage the counselling process more effectively. You will then develop your own personal *style*, from experience.

After the first or 'preparatory' stage, the subsequent stages follow the sequence: *feelings* first, then *new thinking*, leading to *attainable actions*. Though there is a natural progression through the stages, I find in practice that they tend to merge with one another, and to overlap to some extent.

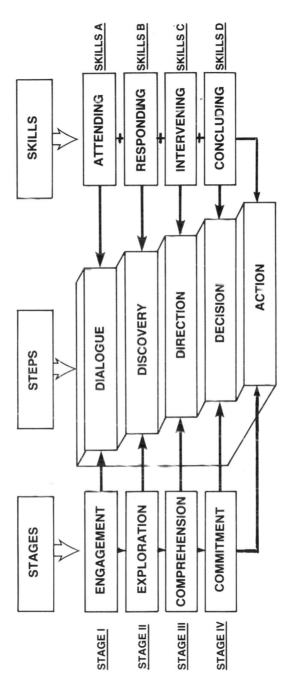

Figure 6: A model of the counselling process: stages, steps and skills.

Likewise, the corresponding skills are cumulative and not associated simply with a single stage. Skills of *attending*, for example, are required right the way through the conversation.

Also, in my experience it is not necessary for all four stages to have happened by the end of a session, or to happen at all, since some colleagues may find the exploratory stage sufficient to satisfy their immediate needs. Having expressed their feelings, and 'got it off their chests' so to speak, they may seek no further help.

Yet if some deeper resolution of a problem is to be achieved, or some opportunity exploited, it is important to complete the sequence at some point in the future (and possibly several times over), since ultimately it is decisions leading to actions which resolve problems.

The Stages and Skills

The four stages of the process, together with their attendant skills, are as follows:

Stage I: Engagement: *commencing dialogue and establishing rapport.*
Question: *'How do you do?'*

The purpose of this preliminary stage is to establish a relationship for helping between you and your colleague, under terms of common agreement and expectation. All the conditions described previously contribute here, in helping to create 'rapport': that mutual sense of personal presence and reciprocal communication which creates a climate of acceptance, security and warmth.

To establish a receptive relationship in which trust can grow may take a little time; but this is well worth spending if successive stages of the counselling process are to prove productive. Colleagues need to feel that you, as their manager, are both 'with' them and 'for' them before they venture to disclose themselves in an open, honest way.

To achieve this reciprocal relationship requires skills of attending, *which continue to be used throughout the encounter.*

Skills A: Attending

Focus on Feelings

Giving undivided attention to another person lies at the heart of counselling. It can of itself often suffice to lighten a load or to resolve a problem, by creating an opportunity for a colleague to discharge pent-up feelings to a receptive listening ear.

This process of 'ventilation' can be doubly productive. Firstly, it can achieve a considerable amount of emotional release, and a lessening of inner tension. Subsequently, this makes space for further feelings and thoughts to come into consciousness, and for new ideas and suggestions to be received.

Until such emotional catharsis has happened, it is rarely possible for rational thought to emerge. Thereafter, a colleague may be enabled to 'move on', as it were, to acknowledge and confront an issue in a new and more realistic way.

You may at first be reluctant to acknowledge a colleague's feelings, or to admit them to the agenda right away, especially if they are negative feelings about yourself or the employing organisation; but it is very important to do this if the counselling process is to proceed.

Posture

In paying attention it helps to adopt a relaxed and open posture, leaning forward slightly perhaps, and maintaining good eye-contact – though not to the extent of a fixed, unwavering stare!

Likewise, 'postural echo' can be useful in creating rapport; that is, unselfconsciously 'pacing' the other person by matching and mirroring to some degree both posture and gesture, and even breathing and tone of voice. However, if you do this too deliberately, it soon becomes mannered and false. The intention is to demonstrate engagement with a colleague, not to mimic him or her, and for this it may not be necessary to use many words.

. . . it helps to adopt a relaxed and open posture . . .

Non-committal 'nodding and grunting' are often enough to confirm that you are attending, accompanied by corroborating movements of your head and hands and the occasional 'echoing back' of your colleague's last spoken words; eg '. . . so I feel quite angry about that'. *'Angry?'*

Body Language

The central skill of attending is that of *listening*. However, being a good listener is not as simple as it sounds. It involves not only hearing, but observation as well, *and* concurrent awareness of your own thoughts and feelings.

Research indicates that less than 20% of direct communication between people relies upon words. The remaining 80% or more is achieved by non-verbal means such as posture, gesture, facial expression and tone-of-voice. The first three of these constitute what is commonly called 'body language' (ie non-vocal means of communication).

You will therefore need to use your eyes as well as your ears when paying attention, to pick up signals sent by your colleague's bodily disposition, movements and mannerisms, adding these to the words you hear.

Mixed Messages

I sometimes find that a colleague's words are saying one thing, whilst all the other signals together are saying something else, quite contrary to the verbal message. This is called 'sending mixed messages'.

Since non-verbal modes outweigh words in the ratio of at least four to one, if the two communications do not correspond then I think it is wise not to place too much

. . . *sending mixed messages*

weight on a colleague's words, but to listen carefully to the 'music' behind them: the so-called hidden agenda; and then to check the accuracy of the verbal statements, pointing out any incongruencies if this is appropriate at the time. It seems to be the case that: 'The body never lies. Only the tongue tells tales'.

Obstacles to Attending

Many things can get in the way of effective attending. Your own body language will send messages to a colleague, which will either enhance or detract from the encounter, no matter what you may say, since it displays your own internal disposition at the time.

You will need to be aware constantly of your own state of *readiness* to receive a colleague and to hear what is being said. If you are pre-occupied by problems of your own, or distracted by concurrent events, you will not have the 'space' within yourself to receive a colleague's revelations, nor to give them that concentration and continuity of attention which good counselling requires.

Likewise, if what a colleague has to say triggers tangential thoughts or anxieties in your own mind, then these should be set aside (or discreetly noted on paper), if the counselling process is to continue.

Lastly, if a colleague's disclosures arouse strong feelings in you, even to the extent of provoking some personal prejudices or past pains, these will effectively block any further constructive work until you can successfully 'own' such feelings and put them to one side. If you cannot do this, then you should say so, and seek help yourself at a later date, to resolve the issues raised.*

*You should not be surprised or alarmed if this happens! It is impossible to predict what personal 'sore spots' a colleague's revelations may touch upon, which may then get in the way of further work together. This is why professional counsellors must constantly be under supervision themselves, to work on such 'emotional imports', if they are to be of continuing help to their clients.

Stage II: Exploration: *discovering the difficulty and defining the problem.*
Question: *'Where are you now?'*

The purpose of this investigative stage is to develop mutual understanding of the issue a colleague brings, to clarify it, define it, and to determine just where a colleague is, ie the present position.

Until this has been recognised and acknowledged, change is unlikely to take place, or new ideas for action considered. Just as emotional release makes way for further feelings to emerge, so a sense of being understood makes movement towards new comprehension possible.

A colleague is looking first of all for a chance to 'tell his or her story' with a view to understanding, which may then promote insight leading to action.

Presenting Problems

Here, it is important to recognise that the problem presented may not always be the 'real' problem. Colleagues come for counselling to talk about themselves: to be received and listened to, accepted, affirmed and understood.

At first they may talk about some issue which seems to be 'bugging' them, for which they are seeking a solution. So it may seem to you too; and you may find yourself tempted to see the situation in the same way, accepting your colleague's definition of the matter at its face value, and perhaps offering some simple solution.

This can sometimes be a mistake. The problems which colleagues bring are usually real ones, requiring resolution; and occasionally they can seem quite simple or straightforward.

To obtain attention however, deeper difficulties are often disguised in socially acceptable clothes: 'acceptable', that is, to both of you, and in keeping with the values, norms and expectations of the surrounding social culture. For example, in present-day British culture, it seems to be socially acceptable to be off work for reasons of ill-health,

So the real problem may be wrapped up . . .

though the causes *of that ill-health could well be found in the work itself or in the circumstances surrounding it.*

Deeper Issues

So the real problem may be wrapped up in something seemingly simple which appears only to require a straightforward solution. This is known as the presenting problem, *and it may well be that both you and your colleague believe it.*

However, my experience suggests that quite often this presenting problem which – to use an angling metaphor – appears like a 'float' on the surface of the water, is tied at some deeper level, below the surface, to something much more important: some 'hook' which is hurting. This deep-down hidden pain or difficulty is the personal problem *which the colleague brings. At a conscious level he or she may be unaware of its existence, or at least be reluctant to admit it, either to him or herself or to others. Yet it may well be the cause of other symptoms on the surface, which will be presented for counselling. Quite often it represents some* relationship *which has gone wrong (or is not working), either in the present or in the painfully remembered past.*

Making the Connection

Where a problem is of this kind, to make the connection is the key to understanding: to uncover a relationship which requires putting right, and to seek ways of righting it. Such relationships could include those which colleagues have with themselves, with each other, with their jobs, their families and friends, and with their managers.

When any important relationship in a person's life is not working, this eventually shows on the surface in some symptom of stress, which inevitably affects performance at work. As a manager you will be concerned to help colleagues to resolve such difficulties, particularly if the 'sore relationship' is within the context of employment: with the job itself, with other colleagues, or even with you personally.

To confront problematic relationships in this way may well be a painful process, and possibly quite costly; yet to do so is likely to be the only way to make progress.

Problems and Opportunities

Not all problems, of course, are of such a negative nature. Some indeed are not so much problems as opportunities for growth in mutual understanding and for the development and deepening of relationships, as mentioned in Chapter 2.

Managers who use counselling skills in a positive, proactive way, without being in the least manipulative or double-minded, can often be surprised at the release of energy and enthusiasm which this engenders in colleagues, as they discover new opportunities and unexpected 'pay-offs' from situations previously perceived as problems.

Skills B: Responding

Whilst listening may be at the core of counselling, it is certainly not its completion, and is not in itself sufficient. To be effective it needs to be listening with empathy, understanding and insight, which in turn need to be conveyed to a colleague. This is called *responding* which means making others aware that they *are* being received, accepted, affirmed and understood.

The skills of responding are very largely those of making suitable *statements* and asking appropriate *questions*.

Statements

I have found the following four types of statement to be helpful in responding to a colleague's disclosures:

- *Paraphrasing:* 'playing back' to someone the gist of what has been said, not 'parrot fashion' but phrased in your own words, to demonstrate understanding of what has been heard, and to check the accuracy of that understanding.

- *Reflecting:* sending back to someone your perception of how that person is feeling, again to demonstrate understanding and to check its accuracy.

- *Focusing:* 'homing in' on some particular point, to help a colleague to be as concrete and specific as possible in what he or she is saying.

- *Summarising:* condensing the story so far into a succinct résumé, to check its accuracy as expressed, heard and understood, and to enable a colleague to move on to the next point at issue.

Questions

Similarly, I have found two types of question helpful in facilitating further exploration and disclosure:

- *Open:* questions which seem more like statements, since they avoid a categorical response like 'Yes' or 'No'. They do not presuppose an answer, nor do they address more than one point at a time. Such questions commonly seem more like invitations to continue talking, commencing with words such as: *'Tell me about . . .'*, *'I notice that . . .'*, or *'It seems as if . . .'*

- *Probes:* direct questions which address a specific point, to provide an opportunity for clarification and confrontation. The purpose in using probes is always to promote a colleague's further understanding, not simply to satisfy a manager's need to know.

Silence

At some point, *silence* may well be the most appropriate response you can make. Silence is searching, and it is sometimes hard to sustain. Nevertheless, the productive capacity of silence can be quite profound.

If you can discipline yourself to 'wait upon' a colleague, by not intruding your own voice for a while, then the colleague can usually be relied upon to tell you all that needs to be known, with only the occasional prompt or question from you. Quite often body language can be sufficient to sustain the conversation: a raised eyebrow, a quizzical smile, a puzzled look, a concerned sigh or a non-committal grunt.

'Silence is searching . . .'

You can only work with what a colleague brings, and forced disclosures generally do no good. On the other hand, disclosures facilitated by silence can often bring colleagues into deeper confrontation with themselves, often with positive consequences. In this way too, you will discover the *power* of active listening, in digging deeper to get the real problem or difficulty out into the open.

Empathy

In responding to a colleague during this stage of exploration, to find out 'where a colleague is' and to identify the problem, *empathy* is all important.

This mysterious word simply means the ability to 'feel with' another person, rather than to 'feel the same as', which is sympathy. It is the capacity to understand another person's position, and to communicate that understanding, without actually joining someone in it. It is a quality of courage coupled with the skills of detached involvement and perceptual sensitivity, which convey to colleagues that you know what it is like to be in their situation, and are available alongside to help.

This is important, since if you permit yourself to be 'hooked' into a colleague's feelings and problems as if these were your own, you will lose all objectivity and cease to be of further use for a while in a counselling capacity. It is all too easy to get 'sucked into sympathy' since this is a natural human response.

Counselling however requires that proper personal and role boundaries are observed and maintained, if the process is to proceed effectively. It requires you to be secure and strong enough in yourself to remain separate from colleagues, whilst entering as fully as possible, by imagination, into their worlds of feelings, meanings and values.

Stage III: Comprehension: *finding new directions towards a desired destination.*
Question: *'Where do you want to be?'*

The purpose of this stage is to discover alternatives for action and to consider the options available. It begins by seeking new perspectives on a problem, thus opening up the possibility of change.

It may be that a colleague does not want to change, in any direction, or is unable to do so without considerable further assistance. If so, then the counselling process may end here. You will not normally wish to force change on a colleague, since the use of managerial authority in counselling is usually inappropriate. Nor will you be able to spend a disproportionate amount of time in lengthy counselling sessions.

More often, when new possibilities for problem-management are realised and new opportunities discovered, you will find that colleagues are energised to pursue them personally as far as they can.

Let me recall here the definitions of counselling I gave earlier and summarised as the process of helping people to help themselves, using their own resources. *A fundamental article of faith held by many who do counselling is that, generally speaking, people have within themselves all that it takes to resolve their own problems, even when some aspect of the situation seems intractable.*

Rescuing

Counselling, like other creative endeavours, is full of pitfalls for the unwary; and a particular danger for the manager is that of rescuing a colleague by assuming personal responsibility for a problem, using such well-worn phrases as: 'Leave it to me' or 'I'll sort it out'.

Occasionally perhaps such action may be appropriate, but as a rule you should resist it. Whilst it may appear to bring immediate relief to a colleague, who may go away muttering thanks, it solves nothing in the longer term. It simply transfers responsibility to you, and leaves your colleague 'stuck' at the same point. Far better to keep the problem where it belongs, in your colleague's hands, having helped him or her to understand it somewhat better.

Referring

At other times, you may come to recognise that a colleague's underlying difficulty is beyond your competence as a manager to contain. Do not be afraid then to suggest that a colleague seeks specialised help elsewhere, either within or beyond the employing organisation (for example, over problems of debt, domestic difficulties, personal ill-health or bereavement).

This is known as referring, which should normally be a joint decision reached by you both, with self-referral by a colleague preferable to any kind of managerial direction. Sometimes, as indicated in Chapter 2, Personnel Departments may be able to offer further help, directly, or in finding sources of specialised counselling.

Work-related or Home-based?

Whether or not a colleague's problem is work-related is at first a side issue. Whilst debt, death, or domestic difficulties may subsequently require or merit help from further afield, you cannot as a manager remain unconcerned about such matters.

It is quite impossible, nor is it realistic or sensible to draw a hard-and-fast line between life at work and life elsewhere, at home, or in leisure pursuits. Life is not lived in compartments, and what happens in one sphere usually produces reverberations in all the others. You engage with your colleagues as 'whole people', and a counselling approach to the problems which beset them provides the best opportunity for a fruitful and constructive discussion of difficulties, leading to new ways of looking at and doing things, and hopefully to new ways of thinking.

Skills C: Intervening

Up to this point in the counselling process, attending and responding will hopefully have established a relationship of honesty, openness and trust between you and your colleague, in which the latter feels free and safe to disclose difficulties in full assurance of a confidential reception and respectful understanding.

For some, this will be sufficient. The opportunity to hear themselves talk out their problems to another person may provide enough relief and insight for them not to need further help. Yet for others some form of *intervention* can be quite crucial in bringing about that shift in thinking required to resolve a problem or to exploit an opportunity.

At this point, to continue listening and responding *without* intervening becomes counter-productive, and both of you can get 'stuck in the same groove'. It becomes important to confront the issues.

Imagination

Imaginative interventions are the creative challenge of counselling. They are risky, since you will be offering a colleague your own understanding and interpretation of a situation, with suggestions (not advice!) as to what he or she might say or do next. They are creative, if you get them right, since the suggestions offered may be just what a colleague needs to make new connections in his or her mind. This usually promotes fresh insight and understanding, and generates considerable forward movement in resolving a difficulty.

Interventions can also be costly, since it takes time to listen in depth to what a colleague is saying, before venturing any insight or interpretation of your own, which may perhaps just 'hit the nail on the head'.

'hit the nail on the head'

Intervention is to counselling what inspiration is to inventing. The intuitive insight, the inspired thought, the logical conclusion, all converge on the critical factor, which is *timing*. It is very much a matter of 'the right word at the right moment', coinciding with your colleague's readiness to receive it.

For this to happen, it is important to maintain constant awareness of what is going on, in yourself and in your colleague, and between you both, in order to seize the appropriate moment when it comes.

Interventions

Interventions can take many forms, including at least the following examples:

- *Reflective summaries:* 'What you seem to be saying is . . .'

- *Suggestive statements:* 'You appear to be very troubled by that . . .'

- *Ventured interpretations:* 'It sounds to me as if . . .'

- *Re-framing thoughts:* 'How about looking at it this way?'

- *Picking out patterns:* 'Putting together what you have said seems to suggest that . . .'

- *Confronting inconsistencies:* 'You say that isn't a problem . . . yet you look very worried to me.'

I think it is important to acknowledge here what you are offering with an intervention; or rather what you are *not* offering, namely a diagnosis of a colleague's difficulty, a prescription for its resolution, or an explanation in terms of your own experience – prefaced by those baneful words: 'It's all because . . . !'

Interventions are intended to help overcome blocks in thinking and to promote shifts in awareness, so that new perspectives may be seen, new ideas considered, and alternatives for action assessed.

However, these cannot be forced. In particular, you should employ probing questions and direct confrontation very cautiously, when you judge that it would help to put the point directly which a colleague might otherwise prefer to avoid. If the pain of confrontation is too great, your colleague will usually deflect the challenge, and you should accept this, recognising that it is your colleague who controls the conversation which you are seeking to conduct.

Self-disclosure, Concreteness and Immediacy

To achieve this depth of encounter with a colleague may require additional skills of sensitivity, concreteness and immediacy, augmented on occasion by a certain amount of well-chosen *self-disclosure*. To know that you too have your problems, pains from the past, and present troubles, without going overboard about them in a reversal of roles, can be very encouraging to a colleague. You also may gain strength from such honest sharing – within the bounds of confidentiality.

Being *concrete* also helps; that is, making specific not general remarks, and staying in the 'here-and-now' of current thoughts and feelings, not allowing colleagues to displace these on to outside events or other people, past, present or future. *Concreteness* is a very useful skill to acquire, since there is in all of us a tendency to avoid direct encounter with the pain behind our particular problems, going off easily into all sorts of tangents and side issues if given the chance to do so.

Likewise, *immediacy* indicates an awareness of and an ability to share personal feelings in the present moment, in a way which reassures a colleague of your genuine concern and willingness to help.

Stage IV: Commitment: *reaching decisions about achievable actions.*
Question: *'How are you going to get there?'*

Goal-Setting

The final stage of the counselling process has to do with helping colleagues to set realistic goals and to work out ways of achieving them. It also involves assessing and sometimes acquiring the resources needed to do so. New insights discovered and new understanding developed during the previous stage need to be translated into action by reaching a decision to do something.

The choice need not be dramatic. There is much to be said for taking small steps to begin with, in resolving any problem or exploiting a new opportunity. Sometimes it can help to describe a desired future state of affairs in terms opposite to those used to represent the problem, 'putting it positively' so to speak, as a goal-statement towards which actions can then be directed.

Equally, it is better not to be over-ambitious in setting goals, the distant achievement of which can seem quite daunting, leading possibly to discouragement and despair. For example, a movement from 'no hope' to 'maybe' can represent a considerable accomplishment in some circumstances.

Learning to be more assertive (not aggressive!) can also bring about rapid change in a positive direction. Above all, Stage IV is a matter of the will: of colleagues' solving their own problems and seizing their opportunities with a determination to do something about them.

Action Plans

Your part here is to help colleagues to make firm commitments and to construct action plans for the future which are specific, realistic and achievable. To do this in your presence can create a further contract for action, *which can be reviewed and revised if necessary at subsequent meetings. There is no need for you to be directive. A simple*

Learning to be more assertive . . .

invitation to a colleague to articulate the next step will often suffice, eg 'What will you do now?'

Reviewing the Resources

In assessing the resources required to achieve change the technique of force-field analysis *has sometimes proved useful; that is, systematically identifying the* restraining forces *and the* facilitating forces *which together, and in opposition to one another, are holding a particular problem in place (see Figure 7).*

By identifying these forces, listing them, and making some estimate of their relative strengths, it may become possible to isolate a few of them for attention and action. Thereafter, by increasing appropriate pressures (or more easily perhaps, by decreasing specific resistances) the point

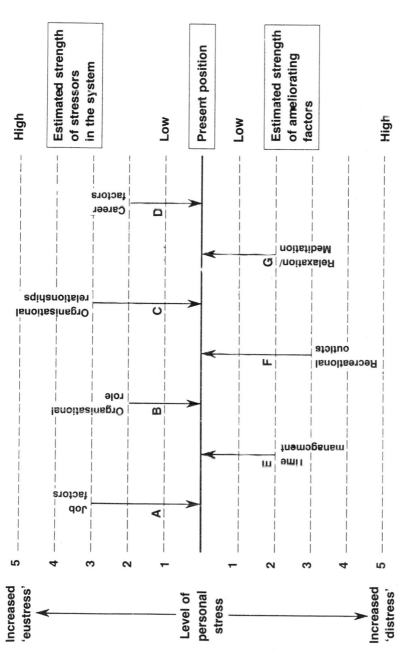

Figure 7: Using force-field analysis to determine levels of personal stress (in this instance, moving towards increased 'distress').

of balance can be shifted between 'hindering forces' and 'helping forces', so that the problem resolves itself.*

'Door-Knob' Syndrome

At this stage, not all colleagues will need the same amount of help. Some may be able to choose well enough for themselves, plan their own actions, and mobilise their own resources. Others may require your continuing support and encouragement, including active intervention to supply additional resources of some kind, as they work through their difficulties and opportunities.

At any point in the counselling process you should be prepared to terminate the conversation, if this is your colleague's choice. However, be wary of the infamous 'door-knob' syndrome – the well known 'By the way . . . ' from a colleague just as he or she is about to leave. This may indicate the real problem which a colleague had come to discuss, but which there isn't time now to disclose. By this neat subconscious ruse, colleagues can get quite a lot of comfort for themselves whilst avoiding the pain of direct confrontation with their difficulties.

It would be wise to seize upon this 'give away' to make another appointment, and not be seduced into spending further time then and there in a hurried and superficial discussion of the real issue.

*It is worth mentioning here that the resolution of one problem quite often makes way for another to emerge, previously unanticipated! This is quite normal, and should surprise no one – though you may feel that 'enough is enough' and that sufficient time has been spent in counselling a particular colleague.

. . . be wary of the infamous 'door-knob' syndrome . . .

Skills D: Concluding

The additional skills needed for the final phase of the counselling process are those required to bring it to a positive conclusion. They include at least the following four:

- *Decision taking:* in collaboration with a colleague, reaching tentative agreements about what positive action a colleague might take to resolve a difficulty or seize an opportunity, having considered and evaluated the options open.

- *Informing and resourcing:* supplying colleagues with information they may need to reach a decision, and taking managerial action if necessary to supply additional resources.

- *Reinforcing and rewarding:* using appropriate feedback (including praise) to encourage and support a colleague in achieving constructive change and 'learning to be different'.

- *Ending the encounter:* being courteous and firm in closing the conversation, giving plenty of advance warning (eg by referring overtly to the time: 'We have about ten minutes left . . .') and concluding on a note of continuity, assuring a colleague of your future availability by offering a further appointment, if necessary.

Continuation

In concluding the conversation it is usually a good idea to 'end before the end': that is to stop the serious talking a short time before the finish, to give colleagues the chance to recover and recollect themselves before departing.

Also I think it is wise not to prolong a counselling conversation beyond the time limit agreed at the start. Far better to break off at a suitable moment, and take up the conversation again at some future date. When this happens you will often find – perhaps to your surprise – that a colleague has 'moved on' quite considerably from the

. . . give a colleague a chance to recover . . .

position he or she described previously. The problem has 'continued to cook' during the intervening period, a testimony to the effectiveness of the counselling process.

Chapter 4

Credentials for Counselling

If you have read thus far you may be forgiven for supposing one of two things about counselling, both equally mistaken:

(a) that it is all common sense, easy and obvious; so what is all the fuss about?

(b) that it is all too technical and difficult, and takes too much time; so why spend further energy on it?

Neither of these responses is realistic. Counselling *does* build on common social skills which most people develop to some degree during their lives; but it requires more than common sense to do it well. Indeed, as I said at the start, well-meaning but uneducated common sense can sometimes do more harm than good; and unskilled counselling *can* occasionally cause damage. Nevertheless, it is not necessary to become a technical expert to do 'general purpose' counselling; and the development of counselling skills *is* well within the competence of many people — including managers.

As I suggested in the Introduction, you may already be well on the way to realising this part of your repertoire of 'core competencies', and an investment in some further training to refine it is likely to prove quite profitable. What you are then in a position to offer to colleagues is simply a service of listening and befriending, supplied with sensitivity and skill, and backed up by specialist resources if required.

Qualifications

What qualifications then should you look for, if you wish to develop yourself further in this field? The immediate answer is 'None', as a manager you are not seeking to become a professional counsellor, accredited perhaps by a national body or licensed to practise by a degree or a diploma.

It is more a question of *qualities*, which you should look for in yourself, or in others whose development you may be supervising. To repeat Michael Reddy's warning, if you are not keen to engage in counselling then maybe it is best left to others. (Whether in reality you can fully avoid it is another matter. The nature of managerial work indicated in the Introduction rather suggests otherwise.)

Qualities

The consensus of research on counselling seems to suggest that beyond knowledge of the counselling *process* and the acquisition of counselling *skills*, the personal *qualities* of the counsellor count for more than anything else in the success of the process. What then, *are* these qualities?

The research literature is full of lists of enviable attributes, some bordering on moral characteristics, some approaching skills, which rather suggest a paragon of such virtue that no manager (or counsellor, for that matter) could hope to emulate! Perhaps the most which you can do is hope to *aim* for some of them, and to be grateful for those positive aspects of personality which by nature you seem to possess.

I describe below *four* attributes which seem to be necessary for successful counselling:

- *Authenticity*, sometimes referred to as 'genuineness': a quality of reality and reliability, trustworthiness and integrity.

- *Approachability*, that is a willingness to be of assistance, to put yourself at a colleague's service and disposal, sometimes to the detriment of other priorities, putting people before things.

- *Acceptance*, including non-possessive warmth towards others and a liking for people generally, coupled with an ability to be tolerant, discreet and sensitive.

- *Respect*, a non-judgemental attitude of support and encouragement which values others for themselves, 'warts and all', and distinguishes the person from the problem.

These are four basic qualities or characteristics which good counsellors require, and which can be cultivated by practice and training, including that essential element: *feedback* from others.

To these four, Michael Reddy adds a fifth:
- *Self-knowledge*, to the extent of knowing your own gifts and abilities, competencies and capacities, strengths and limitations, in a realistic, non-self-conscious way.

Use of the 'Self' in Counselling

Developing self-awareness is a life-long process, which can sometimes be painful but is well worth pursuing. As I suggested earlier, counselling as an approach to managing is just as likely to benefit you as it is your colleagues.

Michael Reddy writes: '*Counselling is in itself a tremendous education in living*'. He goes on to say: '*The best starting point for counsellors is to become involved in counselling, to learn to use themselves as the main tool and then to be aware of how the process is affecting them, and how they can improve.*'[19] It is this 'use of the self' in the service of others which constitutes the core of counselling.

Accountability, Supervision and Support

Like other aspects of managing, counselling colleagues is an activity which you may undertake as part of your contractual role. You undertake it personally, but within the framework of support and supervision which the employing organisation provides.

Qualified counsellors normally submit their work with clients to regular scrutiny, known professionally as 'supervision'. You are more likely to have your performance at work subject to regular 'appraisal'. Whatever the title, the process is essentially the same: that of 'rendering an account of your stewardship to an authorised other', with the opportunity to receive corrective feedback which may help to improve future performance.

Despite this similarity, the practice of accountability differs for managers and for counsellors. Performance appraisal does not intrude upon the contract of confidentiality which you may have with colleagues; nor does it happen as frequently, as a rule, as the meetings between a professional counsellor and a supervisor.

There is need for discrimination here. You may need to find alternative sources of support for yourself (and supervision for your counselling work) if that forthcoming from your own organisation is unsatisfactory or insufficient.

Such sources could include a mutual arrangement with a managerial colleague, on the basis of what is sometimes called 'peer supervision'; or they could involve external agencies to which you may turn from time to time to meet your own needs, such as some of those mentioned at the end of this book. This last point is important, since I cannot stress too strongly that if you are not taking proper care of yourself, then you will hardly be in a position to help others.

These twin themes of accountability and support are brought into particularly sharp focus by the practice of counselling, since without both it is likely to fall into disrepute. Within a working organisation, it is too easily assumed that the framework provided will be sufficient − until there is a casualty, and someone (a manager, maybe) 'slips through the net'.

The Payoff

Among the many benefits which can accrue from the appropriate use of counselling skills at work, Michael Megranahan lists the following:

'● *protection of the organisation's investment in people*

● *improvement in productivity*

● *reduction of accident, sickness and absenteeism rates*

- *improvement in decision making, group cohesiveness and cooperation*
- *improvement in the quality of communication*
- *provision of a mechanism for individual growth and development*
- *release of management time*
- *contribution to an environment of trust and openness.* [20]

Whilst not all of these may immediately be apparent to you (especially the release of your time!), nevertheless it will be the *cumulative* effect of counselling on the quality of working relationships in your organisation which will eventually show itself through indicators such as these.

In particular, the incidence of excessive *stress* and stress related conditions, from whatever cause, is likely to diminish, perhaps quite considerably. As a manager, you do not have to 'do it all' yourself, as I indicated earlier (Chapter 2). Yet you can make a unique contribution from your position as a manager, which perhaps no one else can offer. You will be for some the one person they feel able to turn to in a time of trouble, or when some unforeseen opportunity arises. It puts you in a very privileged position.

Do not assume that counselling is easy work! When you undertake it seriously, you may be surprised to discover how intellectually taxing and emotionally demanding it can be. Yet when it works, and works well, it can be infinitely rewarding, and well worth the time, training and trouble it has taken to be of service to others.

References

1 Mintzberg, H: *The Nature of Managerial Work*, Harper & Row, 1973

2 Stewart, R: *Managers and their Jobs*, Macmillan, 1967

3 Megranahan, M: *Counselling*, Institute of Personnel Management, 1989

4 Reddy, M: *The Manager's Guide to Counselling at Work*, Methuen, 1987

5 Honey, P: *Can You Spare a Moment?*: The Counselling Interview, Video Arts Ltd, 1987

6 Hughes, J M: *Stress – Scourge or Stimulant?*, Nursing Standard, Vol 5; Oct 17 1990

7 Honey, P, op. cit.

8 Reddy, M, op. cit.

9 Rushbrook, L: Editorial in: *Counselling News for Managers*, CEPEC, June 1989

10 Hughes, J M: *Authority, Accountability, Responsibility and Power*, The Training Officer, May 1988

11 Blake, R R & Mouton, J S: *The Managerial Grid III*: Gulf Publishing Co, 1985

12 Burgoyne, J: *Creating the Managerial Portfolio: Building on Competency Approaches to Management Development*, Management Education and Development, Spring 1989

13 Reddy, M, op. cit.

14 Charles-Edwards, D: *Counselling as a Training Resource*, The Training Officer, April 1989

15 Charles-Edwards, D, op. cit.

16 Milne, A R: Article in: *Counselling News for Managers*, CEPEC, June 1984

17 Torrington, D P: *Face to Face in Management*, Prentice-Hall, 1982

18 Egan G: *The Skilled Helper*, Brooks/Cole, 1st edn 1975, 2nd edn 1982

19 Reddy, M, op. cit.

20 Megranahan, M, op. cit.

Brief Bibliography for Further Reading

1 For a brief general introduction to employment counselling, see: Einzig, H A, Evans, R: *'Personal Problems at Work'*, British Association for Counselling, 1990.

2 For an excellent audio-visual introduction to managerial counselling, see: *'Can You Spare a Moment?'*, Video Arts Ltd, 1987, with accompanying text (of same name) by Honey, P.

3 For a wider treatment of the managerial context of counselling, see: Torrington, D: *'Management: Face to Face'*, Prentice-Hall, 1991.

4 For a deeper treatment of the skills required for effective managerial counselling, see: Reddy, M: *'The Manager's Guide to Counselling at Work'*, Methuen, 1987.

5 For an in-depth examination of the process and skills of counselling, see: Egan, G: *'The Skilled Helper'* (4th edn), Brooks/Cole, 1990.

6 For a detailed treatment of interpersonal skills in any setting, see: Hargie, O, (ed): *'A Handbook of Communication Skills'*, Croom Helm, 1986.

7 For a detailed examination of non-verbal communication, see: Pease, A: *'Body Language'*, Sheldon Press, 1984.

8 For a specialised examination of the specific skills of process intervention, see: Heron, J: *'Helping the Client'*, Sage, 1990.

9 For a general treatment of employment counselling and related topics, see: de Board, R: *'Counselling Skills'*, Wildwood House, 1987.

10 For a broad treatment of counselling applied to specific circumstances, see: Megranahan, M: *'Counselling: a Practical Guide for Employers'*, IPM, 1989.

11 For a general overview of counselling from several sources see: Dryden, W, Charles-Edwards, D and Woolfe, R: *'Handbook of Counselling in Britain'*, Tavistock/Routledge, 1989.

12 For a stages and skills approach to training for counselling, see: video-pack: *'Counselling at Work'*, NACAB, 1988.

13 For a training package on counselling skills for managers, see: video-pack: *'Are You Really Helping?'*, CEPEC, 1988.

14 For a comprehensive overview of the subject of 'stress', see: Looker, T and Gregson, O: *'Stresswise'*, Hodder & Stoughton/Headway, 1989.

Sources of Further Information and Training

BAC (British Association for Counselling)
1 Regent Place, Rugby, Warwicks CV21 2PJ
(Tel: 0788 578328)

BACIE (British Association for Commercial & Industrial Education)
16 Park Crescent, London W1N 4AP
(Tel: 071-636 5351)

CEPEC (Outplacement, Training, Career Development Counselling)
67 Jermyn Street, London SW1Y 6NY
(Tel: 071-930 0322)

EAR (Employee Advisory Resource)
Brunel Science Park, Kingston Lane, Uxbridge UB8 3PQ
(Tel: 0895 71155)

ICAS (Independent Counselling and Advisory Service)
PO Box 615, Aspley Guise, Milton Keynes MK17 8DB
(Tel: 0908 582477)

IPM (Institute of Personnel Management)
IPM House, 35 Camp Road, Wimbledon, London SW19 4UX
(Tel: 081-946 9100)

NACAB (National Association of Citizens Advice Bureaux)
115-123 Pentonville Road, London N1 9LZ
(Tel: 071-833 2181)

VIENNA SPIES

ALEX GERLIS

STUDIO 28

Published by Studio 28, 28 Haymarket, London SW1Y 4SP.

ISBN: 978-1-78292-557-6

Also by Alex Gerlis

The Best of Our Spies

The Swiss Spy

The Miracle of Normandy (Kindle Single)

Alex Gerlis

Contents

The author

Alex Gerlis was a BBC journalist for more than 25 years before leaving to concentrate on his writing. In 1994 he helped to produce the BBC coverage from Normandy of the 50th anniversary of D-Day, an event that inspired his first novel, *The Best of Our Spies* (2012).

His second novel, *The Swiss Spy* (2015) is also an espionage thriller set in the Second World War and based on real events. *The Swiss Spy* is a prequel to *The Best of Our Spies*, with the plot revolving around the German plans to invade the Soviet Union in 1941. Both books have featured prominently in the Amazon bestseller charts and between them have received more than 1,200 Amazon reviews. He is also the author of *The Miracle of Normandy*, published in 2014 as a non-fiction Kindle Single.

Vienna Spies features a number of characters from *The Swiss Spy*, notably Major Edgar (who also appears in *The Best of Our Spies*) and the Soviet agent Viktor Krasotkin.

Alex Gerlis lives in London, is married with two daughters and is represented by Gordon Wise at the Curtis Brown literary agency. Now that his team has finally been promoted back to the Football League, he is happy to admit to being a supporter of Grimsby Town – having first seen them play even before England won the World Cup.

Facebook.com/alexgerlisauthor
Twitter: @alex_gerlis
www.alexgerlis.com

List of main characters

Rolf Eder
Austrian, British agent. Alias: Gerd Schuster

Katharina Hoch
German, British agent. Alias: Anna Schuster

Edgar
British intelligence officer

Sir Roland Pearson
Downing Street Intelligence chief

Christopher Porter
Edgar's boss

Basil Remington-Barber
MI6 agent in Switzerland

George Whitlock
Former head of MI6 in Vienna

Crispin Meredith
MI6 trainer

Fowler
MI5 officer at Pentonville

Alex Gerlis

Neville Ponsonby
MI6 agent in Moscow

Vernon Wanslake
British spy in Vienna

Sister Ursula
Nun and British spy in Vienna

Viktor Krasotkin
Russian spy master. Alias: Otto Schneider

Ilia Brodsky
Krasotkin's boss

Johann Koplenig
Chairman of the Communist Party of Austria

Irma
Secret communist and friend of Viktor in Vienna

Paul the plumber
Secret communist in Vienna

Frieda Brauner
Rolf Eder's fiancée and member of Hades resistance cell

Vienna Spies

Joachim Lang
Member of Hades resistance cell. Codename: Acheron

Ernst Lang
Father of Joachim Lang

Manfred Becker
Member of Hades resistance cell. Codename: Styx

Hans
Schoolboy, member of Hades resistance cell

Ján Kuchár
Skipper of Slovak coal barge

Alois
Member of Hades resistance cell at Heinkel factory

Franz Josef Mayer
Former member of Hades resistance cell

Wolfgang Fischer
Former member of Hades resistance cell

Alexei Abelev
NKVD officer

Alex Gerlis

Hubert Leitner
Prominent Austrian politician

Frau Graf
Owner of safe house in Währing

Frau Egger
Concierge in Leopoldstadt (son: Otto Egger)

Walter Baumgartner
German spy at Pentonville Prison

Geoffrey Hayfield-Smith
Baumgartner's lawyer

Wilhelm Fuchs
Contact of Walter Baumgartner in Vienna

Johann Winkler
Manager of hat shop

August Otto Unger
Lawyer and former schoolmate of Rolf Eder

Wolfgang Plaschke
Manager of Bank Leu in Vienna

Vienna Spies

Franzi Landauer
Friend of Frieda Brauner. Alias: Anna Wagner

Karl Strobel
Vienna Gestapo officer

Strasser
Vienna Gestapo officer

Doctor Rudolf
Vienna Gestapo doctor

Franz Josef Huber
Head of Vienna Gestapo (to December 1944)

Rudolf Mildner
Head of Vienna Gestapo (from December 1944)

Andreas Schwarz
Vienna police officer

Dr Peter Sommer
Nazi doctor at children's hospital

Father Bartolomeo
Vatican priest

Sir Percy
British diplomat to the Vatican

George Harman
Surgeon, London

Captain Henry Steele
5th Infantry Regiment, US Army

Montse
Spanish prisoner at Mauthausen

Marie
French prisoner at Mauthausen

Yulia
Russian prisoner at Mauthausen

Vienna Spies

Alex Gerlis

Prologue

Zürich and Linz, March 1944

'Remember, you're supposed to be married to each other, so please act accordingly,' said Basil Remington-Barber. 'Don't give the appearance of being strangers. According to your paperwork you've been married for six years now so one would expect the occasional argument.' He paused to allow himself a little chuckle 'In fact, I can assure you from personal experience that a few cross words every now and then are par for the course!'

The MI6 agent's parting advice was given as they stood at the back of the railway station in Zürich, waiting for the Munich train to board. They had found a quiet spot just along from a kiosk selling newspapers.

At that moment the locomotive on the platform nearest to them let out a loud whistle and a thick cloud of white steam rolled towards them. When it finally ebbed away, Remington-Barber had gone. Rolf glanced around looking for him but Katharina reached out for his arm and pulled him close to her.

'Come on,' she said. 'Let's go to our platform. Smile and laugh occasionally. Maybe you should carry both suitcases. Here, let me straighten your hair.'

***

'She's good and she's brave,' Remington-Barber had assured him in the safe house a few days previously as Rolf struggled to absorb the news that he'd been married since 1938 to someone he'd yet to meet. 'She was actually our agent in Stuttgart, but you never met. She's German but has been in Switzerland since 1941, so for the purposes of her identity she's a Swiss-German, from Zürich. You have a Swiss passport too. Your cover story shows you met in 1936 and married in 1938. You've all of the paperwork for that – and in addition her nursing accreditation goes back to 1932. If anyone bothers to check those records they'll stand up to some scrutiny, though of course one would worry if someone felt the need to check things out to that extent. When you arrive in Vienna, this chap Wolfgang Plaschke will meet you and sort things out.

'The important thing,' he slapped Rolf's knee hard as he made the point 'is for you both to have utter confidence in your cover story. If you believe it then other people are more likely to.'

***

They were aware the initial part of their journey would be the most difficult: crossing the border into Germany would be the first test of their new identities. They'd found themselves in a six-seater compartment with two elderly Swiss ladies and an overweight German businessman. The train came to a noisy halt at Schaffhausen railway station, just on the Swiss side of the border.

The Swiss border guards came through first, checking everyone's papers and were followed into the compartment by the Germans: two uniformed policemen and a Gestapo officer in plain clothes who asked the two Swiss ladies the purpose of their visit to the Reich. *To visit an older sister who lives near Munich.* The

Gestapo officer nodded, returning their passports to them. Everything was in order with the businessman, too, who exchanged enthusiastic 'Heil Hitlers' with the Germans.

'Have you ever visited Vienna?' he asked Rolf.

Rolf shook his head. The Gestapo officer was a small man with an unusually flat nose, and he constantly fidgeted with his collar. He checked Rolf's passport and nodded.

'And the reason you're visiting the Reich?'

'Work. I'm employed by Bank Leu in Zürich and I've been transferred to Vienna. My wife is a nurse and…'

The Gestapo officer handed Rolf's papers back to him and turned to his wife, who handed her passport over. He flicked through her papers, running his finger under his collar as if trying to loosen it. 'Very well then,' he announced, and with a snap of the head he turned on his heels and left the compartment, followed by the two men in uniform.

Katharina squeezed Rolf's knee gently and smiled briefly, and they both made a concerted effort not to look too relieved. A minute later, though, they heard shouting in the corridor outside their compartment and movement further down the carriage. The small Gestapo officer appeared in the doorway of their compartment looking agitated.

'You!' he was pointing at her. 'Come with me!'

Rolf opened his mouth to say something and felt her hand grip his knee tightly, her nails digging through the material of his trousers.

'Come on quick. Leave your bag, hurry up.'

Rolf stood up.

'No! You stay there, only her.'

The two Swiss ladies did their best to avoid looking at Rolf while the German businessman smiled awkwardly. Rolf shifted over to the window seat. He could just see three or four German police officers running across the tracks towards the train. There was the noise of slamming carriage doors and shouting further down the train.

Rolf tried to order his thoughts: evidently she'd been arrested and it was surely only a matter of time before they came for him. The train was still in Switzerland, though only just. As far as he could tell, all the activity was taking part in the front of the train – the part closest to Germany. If he slipped out of the carriage now and moved towards the rear he may be able to escape. It would mean abandoning his companion but what was he meant to do: wait to be arrested with her? He peered out of the window, but couldn't see anything. There was still a commotion further down the train and he decided to leave the compartment, at least to see what was going on. The other passengers would expect him at the very least to wonder what had happened to his wife.

He looked down the corridor and at the end of the carriage saw a German policeman, who pointed at him. 'Get back in your compartment!'

'But my wife... I was...'

'I said, get back in!'

Rolf turned towards the other end of the carriage. A Swiss border policeman was standing there, blocking any exit and nodding towards Rolf, as if to say he should do as he was told. Rolf stumbled back into the compartment, frantic with worry. He felt a wave of fear come over him and there it remained. Two hours out of Zürich, what kind of a mission is that? *A failure, an utter disaster.*

He caught the German businessman looking at him. 'I don't understand what's going on! This must be a misunderstanding.' He did his best to allow what he hoped sounded like an irritated laugh pass his lips.

The businessman shrugged and suddenly became very interested in a magazine he was holding. There was more noise coming from down the carriageway, approaching his compartment. They were coming for him. He shouldn't have remained in the compartment. Surely the Swiss border policeman couldn't have physically prevented him from leaving the train?

Katharina swept into the compartment, a German policeman behind her repeating 'thank you, thank you'. She smiled sweetly at Rolf and the others in the compartment, and sat down next to the man who was meant to be her husband, kissing him softly on the cheek. As she did so the train coughed into life and lurched forward. Rolf looked at her quizzically. 'Are you alright?'

'Yes, thank you dear. An old man had collapsed in a carriage towards the front of the train. They remembered I was a nurse, so asked me to help before the ambulance arrived. I made him comfortable.'

She smiled again and patted Rolf on the thigh and he placed his hand on hers, keeping it there until they reached Munich.

***

At Munich station they had just enough time buy some food

before finding the right platform for their connection to Linz, where they arrived shortly after 6.00 that evening. They found a hotel near the river that looked as if it had been plucked from a glade in the Black Forest. After dinner they returned to their room and sat by the window: they turned off the lights but opened the curtains. There was enough light from the moon for them to look out over the river, the city and the countryside beyond that. They sat there for a while, the previously unspoken tension now evident. In turn they shot glances at the double bed, the only one in the room. They were avoiding looking at each other.

'I'll sleep on the chair,' said Rolf eventually. 'You have the bed.'

She frowned. 'It'll be too uncomfortable, you won't get any sleep. You sleep on top of the bed. I'll get you a couple of blankets.'

'Are you sure? I'll keep these clothes on, obviously.'

She nodded, the only sound the distant rush of water.

'It's a clear night,' said Rolf.

'Possibly too clear: in Stuttgart we used to call these good nights for the bombers.'

Rolf scanned the sky. 'It does look as if Linz has been bombed quite a bit,' he said. 'Maybe they're targeting it because it's Hitler's home town?'

He paused. 'That's the Danube, you know,' he said, pointing at the river. 'It's hard to believe it's the same river that flows through Vienna. It's so much narrower around here – like a stream in comparison.'

'Ah, the Danube,' she said. 'It seems such a romantic and mysterious river. Perhaps we could sail on it tomorrow from here to Vienna and arrive in style!'

They both laughed, the tension of the day lifting just a little.

***

Their arrival at the Westbahnhof in Vienna the next morning was not in any kind of style. A troop train had arrived just before them – Wehrmacht soldiers apparently en-route to the east – and the station was a heaving mass of ill-tempered people pushing in different directions. A group of emaciated labourers in what looked like prison uniform were repairing a damaged wall at the front of the station; some Hitler Youth hurried past them; and they were jostled by a porter pushing two enormous suitcases on a rickety trolley.

As arranged, they waited for Wolfgang Plaschke in the ticket hall, which was jammed with people and so noisy they could hardly make themselves heard. Katharina leaned and shouted in Rolf's ear.

'I said… how on earth will he recognise us? There are so many couples in here.'

'I know,' said Rolf. 'Maybe he thought it'd be quieter at this time.'

They waited patiently for half an hour, having eventually found a vacant bench to sit on. A smartly dressed man appeared in front of them, asking if they might be Herr and Frau Schuster? It was Rolf's new boss, greeting them in a formal manner.

Twenty minutes later they were climbing to the top floor of a small apartment block on Ungargasse in Landstrasse, the 3rd District. Herr Plaschke explained the apartment belonged to his mother-in-law, who was now in a nursing home.

'These days, if a home's left empty for too long it can be appropriated by the authorities, so it makes sense for you to live here. My wife hopes her mother will be able to return one day, but I very much doubt it: she hardly knows who we are when we go to visit her these days.'

***

Herr Plaschke took Rolf for a walk to show him where the bank he'd be working at was based. He returned to the apartment on Ungargasse later that afternoon. His new wife called him into the kitchen, where she turned on the taps.

'I've checked out the place thoroughly, as Basil instructed.' She was speaking quietly against the sound of the water and Rolf had to lean in very close. When their shoulders touched, she didn't flinch. Rolf noticed a distinctive smell of perfume, one so sweet he could taste it on his lips. 'I can't find anything out of order: I'm sure there aren't any recording or listening devices. But I do think any conversations we have about operational matters should be conducted like this, or if we go out for a walk. Do you agree?'

Rolf nodded. Remington-Barber had told them as much.

'Is the bank very far?'

'Not at all: quite a pleasant walk actually,' said Rolf. 'Being back in Vienna's so strange: part of me feels at home, but when I see the troops it's terrible. Plaschke said he'll take me to the employment office to sort out my permit on Monday, then both of us will need to go to another office – he's given me the address –

within two days to make sure all our paperwork's in order. We'll be given identity cards, then we need to register at the Swiss consulate.'

It was just before 11.00 that night when she said she was going to bed. She walked out of the lounge and held the door open for Rolf. He followed her then stood in the little hallway, hesitating.

'Perhaps, um… it'll be best if… I tell you what, I'll take one of the pillows and a couple of blankets, and maybe if I sleep in the lounge – on the sofa?'

Katharina paused for no more than a second or two before fetching some blankets and pillows for Rolf.

'So when do you think we should… you know…?' he said as she handed them to him.

'Do you mean make contact?'

'Yes,' said Rolf. 'And the other matter.'

She shrugged. 'They told us to wait, didn't they – until we're sure it's safe.'

'I know,' said Rolf. 'The problem is I can never imagine feeling safe again in this city.'

Chapter 1

Vienna, August 1941

On paper, Vernon Wanslake was the perfect spy. The more
optimistic types in London certainly thought so. *Mother's from
Salzburg... speaks German with a proper Austrian accent, bright
young man...* they were quick to point out. *But British through and
through... his father's one of us, no politics...* they reassured each
other. *Harrow and Sandhurst... family go to church...* There was a
strong emphasis on that last part, just in case anyone wondered
what kind of émigré he was.

Edgar did his best to point out that espionage is mostly carried
out on the dark streets of hostile cities rather than on paper and,
in his opinion, Vernon Wanslake wasn't quite ready to be sent on
to any streets yet. *I'm not convinced... he's still a bit edgy... needs a
few more months... prone to panic.* But the Germans were halfway
to Moscow and MI6 had precious few agents operating in
Occupied Europe, so Edgar wasn't allowed the luxury of a few
more months. Vernon Wanslake had been dropped into Slovenia,
crossed the border near Klagenfurt and had made his way up to
Vienna.

His cover was decent enough, though Edgar did point out
that was only half the story. The person carrying it needed to be
convincing too. Vernon Wanslake was now Karl Urach, a doctor
from Innsbruck, who was in Vienna for a few days training at the
main teaching hospital. *Gives him a week or two in the city,* they
assured Edgar. *Should be enough for him to see what's going on,*

23

rekindle a few fires, make some contacts, slip out again...

Things went wrong for Vernon Wanslake as soon as he entered Vienna early one August morning in 1941. The house in Brigittenau he'd been assured had a sympathetic landlady and a room for him to stay turned out to have neither. His fallback was a discreet hotel in Alsergrund, the kind where a doctor visiting the nearby hospital would stay. But no sooner had he entered the hotel's small but smart lobby than it became apparent the hotel's main patrons were now SS officers, most accompanied by ladies noticeably younger than themselves.

So Vernon Wanslake walked through the Innere Stadt towards the Danube, trying hard to control his fear and act as normally as possible. He paused for a while by the banks of the Danube Canal, smoking half a dozen cigarettes as he wondered what to do. He realised he had no alternative.

'You use this number only in an emergency, you understand?' George Whitlock had told him at his final briefing. 'It's not for if you've run out of money or fancy a friendly chat.'

Edgar had been even blunter: as they'd left the briefing he'd taken him aside. 'Whitlock shouldn't have given you that contact. Just remember, it's only for the direst of emergencies. There'll be hell to pay otherwise.'

Vernon Wanslake decided his predicament did constitute the direst of emergencies, so he walked to Wien Mitte station and found a payphone near the left-luggage office. 'Only ring this number between 2.00 and 4.00 in the afternoon,' Whitlock had told him when he'd made him memorise it. The telephone rang for longer than Wanslake was comfortable with before it was answered by a female voice, sounding out of breath.

'Hello.'

'I've a bible that needs repairing: a family bible.'

A slight pause, the breathing on the other end of the line was still heavy. 'When?'

'As soon as possible.'

'Are you in the city?'

'Yes.'

Another pause. When the woman next spoke it was in a quieter voice. 'Do you know St Ulrich's church in the 7th District?'

'I can find it.'

'It's on Burggasse. There's a Mass tonight at 5.30. Sit towards the middle of the central aisle. I'll be on my own in the front row of the right-hand aisle. When the service ends, come up to me and introduce yourself as Alfred, and ask if I know where you can get a bible repaired. Do you have a bag with you?'

'Yes.'

'Describe it please – and your coat.'

'It's a long black raincoat. The briefcase is large, very light tan.'

'Keep the briefcase in your left hand all the time. If there's a problem, move it to your right hand.'

'How will I know who you are?'

'I'll be the only nun there.'

***

Sister Ursula called the hospital and told them she'd be late, then hurried to the church, one of the few in the city where she still trusted the priest. Not that she'd tell him anything, but she knew he'd turn a blind eye in a real emergency and she may be able to hide someone at the church overnight – though she wasn't even sure of that now.

Father Josef gave her a nervous look when she entered his office and asked if she could borrow the keys. He handed a bunch over to her before closing the door. 'This'll have to be the last time, you understand? It's getting far too dangerous. You heard what happened in Penzing last week? I can't risk it. I think there are informers at every service. You Daughters of Charity of Saint Vincent de Paul are far too charitable...'

She knew from experience he'd arrive early, calling her on that number meant he was desperate. She climbed the steep stone staircase until she reached the small landing above the sacristy and opened the narrow window that allowed her a clear view of Burggasse – the only route into the church across Sankt-Ulrich-Platz. Just before 5.15 there was a commotion on Burggasse as three or four police cars pulled up and a checkpoint was quickly erected, manned by a mixture of police, Gestapo and SS. They'd started to do this much more recently; it was a way of intimidating church-goers and showing who was in charge in Vienna. A minute or two later she spotted what must be Alfred; a tall, young man wearing a long black raincoat, walking uncertainly as if he was unsure of where he was. In his left hand was a large leather briefcase, light tan. He'd been so absorbed in looking for the church that he didn't spot the checkpoint until he was almost upon it.

Then he panicked.

If he'd been told one thing in his training it was never to turn away from a checkpoint. *That's a sure way of drawing attention to yourself... have confidence in your cover... remember, checkpoints are routine...*

Sister Ursula watched in horror as the young man stood still in the middle of the pavement, unsure of what to do. A queue had now formed and at first he edged towards it then moved away. A policeman signalled for him to join the line, but he continued to hesitate before moving to the side of the pavement and turning around, standing for a while in the shadow of the church before walking backwards for a few steps then walking away – too fast – in the direction he'd come from. As he did so he fumbled with his briefcase, dropping it then picking it up and placing it in his right hand. Two policemen were now shouting at him to stop, but instead of doing so he quickened his pace into something approaching a run. One of the SS men left the checkpoint and ran after him.

Sister Ursula muttered a prayer as she watched, but soon stopped. She knew they'd catch him and she doubted someone who panicked at the sight of a checkpoint would be resilient under interrogation. She'd need to leave the church quickly. As she carefully closed the window she saw Alfred stop in the middle of the road, drop his briefcase and put a hand to his mouth. Moments later he tumbled over, writhing on the ground in agony for nearly half a minute before his body stopped moving and slumped.

The nun didn't wait to see what happened next. She closed the window and hurried down the stairs to the sacristy. She was aware the British gave their agents suicide pills and she was grateful this agent had at least had the presence of mind to use his.

Chapter 2

Vienna, March 1942

Frieda Brauner hadn't seen daylight for a week and sensed she never would do so again.

She was disorientated and her senses so dulled by pain that she'd only the vaguest recollection of what had happened since she'd been brought to the elegant building on Morzinplatz. She did remember leaving the safe house in Meidling on what was probably the Monday morning and checking the street was clear. There was some memory of bumping into an older woman, apologising and possibly bending down to pick up something she'd dropped. After that she seemed to fly, that was the only way she could remember it. She must have been picked up and thrown into the large car that had appeared alongside. Her head was forced face down into the hard leather seat as the car sped through central Vienna to its destination. When it slowed she was forced to sit up: they were turning off Morzinplatz and into Salztorgasse. She realised this was a deliberate act: they wanted her to know where she was being taken, a building she'd be unlikely to leave alive.

A young man with greasy, slicked-back hair and uneven eyebrows had turned around from the front passenger seat and leered at her, his tongue running between yellow teeth, moistening his lips.

'Welcome to the Vienna Gestapo,' he said.

The car pulled into a dark courtyard and she was hauled out

into the building, where she was blindfolded and marched down a flight of narrow stairs. According to the rumours going around Vienna, prisoners were either taken to the basement or to the level below. The basement was nicknamed hell – which of course was ironic in her particular circumstances. Apparently some people did survive the basement, though only after a fashion, and what happened after that was another matter. For most of them, the basement was a staging post on the way to Mauthausen. But the level below the basement was reputed to be far worse. According to those same rumours, no one had ever survived it.

At the bottom of the first flight of stairs she'd been dragged along a corridor before being pushed against a rough wall: the basement. She heard screaming and a series of dull, thudding noises, followed by what sounded like metallic scraping. Then a noisy metal door alongside her was unlocked and she was dragged down another series of steps. The level below the basement. *Worse than hell.*

She could recall being pulled through a series of metal doors, and becoming aware of an uneven floor and a pervading sense of damp. But there'd been no sounds to be heard, other than the occasional drip, and her own footsteps and those around her. Another metal door opened and her blindfold was removed before she was pushed in and the door slammed shut.

There was no light in the room, no window as far as she could make out. Even after a few hours there was nothing to help her eyes acclimatise. After a while she had an approximate idea of its dimensions: six steps long, four steps wide, the ceiling too high to touch. Along one of the walls was a rough wooden bench that was just wide enough for her to lie on, but there was no mattress or blankets. Nor was there a toilet.

And there she remained, for perhaps three days, possibly four. Twice a day the cell door would open, and a bowl of water and a plate of dry bread would be pushed in.

As the terror of the first few hours abated she felt an odd sense of relief. To have remained free for the four years since the Germans had rolled into Vienna was something of a miracle, so while being arrested had been a shock it wasn't completely unexpected. The one thing they all knew and reminded each other of all the time was what to do in the event of being arrested. *Reveal nothing for as long as possible. Every minute will count; every hour could save a comrade's life. The longer you can hold out, the more chance the others will have to save themselves.* So she'd expected the interrogation to begin quickly and the fact it hadn't was a source of some comfort.

But after a day or so, that small comfort was replaced by confusion. Why would the Gestapo wait so long? They, more than anyone, would know how important it was to prise information from her as soon as possible. After a while, the fact they weren't doing so brought its own terror, one that wrapped itself around her in the dark and damp dungeon.

By the time they came for her she'd developed a fever, unbearably hot one minute, chilled to her bones the next: her dress was soiled and drenched with sweat, and she couldn't stop trembling. She'd no idea whether it was day or night, let alone what day of the week it was. The cell door had opened and she'd been instructed to come out. She had to close her eyes in the corridor as they were so unused to the light, but then they blindfolded her and she was dragged along a corridor into a warm room where she was forced into a chair and the blindfold was removed.

She was aware of people around her, but no one said a word and it was a few minutes before her eyes could focus properly. In front of her a stocky man looking very pleased with himself was leaning back in a chair, his arms folded high on his chest. A taller, younger man was standing behind him. She could just make out two people on either side of her. The stocky man had a short, pointed, dirty-yellow beard that he played with as he studied her, smoothing out his moustache as if he was keen she admired it.

'Your name?'

'Dreschner. Maria Dreschner.' Her voice sounded hoarse, it was the first time she'd used it since arriving at Morzinplatz.

The man continued to stare at her, nodding very slightly as if that was the answer he was expecting. 'Yes, yes, I can read you know. Your paperwork says you're Maria Dreschner but we know you're not Maria Dreschner. We know your real name but I need you to tell us what it is. That way, I'll know you're being honest and it'll be a good way to start our... acquaintance.'

He looked at her, slightly lowering his head and raising his eyebrows, as if to say 'understand?' His accent was coarse, certainly not Viennese. He wasn't German either. As far as she could tell he was from Carinthia or somewhere near there: from the south of Austria, or what used to be Austria.

'How about...?' He was edging his chair closer to hers, now he was no more than a foot away. There was an unpleasant smell as he came closer.

'... How about if I tell you your first name and you tell me the rest? It'll be like a game.' He raised his eyebrows and allowed a brief smile, as if this really was a game and he was enjoying playing it.

She shrugged, desperately trying to work out what to do. *Always give them a little something at first*, she'd been told. Did her real name count as a little something?

'Frieda,' he said. He'd shouted it out in a dramatic fashion, like an actor. 'Is that correct?'

Her head dropped and she could feel the room moving slowly around her. Someone prodded her sharply in the back.

'Is that correct?' The man was shouting at her.

'Is what correct?'

'Frieda. It's your first name, yes?'

She nodded.

'Good. And now...' his chair edged even closer so his knees were touching hers, 'you tell me your full name. Remember the game?'

Her whole body slumped in the chair and it took three or four prods in her back before she was able to sit up again. It sounded as if they knew her name, but to admit it would feel like a betrayal. At least it would only be herself she was betraying. She cleared her throat and spoke softly.

'Brauner.'

'I can't hear you!'

'Brauner. My name is Frieda Brauner.'

'Good. And my name is Strobel. Kriminaldirektor Karl Strobel.' He emphasised his Gestapo rank with pride and in such a manner that she'd be in no doubt whose company she was in. 'As well as knowing your name, we also know you're a member of a Communist resistance cell, so I'd be obliged if you could tell me the names and addresses of the other members in that cell... oh, and its name.'

She felt the fear rise in her. She hesitated for as long as she could in the hope it'd appear her answer was a reluctant one.

'Franz Josef...'

'Franz Josef who?'

Another pause. She could feel herself weeping now and she allowed the tears to flow freely. They could help. 'Mayer. I believe: Franz Josef Mayer. And another man called Wolfgang.'

Strobel didn't look impressed. She hadn't expected him to.

'Surname?' he asked wearily.

'Fischer, if I remember right. They're the only ones I know: Franz Josef Mayer and Wolfgang Fischer. But I promise you, I was a messenger: no more than that and, even then, only on a few occasions. I've no idea of the name of the cell; I didn't even know there was a cell. I wish I could help...'

For the first time Strobel showed some emotion, leaning back in his chair and laughing raucously. The taller, younger man behind him joined in obediently, as did the other people in the room who she couldn't see. When he stopped laughing he jumped out of his chair and stood directly in front of her, bending his short body so his face was just inches from hers. When he shouted, specks of spit sprayed over her face.

'Do you think we're fools? Franz Josef Mayer and Wolfgang Fischer were arrested months ago – and you know that. Fischer died in this very room. Mayer didn't even make it this far. We know there were at least five others, including you. So what you'll do now is tell me those other four names.'

She was shocked at how quickly the emotion swept over her. She could see now why they'd left her in the cell for so long: she wasn't prepared for this. Her body was weak and her mind was going. Tears filled her eyes and her body shook violently. The names of the other four were forming on her lips and she had to bite her tongue to stop herself saying anything. She shook her head. Behind her she could hear a scraping noise.

'We'd hoped the few days we allowed you to have on your own would prepare you for this, but evidently not. Normally at this point we'd attempt some of our gentler methods of persuasion in the hope you'd tell us the names but I can see that may be a waste of time. The names?'

She shook her head, trying to make sense of what he was talking about.

'Franz Josef Mayer and Wolfgang Fischer,' Frieda repeated. 'I don't know of anyone else. I was only a messenger, I told you. I did see a woman once or twice, but I was never told her name. She was older than me. She was tall with dark grey hair.'

'Stand up.'

She stood, holding on to the back of the chair for support. When she turned around, she saw what appeared to be a large examination couch, with various straps and bars attached to it. Two men in uniform were undoing the straps. Two women came and stood on either side of her. Strobel nodded at the younger man then at her.

'Get undressed.'

'What?'

'Unless you're prepared to give me those four names now then get undressed.'

The younger man had dark blond hair that dropped over his bright blue eyes. He couldn't have been more than 25 and he reminded her of her younger brother. He smiled as he removed his jacket and shirt, and unbuckled his belt.

'I've no idea what names you want. I've told you, I was just a messenger. Please, you have to believe me!'

'Go on Strasser, get on with it.'

***

After Strasser had finished with her for the second time they left her alone in the room, still strapped tight to the table. Her legs were splayed apart, attached to the bars jutting up from its sides. Her body was naked and bruised. Strangely, she no longer seemed to have the fever and the pain wasn't as bad as it had been, but the humiliation was worse. The bright lights trained on her face felt as though they were burning her. Even when she shut her eyes the light was still unbearable.

They'd all gathered around the table, watching. Strobel had seemed quite excited throughout; breathing noisily, his face bright red with a thin smile and a glow of sweat on his forehead. As Strasser got dressed, Strobel stayed next to her, his hand stroking the inside of her thigh, his sweaty fingers gradually creeping higher.

'Think about it. We'll be back. Just four names.'

The fact she hadn't given the names was of little consolation.

***

They'd returned the next day. 'It's Friday morning, Frieda,' Strobel announced, his eyes sweeping up and down her naked body as he removed his raincoat and carefully folded it before handing it to someone behind him. 'By the end of the day you'll have told us everything we need to know, then I can enjoy the hunting I've planned for the weekend. We need the names and addresses of the other four people along with the name of the cell, so just get on with it. You know what we're capable of now.'

Strobel was accompanied by Strasser, the one who'd raped her the previous day. They both watched as two other men in uniform came in and unstrapped her from the table. The relief she felt from the pain and discomfort was short-lived. No sooner had she collapsed onto the floor than Strobel took a running kick at her, his boot connecting with her throat. As she twisted on the floor, he stamped hard on her back. She must have blacked out after that because her next memory was of being hauled onto a wooden chair and strapped to it. She was coughing blood and unsure whether she could feel her legs.

After that, things got worse.

***

A shade before 9.30 on most weekday mornings a hush would

quickly descend over a long, wood-panelled office on the third floor of the elegant building on Morzinplatz. The office was on the Franz-Josefs-Kai side of the building, the Danube Canal comfortably falling within its shadow and the mighty Danube itself a couple of hundred yards beyond that.

Most of the staff had been at work since well before 9.00 – though for most of them the first hour or so was a sociable time as much as anything else, given to drinking coffee, sharing gossip, dividing the minor spoils of war and indulging in various games of office politics.

That would stop with a warning telephone call from the ground-floor reception. A minute or so later they'd hear the swing doors at the end of the corridor crash open, by which time the office workers were now busy on their telephones or poring over reports.

This was the sight that would greet the stocky figure of Kriminaldirektor Karl Strobel as he marched into the office, doing his best to rise above the five foot four inches nature had cruelly dealt him and for which he'd never forgiven it. A large secretary wearing a severe black suit and a matching expression would follow in his wake, along with one or two officers eager for an early audience.

Acknowledging the 'Herr Kriminaldirektors' with only the curtest of nods, he'd stride between the rows of desks to his office, the door of which would be held open by another secretary, her head slightly bowed.

On this particular Monday morning he paused at one of the desks close to his office and spoke to the young man behind it, who was in the process of quickly rising to his feet.

'Did you manage to get the information out of her, Kriminaloberassistent Strasser?'

'Not yet sir.'

'Is she still alive, Strasser?'

Strasser was now standing awkwardly in front of Strobel, aware his height would be a cause of some embarrassment. He edged further away.

'Yes, Herr Kriminaldirektor.'

'And yet she's said nothing?'

The younger man shook his head.

'You'd better come into my office, Strasser. Now!'

Strobel's shouting caused the office to fall silent. The small group that had gathered expectantly behind him backed away, with the exception of the large secretary in the severe suit. Strasser followed Strobel into his office, with its magnificent desk taken from a Jewish-owned apartment in the 9th District and other fine pieces of furniture similarly acquired. Strobel stood by the window, staring over the canal towards Donaustrasse and the enormous flak towers of the Augarten in the distance.

'So, you weren't able to get her to say anything, Strasser?'

'Nothing that makes any sense, Herr Kriminaldirektor. I'm afraid that since you last interrogated her on Friday she's been largely incoherent. The medics gave her an injection on Saturday and that brought her to her senses for a while, but even then...'

'I can't emphasise enough how important it is we break this resistance cell, Strasser. They've been operating for at least three or four years, and we should never have allowed them to continue for so long. We've already dealt with Mayer and Fischer, and now we have Frieda Brauner, but we have to find out who the others are. How hard did you actually try, Strasser?'

'I tried my best, Herr Kriminaldirektor, but you'll appreciate the more persuasive I was, the less she responded. Her injuries really are very severe. Doctor Rudolf says she probably has some paralysis from the injury to her spine, but the most serious injury is a collapsed windpipe. It's a very...'

'What's this, Strasser? Are you a nurse all of a sudden? It can't be difficult to get a woman like that to give us the information we need, surely? In fact...'

'I know sir, but you yourself tried to do so on Thursday and Friday and...'

'Don't interrupt me, Strasser! You're impudent as well as incompetent. Tell them to get her ready and I'll go down and deal with her myself.'

***

Frieda Brauner was still on the floor below the basement, but she'd now been moved into what was, in effect, a hospital room. Doctor Rudolf, who tended her, was an elderly man, some years past the age when he'd expected to retire. He was now enjoying a status denied him during an undistinguished career blighted by drink and what he perceived as the scheming ambition of the Jewish doctors in the hospital where he worked. Now, as a Gestapo doctor, he'd become skilled at preventing people from dying inconveniently early.

'Tell me about Frieda Brauner,' said Strobel.

'She's very ill, Herr Kriminaldirektor,' replied Rudolf.

'So I gather. But you've kept her alive?'

'After a fashion, yes,' said Rudolf. 'The most severe injury is to her windpipe. Tracheal injuries like hers are often fatal. It's caused complications in her lungs and she's having increasing difficulty breathing: the trauma has caused the tracheal cartridge to tear and she needs an operation. She was in a very bad state on Friday night when my medics first saw her and they called me in yesterday. I carried out a procedure on her, but it was only temporary. She's a very sick woman. She needs to be transferred to hospital and even then her chances of survival are…'

'That's out of the question, Rudolf. I need her to give us information today. Can you get her in a state to do that?'

The elderly doctor looked at Strobel over the top of his half-moon shaped spectacles. 'With the very greatest of respect, Herr Kriminaldirektor,' he said. 'If you needed her to be in a state to talk, that should have been a consideration last week. My understanding is that when she came here she was healthy. It's unreasonable to expect the Gestapo medical service to perform miracles. Surely, if a prisoner is so important…'

Strobel stormed out of the doctor's office while he was still talking and marched down the corridor to Frieda's room, motioning for Strasser to join him. The prisoner was shackled to the bed, her skin almost as pale as the white sheet she lay on, and her breathing was uneven and noisy. Strobel knelt beside her and gripped her wrists.

'Tell me the names, Frieda, just the names. Then I promise

we'll give you something to make you feel more comfortable.'

Frieda opened her eyes and took a moment or two to focus. She blinked rapidly and silently mouthed a word. Strobel leaned over her, his ear almost touching her mouth.

'Water! She's saying water, Strasser. Bring a glass. Get a move on.'

Strobel gently held the glass of water to her lips and raised her head from the pillow, allowing her to sip from it. When she'd finished, he propped her up against the headboard and stroked her hair.

'Come on, Frieda, the names. Just give me the four names then you can rest.'

The woman's eyes half-opened, still not properly focusing. Strobel signalled for Strasser to turn off the main light then wiped her brow with his handkerchief. She was trying to say something – her mouth was moving but no noise came out. He allowed her some more water and was then able to make out the very faintest of whispers.

'She's trying to say something, Strasser. Get your notebook out. Come on Frieda, the names.'

It was a while before she spoke: it was louder than a whisper, but in a voice that was weak and cracked.

'"L", Strasser, she's saying the letter "L". Write it down'. Is that right, Frieda?'

She nodded then glanced in the direction of the glass of water. Strobel allowed her another sip.

'"E" – the letter "E". Is that right? Good. You're writing all this down Strasser? What's next?'

This carried on for the best part of an hour: the woman whispering a letter to Strobel, nodding or shaking her head when the Gestapo man repeated it and, only when it was correct, being allowed a sip of water. There were frequent pauses during which Frieda's head would sink back on the pillow and she appeared to have given up. But Strobel was surprisingly patient: he allowed her just enough time to recover before carefully raising her up and holding the glass to her lips.

'Carry on Frieda, carry on please...'

When she completed the fourth name, Strobel grabbed the book from Strasser and studied it for a minute or so.

'Are these the names Frieda? Are you sure?'

She nodded her head.

'They don't make sense. Here, have some more water.'

Strobel's hand was shaking and instead of allowing her to sip from the glass he spilled most of down her neck.

'Come on, tell me what it means! You're making fools of us!' His manner was no longer gentle and persuasive. His voice was angry and loud. She stared beyond him, saying nothing. Strobel grabbed her chin in his hand and forced her to look at him. Still she said nothing, closing her eyes. With the back of his hand he slapped her face hard, causing her to open her eyes wide, a look of panic set on her face.

'Tell me what this all means – and...'

She made a sound. He leaned closer. She repeated the word.

'What's she saying, Strasser? Say it again Frieda.'

She spoke again.

'I think she'd saying "Hades", sir,' said Strasser. 'That's what it sounds like.'

She repeated the word: this time it was clear: "Hades". It was the first word she'd spoken above a whisper.

'What's Hades?'

'I believe it's another word for hell, sir.'

Strobel stood up, looking furious.

'Hell? You're telling me to go to hell, you bitch?'

As he spoke, there was a cackling sound from the bed and Doctor Rudolf, who'd been hovering nervously in the doorway, moved swiftly to the bedside, just in time for Frieda to rise before dropping back, dead before her head hit the pillow.

***

By the time they arrived back in his office Strobel was being more conciliatory towards young Strasser. He realised, though he'd never admit it, that if it weren't for his violence on the Friday they may now have had the proper names from Frieda. Now she was dead. Strobel took Strasser's notebook and held it at different angles, as if that could throw some meaning on the four names she'd given.

'They're not German names, are they sir?'

'Obviously not, Strasser. I'd worked that out.'

'They could be code names, sir. If only we'd had a bit more time with her, I reckon she'd have told us everything!'

'It was a miracle she told us anything Strasser. It's a good job I haven't lost my touch – this department simply wouldn't function without me. I've no idea what you were up to over the weekend.

We lost two valuable days.'

Strasser had now copied the four names out onto a separate sheet of paper, spacing the letters out carefully.

'They look as if they could be Latin or Greek, Herr Kriminaldirektor.'

'Possibly, possibly... You'll need to go and check it out somewhere. Find an expert... there must be someone in Vienna. This is meant to be a cultured city after all.'

'How about the university, sir? There must be a classics department there.'

'Well let's hope it's not one of those departments where all the staff were Jews and communists. You'd better get a move on.'

***

Karl Strobel paced around his office, making a conscious attempt to calm himself down. Normally a weekend's hunting would have had that effect, but he knew he'd allowed his temper to get the better of him on the Friday. If he'd not attacked the woman so viciously she'd probably have confessed all.

Through the frosted glass in his office door he could just about make out movement beyond it, the blurred dark shapes of the 70 staff who worked for him. He was proud of what he'd achieved: childhood poverty in Carinthia; his father killed in the Great War; then a series of dead-end jobs. He was drifting through life until he'd joined the Nazi Party when it started in Austria in 1924 and from that moment on his life began to have some meaning. He'd started to command respect; his brute strength and cunning more than compensated for his lack of intellect and wealth. And so he'd climbed through the ranks of the Nazi Party. After the failed putsch of 1934 he'd spent a few months in prison, which did his reputation no harm. He came out to find he was one of nearly half a million jobless in Austria, but he'd continued to rise through the ranks of the Nazi Party and when the Germans marched into Austria in March 1938, Strobel joined the Vienna Gestapo. By the time the war started he headed section IVA, which was responsible for finding communists, liberals and saboteurs who somehow still existed in Vienna four years after the Nazis had been so joyfully welcomed into the city.

But recently life had become more difficult for Strobel. He was under pressure. What was it Huber had said to him the other week? 'Your job should be an easy one, Strobel: finding communists and resistance cells in Vienna should be like spotting the full moon. It's not as if you're in Paris or Prague. Maybe a spell in the east will show you what the real world's like. Find that cell or else you'd better start packing some warm clothing.'

All well and good for Franz Huber to say that: the Bavarian might well be in charge of the Gestapo here in Vienna but it wasn't as if he did much in the way of real work himself. Strobel began to feel quite sick again. He was no coward, he was brave and tough – he was a hunter after all – but he'd heard such terrible things about the east. Apart from anything else, his talents would be wasted there. They were needed here in Vienna. He was interrupted by a knock at the door: tentative at first then louder as it was repeated. It was Strasser, who was looking very pleased with himself.

'You have something?'

'Possibly sir. A very helpful lecturer at the university looked at the list and the names made sense to him as soon as he saw them.'

'Go on.'

The younger man removed a notebook from his jacket pocket and thumbed through the pages. 'They're all rivers, sir.'

'What are?'

'Those words Frieda gave us: Lethe, Acheron, Cocytus and Styx. The lecturer recognised them straight away. He's to be trusted by the way, sir – he's a party member and he told me about a lecturer in the physics department he suspects may have a Jewish grandfather.'

Strobel shook his head as if he was missing something. 'And where are these rivers, Strasser? They don't sound like they're anywhere in the Reich.'

'Hell, sir. They're all the rivers of Hades – the underworld. That must have been why Frieda said "Hades" just before she died.'

Chapter 3

Bern, May 1942

For Basil Remington-Barber, the first Monday of each month was sacrosanct. More to the point, lunchtime on the first Monday of each month was sacrosanct and, inevitably, what little remained of its afternoon.

So, a shade before 12.30 on that first Monday of May, MI6's head of station at the British Embassy in Bern placed the papers on his desk in a safe and prepared to leave his office, ostensibly that of the Commercial attaché. He drew the blinds and carefully locked the door to his office before saying goodbye to his secretary in the outer office and walking down to the ground floor, a definite spring to his step. He'd leave the embassy in Thunstrasse in the east of the city and walk towards the Old Town, allowing plenty of time to ensure he wasn't being followed. All being well, he'd then cross the River Aar on Kirchenfeldbrücke, his favourite bridge in Bern, which he never tired of pointing out to people was built by a British company ('1883 – just a little before my time!').

Once across the bridge it would be a short walk through the Old Town to Kreuzgasse where, in a basement deep beneath a magnificent medieval building, was the finest restaurant Remington-Barber had ever been to. It was more like a private dining club: customers were only admitted with a prior reservation and were required to ring a bell to be admitted by an elderly man in a heavy dark suit. A guest would then be escorted to a table, following the suited man through a network of low-ceilinged corridors. Each table was set into its own alcove from which it was impossible to either see or hear anything of any of the other tables.

The cuisine was French, 'but better than anything you can get in France these days', as his host never failed to remark. It was rare for Remington-Barber not to start with foie gras followed by either venison or veal for his main course. But the highlight of the meal was the wine, always a different red from one of the finest French vineyards. The wine was never ordered, as such. A bottle would appear before each course, invariably covered in a layer of dust testifying to its vintage. And after the dessert and coffee, a bottle of Bas Armagnac would be produced. It was quite the most perfect drink Remington-Barber had ever experienced: sharp enough at first for the full flavour to be appreciated then a warm sensation of wellbeing would spread through him and, for the next two or three hours, he'd oblige his generous host with as much information as he felt able to share, only just managing to stay on the safe side of discretion.

His host was an improbably young American called Jack J Clarke who ran what passed for the US intelligence operation out of its embassy in Bern. Jack J Clarke had arrived in the Swiss capital at the beginning of the year, just a month after the US had entered the war. He went about his role with an air of bemusement and confusion, his qualifications for the job apparently having more to do with his father's generosity to President Roosevelt than any obvious skills or experience in intelligence. But his operation was a well-funded one and he did have a willingness to learn. He came to rely heavily on Remington-Barber: in return for lunch, the older man would throw titbits of intelligence to his younger counterpart. *Whatever you do Basil, show willing*, the Ambassador had told him soon after America joined the war and Jack J Clarke arrived in town. *Co-operate with them: make them feel wanted. Winston absolutely insists on it.*

But on this first Monday of May not one drop of Bas Armagnac passed his lips. Remington-Barber didn't cross into the Old Town and got nowhere near the restaurant beneath the medieval building on Kreuzgasse. He didn't even make it as far as the Kirchenfeldbrücke. In fact, Remington-Barber didn't even leave the embassy. He was about to leave the secure part of the ground floor when he was approached by one of the security officers.

'Someone to see you, sir. Insists on seeing you today.'

'Impossible, Jarvis. I've an important meeting. Marjorie's in the office. Ask her to come down and make an appointment with him.'

'It's a lady, sir. She said to tell you she's from Germany, sir. She seems awfully nervous, sir.'

'Has she given a name?'

'She just said to say the word "Milo" to you, sir.'

Remington-Barber didn't reply as he did his best to compose himself before gently pushing open the door that led into the reception just far enough for him to be able to see in. Sitting on a bench in the shadows to the side of the waiting area was a lady in her early thirties; elegant and composed, her gloved hands neatly folded on her lap. Though it was hard to make out her features, he had little doubt it was her. Remington-Barber stood back against the wall and breathed deeply. Until that moment he'd believed the person waiting for him in reception had been killed by the Gestapo in Stuttgart more than a year ago.

Five minutes later lunch had been cancelled and she was sitting opposite him in his office. 'Milo,' he said, repeating her code name a number of times as he reassured himself he wasn't sitting in the same room as a ghost. 'I thought you were dead, Milo. Tell me what happened.'

Katharina Hoch, the woman Remington-Barber was calling Milo, was sitting very still, a nervous smile on her face. Her dark hair was immaculate and she was wearing bright-red lipstick. When she spoke it was very quietly and in German: Remington-Barber had to lean across his desk to catch everything she said.

'I very nearly *was* dead, but I managed to get out of Germany. May I smoke?'

'Of course, please.' Remington-Barber's hands were shaking as he fumbled for a lighter and held the flame unsteadily in front of her. She'd removed her gloves now and one of her bare hands clasped the English diplomat's as she lit her cigarette.

'I managed to escape from Stuttgart that day. I came straight to Switzerland, by train.'

'But that was over a year ago, Katharina. Why on earth did you wait till now to contact me?' Where did you go once you got into Switzerland?'

'I went to Lucerne,' said Katharina. 'I've a friend there, a very close friend I totally trust. She left Germany after '33 and married a Swiss man. I've been staying with her ever since.'

'But why didn't you contact me?'

'Because I didn't want to do anything till I'd heard what'd happened to my brother. When we parted at Stuttgart station we agreed we'd head in separate directions. It was only last Friday I received a telegram from him in Barcelona. I don't know all his circumstances, but he's safe. Until I'd heard from him, I couldn't trust anyone. Not even the British, Mr Remington-Barber.'

Katharina paused and took one final drag on her cigarette before stubbing it out in a heavy glass ashtray on the desk. 'Do you consider it too early for a drink, Mr Remington-Barber? I know the English have rules about these things.'

He was grateful for the opportunity and poured two measures of whisky, his somewhat more generous than hers. It was as welcome as the Bas Armagnac he'd have been drinking that afternoon in more expected circumstances.

Katharina smiled for the first time, her teeth flashing behind the bright-red lipstick. When she'd finished speaking she held her arms out, as if to say, 'And here I am.'

'Do you need money?'

'Well, I've obviously not been able to get a job and my friend…'

The diplomat stopped her speaking. 'Naturally we owe you money. You're not to worry. Are you willing to continue working for us?'

She nodded.

'You're sure, are you – after what you've been through?'

'I'm sure.'

'Good. I'll sort you out with some decent papers. We'd better get you a Swiss identity. You'll appreciate that takes time.'

'When would I start working for you?'

'Possibly not for a while,' said Remington-Barber. 'But don't worry. I'm sure something will crop up.'

'In the meantime, I'd like to do something useful,' said Katharina. 'I've been so bored this past year.'

'Am I correct in recalling that you trained as a nurse, Fraulein Hoch – before you worked at the hotel?'

'That's right, you've a good memory. I completed my training but only worked in a hospital for a few months. I decided I'd rather work in a hotel.'

'I'll sort your Swiss identity out as soon as possible and make sure it includes nursing accreditation. Get a job in a hospital: you never know when it'll come in handy.'

Chapter 4

London, July 1943

The second Tuesday of July was just minutes old when the police car sent to collect him sped past Kings Cross station and turned left, accelerating hard as it headed north up the Caledonian Road. The little moon there was that night remained mostly hidden behind banks of cloud, the otherwise black sky punctuated by the searchlight beams tracking it. A few minutes earlier, as he'd waited outside his flat behind Victoria Street, he'd heard the sound of anti-aircraft fire in the far distance and the noise of heavy explosions to the north east.

The man sitting next to him in the back seat shifted uncomfortably close. He'd met him before, but he was the type of person whose name you easily forgot: Simons, or Simmond or something like that – a civil servant elevated way beyond his natural levels of competence thanks to the war. Now Simons or Simmond leaned even nearer, his sour breath an unpleasant mixture of stale milk, strong tobacco and poor hygiene.

'Sorry about this Edgar. It may turn out to be a wild goose chase.'

'Sorry about what?' Edgar edged closer to the door but the man from the Home Office edged along with him.

'About waking you and dragging you along here and all that.'

Edgar shrugged. He was used to the likes of Simons or Simmond and the way they acted with Edgar and others from MI6: a mixture of uncertainty and awe.

'And apologies for asking you this, Edgar, but you're fluent in German, aren't you? Porter said you'd be just the chap.'

'I'm fluent in German, yes.'

There was a pause, during which the man from the Home Office noisily wiped his nose first with one sleeve then the other. 'How fluent, if you don't mind me asking?'

'Fluent,' replied Edgar, angling his head towards the window, making it clear he was in no mood to be any more helpful than he needed to be.

'I know, but there's fluent… and fluent.' The man from the Home Office wasn't giving up.

'Perhaps you could explain the difference between fluent and fluent, eh? They sound very much the same to me.'

'What I mean… what I'm trying to say… is, well, are you fluent enough to understand every nuance of a native German speaker?' He heavily emphasised the word 'nuance' as if especially pleased with it.

Edgar turned round to face Simons or Simmond, whose shoulder was now more or less touching his. 'Yes.'

'Good. Porter said you speak it like a native. When were you last there, if I may ask?'

'Where?'

'Germany.'

Edgar turned to face the Home Office man once again. 'Two years ago.'

'Good heavens!'

***

Pentonville Prison was set directly on the Caledonian Road, behind surprisingly low walls. Edgar and his escort were expected: a police officer at the gate waved the Jaguar through and directed it to an inner courtyard, where a man in a suit was waiting for them. They were taken to a narrow room on the ground floor of A Block, where half a dozen men were crammed around a narrow table, with two empty chairs waiting for them. The air was thick with smoke and in the yellow glow cast by the single lightbulb everyone appeared unnaturally pale. It reminded Edgar of one of those ghastly séances his mother had insisted on going to after his father died.

Fowler from MI5 did the introductions: MI5, MI6, Special Branch and the Home Office. The final man he introduced was the governor of the prison, who made a meal of coughing and clearing his throat before he spoke. 'Walter Baumgartner was arrested in March this year as a German spy and tried *in camera* at the Old Bailey last month,' he said. 'He was found guilty of espionage on the 18th June and sentenced to death, after which he was transferred here. He's due to be executed at 9.00 this morning.' The governor paused, coughed nosily once more and peered at a fob watch on a chain he'd produced from his jacket pocket. 'In a little more than eight hours' time,' he added.

A brief silence followed before Fowler from MI5 spoke. 'And maybe you could tell us what's happened in the past few hours that's led to us all being assembled here?'

'Baumgartner only heard yesterday afternoon that his final appeal for clemency had been turned down,' said the governor. 'His solicitor came to see him with the letter from the Home

Secretary and explained there was nothing more that could be done. In my experience, at this point, most men resign themselves to their fate or at least withdraw into themselves. Not Baumgartner. He's been no end of trouble and at one stage had to be restrained by the warders. He refused to see a priest and wouldn't write any last letters. Then at around 7.00 last night he insisted on seeing me alone. He told me he'd important information to pass on to British intelligence and insisted on someone being brought to the prison to see him. I asked him to give me some idea of what he was on about, but he was adamant he'd only speak to someone from intelligence and he refuses to see anyone from either Special Branch or MI5 as he blames them for the predicament he's in. He wants to see someone from MI6, which is why you're here Edgar. I must say that these circumstances are really most unusual.'

'I think there's a rather crucial point you omitted?' said Fowler.

'You're quite right, I'm sorry,' said the governor. 'Baumgartner says he's important information to pass on to our intelligence service. His condition for this is he's granted a reprieve.'

There was loud muttering around the table. The man from Home Office, who was clearly senior to Simons or Simmond, was red-faced with anger when he spoke. 'That's completely out of order and I can assure you it can't possibly be permitted to happen. The judicial process had been followed and, unlike the Nazis, we're bound by the rule of law. Once the Home Secretary has turned down an appeal for clemency then no grounds remain for it to be overturned. What's more, his solicitor will know that and will undoubtedly advise him accordingly.'

'But at the very least,' said Fowler from MI5, 'we need to hear what he has to say. It's for us' – he was now staring directly at the man from the Home Office – 'to judge the value of what intelligence he may have to offer. I would remind you that good intelligence can save many thousands of lives and can have a significant impact on the outcome of the war. Edgar, you'll need to go in and see him to hear what he has to say. Then we can form a view.'

The man from the Home Office was half out of his chair, his fists banging the table. 'But this is ridiculous! Why's this man decided to tell us this now? He's so desperate to save his skin that he's going to come up with some nonsense we'll be expected to believe. I can't believe we're playing along with this charade!'

'May I speak?' Edgar's voice wasn't loud but it had an unusual authority to it, one that caused everyone in the room to turn their attention to him. 'My colleague from the Security Service is quite correct, good intelligence is worth its weight in gold, it's hard to underestimate how vital it can be to the war effort. At the very least I need to assess what he has to say then we can decide what to do. And I can assure you...' Edgar was now looking directly at the man from the Home Office, '... I'm most experienced at knowing when someone's telling me the truth and when they're lying.'

***

The governor escorted Edgar to the condemned cell on the first floor of A Block. Two dark-suited wardens were outside the cell and, on the governor's instructions, unlocked it. Two more guards were at a table in the surprisingly large cell, both facing a man who was sitting on the bed, his head in his hands.

'Get up, Baumgartner,' said the governor. 'You asked to see someone. Here he is.'

The man who rose from the bed was of medium height and an average build, his dark, lank hair not unlike that of his fellow Austrian Adolf Hitler, but he was clean-shaven. His complexion was almost white, as if fear had already taken a grip on him. His eyes, mouth, nose and even ears all had a red hue to them.

'Thank you, you can all leave now,' Edgar said to the governor.

'I'm afraid we're not allowed to leave a condemned man alone.'

'He won't be on his own. I'm here.'

'It has to be just the two of us,' said Baumgartner, his voice higher-pitched than Edgar had expected; his English heavily accented.

'You have a peephole in the door: observe us through that,' said Edgar. 'I'll call out if I need you. But I promise you I'm very capable of looking after myself.'

The governor looked Edgar up and down: more than six feet tall and well-built. *Alright.*

Once they were alone, the two men sat on either side of the wooden table. Edgar glanced at his watch and removed a leather notebook and fountain pen from his jacket pocket. From another pocket he took out a silver cigarette case and offered one to the Austrian, who gratefully accepted. Edgar waited until they were both halfway through their cigarettes before he spoke. Until then he'd been carefully observing the other man through the blue-brown smoke.

'Tell me your story, Baumgartner.' Edgar spoke in German

and when the Austrian replied in the same language he sounded more confident, his voice sounding more natural in the familiar Viennese sing-song accent.

'I'm from Vienna, where I used to work for the von Rothschild Bank,' he said. 'I was an official in a department that handled the accounts of important private clients. The bank was owned by Jews and many of its clients were Jewish, but I was actually a member of the Nazi Party – I'd joined in 1934 after the failed putsch. I joined because I felt Austria needed firm direction and I was worried about the Communists, but I wasn't a very active member. Naturally, I kept my membership secret; it wasn't something my employers would have approved of.'

Baumgartner paused while Edgar lit another cigarette for him. He noticed the Austrian's hands were trembling violently as he held it to the flame.

'After the Anschluss in March 1938 the bank came under state control because of its Jewish ownership – and eventually it was sold to a German bank called Merck, Fink,' Baumgartner continued. 'Soon after that, I got a new job. Because of my membership of the Nazi Party I was appointed to what's known as the Special Office, which is another name for Section IVB4 of the Gestapo – the section that deals with Jewish affairs. We were based in the Vienna Gestapo headquarters in the old Hotel Metropole on Morzinplatz. I don't know if you know Vienna, but Morzinplatz is on the banks of the Danube Canal, a very agreeable location. My role was to assist in the confiscation of Jewish assets. I was in a very good position to identify them then arrange for them to be assigned to the state. May I have another cigarette please?'

Baumgartner had only half-finished his previous one, but as he'd been talking he'd jabbed it out in the tin ashtray in front of him. He leaned close to Edgar as the Englishman lit his cigarette. For a moment or two, the Austrian's face was no more than an inch or two from his and Edgar was able to look into the unblinking eyes, red-rimmed and bloodshot, full of fear but hard with determination.

'I have to confess I retained some assets for myself – jewellery, gold, cash and details of accounts. Everyone in the Special Office seemed to be doing that, but the mistake I made was that I failed to be generous enough to my superiors. Eventually I was caught and given a stark choice: to face trial and a long prison sentence, or to co-operate. They told me I'd impressed them with my efficiency and manner, and with my ability to speak English they thought I'd be suitable for espionage work. This was how I became a Nazi spy.

'I was given training and the identity of a Jew from Munich, can you believe? Arrangements were made for me to travel to Britain in early 1940. It was still possible then – the problem for Jews wishing to flee Germany was getting the papers to leave, which of course wasn't a problem for me. I was able to secure a passage from France to England. But I'd no intention whatsoever of being a Nazi spy, that seemed to me to be far too dangerous an occupation and, in any case, I'd already made my own arrangements.'

There was a long silence. Edgar looked around the room, with its low bed, stained sink and chamber pot beneath it, the window set high in the wall; an appropriately miserable place to spend your last hours on earth. He knew better than to hurry the man sitting opposite him: it was a sight he was familiar with, the card player deciding when to reveal the rest of his hand.

'The Gestapo had found me in possession of Jewish assets worth around 1,000 pounds in British money. But they didn't know I'd also managed to hide a set of papers that belonged to a former client of mine; a Jewish businessman from Vienna called Leo Frankl. Frankl was a prominent figure in Vienna and he knew he was in danger. In late 1938 he planned to leave Austria under an Aryan identity and travel to Zürich, where I'd meet him and hand over the paperwork he'd entrusted to me – his passport and other documents, including proof of funds he'd deposited at the Lombard Street branch of Martins Bank in the City of London.'

Baumgartner paused and looked up nervously at Edgar, unsure of whether to continue. He only did so after edging his chair away from the table, as if putting himself out of the Englishman's reach.

'I know you'll think badly of me for what I'm about to say, but if nothing else then at least it should show I'm telling the truth – why else would I incriminate myself? I'm ashamed to say that before Frankl could escape to Switzerland, I told the Gestapo of his plans and he was arrested. Apparently he died soon after.'

'On the boat to England I destroyed the identity the Nazis had given me and used that of Leo Frankl to enter the country. The Nazis never heard from me again. I kept to myself and avoided mixing with Jews. I had to report to the local police station twice a week, but I had no other obligations other than that. I even found myself a job as a bookkeeper at a department store in central London. Fortunately for me, Herr Frankl had no immediate family, so I was able to withdraw the money from Martins Bank and live a discreet but well-funded life as a Jewish refugee in London. That was how I lived for almost three years.

'All this changed in March. One Sunday morning I was enjoying a pleasant stroll in Regents Park when, apparently, I was spotted by a former client of mine – a Jew I should add – from the von Rothschild Bank. He not only recognised me as Walter Baumgartner, but was also well aware I'd been working for the Gestapo. He followed me back to my apartment then went to the police. I was arrested and they were able to establish that, whoever I was, I wasn't Leo Frankl. A former neighbour of his and a distant cousin lived in London, and they were brought along to disprove my identity, along with the former client from the bank. I admitted I was Walter Baumgartner and thought the matter wouldn't be treated too seriously. I thought they'd charge me with having used a false identity. But, foolishly, I'd retained some of the espionage equipment the Germans had given me, including invisible ink and addresses in Sweden to write to, and when the police searched my apartment they found that. I was a fool. I don't know why I kept those. If I hadn't, they'd have had no evidence against me.

'Even then, my solicitor assured me that, as I'd not actually committed any espionage in England, I'd only receive a prison sentence. Even after I was sentenced to death he was still optimistic I'd be reprieved. You can't imagine the shock when I heard yesterday there was no chance of that. So now I've a proposal to make, in exchange for my life.'

Edgar leaned back in the small chair and nodded at the Austrian. *Continue.*

'The Nazis didn't recover all the assets I stole from the Jews.

There are more in a strongbox hidden in Vienna. I can tell you where that is.' He looked at Edgar, trying to gauge his reaction.

'What assets?'

'Cash and jewellery.'

'Total value?'

Baumgartner closed his eyes, trying to calculate how much money he was talking about. 'Approximately the equivalent of 950 pounds sterling, possibly closer to 1,000.'

'In Reichsmarks?'

'Mostly. A small amount in Swiss Francs.'

'You're offering a bit of money and jewellery in exchange for your life?'

The Austrian offered a thin smile, a theatrical shrug of the shoulders and shook his head. 'I'm not naive; there's more than that, much more. I have an acquaintance in Vienna with whom I was what you may call a collaborator in various ventures. We believed in protecting ourselves and using any means to do so. My friend runs a specialised business: he procures people for his clients to sleep with. By 1939 most of his clientele were senior SS and Gestapo officers, and important Austrian Nazi officials. And their tastes were very extreme, if that's the right word. The Nazis seemed to have a taste for younger people and my friend was able to provide those; girls and boys, mostly around the age of 15, 16 – some younger. Very unpleasant, please don't get me wrong – it's not something I was directly involved in or even approved of. But my friend was clever. He had an apartment on Schulerstrasse, behind the cathedral, where he arranged for his clients to meet with the boys and girls. And he took the precaution of installing hidden cameras there, so he was able to photograph many of the Nazis in the most compromising of positions. He called them his insurance policies. There are copies of these photographs in my strongbox. That's valuable information, wouldn't you agree?'

Edgar had been making notes. He continued to write for a while before looking up at the Austrian. 'And what else?'

'How do you know there's anything else?'

'Because you're negotiating with me for your life, Herr Baumgartner, and in my considerable experience people in your position don't offer everything all at once.'

'Have I not offered enough?'

Edgar shrugged. 'Some money, a bit of jewellery and a few dirty photographs? That's not enough to save your life, I'm afraid.'

'There are two guns in the strongbox as well.'

'What type?'

'Semi-automatic pistols, Steyr-Hahns: Austrian army issue, from when we still had an army of our own. They're less than five years old and in excellent condition.'

'Ammunition?'

The Austrian nodded.

'Describe it.'

'Eight-round magazines, more than a hundred of them.'

Edgar said nothing while he lit another cigarette, this time not offering one to the man opposite him, who was beginning to look and sound desperate. 'Just say we were interested, Herr Baumgartner – how would we get our hands on the strongbox?'

Baumgartner shifted uncomfortably in his chair then lowered his head to the table, between his handcuffed hands. When he eventually peered up, his eyes were even more bloodshot and his lips were quivering. He nodded towards Edgar's cigarettes and allowed the Englishman to light another one for him.

'The strongbox has been hidden for us by a mutual acquaintance, a man called Johann,' he said. 'In return for hiding the box, we deposited a large sum of money for him in a safety deposit box at the Creditanstalt bank in the 1st District, the main branch in Schottengasse. That box contains the equivalent of some 300 pounds sterling in Reichsmarks and requires four keys to open it. I have one, my friend has one and Johann has one. When someone presents themselves at Creditanstalt with the three keys, the bank will produce the fourth: that's the only way they'll allow access to the box. Apparently, it's a system they've devised over many years because of Viennese families arguing with each other.'

'Hang on,' said Edgar. 'Why didn't you simply put everything in this safety deposit box in the bank, rather than involving Johann?'

'Once the Nazis came to power the banks were required to be much stricter about what was being kept in their deposit boxes. Managers had to show they were aware of their contents. It's alright for them to say a box contains cash or papers, but clearly guns…'

'So where's your key, Herr Baumgartner?'

The Austrian shrugged his shoulders. 'If I'm reprieved I'll tell you.'

'And how do I know you'll be telling the truth, Herr Baumgartner? You're six hours from your execution; surely you'll do anything you can just to save your life?'

'That's true, but if you act on the information I give you and find it's not true then the deal will be null and void, and no doubt you'll wish to proceed with the execution at some point in the future. You'll know where I am.'

'And how will you know to trust us?'

'The letter telling me I wasn't being reprieved was personally signed by the Home Secretary, Mr Morrison. I want a letter signed by him saying I am now reprieved. And I want one other thing with it, Mr Edgar: a magnifying glass.'

**

It was 3.15 when Edgar returned to the room on the ground floor of A Block and explained what Baumgartner had told him. The men from the Home Office shook their heads while Fowler from MI5 nodded appreciatively. The officer from Special Branch and the prison governor remained impassive. The Home Office man was the first to speak.

'I can't see any possible grounds for commuting the death sentence, certainly not now the Home Secretary has rejected Baumgartner's plea for clemency. Even if there were grounds for considering it, what's he offered – some money, jewellery, a couple of pistols and some filthy photographs? We can't advise the Home Secretary to issue such a letter on those grounds. We may as well dispense with the courts and run things like the Nazis do.'

'I'm sorry, I'm not sure I remember your name?' Edgar was addressing the Home Office man, the one who was the superior of Simons or Simmond. Edgar peered at him as if he'd only just noticed he was in the room.

'Otter. Martin Otter.'

'I take it, Mr Otter, that you've never served in the field of intelligence?'

Otter nodded tentatively.

'So you'll have no idea of the extremely perilous and exposed nature of operating in enemy territory,' Edgar continued. 'The agents we have operating inside Occupied Europe have very few resources they can rely upon, but at least they do get some help from resistance groups and sympathetic members of the local population. But the few agents we have operating inside the German Reich – which Austria is now part of – are in an even more dangerous predicament because they can't rely on any assistance from the civilian population and there's no resistance to speak of. If what Herr Baumgartner has told us is true, then I can't tell you how valuable the contents of this strongbox would be. Agents need money, they need weapons and, above all, they need intelligence. You can't appreciate unless you've worked in this area how hard these are to come by in hostile territory. Taking large sums of money and weapons into Austria is risky in the extreme: knowing where they're stashed away would make an enormous difference.'

They argued until the clock behind the governor edged past 4.00: the Home Office adamant no reprieve could be offered, the two intelligence services insisting it was in British interests to do so. At 4.05, Edgar asked the governor if he could use a telephone. Twenty minutes later he returned to the room.

'Mr Otter? The Home Secretary would like a word with you.'

A palpably crestfallen Otter returned to the room less than five minutes later, with all the appearance of a defeated man.

'The letter from the Home Secretary will be ready within the hour I'm assured,' he said. 'A police car will collect it from the Home Office.'

The least surprised person in the room was Edgar. 'We need to get Baumgartner's solicitor along here as soon as possible,' he said. 'And a magnifying glass.'

**

Walter Baumgartner's solicitor padded into the meeting room at 5.45 – around the time the first hints of the early morning sun were beginning to break through the fast-disappearing night clouds. Geoffrey Hayfield-Smyth was an extraordinary looking man: at least as tall as Edgar, but his painfully thin frame was quite hunched. He was bald apart from two wild tufts of hair on either side of his head and his eyes were sunk deep into their sockets, which in turn were overhung with thick eyebrows. His chin, which was specked with shaving rashes, merged into a long neck. This all contributed to a startled appearance. When he spoke it was in the kind of well-educated voice keen for the listener to understand the speaker's innate superiority.

'Why have I been brought here at this time? The execution is not until 9.00. My instructions had been to arrive at 8.00.' Hayfield-Smyth had been speaking to the governor, but it was Edgar who replied.

'Mr Hayfield-Smyth, my name is Edgar and I represent a

Government intelligence agency. Since you last saw Herr Baumgartner yesterday he's been in touch with us to offer some important information.'

'You mean you saw him without me being present?'

'Under wartime regulations, Mr Hayfield-Smyth, you do not have the right to be present when a prisoner is being questioned by either of the intelligence services, I'm sure you're aware of that. Can I ask, do you have with you the letter from Mr Morrison informing you the appeal for clemency has been rejected?'

The solicitor rummaged around in his briefcase and handed an envelope to Edgar, who opened it and read the letter. From another envelope, Edgar produced another letter and handed it to Hayfield-Smyth.

'Would you care to read this please?'

'Out loud?'

'If you please.'

The solicitor glanced at the letter with a growing look of shock on his face then cleared his throat before reading at what sounded like dictation speed.

'Dear Mr Hayfield-Smyth,

'I am writing subsequent to my letter of the 12th, informing you that I saw no grounds to justify not proceeding with the execution of your client, Walter Baumgartner. It has since come to the attention of the Home Office that your client has been able to be of very considerable assistance to His Majesty's Government and, in light of this development

I am pleased to inform you that I have reviewed my original decision and am now able to commute the original sentence from one of death to a term of 18 years imprisonment. I would be grateful if you could inform your client of this decision without delay.

Yours sincerely,
Herbert Morrison
Home Secretary

Long after he'd finished reading the letter, Hayfield-Smyth continued to stare at it in apparent disbelief. He looked around the room: at Edgar, at the prison governor, the two men from the Home Office and the man from MI5.

'And this is genuine, is it?'

'It's quite genuine, Mr Hayfield-Smyth. The Home Secretary himself signed the letter less than an hour ago. What you'll need to do is accompany myself and the governor up to see Herr Baumgartner, where you'll assure him of the veracity of this letter and that his life has been reprieved.'

The solicitor read the letter once more then allowed his head to drop in a resigned manner. He started to speak, then shook his head.

'The point is,' said Edgar, leaning over to Hayfield-Smyth, 'your client has been able to indicate he can be of considerable help to us. But he'll only do so when he's satisfied he'll not be executed.'

***

It was a little after 8.30 when they entered the condemned cell. It was already a warm July morning and blades of sunlight were piercing through the high window, giving the room an ethereal quality. Baumgartner was sitting at the table, playing cards with one of the three wardens in the room. He sat up with a start when the governor entered the room, Edgar and Hayfield-Smyth in his wake. Edgar noticed the prisoner was peering behind them, clearly concerned at whoever may be following. The governor instructed the warders to leave the cell and wait in the corridor. Edgar had to nudge Hayfield-Smyth to sit down in front of his client. When he finally did so, he removed the letter from the Home Secretary and showed it to the man sitting opposite him.

'It's a letter granting you a reprieve, Herr Baumgartner.'

Edgar wasn't sure how convincing Hayfield-Smyth sounded. The Austrian said little, but he did lean over to the small table beside his bed to collect a dictionary. For a few minutes he carefully read the letter, from time to time checking the translation.

'And this is official?'

The solicitor hesitated before nodding.

'It couldn't be more official, Herr Baumgartner,' added Edgar. From his pocket he removed a magnifying glass and handed it to the Austrian.

'Ah, you remembered. Good. Mr Hayfield-Smyth, please could I see the letter you showed me yesterday?'

For a few minutes Baumgartner examined both letters, nodding silently to himself. 'What I'd not told you was I'm an expert in checking documents. When I worked for the von Rothschild Bank I was often the person who examined documents in case they were forgeries. Not only can I distinguish a fake signature from a genuine one, but I can also tell if a letter has been typed on the same machine. These two letters have been typed on the same machine, on the same paper and signed by the same person.'

'So you're satisfied, Herr Baumgartner?'

'What is the time please? I cannot understand why I'm not allowed a watch or why there's no clock in here.'

'I'm afraid it's our practice not to have clocks or watches in a condemned cell,' said the governor.

'So I'm still a condemned man?'

'No,' said Edgar calmly. 'That letter makes it clear you've been reprieved, does it not Mr Hayfield-Smyth?'

Hayfield-Smyth nodded slowly.

'So what's the time?'

'Ten to nine.'

'I need more time to think. Come back in an hour.'

***

An hour later Edgar was on his own in the condemned cell with the Austrian, who no longer looked as if he was consumed by fear. 'For some reason, I trust you,' he said.

'Thank you,' said Edgar.

'But then, it's not as if I have much alternative, is it?'

Edgar said nothing. His experience told him that when the fish had the bait in its mouth, he should stop pulling.

'You've still got your notebook?' asked Baumgartner.

Edgar nodded and removed it from his pocket then placed it on the table between them, his pen poised.

'Good, listen carefully. The friend I told you about is called Wilhelm. To make contact with him, go to the Café Demel on Kohlmarkt, very near the Hofburg Palace. Wilhelm breakfasts at Demel every morning: he never arrives before 9.00 but is always there by 9.30. He sits at a small table that's on its own towards the back, in front of the kitchen where they prepare the pastries – which you can see through the glass windows. He's a tall man, about your height but much thinner and he wears round spectacles. He's around 35, but looks younger. He'll drink a lot of coffee – or whatever they're calling coffee these days – and smoke non-stop. Can I have a piece of paper, please?'

Edgar tore a sheet out of his notebook and passed it to the Austrian, who wrote a few words on it and handed it back to Edgar.

'When you see him, ask one of the waitresses to pass this note to him. He'll know then he's to trust you, or whoever you send. Follow him from the restaurant and arrange when to go to the location of the strongbox, each with your own key.'

'And where's your key?'

'May I have another sheet of paper?'

From his briefcase Edgar found a large plain sheet of paper and a pencil. He placed both on the table in front of Baumgartner.

'In the 10th District there's a church called St Anton of Padua. It's a Catholic church – most of them in Vienna are. The church is just off Favoriten Strasse and is easy to find, it's a simple tram ride from the centre. The church has rather attractive gardens surrounding it and towards the rear, close to Antonsplatz, is a statue of St Anton. Now, look at my diagram, here – about one yard in this line from the statue, I've buried the key. It's wrapped in oilskin and buried in a small tin. Poke a spike down until you hit the tin then dig it out with a trowel. Because of its position near the statue, the person retrieving the key can kneel down and look as if they're praying. There'll be another key in the tin, for a padlock that's on the strongbox.'

Baumgartner finished the diagram and pushed the sheet of paper towards Edgar.

'The strongbox itself is hidden somewhere in a hat shop on Wiedner Hauptstrasse in the 4th District, just to the south of the Opern Ring – just a block or two away from the *naschmarkt*. Wilhelm will accompany you or your representative, but I ask there are no more than two of you. The store opens at 8.30 in the morning, but for the first hour Johann is alone, every day apart from Wednesdays. He's short and rather fat, and walks with a very bad limp – an injury from the Great War – so there's no chance he's been conscripted. Johann knows he's only to allow access to the strongbox if Wilhelm is present; it's another measure we've agreed to ensure one of us doesn't take the box without the other being there. Wilhelm should introduce the other person as his friend from Gleisdorf, which is a town near Graz. Johann will ask what kind of a hat they'd like and they must respond by saying they'd like a hat that's suitable for both church and hunting. You have all that?'

Edgar glanced up from his note-taking, his cigarette still lit between his lips.

'Johann will then show Wilhelm and the other person to where the strongbox is. At this point you hand over the two bank keys to him. He'll go back into the shop and you and Wilhelm can open the box, remove the contents then leave.'

'And that's it?'

'That's it: money, gold, jewellery, the photographs, guns… is that not enough?' Baumgartner leaned back in his chair. 'Do you have the time?'

Edgar checked his watch. 'It's just gone 10.20.'

The Austrian chuckled. 'I should have been dead over an hour ago!'

Edgar smiled.

'I'd be relieved if they could move me out of this cell as soon as possible. You'll understand I feel rather uncomfortable here.'

***

In the room on the ground floor Edgar was brief and to the point, and when he'd finished the man called Otter from the Home Office sounded affronted.

'So you won't tell us what he actually said?'

Edgar shook his head.

'In the world of intelligence it's a case of who needs to know, Mr Otter,' said Fowler from MI5. 'And I'm afraid you don't. The point is Edgar's satisfied. That's enough.'

'Right then,' said the governor, rising slowly from his chair and gathering his papers from in front of him. 'I think we all know what needs to happen now. Edgar, will you be joining us?'

Edgar shrugged. 'I think I'd better.'

Edgar, Fowler and Otter followed the governor as he left the room, and waited in a corridor while he entered a small office, emerging minutes later with a shocked-looking Hayfield-Smyth. The five of them silently climbed the stairs to the first floor and through a series of doors until they found themselves in the narrow corridor outside the condemned cell. Edgar noticed Otter had a hand on the solicitor's elbow, as if supporting him. There they waited for a few minutes, the governor looking at his watch throughout. At 10.59 a door at the end of the corridor opened and a warden led two men in civilian clothes towards them. The first man was short and dapper, the man behind him much taller and thicker-set. The first man nodded to the governor, who looked once more at his watch and waited a few seconds before nodding.

Even Edgar marvelled at the speed and efficiency of what happened next. The governor opened the cell door and the two men in suits entered very fast, the others following.

Walter Baumgartner appeared to have just stood up. Two of the guards moved to either side of him and the short, dapper man walked smartly behind a clearly startled Baumgartner with a leather strap in his hand. He quickly tied the Austrian's hands behind his back and said, 'Follow me'. While this was going on, a door on a side wall had been opened and Baumgartner was now being marched through it. Edgar, along with the governor, Hayfield-Smyth and Otter from the Home Office followed. They were now in a large room, most of which was taken up with a wooden platform, around which there was room for people to stand behind wooden railings. Edgar noticed a few people already there. Above the platform, hung from a beam, was a gleaming white rope with a stiff noose at its end.

Only then, when he saw the rope, did Baumgartner react. *Nein! Sie liegen Bastarde! Verdammt nochmal!*

The two wardens positioned the Austrian on a 'T' chalked on the floor. As they did that, the tall man in a suit was strapping Baumgartner's ankles together. He was still shouting '*nein*', and looking around the room and beginning to struggle. For a second, no more than that, his eyes locked on Edgar's, furious with loathing. The shorter man now produced a white hood from his pocket and pulled it over Baumgartner's head. In what seemed like the same move, he placed the noose over the man's head, tightening its knot below the left ear. Within a second the hangman sprang back, reached over to a lever and pulled it hard. There was a bang as the trapdoors opened and the body of Walter Baumgartner shot from sight. All that remained visible was the white rope, now taut and slowly swaying.

For a few seconds there was complete silence. The short man broke it when he spoke to the governor. 'How long?'

'Twenty-three seconds.'

The hangman shook his head. 'Longer than usual I'm afraid sir: that two-hour delay didn't help. Anyone know what he was saying?'

'Gist is he wasn't altogether happy with us,' said Edgar, his voice less confident than usual. 'Called us bastards. And liars.'

***

Ten minutes later in the governor's office the small group who'd witnessed the execution sat in silence; glasses of whisky trembling gently in their hands and spirals of cigarette smoke rising above them.

'Well, he was right, wasn't he?'

'Who was, Otter?'

'Baumgartner. You said he called us liars and bastards. We were.'

Edgar looked nonplussed. 'Well, that's our line of work, is it not? End justifies the means and all that. It was the only way of getting the information he was offering, you know that Otter. Even the Home Secretary understood what we were doing, which is why he agreed to the letter. It could result in saving many British lives. What Baumgartner had to tell us could turn out to be of the most enormous help to our network in Vienna.'

Everyone had now stood up, ready to leave. Edgar walked over to the solicitor. 'One thing, Mr Hayfield-Smyth: that letter from the Home Secretary, about the reprieve…'

'What about it?'

'Could you give it to me please?'

***

Edgar and Fowler left the prison together, the glorious sunshine bouncing off Pentonville's walls. 'Unnaturally quiet, isn't it Fowler?'

'Always like this on the day of an execution apparently, Edgar: no doubt gets the prisoners thinking about their own mortality.'

'Not just the prisoners,' said Edgar. 'Come on, we ought to

find a taxi on the Caledonian Road. That chap from the Home Office offered me a lift back but I couldn't bear the thought of another minute in his company.'

'Quite understand, but no need for a taxi,' said Fowler. 'The number 14 bus goes direct to Piccadilly Circus. Look Edgar, I'm not questioning what happened, but I presume it was absolutely necessary to go ahead with the execution? I'm just worried if this gets out, somehow. Baumgartner did give us all that information, after all.'

'Completely necessary: assuming what he told us was true, we could hardly risk having him alive and jeopardising that information, could we? Who knows who he'd tell? Too many fascists in the prison system.'

They'd now reached the bus stop. 'Well, let's hope he was telling the truth,' said Fowler.

A number 14 bus showing Putney as its destination was pulling in.

'Oh, he was telling the truth alright.'

'How do you know?'

'Gut instinct – I've learnt to sense when someone's lying. Must be the same with you, Fowler. Plus his reaction when he realised he was about to die: he was genuinely aggrieved. And also, if he was lying, I think he'd have embellished a lot more – offered us the crown jewels, so to speak.'

'Well, so long as it's of some help. Every little bit counts, eh? One other thing Edgar: you mentioned about our network in Vienna. I didn't realise we still have one there?'

Edgar waited until they'd seated themselves on the top deck, out of the earshot of other passengers, before replying.

'That's the thing Fowler: we don't.' Edgar removed his wide-brimmed trilby and placed it carefully on his lap. 'Not yet, at any rate.'

Chapter 5

Vienna and the Vatican, December 1943

In the second half of 1943, somewhere between the fourth full summer of the war and its fifth winter, Sister Ursula was overwhelmed with such a profound sense of fear and self-doubt that she abandoned her resistance work.

She would, she decided, avoid any contact with the British: she'd not go anywhere near the dead-letter drops, she'd keep away from the other places where messages might be passed on to her and she'd ignore the one or two remaining contacts she'd been nurturing. The best course of action, she concluded, was to do nothing and hopefully they'd forget about her and leave her alone. She had, she reasoned, done her bit. No one could accuse her of cowardice.

Until she stopped working for the British she'd not quite appreciated the impact doing so had been having on her. The fear that overwhelmed her had been easier to deal with because it was more understandable, more tangible. She was working as an agent for British intelligence in a city that rivalled and possibly outdid Munich in its enthusiasm for the Nazis. Her nun's habits offered little protection: since their arrival in 1938 the Nazis had been increasingly hostile to the Catholic Church. At best it was something of a disguise; people still associated nuns with innocence and treated them with a degree of respect. It would have been more worrying had she not been fearful.

But the self-doubt was far more difficult for her to understand

and cope with. She wondered why she was risking her life and possibly putting colleagues in danger. She reached the stage where she was constantly questioning her own motives. She asked her Mother Superior whether it was possible for a person to be truly altruistic. 'If someone devotes their life to others,' Mother Superior had told her, 'then we can't deny that somewhere in their soul they're getting some kind of satisfaction from that. Maybe that's God's reward. We shouldn't question it.'

She was assured, too, at confession. 'Ah, is it an indulgence to help others because in doing so one gets a sense of having done good? I'm asked that question many times.'

The confession box had a musty, unpleasant odour to it and the priest on the other side of the grille was elderly and had kept blowing his nose loudly. She'd an urge to tell him the good she was doing went far beyond her devotion to prayer and charity, and exceeded her tireless nursing of the sick. He'd have been horrified if she'd confided in him just a small amount of her activities: how she helped people escape from the Nazis, how she carried messages and even weapons. How some of the people she helped were probably communists, certainly atheists. But she'd have no more confided in him than she would have written to the Vienna Gestapo to inform them of her activities. She simply said nothing more other than how she felt her soul was in torment.

'Remember the wise words of Silouan of Athos,' the priest told her. He sounded as if he was chewing as he spoke. 'Keep thy mind in hell and despair not.'

And by December she felt better: her appetite had returned, she was sleeping better in the little time she had for it and she felt more fulfilled by her work at the hospital. She was, she realised, a very good nurse. Perhaps a better nurse than she was a nun, certainly a better nurse than a spy.

But if at any time during those three months she'd allowed herself to be honest with herself she'd have perhaps admitted that as good as she was at being a nurse and a nun, the world of espionage was one she feared she could never truly leave.

And sure enough, she was now back in it. She'd crossed the Gürtel, Vienna's outer ring road, and into the more desirable area on the outskirts of the city on the way to the Vienna Woods. Here there were more trees and parks and the houses were bigger and liked to style themselves as villas.

And one of those villas was a safe house.

***

The priest hurried from his office in the Palazzo del Sant' Uffizio on the southern edge of Vatican City and, despite the heavy rain, headed into Saint Peter's Square. It was early in the afternoon at the beginning of December and the vast square had small groups of pilgrims and other visitors dotted around it. It was quite busy towards the centre, where people were grouped more closely together and Father Bartolomeo made a point of moving into the crowd. Once he was surrounded by people, he put on a *capello romano* hat that, with its round crown and wide brim, helped make him indistinguishable – he hoped – from any other priest hurrying around the Vatican. He couldn't be sure he wasn't being followed, but these days he worked on the assumption that he was. It was safer that way.

Going through Saint Peter's and the Apostolic Palace would have been a quicker and certainly a drier route to where he was going, but he'd have been more exposed and far easier to follow in the wide, long corridors. He moved to the north side of the square, mingling briefly with another group of visitors outside the Colonatto del Bernini before moving through the colonnades, past the barracks of the Swiss Guard and into Via del Belvedere. He was now in what they called the business end of the Vatican, away from the public eye and where many of the routine functions of this tiny city state were carried out. He made a point of stopping at the telegram office to check if anything was waiting for him then left through a side door, emerging into a rain-soaked Via della Posta. Halfway down the street was a building with a larger array of brass nameplates and bells than its neighbours. As he was about to press one of the bells the large front door opened and an elderly bishop hobbled out. Father Bartolomeo slipped through the open door and climbed the steep stairs to the apartment on the top floor that, according to a fading notice taped to the frosted glass door was the British Diplomatic Mission to the Holy See. A dark-suited valet let him in and took him into an office where an older man, also in a dark suit, was waiting for him.

'Are you well Father Bartolomeo?'

'I am Sir Percy, thank you. And you, I trust?'

The British Minister to Vatican nodded. The valet had come in and poured whisky for the two men then left. 'I received the message you need to see me, urgently,' said the priest. 'Is it about the pilots?'

'No, I think all's well with them. I don't know how you keep finding these houses Father, but we admire your resourcefulness. I need to discuss a more pressing matter with you...'

The British diplomat pulled his jacket tightly around him as if he was cold and leaned towards the priest. 'I know I've said this to you many times, Father, but we really are most terribly grateful for everything you do. We realise just how dangerous it is. I'm afraid that what we're about to ask of you may be even more dangerous. We've had a message from London...' He hesitated, struggling to phrase what he was about to say correctly. 'Let me ask you a question first, Father: how easy would it be for you to travel to Vienna?'

The priest closed his eyes for a moment, somewhere between prayer and thought. 'Easy may not be the best word. It's possible, certainly. Of course the Vatican sends emissaries to the Cardinal in Vienna on a frequent basis, perhaps two or three times a month. If...'

'... Could you become one of those emissaries?'

'I see no reason why not: I'm a Vatican diplomat and travel under a diplomatic passport. I know the Bishop who's in charge of these matters... he's also from Turin and knows my uncle well. I could approach him...'

'You'd need to do this in a way that wouldn't arouse suspicion.'

'Of course: but I've done this before. I'd mention to him I could do with being away from Rome for a few days and ask where he needs to send people to. That tends to be the way it works. From my experience he'll mention a few places and there's a chance Vienna will be one of them, so it'll appear he's offering

Vienna to me rather than me mentioning it, if you get what I mean. It won't be easy though. You should know that relations between the church in Austria and the Nazis are very bad: Cardinal Innitzer strongly resents the way the Nazis have diminished the authority of the church and he's been quite outspoken. I understand visits there tend to be quite… tense. But with my diplomatic cover, it could be possible.'

'When could you approach this Bishop?'

'Tomorrow morning.'

'Good. Before I explain what we'd like you to do in Vienna, I need to give you more background. Does the name Hubert Leitner mean anything to you?'

The priest leaned back in his chair and frowned, slowly shaking his head. 'I'm afraid not.'

'Don't worry,' said Sir Percy. 'All you need to know is that, before the Anschluss, Hubert Leitner was perhaps the most respected politician in Austria. He'd been a senior officer in the Austro-Hungarian army in the Great War, where he fought with great distinction and was regarded as a hero. After the war he went into politics: he was a leading member of the Christian Social Party, which was strongly opposed to a union with Germany. When Austria became a one-party fascist state under Dollfuss, Leitner resigned from the Christian Social Party, forged links with the Social Democrats, and spoke out against Dollfuss and the Nazis. He had an enormous amount of public respect and was imprisoned once or twice, but never for very long. However, as soon as the Nazis took over in March 1938, he disappeared. No one had the faintest idea what'd happened to him, apart from an unconfirmed report he'd been killed trying to cross into Slovenia, in 1940.'

'This is most interesting, Sir Percy, but I'm not sure why you're telling me. Do I really need to know it? I can't be here for too long.'

'Bear with me,' said Sir Percy patiently. 'A few days ago our Head of Station in Bern was approached by a Swiss diplomat based in Vienna with an important message for British intelligence. According to this diplomat, not only is Leitner alive and well, but he's in Vienna, where he's been in hiding since the war began. This Swiss diplomat had been looking after him in a safe house but now he's been transferred away from Vienna there's some concern Leitner will have to leave too.'

'And you want me to... rescue him?' The priest sounded alarmed and stood up, walking over to the window and looking out of it. Instead of returning to his seat he paced around the room as Sir Percy continued.

'No, no, no – nothing like that' said the British diplomat. 'Apart from any other consideration, it'd be far too dangerous to try to get Leitner out of Vienna. The man's in his seventies and is very well-known. No. There's someone in Vienna who works for us, but we need to get in contact with this person and they'll move him to another safe house. But first, we need to get all this information to that person – about Leitner, where he is and all that. We're asking you to go to Vienna and pass that message on. It has to be done in person, there can be nothing on paper, which is why I've given you all the background: you'll need to memorise the address of where Leitner is at the moment.'

***

A fortnight later, as Vienna made some half-hearted gestures towards Christmas, Father Bartolomeo found himself in the city's Archbishop's Palace, on the other side of Schulerstrasse from the mighty Stephansdom cathedral. It was late in the afternoon, already dark and he'd arrived in Vienna an hour previously. He had left Rome early that morning: a Deutsche Lufthansa flight lasting nearly four hours from Rome to Munich, then a surprisingly straightforward train journey from Bavaria. He'd been taken immediately into an audience with Cardinal Innitzer, waiting during an awkward silence in his study while the Cardinal opened a series of sealed letters from the Vatican, glancing suspiciously up at Father Bartolomeo as he did so. Soon after the German takeover of Austria the Cardinal had famously announced to a congregation of thousands at the cathedral that 'our Fuhrer is Christ'. That had earned him the wrath of the Nazis and now he trusted no one. Father Bartolomeo knew the feeling.

After evening Mass and dinner he retired to a lounge in the palace with a Bishop he knew from Rome and some of the priests on the Cardinal's staff. As the priests drifted away, one by one, the Bishop gestured for Father Bartolomeo to join him in a corner, by a large and uncomfortably hot fire.

'We live in very testing times, Father Bartolomeo.' The Bishop reminded Father Bartolomeo of a medieval monk: a rotund figure, bald, with a weathered face and the trace of a beard. The Bishop said no more for a while, gazing into the fire, the flames from it reflecting in his unblinking eyes and picking out thin threads of red veins on his face. 'When I knew you in Rome, you were a man with a strong social conscience. Is that still the case?'

'I'm not sure what you mean, My Lord.'

The Bishop turned around, checking the room was now empty. He leaned closer towards the priest. 'I know you're a discreet and careful man, Father Bartolomeo, but I also know you had views, shall we say, on the situation in Europe. You don't need to respond, I trust you. The situation here is dreadful: do you know, we receive reports every day about the old and the sick simply disappearing from the places where they're meant to be cared for. It's no secret the Nazis have a euthanasia programme: they simply dispose of people they regard as being a burden. Whenever any of our priests or nuns complain about it, they're arrested and some have even been killed. It is all so un-Christian.'

'And what about the Jews?'

The Bishop shrugged, as if to indicate this was less of his concern. 'There are hardly any left in Vienna.' He held his hands outward, palms down and moved them across his body. *Finished.*

'Your visit here... you're not just a messenger, are you Father? I'd have thought you're too senior for that.'

It was now Father Bartolomeo's turn to look around to reassure himself they were alone in the room. 'I'm told there's a convent of the Daughters of Charity of Saint Vincent de Paul in the 9th District my Lord...' he said in a tentative tone, letting the sentence remain unfinished, hoping the Bishop would do it for him. The older man said nothing but did raise his eyebrows. 'If I um... wanted... needed... to contact one of the sisters there...?'

The Bishop sighed and dropped his head slightly: *I thought as much.* 'Then it'd be safer for you to meet her here. You mustn't leave the Palace; you'll almost certainly be followed. I'll send a messenger.'

***

After Mass the following morning, Sister Ursula was taken aside by her Mother Superior as she entered the refectory for breakfast: she'd been summoned to the Archbishop's Palace; she was to go immediately. The Mother Superior placed a hand on her shoulder and gave her the puzzled and concerned look she always did when she suspected Sister Ursula was up to something. 'Be careful, Sister.'

An hour later Sister Ursula was in a small study at the back of the palace, sitting opposite a priest she was told was 'from Rome'. She'd been given no name and she studied him carefully as he walked around the room, checking the windows were closed and the door shut. She remembered a vet telling her that, after they'd passed the kitten stage, cats had two distinct phases to their lives: they were young then they were old. She'd come to believe the same applied to priests: when they were in their twenties they looked as if they were in their mid-thirties and this appearance would remain – seemingly unchanged – until their mid-fifties. Sometime after that, they would quite suddenly take on the appearance of an old man. There seemed to be no middle age, nothing in between, no discernible ageing process. The priest who now sat down opposite her looked in his mid-thirties, with a paler complexion than she'd have expected of an Italian, but thick black hair and dark eyes. A good-looking man, were she ever to admit to such feelings.

'You don't speak Italian I suppose?' He was speaking to her in heavily accented German. She shook her head.

The priest coughed and closed his eyes, taking care with what he was about to say. 'I bring you greetings from Doctor Huber. I understand you worked with him in the past?' He spoke slowly and, as if he was reading, the intonation not quite right.

Since the early morning summons to the Palace, Sister Ursula had feared this: they'd returned. She could, however, at this point choose to fail to respond in the expected way to the first part of this coded message, in which case the other person would have instructions to abandon the dialogue. She also had the option of an answer that would indicate she was in danger, that she'd been compromised. Either way, they'd then leave her alone. She felt her throat tighten, her heart beat faster, and the fear and self-doubt begin to return.

She chose the other way. 'Yes, I remember Doctor Huber: an anaesthetist, a fine man.'

The priest looked relieved. Her answer had been a long time coming but it was the correct one. 'And his two daughters asked to be remembered to you too. Do you recall their names?'

'Margarete and Ingrid, if I remember correctly. And his wife... please remind me of her name?'

The priest smiled, the exchange was going as Sir Percy had told him it would if all was well. 'I understand Frau Huber's first name is Emilie.'

The nun nodded: *correct*.

Father Bartolomeo paused, realising just how nervous he'd been. He exhaled, as if he'd been holding his breath and wiped beads of sweat from his forehead with the back of his shaking hand. 'Is all well with you, Sister? My friends say they've not heard from you in a while.'

'All's well with me, thank you Father.'

'The lack of contact… perhaps there's a reason?'

'As I say, all's well with me, thank you.'

'Good, in that case I have instructions for you. You're to listen very carefully and memorise the details.'

***

It was two days before Sister Ursula travelled to Währing, the 18th District. The priest from Rome had insisted her visit was urgent, but she was determined to do nothing that could arouse suspicion, so she waited until she had a day off from the hospital. In the old days her absence from the convent would have been noticed and even remarked upon, but these were no longer the old days.

She took a series of trams into Währing, managing to avoid conversation with any of her fellow passengers. If anyone showed signs of wanting to talk – which some people took the nun's habit as an invitation to do – they'd soon notice her eyes were closed in prayer and her lips moving with it, her fingers toying with the rosary.

She left the last tram some way before her destination then walked the last few streets to ensure she wasn't being followed. It was a crisp, clear morning and noticeably quieter than in the centre of the city. She found the address she'd memorised: it was detached, in a comfortable road alongside the Türkenschanzpark, its front shaded and almost concealed by trees. It was also slightly shabby, so typical of Vienna these days. Such a smart city before the war, she thought, people took such pride in everything. Now that wasn't such a priority.

The house is owned by a Frau Graf: we understand she's in her sixties. It's her you're to see, no one else.

The door was opened by a stout girl in her twenties with what sounded like a Carinthian accent. She'd find Frau Graf, she said, appearing resentful at having to interrupt her housework. When Frau Graf finally appeared she was a tiny figure who looked to be more in her seventies than her sixties. She had that refined appearance so common among Viennese women, but like so many of them these days, she wasn't quite as well-maintained as she once would have been. Like her house.

She ushered the nun into a lounge at the back of the house and told the maid they weren't to be disturbed. Frau Graf perched on the end of a settee, tense and looking quizzically at her unexpected visitor. 'How can I help you, Sister?'

'I understand you take in lodgers? I've been told to tell you I have a nephew from Graz who may require accommodation.'

Frau Graf's shoulders sagged in relief. 'Oh thank goodness. Do you know how long I've been waiting for someone to come along and say those words? I'll tell you...' she paused and beckoned the nun closer to her, speaking now in a whisper. 'I've had Herr Leitner here for nearly two years, two years! Can you imagine? When the Swiss diplomat asked me, it was to be for a few weeks. But what could I do? His father had been a dear friend of my late husband's when he studied in Zürich and I felt obliged to help: he asked me in such a way that I couldn't refuse, he was so persuasive. Of course I was – I am – a great admirer of Herr Leitner. But the strain of hiding him here has been terrible and, I have to tell you, he's, how can I put it… difficult. I don't want to speak out of order but he's what my mother used to call grumpy. That was the word she used to describe my father when he came home from work and Herr Leitner is just like that: grumpy. Nothing's ever quite good enough, you know? One day he…'

'Frau Graf …'

'No one knows, you realise? None of my family, my friends, no one. Heidi, the maid – she's no idea. Herr Leitner is in the attic so she doesn't go there, but on the days she does clean upstairs he hides. The strain has been terrible…'

'And no one suspects?' Sister Ursula was shocked at how indiscreet Frau Graf was being.

'Of course not. You live in Vienna, Sister?'

'Yes.'

'Then you'll know that if people suspect anything they'll inform. I trust no one, not even my own sister. I've become so secretive with her that she's convinced I'm turning odd, just like our mother did. Perhaps it's best for her to think that.'

'I understand Herr Leitner has to leave here?'

'Yes!' Frau Graf leaned forward and clasped the nun's hands in hers. 'I'm so relieved. I'm so grateful to you.'

'But if no one suspects anything, isn't he safer here?'

'But the diplomat promised he'd be moved!' She sounded quite offended now, even angry. 'He said he wouldn't be able to visit any more and I relied on him – he gave me money to help buy food, you understand. Also, I'm not sure I like the way Herr Leitner looks at me sometimes. I'm not suggesting anything improper, of course not, but sometimes... I feel uncomfortable. Then a few weeks ago I had a letter from the authorities. Because I live here on my own and have three spare bedrooms, well – they want to accommodate people here because of the bombing in the city. It might even be soldiers, who knows? It's essential he's moved.'

Frau Graf began sobbing and Sister Ursula went to sit next to her on the settee. She reassured her that of course Herr Leitner would be moved, she'd make arrangements as soon as possible. Could she see Herr Leitner, possibly?

'Wait until Heidi leaves,' said Frau Graf, more composed now.

It was close to lunchtime when the maid left and Frau Graf took Sister Ursula up to the top floor of the house, having first paused on the first-floor landing where Frau Graf pressed a bell hidden behind a painting. *That's to alert him: one ring and he knows it's me coming up, two rings for danger.* She unlocked the attic door and Sister Ursula recognised the old man standing hunched in the middle of the attic, but only just. She'd never been very interested in politics, but she'd always admired Hubert Leitner for his obvious integrity and his determination for Austria to be free and independent. The man she remembered from newspaper photographs and newsreel had been younger, his bearing more upright, his hair fuller and darker, and his complexion less pale.

'The Sister has come to take you to a safer place, Herr Leitner,' said Frau Graf in a slightly bossy tone.

The old man gestured for the nun to sit down on one of the two small armchairs in the attic, which appeared to be a series of small, interconnecting rooms with heavily sloping ceilings. He had particularly small eyes and they darted around the room, taking everything in: Frau Graf, the nun and the space behind them in case anyone else might be there. He didn't look wholly trusting. 'Today? I'll be leaving today?'

Frau Graf looked at Sister Ursula, clearly hoping she was going to say yes.

'I need perhaps two or three days to arrange it. Frau Graf, I hope you'll understand if I ask you to leave? I need to discuss some arrangements with Herr Leitner and for your own safety, if for no other consideration, it's best you know nothing of what we discuss.'

She waited a few minutes until she was satisfied Frau Graf had descended the stairs. 'How long have you been here, Herr Leitner?'

'Around two years, Sister. I can tell you exactly, if you wish. Why do you ask?' His voice sounded as distrusting as his eyes had looked.

'There's something important I need to tell you first: I'm working on behalf of the British Government. I've been told to tell you that in due course they'll be in touch with you. Do you understand that?'

Leitner nodded, his eyes darting around the room again.

'You understand that you need to be moved? It seems this house may not be safe for much longer. I've somewhere in mind that'll be safer. But I fear it won't be an improvement on where you are now in terms of comfort. Would you have a problem being underground, where you wouldn't see any daylight?'

The old man shrugged and coughed nosily, pausing to spit into a dirty handkerchief before replying. 'As long as I'm safe. I've begun to feel increasingly less safe here for the last few months.

Frau Graf is a nervous woman, as you may have noticed. I've my doubts about how much longer she can be relied upon. Can I ask you this one question, the place you're taking me to – will it be in Austria?'

'Oh yes, sir. It'd be too risky to take you very far.'

***

Sister Ursula left the house in Währing at lunchtime, declining Frau Graf's offer to join her for a meal and promising she'd return before the end of the week. 'You'll receive a telephone call, informing you of the time of a furniture delivery,' she instructed her. 'Please make sure Herr Leitner is ready that day and that no one else is here.'

She travelled back into the city, again on a series of trams. The final one took her over the Danube Canal into Leopoldstadt, from where it was a short walk to her destination. Once there she remained with the woman and the man for over an hour. *We understand, we're prepared... maybe allow us another day or two? A van? Yes that's possible, again, in a day or two...*

It was three days later when a battered Daimler van rattled its way round the Gürtel and headed noisily into Währing. The van's dark-cream colour was losing a battle with rust and it looked slightly shabbier than would have been expected in this district, but then all of the decent vans and lorries had been pressed into military service. The van pulled up alongside the house by the Türkenschanzpark then reversed very carefully into the drive so its rear doors were almost flush with the front door of the house. The driver rang the front-door bell and it was opened quickly by Frau Graf.

'I have the chair you ordered. Are you on your own?'

Frau Graf nodded.

'No problem,' said the driver. 'I can carry it in myself.' He opened the rear doors of the van. Crouching behind a small upholstered chair was Sister Ursula, who nodded and smiled at Frau Graf. *Everything's well.*

The driver carried the chair into the house, Frau Graf looking at it with a degree of distaste. With its frayed embroidery and chipped legs it was clearly not the kind of chair she'd have in her house, but that was the least of her considerations. After the driver had carried it into the lounge he spoke in an urgent manner. 'Is he ready?'

'Yes.'

'Get him down now. We need to move fast.'

A minute later Frau Graf came down the stairs with Leitner slowly following her, the brim of a dark Homburg shading much of his face and a woollen scarf wrapped up to his nose. He was carrying a small case and paused in the hall to shake Frau Graf's hand in a formal manner. His voice was muffled somewhat by the scarf.

'Thank you, Frau Graf, you don't understand…'

'Quick,' said the driver. 'We need to move. Someone could turn up.'

'Just one thing,' said Leitner as he climbed awkwardly into the back of the van. 'I left another bag on the landing. It has books in it. Please could I take that too?'

The driver and the nun looked at each other, and the nun nodded.

'Alright then, you'll probably need them.'

Chapter 6

Moscow, December 1943

'A pleasant journey, I trust?'

Christopher Porter fixed the man sitting opposite him with as disapproving a glare as he could muster in the circumstances, which wasn't easy given his eyelashes felt as if they were still frozen together. The room on the second floor of the British Embassy on Sofiyskaya Naberezhnaya was allegedly heated, but the man from London was impervious to warmth. He couldn't imagine ever being warm again and worried that, when he spoke, his teeth would chatter. Because he couldn't stop shivering he held his hands clasped tightly behind his back as he paced around the room.

'The convoy left Loch Ewe on 22nd November, 15 ships in total. The voyage comprised the 11 longest and coldest days of my life, seeing as you ask, Neville. I never imagined one could be so cold and survive. It gets into every part of your body like little blocks of ice and stays there: I can still feel it now. I was on *HMS Beagle*: brought a couple of volumes of Trollope with me, barely managed a chapter. Apparently there was a pack of U-boats lurking around the Norwegian Sea, but somehow we managed to avoid them.'

'Well, I'm sorry, Christopher. Yours was only the second convoy to come over since February, it was never going to be an easy journey. At least you weren't attacked. We've lost so many ships on the convoys. It breaks my heart.'

'I know, one should be grateful. Now then, Neville, your cables were very vague. Why exactly did you need me to risk my life and come over here?'

There was a pause as Neville Ponsonby left his chair and walked over to the window. He turned and looked out of it, the Kremlin ahead of him with the colourful domes of Saint Basil's Cathedral to his right and the hints of Red Square beyond that. Ponsonby's hands were thrust deep into his pockets and his shoulders slumped. When he finally turned around he looked troubled.

'I hope I'm not going to get into trouble for this, Christopher.'

'In trouble for what, Neville?'

'The thing about with working for the Service while based at an embassy is that one really is caught between a rock and a hard place. I know my primary loyalty is to the Service, I understand that, but one can't ignore the fact one works with our diplomatic colleagues on a daily basis. The truth is we tend to see from entirely different perspectives. The principles and the priorities of the diplomatic service are somewhat different to those of the intelligence service.'

Ponsonby wiped his now glistening forehead and sighed.

'I do understand, Neville,' said Porter. 'But do remember we're your masters. The fact there's something of a conflict between diplomacy and intelligence is nothing new: we have to handle that every day. I promise you, if there's any flak from this, we'll back you as we always do. Now, what is it?'

Ponsonby pushed a manila folder across his desk towards Porter. 'Are you familiar with this?'

Porter put on a pair of reading glasses and studied the front page. 'The Moscow Declaration? Yes. Eden signed it back in October, didn't he?'

'On the 30th October, to be precise, five weeks ago. Eden came over here especially for the negotiations. There are actually four parts to the Declaration, but this is the one I want to discuss.' Ponsonby turned over the pages of the document and angled the page towards Porter.

'The Declaration on Austria?'

'That's correct. We signed it along with the Americans and the Soviets.'

Porter picked the document up and put on his spectacles. 'Let me read it – I need to remind myself.'

'The governments of the United Kingdom, the Soviet Union and the United States of America are agreed that Austria, the first free country to fall victim to Hitlerite aggression, shall be liberated from German domination.

'They regard the annexation imposed on Austria by Germany on March 15th, 1938, as null and void. They consider themselves in no way bound by any charges effected in Austria since that date. They declare that they wish to see re-established a free and independent Austria and thereby to open the way for the Austrian people themselves, as well as those neighbouring states that will be faced with similar problems, to find that political and economic security which is the only basis for lasting peace. Austria is reminded, however, that she has a responsibility, which she cannot evade, for participation in the war at the side of Hitlerite Germany, and that in the final settlement account will inevitably be taken of her own contribution to her liberation.'

'Sounds eminently sensible to me, Neville,' said Porter as he pushed the document back across the desk.

'The problem isn't in the text of the Declaration, which Eden and Winston are apparently very happy with – and the Americans, of course. So's the embassy, I have to say. Sir Archibald is cock-a-hoop about it, taking as much credit as he can decently manage. The Foreign Office was insistent that, if nothing else, the declaration states Austria should be re-established after the war – and as a neutral country. Since Stalingrad, the feeling is that the tide of the war has turned against the Nazis and so we've been thinking about Europe after the war, you're as aware of that as I am. Their major concern about Austria is that it may fall within the Soviet sphere of influence. After all, look at this map.'

Ponsonby walked over to a large map of Europe on the wall behind Porter. 'Here, Vienna: we may think of Austria as being in Central Europe, but Vienna is further to the east than we perhaps appreciate. East of Prague, far closer to the Soviet border than the French one. So an agreement that Austria remains neutral after the war was seen as an absolute priority.'

They walked back to the desk and Porter picked up the document.

'Which is what it says here – "a free and independent Austria": I'm not sure I see the problem Neville.'

'Archie and the rest of them here are so pleased with themselves over the Declaration they won't hear a word against it. But since it's been signed I've been picking up all kinds of intelligence here in Moscow. In a nutshell, the Soviets are as thrilled as we are about the Declaration, but that's because they feel it's lulled us into a false sense of reassurance over Austria. The truth is they have no intention whatsoever of abiding by it. Remember the map, Christopher. They see Austria as part of their territory. They'll not allow it to be neutral or cede it to us, and the way things are going, there's a good chance the Red Army will reach Vienna first. And once they get there they won't leave.'

'You say you've been picking up all kinds of intelligence. What do you mean by that – gossip and that kind of thing?'

'Good heavens, Christopher, no: Moscow isn't that kind of a city. People don't gossip here, they barely talk. The NKVD hears everything, or at least people assume they do. But don't forget I've been here since 1937 and I've built up a damn good network of contacts in that time. Many of them have disappeared, of course, but since the Nazis invaded in 1941 it's been much easier. I know people in all the key ministries, even a couple in the Party. I'm not naïve, I'm quite aware they're not doing it to help us but more to help themselves, for whatever reasons. But they're all saying the same thing: the Kremlin is convinced they've pulled a fast one on us and the Americans, and as far as Molotov's concerned, there's about as much chance of him allowing Austria to remain neutral as there is of Stalin turning up at Lords and asking to use the nets.'

'And you say the Ambassador and everyone else here is unaware of that?'

'Not as such: they don't trust the Soviets entirely of course – they're not fools. But neither do they want to rock the boat. They know Winston regards the alliance with the Soviet Union as the cornerstone of our foreign policy, so they won't hear a word against them. That's why I felt you needed to come over here to be told.'

'That's all very interesting, Neville, but how are they actually going to achieve it? An awful lot's bound to happen between now and whenever we liberate Austria. The Soviets can't be sure of having things their own way, can they?'

Ponsonby leaned across the desk, gesturing for Porter to come closer to him. Their heads were now alongside each other and when Ponsonby spoke it was no more than a whisper.

'I have a contact called Darya who's an excellent source of intelligence, but I only hear from her once in a blue moon. When she wants to tell me something, she finds me: I've no way of contacting her. Now then, when top Soviet agents come back to Moscow after a time abroad they do one of two things with them: the ones they're unhappy with end up in the Lubyanka and never leave it, but those they're pleased with are put up in a dacha outside Moscow and treated like princes.

'Darya looks after them while they're in the dacha. I'm not sure what she gets up to, I don't like to ask, but I do know she gets very close to some of them, as it were. In the middle of November – a fortnight or so after the Moscow Agreement was signed – she stopped me as I was walking to my apartment. She was taking a big risk, but what she had to say was urgent. She told me there's one particular agent who's visited the dacha several times over the years; she says he's one of their top agents. She knows him as Vitaly, though that's a name he uses at the dacha. I get the impression he's especially close to her – so much so that he confides in her more than agents usually do. He'd been at the dacha the previous week and told her his next mission will be so dangerous he's unsure if he'll ever see her again.'

'And where's he being sent?'

'Vienna.'

'When?'

'As soon as possible, apparently. It can't be a coincidence. They must have brought this chap back as soon as the Moscow Declaration was signed and, if he's indeed one of their top chaps, they'll want him to start preparing the ground for them in Vienna.'

'Are you sure we can trust what she says?'

Ponsonby shrugged. 'She's been a source of mine for a number of years and she's never been wrong. I've no reason to think this is either disinformation or that she's been compromised. We've an agreed phrase she'd use if she's in trouble and she didn't use it.'

'And we've no name for this chap?'

'Other than Vitaly, no.'

'Can she at least provide a description of him?'

For the first time since Porter had arrived at the embassy, Ponsonby smiled. He walked over to his bookcase and selected a volume of *Das Kapital* from the top shelf then placed it on the desk in front of Porter, pointedly tapping the cover.

'What's this about, Neville? Please don't tell me you've gone over to the other side?'

'Turn to the beginning of Chapter Eight; the one entitled "Constant Capital and Variable Capital".'

'Please don't play games with me, Neville. I'm really not in the mood for Marx.'

'I think you'll find it worth your while: between the end of Chapter Seven and the start of Chapter Eight, there's a photograph of Vitaly.'

Vienna Spies

***

Christopher Porter was still in state of shock as he left Moscow on the Wednesday morning. He remained in that same state when he crossed the border into Finland early the following morning and he wasn't much better when he arrived in Stockholm a day later. He remained in an MI6 safe house until the following Tuesday, sending a series of increasingly urgent messages back to London.

I've got the bloody photograph with me and I'm not prepared to risk travelling with it on a boat. Remember, I've seen the bloody thing. I know it's him for Christ's sake!

Early on the Tuesday morning he took a Swedish Intercontinental Airlines flight from Bromma Airport in Stockholm to Perth. At Scone Aerodrome, an RAF Avro Lancastrian from Transport Command was waiting on the tarmac with its engines running to fly him straight down to London.

For the first time since he'd seen the photograph in Ponsonby's office, Porter began to relax. London, it seemed, had finally got the message. For the umpteenth time, he patted his breast pocket to check the photograph was still safe.

Now they'd have to do something about it.

Maybe it hadn't been such a bad journey after all.

Chapter 7

Moscow and London, December 1943

Viktor Krasotkin wished he shared the confidence his masters had in him.

It's because we trust you, they kept telling him. *It's because you're so good. We know you won't fail.*

He used to be so confident – it was impossible to undertake these missions without believing absolutely in what you were doing. But now he wasn't so sure. He'd been recalled to Moscow in the first week of November: by then the Comintern for which he'd worked no longer suited Stalin's purposes so it had been dissolved and Viktor found himself working for the intelligence arm of the NKVD, though most of the people in Moscow were ones he'd worked for before. However, some things had changed. The briefing from what turned out to be a bunch of idiots had been a long way from its usual standard, with none of the thoroughness he was used to. Then there was the debacle over his identity.

'You'll be a Slovak,' they told him, 'an engineer from Bratislava.'

'Are you mad? I don't speak Slovak!'

'But you speak Czech,' one of the idiots said.

'Yes, but not fluently and, though it's similar to Slovak, it's not the same. Vienna is just a few miles from the Slovakian border: sooner or later I'm bound to bump into Slovaks.'

They returned to the dacha the following day, the three idiots looking pleased with themselves as they spread a selection of documents on the table in front of him, his photograph staring out from some of them.

'Who's this?'

'Alain Vercher,' said the same idiot who'd thought he could be a Slovak engineer. 'Apparently many French workers have been sent to Vienna to work in the factories. You'll be one of them: your French is good enough, no?'

Viktor looked shocked then broke into laughter. 'And you think a French worker sent to Vienna is just going to be able to wander around the city, without arousing attention? They'll be slave labour and watched all the time. You'll have to do better than this.'

'It's a solid identity, it...'

'I tell you what,' Viktor interrupted. 'How about I go as an Englishman? My first name could be Winston and maybe you could get me one of those silly round hats that English gentlemen wear. That shouldn't attract too much suspicion in Vienna, should it? I'm sorry, but this isn't good enough.'

The three men opposite him looked stunned, and looked at each other then back at him. No one spoke to them like that: ever. 'Are you refusing to serve, comrade?'

The self-control Viktor had exercised for many years snapped. He leaned across the table and effortlessly grabbed the idiot by the collar, pulling his now crimson-red face to within an inch of his. The man was making a choking noise, his eyes bulging. 'Refuse to serve? When have I ever refused to serve? I've served in enemy territory for all these years and done everything I've been asked to do while you've been doing nothing more dangerous than cross an empty road. I'm your best agent left out there. I realise I'm not indispensible, but I'm a thousand times more indispensible than you are!'

He pushed the man hard back into his chair, watching as he struggled to regain his breath. The other two sat very still on either side of him, their faces white with fear, avoiding eye contact with Viktor.

He knew if they were going to come for him they'd do it at night, so he sent Darya away, anxious she shouldn't be caught up in any of this. He began to write a letter to the wife and daughter he hadn't seen for more than 13 years, but he'd no idea what to say and abandoned it, burning the paper in the fire. He'd shown emotion, which was unforgiveable, and he'd broken the cardinal rules of the service, ones he always demanded of others.

Never question; never discuss; never hesitate.

***

It was 9.00 on the morning of Wednesday 15th December and the freezing cold that had gripped Christopher Porter since he'd set off for Moscow three weeks previously had now been replaced by overwhelming exhaustion. Apart from a few hours here and there in Stockholm, he'd hardly slept since Moscow and, now back in London, he was doing all he could to stay awake.

In an ideal world he'd have taken the day off to allow himself a decent sleep, an indulgent hot bath, a decent breakfast at his club and perhaps an overdue visit to his barber on Jermyn Street. But since the revelation in Neville Ponsonby's office, his was certainly no longer an ideal world. Instead, he was in a cramped and stuffy secure room, high above St James' Square. Sir Roland Pearson was present because Downing Street had begun to take a dim view of Porter's department's tendency to withhold from other agencies intelligence they believed only they should be privy to. Edgar was there, of course, along with George Whitlock, looking worse than ever but insisting he was still Head of Station in Vienna even though he hadn't been in the city for more than five years.

'Your message was that this is an urgent meeting, Porter.' *And it had better be*, unspoken but implicit.

Porter stood up, increasing his chances of staying awake.

'I returned from Moscow yesterday. To be wholly accurate, I returned from Stockholm yesterday. It took me the best part of a week to get back from Moscow. It wasn't that much quicker than by convoy, though a damn sight safer – and warmer.'

'We weren't actually aware you were going to Moscow until you were halfway there, Porter,' said Sir Roland.

'I think I may have sent the cable just before the convoy left Scotland. I do apologise for that, Sir Roland, but it was terribly unclear as to when it would leave: it all depended on how long it would take for the convoy to form and for its close escort to arrive.'

'Hardly a reason for not informing me of your visit before you left,' said Sir Roland. 'And do you now feel able to share with us the purpose of this visit?'

'That's why I've asked you all here at such short notice. Neville Ponsonby had asked to see me as a matter of some urgency, but obviously it was impossible in the circumstances for him to say why, hence my visit. I didn't feel this was something I needed to clear with you, Sir Roland. I considered it a routine operational matter, not one you'd want to be bothered with. Ponsonby has something of a history of jumping the starter's gun and I couldn't be sure this wasn't another of those occasions: a false alarm in other words. I didn't want to waste your time if it was. As it transpired, it wasn't a wasted journey.'

Porter paused for a moment, picking up a cup of now lukewarm tea from the table and sipping from it. His hands were shaking and his eyes felt heavy. Edgar slid a silver cigarette case over to him and he happily helped himself to one, his hands still shaking as he lit it.

'You'll be aware, Sir Roland, that this country, along with the United States and the Soviet Union, signed a declaration in Moscow at the end of October,' said Porter. 'The declaration covered a number of issues to be dealt with after the war, but the one Ponsonby was most concerned about was this one, the Declaration on Austria. I've taken the liberty of obtaining copies for you. I'm not sure if you've seen it, Edgar, nor you, George.'

From his briefcase he removed three single sheets of paper, each headed 'Declaration on Austria'. He distributed them around the table and allowed a minute or so for the others to read the short statement.

'As you can see,' continued Porter. 'The Declaration guarantees Austria's neutrality, with all three parties agreeing it should be a free and independent state after the war. Since the declaration was signed, Ponsonby has picked up quite a lot of talk in Moscow that the Soviets have no intention of honouring this agreement. In short, they don't envisage Austria being neutral but rather very much falling within their sphere of influence.'

'You say "a lot of talk",' said Sir Roland. 'What precisely do you mean by that? Gossip?'

'Intelligence, Sir Roland.'

'Specific intelligence?'

'Well...'

'Well then,' said Sir Roland, gathering his papers in front of him and preparing to leave. 'A complete waste of time. Ponsonby brought you all the way to Moscow to share some half-baked gossip. Maybe he was lonely, I don't know – wanted a friend to pop over and have a reassuring chat, something like that. What you need to be aware of is this: Winston quite rightly sees the Moscow Declaration as a very important diplomatic achievement. He's delighted with it. It's a real feather in Eden's cap and this bitching behind the back of the Foreign Office has got to stop. Sooner or later this wretched war will come to an end and, the way things are going, we shall be the victors, along with the Soviets. We have to think of the peace that follows.

'The problem with you chaps in intelligence,' – Sir Roland paused and made a dismissive sweeping gesture around the table, as if to emphasise that what he was saying applied to all of them – 'is that for you the difference between war and peace is of almost academic interest. Once this war ends you'll no doubt begin to start worrying about the next one: by the sounds of it, you've already started to do so. I understand that, it's part of your job. But I'm not prepared to have the Moscow Declaration undermined on the basis of little more than chit-chat. You see...'

'... I'm sorry to interrupt Sir Roland,' said Porter. 'But I have to say that was certainly my view at first. However, Neville

Ponsonby is no fool: he wouldn't still be in Moscow if he was. He had something much more specific to tell me and he'd very good reason to feel the need to do so in person. He has a very reliable source who approached him shortly after the Declaration was signed. According to her, one of the Soviet Union's top agents was recently recalled to Moscow. The agent – who she knows as Vitaly – is being prepared for a very special mission. He's to be sent to Vienna. If true, it would of course lend some credence to the view that they wish to undermine Austrian neutrality.'

'But is that all, just the name Vitaly? As I say, little more than chit-chat,' said Sir Roland, now putting his papers back into his briefcase.

'Hang on, please.'

Porter opened his own briefcase and from a compartment inside the lining extracted an envelope, from which he produced a photograph. He passed it first to Whitlock who peered at it and shook his head before passing it on to Sir Roland, who did likewise.

But it was a very different story when it was passed to Edgar, who until that moment had been sitting quietly, apparently not terribly interested in the meeting. He bolted upright from what had been an almost slouching position and held the photograph tightly, a look of shock on his face. From his pocket he whipped out a pair of reading glasses and studied it more closely, turning it slightly to the left then tilting it upwards, all the time his eyebrows raised in apparent disbelief. He stood up, angling the picture towards the light, his eyes wide open, with a look of sheer surprise and not a small amount of fear.

'Well I never,' he said eventually. 'And this picture…'

'Ponsonby's source took it at the dacha where this Vitaly is staying, quite recently – in the last couple of weeks we believe.'

There was a tense silence in the room. Porter allowed a smug appearance to rest briefly but pointedly upon him, while Sir Roland and Whitlock looked confused. Edgar shook his head in continued disbelief.

'Jesus Christ,' he muttered, now looking agitated. 'Jesus... Christ.'

'You know him?' said Sir Roland.

'Jesus Christ? No, not as such... But as for the chap in this photograph...' Edgar was waving the picture quite aggressively. '... Well I certainly know him. It's Viktor Krasotkin. If this is the man the Soviets are planning to send in to Vienna, then you can tell Winston we have a very serious problem.'

Edgar had a reputation as being a man of few words. He rarely showed any emotion, beyond a general air of irritation and generally having something better to do with his time. So his excited reaction at seeing the photograph ensured the undivided attention of the other people in the room. Sir Roland looked startled and some colour returned to Whitlock's face.

'You're sure it's this chap?' asked Sir Roland.

'I certainly am,' said Porter. 'I've only ever seen photographs of him but I recognised him straight away. It's a good picture, decent light and all that. Apparently he was dozing at the time, which was why she was able to risk taking the picture. Admittedly his eyes are closed, but I'm not sure that detracts from it. Edgar?'

'Doesn't detract from it at all,' said Edgar. 'No question this is Krasotkin. I've seen him in person, though from a distance. But

I've also seen plenty of photographs of him: Hurst's team took some especially good ones of him in Paris in '39 and we have plenty of him in Switzerland in '40 and '41. Do you remember that double agent we were running from Switzerland, Sir Roland?'

'Henry something or other wasn't it?'

'Henry Hunter – also known as Henri Hesse,' said Edgar. 'The Soviets recruited him as early as 1929 or 1930, we can't be absolutely sure. We ran him as a double agent, not that he was aware of it. We even got him into Germany – and out again, somehow. He was an extremely useful conduit for us to pass on information that suited us to the Soviets. Well, Viktor Krasotkin was his handler, perhaps from when he was recruited – and remained so until Hunter's... demise in 1941.'

Edgar removed his jacket and carefully chose a cigarette from his silver case, spending some time examining its tip for no apparent reason. He allowed a few puffs of smoke to travel the short distance towards the ceiling and watched them dissolve before picking up the photograph, holding it with the reverse facing him so the others could see the picture.

'So, who is Viktor Krasotkin?' He turned the photograph around so he could see the face. 'He's a quite remarkable person: he has the ability to operate undercover and in different guises throughout Europe. He speaks a number of languages and is fluent in French and German, to the extent that he can pass as a native in those countries. He's a big man, but has the ability to not stand out in a crowd: there are times when very experienced teams of ours have followed him and he's simply disappeared. We know for certain he was in France for most of '39 to '41, but he was also in

Switzerland during that period. We're fairly sure that in late '39 he went back to Moscow, but not for long: he soon returned to Western Europe. The very fact he's survived so long is a testament not only to his own skills, but also to the way he's regarded by his masters. Moscow tends to see senior agents as being disposable because they lose trust in people who've operated away from the Soviet Union for long periods of time: they're concerned they'll lose a connection with the motherland and start to affect bourgeois tendencies.'

'All of which means, Sir Roland,' said Porter, 'that Krasotkin is perhaps their top agent. Sending him into Vienna is a clear sign Austria is a priority for them. They wouldn't waste one of their top men there if it wasn't.'

The silence around the table was interrupted only by the sound of Sir Roland drumming his fingers on its surface and Whitlock's cough. It was Sir Roland who spoke first.

'Assuming all this is true – and I've no reason to doubt it – then it's one thing the Soviets calling this Krasotkin back to Moscow to send him to Vienna and no doubt set up a clandestine operation there. But actually getting him to Vienna is quite another thing. I...'

'He'll get there, don't you worry about that,' interrupted Edgar. 'Please don't countenance him failing to do so.'

'What makes you so sure Edgar?'

'Because Viktor is Viktor, Sir Roland. If they need him in Vienna, he'll get there. It's in our interests to assume he'll be operating from there very soon. He may even be there now. Who knows?'

'I shall of course let Winston know about this,' said Sir Roland. 'But I know what he'll say: do what we can to observe him in Vienna and counter whatever he's up to there. You're frowning, Porter. Whatever's the matter?'

'We hardly have anyone left in Vienna, Sir Roland. George ran it, as you know, and he's sitting here.'

'What do you mean by hardly anyone?' Sir Roland sounded incredulous.

'There's the nun, Sir Roland,' said Porter. 'But she's not been terribly willing recently. That chap Wanslake barely lasted a day and that was more than two years ago. That's it really.'

'Hardly anyone, Porter? That sounds like no one!' said Sir Roland. 'You need to remedy that pretty damn quick. Get someone reliable into Vienna. We need to know if Krasotkin is there and, if so, what he's up to. When I brief Winston I'll tell him you have this in hand. Now, if you'll excuse me I have to…'

'Could I ask you to remain for a while, Sir Roland?' Edgar spoke so firmly that Sir Roland obediently sat down from his half-standing position.

'It's in connection with what you've just said,' said Edgar. 'I agree that, having heard what Christopher has had to say, we do need to get someone into Vienna. But what I'm about to tell you will show that's now even more imperative. Sir Roland, Christopher – I hope you'll excuse the fact I'm rather springing what I'm about to say on you, but this really is the first opportunity to do so. George is aware of it though.'

From a folder in front of him Edgar removed a photograph of a distinguished man. 'You're aware of who Hubert Leitner is?'

'Of course,' said Sir Roland. Porter nodded in concurrence.

'No one had heard anything about Leitner since late '38, soon after the Nazis moved in to Austria. There were rumours he'd been killed trying to cross the border in Slovenia but nothing we could be sure of. Naturally we have a very active interest in him: he's undoubtedly Austria's most important and most respected politician. And it appears we may have found him.'

'Really?' Sir Roland and Porter spoke in unison.

'Basil Remington-Barber was approached in Bern by a Swiss diplomat who'd been based at the Swiss consulate in Vienna. This chap had been in contact with Leitner in Vienna and had even arranged a safe house for him. Now the diplomat is being transferred to Madrid, so he's asked us to look after Leitner – who, it seems, wishes to work with us. That, of course, is something of a coup: whatever happens, we must make sure neither the Nazis nor the Communists get their hands on him. First priority is to move Leitner to another safe house, one only we know about. We've managed to get George's nun working on that but how much we can rely on her in the future, I'm really not sure…'

'One cannot overestimate,' said Whitlock, in between coughing, 'just how important this is. In my opinion, it's vital we get to Leitner as soon as possible. We've heard what Christopher has to say about the Soviets' designs on Austria. If this chap Krasotkin gets to Vienna before we do, there's every chance they'll get hold of Leitner first too.'

'All the more reason,' said Sir Roland, 'for us to get someone into Vienna to look after Leitner. Do we really have no one left there, George?'

Whitlock shook his head, which caused another outburst of coughing.

'We can't leave an open goal like this for the Soviets,' said Porter. 'Surely, there must be someone?'

Edgar had his head buried in his heads, thinking hard. He removed his hands and tapped the silver cigarette case on the table. 'Do you know what? I think I may well have just the man.'

***

They all agreed it was the closest thing there was to a good idea, though they were hardly brimming with enthusiasm about it.

'He's not exactly a front-line agent though, is he?' said Sir Roland. 'Doesn't sound like much of a match for this Krasotkin.'

Porter took a similar downbeat view. 'Well, I suppose he'll do… if there's really no one else. What do you think, George? He was your find, after all.'

Whitlock shifted upright in his chair, a hacking and prolonged cough delaying his response.

'I did recruit him, but never saw him as an agent as such: certainly not one operating on his own. He's typical of the kind of chap one recruits locally: enthusiastic enough, happy to help out, running errands and carrying messages – that kind of thing. He left Austria in '38 and went to Switzerland. I was happy to recommend him to Basil. But I'm not sure…'

'I understand all that,' said Edgar. 'But do remember I worked with him quite closely in Switzerland and he came into Germany with me in '41, so he's been tested in the field. And he's from

Vienna, of course. That counts for an awful lot.'

The discussion went on for another hour: the pros and the cons; the ifs and the buts; on the one hand then the other. It was Porter who wrapped up the discussion.

'I'll tell you what I'll do. If you can get him over here, Edgar, and we can put him through a maximum two month's hard training, then I'll sanction sending him out there. But he's got to come through the training with flying colours mind. No muddling through.'

Chapter 8

Moscow, Sweden, Germany and Vienna, January 1944

They didn't come for Viktor Krasotkin that night, nor the next day and the night after that, but he remained convinced he'd gone too far and his days were numbered. *Never question; never discuss; never hesitate.*

Sure enough, two days later his boss turned up, a large black ZIS-101 pulling up outside the dacha. Viktor watched the driver let him out of the front passenger door and spotted two figures who'd remained seated in the back of the car. He felt his heartbeat quicken and he bit the inside of his lip so hard his mouth tasted of blood.

Ilia Brodsky was a slight, wiry-looking man with a scar running from under his left eye to beneath his chin. The gossip was he currently had the ear of Stalin, which meant Brodsky's days were probably numbered. He reminded Viktor of the Jewish cobbler in his town just after the Revolution, but he knew better than to mention that. There was a rumour his grandfather had been a rabbi, but Viktor had never mentioned that either.

Brodsky stood in the doorway and said nothing, other than telling Viktor they were going outside. They walked along the lane outside the dacha, the heavy snow making all around them silent. Viktor was convinced this was how they'd eliminate him, away from the dacha, a quick bullet that would hardly be heard beyond the snow-covered trees: he'd know nothing. There were worse ways to go; at least it would be quick, they owed him that. He didn't turn around, but he was certain the two men from the car would be behind them, getting close enough for a good shot.

Viktor and Brodsky walked for quite a while, past the other dachas and away from the road that led to Moscow. The sharp sound of their boots crunching on the snow seemed to reverberate around them. Despite a bitter wind blowing almost silently into them, Viktor could feel himself becoming uncomfortably hot and clammy. He loosened the black silk scarf around his neck. He'd bought it a few years previously at Galeries Lafayette in Paris and for some reason he found himself worrying that the scarf, of which he was especially fond, would become blood-stained when they shot him.

'What happened the other day was a serious breach of acceptable conduct.' Brodsky broke the silence, speaking as if reading from an official document. The phrase meant he'd committed a serious political crime. To Viktor, it sounded like a judge intoning a death sentence and he began to feel dizzy and his throat tightened: the bullet would come any moment now. He could make a run for it, but Brodsky's men would get him and, in any case, his legs now felt leaden.

Brodsky patted the bigger man hard on the back, causing Viktor to jump. 'However unacceptable your actions were,' he said, 'there are extenuating circumstances. But they will not be repeated. You understand?'

Viktor nodded, trying hard to disguise the relief beginning to sweep through him.

'They were out of order. They should have been more professional and briefed you properly. They should have shown you the respect you deserve.'

'I don't want any more to do with them, I...'

Brodsky held his hand out to stop him talking. 'You don't need to worry: one of them has already been eliminated and the other two have been sent to fight on the German front. As for your identity, I've been thinking. You'll be an Austrian, from Vienna.'

They carried on walking for a while, Viktor so relieved he didn't bother to argue. They came to where the snow had drifted above knee height, blocking their path, and they paused. 'Let's go back indoors,' said Brodsky.

Which was how Viktor Krasotkin came to be Otto Schneider. He had to admit it was an inspired idea. *Hide in full view*, they'd told them at training school. So he spent a month in another dacha in the company of an elderly husband and wife – Party members in exile from Vienna who fussed over him like indulgent parents. He was immersed in everything Viennese; the dacha was nicknamed Little Vienna. They spoke nothing but German, which he was fluent in anyway and he breathed in their Viennese accents and habits, mimicked their nuances of speech, ate their cakes, pored over maps of the city, and studied photographs and newsreel of it. Otto Schneider's cover story was that he'd spent many years in Germany and Switzerland, which accounted for his less-than-perfect accent, but even the comrades from Vienna admitted it was good.

***

Once they'd agreed on his new identity he'd been driven from the dacha into the centre of Moscow and to a monstrosity of a building that took up the whole of a block just to the north of the Kremlin. An ancient elevator took him to one of the upper floors where Brodsky was waiting for him.

'You're going to meet the Central Committee of the Communist Party of Austria,' said Brodsky 'The chairman is Johann Koplenig. They've been here since 1939. Listen to what they have to say and ask any questions you want.'

Viktor sat in the shadows so none of the men in front of him could make out his features. Brodsky sat to his left. Ahead of them were seven unhealthy-looking men in ill-fitting suits. Comrade Koplenig nervously spluttered out something about the Revolution, the ideals of Marxist-Leninism, the leadership of Comrade Stalin, the heroism of the Red Army and the imminent defeat of the Nazi menace. When he finished, he wiped away the perspiration that had gathered on his forehead and glanced anxiously at Brodsky. *The man who currently had the ear of Stalin.*

There was a long silence after this. Viktor didn't know if he was meant to speak but did so anyway. 'You didn't mention the working class, comrade,' he said mischievously. 'Why ever not?'

Comrade Koplenig was profuse in his apologies. *No offence had been intended, naturally the role of the proletariat...* He looked pleadingly at Brodsky, whose features remained fixed. The Central Committee members all shifted anxiously in their chairs, fearful as ever about Siberia. They knew they survived only because they were slightly more useful here in Moscow.

'Do we have any comrades left in Vienna?'

The seven men again shifted uncomfortably, in unison. A man

sitting next to the chairman replied. 'We've lost so many comrades. Even after the Anschluss and the start of the war we still had thousands in Vienna – it was the KPO's stronghold, I'm sure you know that. Many have been conscripted and, of those who were left in Vienna, virtually all have been captured. The Viennese Gestapo is very, very effective. As much as it pains me to say this, our fellow Austrians have shown themselves to be even more enthusiastic Nazis than the Germans.'

'What the comrade means to tell you,' said Brodsky, his stare still fixed on the men in front of him, 'is that many of his former comrades have defected to the Nazis. That's so, yes?'

'I am afraid it is. All the leadership that remained in Vienna has been wiped out. Many comrades have been sent in to help the resistance – from Yugoslavia, from Slovenia, even from Turkey. But none of them have survived more than a week or so.'

'Betrayed,' said Brodsky, looking at the men in front of him as if he blamed them.

'So there's no one left?'

Another man spoke. He was sitting at the end of the row and looked slightly younger than the rest. 'There'll still be a number of comrades remaining, but they'll be ones who were neither very active or who used false names when joining the Party – that wasn't uncommon, especially after the KPO was outlawed in May '33. We know there are a few minor acts of resistance taking place – machinery being interfered with, anti-Nazi messages being left in public places. These will be people who aren't known to have any association with the KPO, so they'll be hard to find.'

'That's helpful,' said Viktor sarcastically.

'There are some districts where you're more likely to find help than others,' said the man at the end of the row. 'Try Margareten, the 5th district.'

'The 17th – Hernals – is worth trying too,' said another man.

'And the 20th, Brigittenau,' said one more. 'My old district.'

'I'd say the factories are still the best places to find comrades,' said Koplenig. 'We think some of them may even have secret KPÖ cells, but they'll be so secret it'll be near-impossible to penetrate them. But if it was me, I'd maybe try some of the bars around the factories... I don't know.'

Brodsky stood up, a clear signal the meeting was over. The seven members of the Central Committee of the KPÖ hurried to their feet. The man at the end, the younger one and the one who'd been most confident, spoke.

'There is one other thing.' Everyone sat down as fast as they'd got up. 'In Floridsdorf, the 21st District, there's a large locomotive works. It employs many thousands of men, even some women. We did hear they were having so much trouble getting workers they've been bringing them in from France. We believe some comrades volunteered to go there from France, including comrades who'd fled there in the thirties.'

Viktor nodded. At last, something helpful.

'And there's a large Labour Exchange in Favoriten in the 10th District, in the south of the city,' said the man sitting next to the Chairman. 'That may be a place to start.'

When they'd left the meeting, Brodsky took him aside. 'When were you last in Vienna, Viktor?'

''37.'

'And before that?'

'I was there quite often during the thirties.'

'I know you Viktor; you're too good not to have contacts there who'll still be around, people who've never had anything to do with the Party and we don't know about. That's why you're so good; you'll have your own people. You've never made the mistake of trusting people, have you?'

Viktor shrugged. 'That's why you and I have survived, isn't it?'

***

He was still in Moscow on 14th January when the latest Red Army offensive began and they were so pleased with how things were going that someone had the clever idea of getting him into Vienna through the eastern front. *Another idiot.*

'Are you mad?'

'But comrade, the Red Army is fighting a heroic battle and defeating the enemy every hour of every day. You can cross the front line and reach Vienna through Hungary or Slovakia.'

'The front line in the Ukraine isn't even close to Galicia yet. What am I meant to do? Walk through ploughed fields for a month and pretend I'm a Viennese travelling salesman who got on the wrong train?'

'It was just an idea. Maybe in a week or so the Red Army will already be in Hungary.'

'And maybe they'll have reached the United States,' spat Viktor. 'Don't believe everything you read in *The Red Star*, comrade. I've another idea: get me to Sweden and I'll do the rest. Just make sure I have plenty of krona though – and Reichsmarks, of course.'

Always better to do things yourself.

They got him into Sweden and, once there, he made his own way down to Malmo on the south coast. He booked himself into a room above a bar-cum-brothel near the port and stayed there for a few days, getting a feel for the port and the girls. Eventually he trusted one enough, a pretty girl from Poland, no more than 20 and with the saddest eyes he had ever seen.

Find me a Swedish ship sailing to Germany, one leaving in the next day or two. Not a small ship, mind, nor too big. Just get me the information and find out where the captain hangs out. I'll do the rest.

She found a suitable ship: a medium-sized Swedish steamer taking a cargo of iron ore into Rostock, leaving the next day on the evening tide. The captain, she said, was already at a bar around the corner hiring crew. When Viktor got there, he was surprised to see the captain looked more like a shopkeeper than a ship's captain: short and slim with a neat moustache and a generally suspicious air about him. The girl in the brothel had told him she understood the captain spoke good German. His air of suspicion increased somewhat when Viktor emerged from the shadows at the back of the bar as the captain walked past and asked, in German, if they could speak in private.

'You want work? I've hired everyone I need now.'

'I need to get to Rostock.'

'When?'

'When you sail tomorrow.'

'I'm not a passenger ship.'

'I have proper German papers, obviously...'

'… Obviously.'

'… I need to return to Germany as soon as possible. I have a… lady friend in Sweden and my wife's become suspicious, if you understand.'

The captain didn't look as if he believed a word he said, but that look changed soon enough when Viktor opened his jacket to allow the captain a glimpse of high-denomination krona notes. He'd calculated it would be at least two months' salary for the captain – maybe three. In Viktor's experience, less than two was too little for a bribe, whereas much more than three aroused undue suspicion.

'Promise me you're not doing anything illegal.'

'Of course not!' said Viktor, managing to look suitably shocked. 'Just get me on board and let me know when it's safe to leave the boat in Rostock. That's all.'

And that was all. When they left Malmo the following evening the captain kept him in his cabin and even let him have his bed. The voyage through the Orseund Sound and down the Baltic was a short one and it was still dark when they sailed past the batteries of anti-aircraft guns into Rostock harbour the following morning. Viktor left the ship almost straight away, disappearing into the heavy mist as the boat was still being tied up and just before the harbour police came on board. By 8.00 he was on a train to Berlin and by lunchtime was bound for Munich, grateful the Allied bombers hadn't disrupted his journey. He stayed in Munich Hauptbahnhof that night, preferring the safety and anonymity of the bomb shelter beneath the station to a hotel. There was a train to Vienna first thing, across a border that no longer existed. It was

early afternoon when the train pulled into Westbahnhof: Vienna was as certain of itself as ever and, like all the Hapsburg capitals, undeniably beautiful.

Now the hard work would begin.

***

Viktor had to keep reminding himself that Austria hadn't existed as a nation since the spring of 1938, when the country had so enthusiastically allowed itself to be swallowed up into the Reich. For a while it had been known as Ostmark, but now it was just a collection of seven Danube and Alpine provinces and he was in one of them, Greater Vienna. So much to remember, there always was. His ability to move from one country to another and assume completely different personas hadn't failed him yet, although effortlessly absorbing a new identity now felt more perilous. Just staying alive and avoiding capture was becoming an achievement in itself. He was only 45, yet he felt the years catching up on him.

He left Westbahnhof through the Mariahilfer Strasse exit and headed north in the direction of the 1st District. It was a long walk and it gave him time to get a feel for the city after all the years. It also gave him time to think. The Central Committee members had given him some food for thought: possible cells or just individual comrades in the factories around the 17th, 20th and 21st Districts, all in the north of the city. And then the Labour Exchange, in Favoriten, closer to where he was now. But, of course, Brodsky had been correct. *I know you Viktor; you're too good not to have contacts there who'll still be around, people who've never had*

131

anything to do with the Party.

He wished he could share Brodsky's confidence that they'd still be around and, even if they were, that they could still be trusted. But there was one, someone he'd have happily walked from Moscow to Vienna to see just one more time, and it didn't occur to him, not for a single second, they couldn't be trusted.

Just before Mariahilfer Strasse reached the Opern Ring he turned into Getreidemarkt, which all felt familiar, then through the Naschmarkt, which didn't. The famous food market was still open, but with very little food in it. Small groups of soldiers in their long grey coats were milling around, eyeing what food there was on the stalls suspiciously. By one bearing a sad array of old-looking vegetables, a policeman was pestering the stall-holder. From the Naschmarkt it was across to Schleifmuhlgasse and, just off it, the familiar square with the elegant apartment blocks set around it.

Although it was only just mid-afternoon the light was beginning to fade, and people were hurrying that little bit faster. The lights in the shops, though not bright, were just enough to make him feel a bit more exposed. From the street he could see the apartment: there was no mistaking it and as far as he could tell it was dark.

He walked around the block and into Wiedner Hauptstrasse, rehearsing his story and checking it had no flaws. *I was given an address in Schikandergasse for possible lodgings, is this the correct place?* If it was a stranger in the apartment they'd hopefully suspect nothing and point him to the parallel street, and he'd be apologetic and make a feeble joke about all these streets beginning with 'S'

and remember his 'Heil Hitler' as he calmly walked away.

He walked up to Karlsplatz, now beginning to feel self-conscious with his small case, still not wanting to arrive at the apartment too early. He also knew he needed to leave himself enough time to find somewhere else if they weren't there: he'd have to head to the north of the city before the curfew and find a lodging house in one of those districts that apparently still had a very, very faint hue of Red Vienna about them.

By the time he entered the little square through its northern opening it was much darker than before and quite a few of the apartments were now illuminated. He was sure the apartment he was going to did have a light on, behind a set of curtains. Ideally he'd have waited a bit longer, standing back in the shadows of a nearby entrance and observing the apartment, but time was pressing. He wrapped his black silk scarf around the lower part of his face and strode confidently across the square and into the building where the smell – a mixture of soup and strong disinfectant – was so familiar it felt as if he'd been there only the day before. He climbed quickly to the top floor. The landing felt the same, a window overlooking the square, one apartment straight ahead of the stairs and two more on either side of it. There was no name on the door, there never was, just a brass bell that he always joked was so loud it could be heard on the other side of the Danube.

It still was.

She opened the door and, as he loosened his scarf, she staggered back in such shock he thought she was going to collapse. Even though he couldn't be sure she was alone, he quickly followed her in, closing the door behind him. She'd backed into the doorway of the lounge where she stopped, her hand cupped to her mouth, her skin white and tears filling her eyes. She mouthed his name. He went up to her and held her tightly to him, talking quietly but urgently into her ear. 'Are you alone?'

'Yes, yes!'

'Where is he?'

'France. He's based at army headquarters in Paris. He was back last week; he won't be here again for weeks, months maybe. But it's not safe Viktor.'

'Listen carefully. If anyone comes in or asks, my name is Otto Schneider and I'm looking for lodgings, you understand? I thought I had an address nearby and got confused. Understand?'

She nodded and, still shocked, led him into the neat lounge, with the immaculate embroidered covers on the chairs and the fine Bohemian glassware on the sides; the elegant French-polished sideboard with its photographs of a man in uniform; and the tapestries on the wall alongside the dark oil painting of a supposed relative of her husband. She sat down in the armchair then got straight up again.

Something to drink… perhaps to eat? Even as the wife of an officer I have very little these days, but he brought food back from Paris. Some cheese perhaps? I have some pastries. And cognac, you'd like a cognac?

She was talking fast as she fussed over him, her face now red and the tears still flowing. She couldn't take her eyes off him and nor could he stop looking at her.

Viktor sat her down. 'You have to listen carefully, Irma. I know how dangerous this is: I'll not stay here long. No one saw me enter, I'm certain of that. Let me stay one night, maybe two – I won't leave the apartment during that time so no one'll know I'm here, like the old days, eh? In the meantime you can make some enquiries for me and help me like before, then I'll move on.'

'Just like the old days,' she said, smiling and dabbing her eyes.

'Yes, just like the old days,' he said, standing up and leading her towards the bedroom. 'In more ways than one.'

***

When Viktor first met Irma in early 1934 she was a beautiful girl who looked considerably younger than her late twenties. She was engaged to an army officer 10 years older than her whom she married months later, but in what was probably a passing gesture at youthful rebellion she'd attended a clandestine meeting organised by the KPO. A friend of a friend of someone she worked with had told her about it, that kind of thing. Viktor saw these people at every meeting – the KPO attracted them like flies, all the Communist Parties around Europe did in those days. It was fashionable, people were attracted by the danger and the excitement and a passing sense of injustice. They rarely lasted more than a meeting or two.

The Comintern political officers would oversee the different organisations, making sure they followed Moscow's line. In the case of the KPO, the line was quite clear: no co-operation whatsoever with the Social Democrats, active resistance to the Nazi threat and no compromise on Austria's independence. Then came the Communist International congress in 1935, which decided the Social Democrats weren't so bad after all and it was now party policy to co-operate with them in defeating fascism. Agents once again fanned out around Europe to make sure the comrades were aware of this new policy.

And Viktor, as always, followed unseen. He'd remain in the background while the political officers enforced the party line and he'd be there to spot likely recruits or follow up on ones his agents had picked out. France was fine and he'd had some success in Switzerland, but Austria was harder for some reason. The KPO members were so committed that none of them were suitable enough to work for him.

But Irma was different: from a good family, church-going, elegant and sophisticated, and about to marry into the military hierarchy. But more than that was the way she touched Viktor's soul, in a way no one else had, not even the wife and daughter he hadn't seen since 1930 and doubted he'd ever see again. Irma understood him and he understood her. They didn't need to speak or explain themselves to each other; it was enough to be in each other's company on the occasions when he was able to arrange it and when she could do so without attracting the attention of her husband.

Her inability to have children brought her closer to him and, because he didn't want to compromise their relationship, he asked little of her. Occasionally he'd get her to deliver a letter or give a message to someone, but it was a very minor role. He protected her.

But if Irma had looked 10 years younger when he first met her in 1934, she was now not only 10 years older but looked a full decade older than she actually was – as if she were in her late forties. Her face was still beautiful, but it was now lined; her hair was turning grey and no longer as immaculate as it once was. He hadn't mentioned his mission on the first evening, or that night or the next morning. But the following afternoon he told her why he was in Vienna and he needed her help. 'I need to find comrades who can work with me, people who can be trusted.'

'But everyone's a Nazi now,' she replied. 'Even I had to join the Nazi Party, my husband insisted – he said he'd miss out on a promotion otherwise. I've had nothing to do with communists since I last saw you, in 1937. No one has any idea about my involvement then.'

They thought carefully, wracking their brains about who they could approach, but they could think of no one. He would, he decided, have to risk going up to Floridsdorf to find a likely bar and watch people: maybe he would recognise someone; maybe his instinct would come to his aid as it so often did.

That evening she was busy in the kitchen and he was resting on the bed when he heard her cry out, which worried him. There was a danger the neighbours could hear and since he'd arrived at the apartment they'd barely spoken above a whisper.

He rushed into the kitchen and she grabbed him by the arm.

'I know who can help! It's so obvious I don't know why I didn't think of it before! Do you remember Paul the plumber?'

Viktor remembered the bright young man who was on the District Committee of the KPO in the 12th District, Meidling. Viktor had high hopes for him and, as he'd joined the party under an alias, Viktor had persuaded him to leave to try and get a job in an armaments factory. But Paul's wife died suddenly and he was left on his own with a young son and no other family to help look after him. Paul asked to be excused working for the Party, but Viktor refused. *The Party comes first, you know that.* But Irma had pleaded with him: *have a heart for once, just this once. Think of this poor man and his little boy. You never know when this kindness may be repaid.*

So Viktor had gone against his better judgement and allowed Paul to resume a normal life, with no obligation to the KPO. He worked as a plumber and that was the last he'd heard of him.

'He's still around,' said Irma. 'I felt so sorry for him that I kept his details and, if ever I needed a plumber or a friend did, I'd call. I heard he was conscripted but was invalided out, but he's still around.'

'How do you know that, Irma?'

'Because only the other week a friend of mine told me he'd been around to fix a blocked sink and how efficient he was. She said he sent his regards to me.'

***

Irma rang the communal telephone number Paul the plumber shared with a dozen or so other apartments in his block and the person who answered promised to get the message to him. 'Broken tap, yes I've got that... Irma, yes I've got that too... And the address, yes, yes, I've got that.'

Paul arrived the following morning. Viktor had watched him from behind the net curtain in the lounge as he crossed the square and he carried on watching for a few minutes after that: he was sure no one had followed Paul, and no one was watching the apartments. He waited until he was already at work on the tap in the bathroom before going in: from the look on his face, had he not been kneeling already he'd have fallen down. A minute later all three of them were sitting around the table in the kitchen.

'I never thought I'd see you again,' said Paul. 'I was pleased it was that way, if I'm honest. Things became so dangerous here after the KPO was banned, and with the Nazis... I was just grateful you'd allowed me to leave the party. I kept my head down, worked whenever I could and looked after Joachim. Because of Joachim's age – he was only seven when the war started – I managed to avoid conscription until 1941. When I did join up, I was sent to Poland, but I was shot during Operation Barbarossa. The bullet hit my thigh and the injury looked much worse than it actually was, but it was enough for me to be discharged. The irony of it all, me a communist, being hit by a Red Army bullet that put me out of action!'

'You're still a communist then?'

'Of course! I've just not been very active... Well, to be honest, I haven't been active at all. So many comrades – those that stayed in Vienna – have been arrested or just disappeared. Dozens of them have been killed and others have been sent to this dreadful place called Mauthausen. That's where they send the Jews and other prisoners.'

'Do you have any contacts – from the KPO, I mean – other comrades?'

Paul remained silent, his hands clenched in front of him on the table. 'I know I can trust you and Irma, but I can't trust anyone else. That's how I've survived. Even my son, I can't trust him. Joachim's 12 now and he's in the junior section of the Hitler Youth. He comes home from school and tells me all these terrible things, and I know I have to pretend to agree with him. I've no doubt if I disagreed with him or if he heard me saying anything against the Nazis, he'd report me. It happens. So, in answer to your question, yes I do still have a few contacts. They're people I knew before the war, but they're like me, just keeping their heads down... I don't know...'

'People who could help me?'

'Possibly,' said Paul. 'But you need to understand two things. First of all, the vast majority of people in this city, and in the whole of what was Austria, are perfectly happy with the Nazis being in power. If you asked a thousand people in private what they thought of the Nazis, they'd have no problem. Maybe one would, but even then you couldn't be sure.

'But you also need to realise what a dangerous enemy we have in the Gestapo,' he continued. 'They're very effective. You remember the old Hotel Metropole on Morzinplatz, near the Danube Canal?'

Viktor nodded.

'That's where they're based. They have a department there that concentrates on finding enemies of the state, as they call them. It's headed by a brutal bastard, Karl Strobel. He's been very effective. Have you heard of V-Leute, Irma?'

Irma nodded.

'It stands for Vertrauensleute. They're the special informers who infiltrate all kinds of groups and betray them to the Gestapo. Even church congregations have V-Leute, apartment blocks, workplaces, bars… They're everywhere. So many people – not just comrades – have been caught out that way. If someone moans in a queue about the quality of meat, there'll be another person there to inform on them. I assume anyone I meet is a V-Leute, it's safer that way. Even my former comrades, the ones you asked me about, I don't know if they're V-Leute or have been turned since we last met. So I'm very cautious, I never discuss anything.'

There was a long silence. Irma looked at Viktor across the table, her eyes imploring him: *please don't*. Paul remained with his head bowed.

'That all has to change Paul, you know that don't you?' said Viktor. 'We have to take a risk.'

Chapter 9

Southern England, January and February 1944

On the morning of Friday 4th February, Edgar left his apartment just behind Victoria Street and decided, as it was such a fine day, to walk down to Grosvenor Place, from where he caught the number 16 bus. The journey took him past Hyde Park and onto Edgware Road, from where it was a short walk to Paddington Station, which these days felt more like a marshalling yard than a passenger station after a number of visits from the Luftwaffe had given Great Western Railways an excuse for their trains not running on time.

The 9.11 to Marlow did leave on time but there was a long delay at Maidenhead while he waited for his second connection and another at Bourne End for the short ride to his destination. It was almost 10.45 when he arrived.

Crispin Meredith was waiting for him outside Marlow station in a black Morris 25 Saloon that looked as if it had been waxed that very morning. Edgar had barely sat down in the red leather passenger seat and hadn't properly closed the door when the car pulled away.

'In a hurry, Crispin?'

'Time and tide wait for no man, Edgar, you should know that.'

'I don't think Chaucer meant to endorse endangering life like that though.'

Meredith insisted on driving with his window down, which meant Edgar had to wrap his coat tightly around him and the conversation during the journey was mostly shouted.

'I said… how's he getting on, Crispin? Do you really have to have that window open?'

'Fresh air's good for you, Edgar, weren't you taught that at Prep School?'

'I never went to one. You were going to tell me how Rolf's getting on.'

***

Some four weeks previously, at around 2.00 on a bitterly cold and frost-covered morning, a good-looking and energetic Austrian called Rolf Eder had arrived at RAF Tangmere in Sussex. It was a clear night, lit by a full moon, and once the Lysander that had just flown him in from France came to a noisy halt alongside the cars waiting on the edge of the tarmac Rolf bounded down the ladder fixed to the plane's port side, his blond hair catching the breeze.

One of the RAF ground crew helped him to the ground then shepherded him over to the cars, where two men were waiting to greet him. The reunion was an enthusiastic one. George Whitlock had originally recruited Rolf some years ago in Vienna, and Edgar had worked with him in Switzerland and Germany in 1941. Rolf was in his thirties, though he looked younger, and had classic Aryan features: blond hair and blue eyes. These eyes glanced around him, trying to take in his first-ever views of England. He could be forgiven for looking somewhat bemused: just over a week before he'd been suddenly informed by Basil Remington-Barber that he was about to be sent from Switzerland to England, where he'd be trained for a secret mission in his native Austria. Three days after that he was smuggled over the border into France.

After a good deal of handshaking and shoulder-slapping the three men climbed into the car. 'I know it's late, Rolf, but we can't hang around here. People know we fly secret agents in and out on the Lysanders, so protocol dictates the fewer people who see you the better. We'll head straight to where your training will take place.'

***

Crispin Meredith reluctantly dropped the speed and wound up his window. 'How's Rolf getting on? Yes, very well. He's a bright chap, takes it all in. Most pleasant too.'

'I meant more specifically... I say, Crispin, can you slow down a little bit? It doesn't matter if we get there a couple of minutes later, surely?'

'It does actually, Edgar. You gave me two months to train a chap who'd never so much as held a gun in his life and doesn't know one end of a radio transmitter from the other. We've had to start from scratch with him.'

'So will he make it?'

'You told me he'll have to.'

They'd headed north west from Marlow, and the drive to the isolated house at the end of a long and narrow track took another 20 minutes. George Whitlock met them at the front door, looking better than Edgar had seen him for some time.

'It's nice and warm here, Edgar, and I eat two decent meals a day. I think I must have been rather neglecting myself.'

'Rolf's on shooting practice at the moment,' said Meredith. 'He'll join us for lunch. You want to know if he'll be ready by the end of the month, you said that's the absolute deadline?'

Edgar nodded. 'And will he be?'

'He'll certainly be considerably more ready than when he arrived, but I suppose that's axiomatic. George tells me you want him to set up and run a unit in Vienna?'

'Ideally. At the very least he needs to be able to operate on his own with a reasonable degree of effectiveness and survive long enough so it's not an entirely wasted journey.'

'He'll know the basics. Though I do tend to share George's view that he may lack a degree of... steel...'

'I think what I mean,' said Whitlock, 'is that I recruited him as a helper and I'm still not convinced he can make the transition to be an agent in his own right. I wonder if we're expecting too much of him?'

'Remember though,' said Edgar, 'at the risk of going over old ground, he may have been little more than a messenger with you, but he was in the field with me in Germany. He helped escort a very important man and his documents out into Switzerland. I think you underestimate him.'

'Beginner's luck?'

'The same could be said of all of us,' said Edgar. 'In any case, one really never knows until one's tested, thrown into the deep end so to speak. Another consideration is that we've no one else. He'll have to be ready. Now then, is it time for lunch? I'd like to spend some time with Rolf, see how he's faring.'

'Before we bring him in, Edgar, there's something that needs addressing,' said Meredith. 'George, perhaps you'd like to explain?'

Whitlock coughed noisily for a while before he began to speak. 'Poor old Rolf has a weak spot. I always look for that and I'm afraid in his case it's not been terribly hard to find.'

'Go on,' said Edgar.

'He had a fiancée in Vienna, a girl called Frieda,' said Whitlock. 'I knew her: surprised she was his type. A dentist, bit older than him. Rather opinionated and almost certainly a communist. I thought they'd split up and that was one of the reasons he'd left Austria, but he still seems smitten with her.'

'Has he been crying on your shoulder, George?'

'Not mine. There's a girl here called Lucy, she's a cook-cum-housekeeper. Very pretty thing. I encourage her to get close to the chaps, flirt a bit… see what they tell her. She only needed to smile at poor old Rolf and he opened up his heart to her. Evidently he's still in love with Frieda, desperate to find out what's happened to her. As I say, it's a weak spot.'

Edgar nodded. 'And that's all?'

'No,' said Meredith. 'There's another matter, perhaps more serious. Sending a Viennese into his home town is enormously helpful, I realise that. The Viennese are a breed apart, quite unlike other Austrians, let alone other German-speakers. He knows his way around, he understands the city and, even though he's been away for five years now, he'll be alert to its dangers. He'll know when something's not quite right. I know we're planning to give him Swiss identity and he can certainly manage to speak standard German now with a Zürich accent, but that's not the point. It doesn't solve the problem. He can't get out of his mind that someone will recognise him: a neighbour, friend, former schoolmate, even a distant relative. To be frank with you, even though it's five years since I've last seen him, he's hardly changed at all. And it's not as if we can dismiss this as an unfounded fear of his. One can't spend nearly 25 years in a place and expect not to be spotted in it sooner or later.'

'I appreciate that, George,' said Edgar. 'But on balance the advantages of sending him there outweigh what drawbacks there are.'

'The point is though,' said Meredith, 'is it's affecting his confidence. One of the most important aspects of our training is that an agent has to have complete confidence in their new identity. He has to totally believe he's plausible. If he's going to arrive in Vienna then worry that each time he turns a corner he's going to bump into someone who knows him, that's going affect his behaviour. I can tell how worried he is.'

'I realise that, but I'm not sure what we can do about it.'

'That's what I thought too, Edgar, but I do have an idea...'

***

The following Monday morning Edgar was impatiently waiting outside the front door of a large house on Wimpole Street in the heart of London, studying an impressive collection of brass plates as he waited for the building to open. When it finally did, just after 8.00, he went to the third floor, where he found the consulting room of George Harman, Surgeon.

A distinguished-looking man with a dark complexion and gold-rimmed glasses greeted him, and took him into a small lounge.

'I understand you were expecting me, Dr Harman?'

'Mr Harman,' said the man in a well-spoken voice that nonetheless failed to disguise a Germanic ring to it. 'In this country, a surgeon is a Mister. In Germany I was a Doctor: Dr Georg Häumann. Now I'm plain Mr George Harman. When I came here I felt I'd been demoted! Yes, I was expecting you, Mr Edgar: a most mysterious call. But please, how can I help?'

'I'm afraid that much of what I have to say – and why – will remain a mystery, but I'm sure you understand. I can only tell you this: I represent an agency of the British Government. The request I'm about to make is highly confidential. You must never utter a word about it to anyone, not even your wife or close colleagues. Do you understand?'

'If only I had the opportunity to tell my wife, Mr Edgar,' said Harman. 'I left Germany in 1937 when Jews were forbidden to practice as doctors, or at least forbidden from treating Aryan patients. My wife and three children remained in Germany. She had elderly parents and the idea was that I'd establish myself here and she'd follow.'

Harman paused and removed his spectacles, vigorously polishing them for a while with a handkerchief from his top pocket. When he resumed speaking it was more quickly than before, as if it was painful to dwell on the words.

'Needless to say, she left it too late. It was still possible to leave after '39, but it became increasingly difficult then impossible. I've not heard a word from them since January 1940 – January 14th. I deal with it by concentrating on my work. An opportunity to assist the British Government is a most welcome one indeed. Tell me how I can help.'

'I'm sorry to hear that, Mr Harman,' Edgar coughed. 'My department made various enquiries among the senior ranks of the medical profession over the weekend and we've been given to understand you're a leading exponent of the branch of surgery that alters a person's appearance. Is that correct?'

'It's good of people to think that and they're most probably correct. This branch of surgery is a very specialist one and was much more advanced in Germany than in this country, though there's some very impressive reconstructive surgery now being carried out in Britain. I know there are some remarkable results with RAF aircrew that have been burnt and disfigured. Nonetheless, I've specialised in this area for some 15 years and would like to think, without being boastful, I do have a degree of expertise.'

'My question is this, how easy is it to change someone's appearance?'

'It depends,' said Harman. 'I can surgically alter anyone's appearance, but with some people it's easier than with others. I'd need to meet the patient.'

Edgar opened his briefcase and removed a series of photographs of Rolf from every angle, which he fanned out on the table in front of the surgeon.

'This is the patient.'

Harman put his glasses back on and carefully studied the photographs, taking them over to his desk and holding them under an angle poise lamp.

'A suitable patient in some respects, I'd say,' he said eventually.

'The ears?'

'They'd be the most apparent feature. They're most pronounced.'

'And can anything be done about that?'

'Absolutely, Mr Edgar. I'd have to examine the patient first, but I'd say he's an excellent candidate for otoplasty, which is the surgical procedure to pin back the ears. You'll understand I'm putting it in layman's terms.'

'Is it a complicated operation?'

'I wouldn't find it complicated to perform, no.'

'And what would the effect be?'

'Quite significant. Colleagues who work in other fields have discovered that one of the ways we subconsciously recognise people is through the shape and position of their ears. In the case of this person, his ears stick out to such a degree that reverting them to what would be a normal angle would have a marked effect.'

'So that even someone who knows him very well may not recognise him?'

Harman hesitated, frowning then raising his eyebrows.

'I'm not sure I'd go quite as far as that. It would certainly alter their appearance, but probably not to the extent that someone who knows them well wouldn't recognise them at all. The best one can probably hope for is that it would make someone unsure. To make them unrecognisable, you'd need to combine the otoplasty with another form of facial reconstructive surgery.'

Edgar leaned over and looked at the photographs.

'What about the nose, isn't there surgery that can alter the shape of a nose?'

'Rhinoplasty, but I'm not sure your patient would be a suitable candidate.'

'Why not?'

'First of all, there's nothing wrong with his nose, it's actually a perfect nose in almost every respect. There would be ethical issues that would arise about performing rhinoplasty in this instance. However...'

'But Mr Harman, you need to understand that...'

'Please let me finish. I know what you were about to say. No doubt this is an issue of national importance and such a consideration may override other ones, I understand that. However, there's a more important consideration. Can I ask you a question?'

'Go on.'

'How soon would you like this surgery to be carried out?'

'As soon as possible: this patient needs to travel by the end of the month.'

'Really?' Harman had removed his spectacles again and was staring at Edgar as if he was slightly mad.

'Is that a problem?'

'It is indeed: otoplasty takes four to six weeks to recover from, I'd say much closer to six weeks. Rhinoplasty will take far longer than that – it involves breaking the nasal bone and there will be severe bruising for many weeks.'

Edgar looked deflated. 'And you say the otoplasty may not be enough in itself to alter his appearance?'

Harman nodded then picked up one of the photographs again,

studying it carefully. 'There is another option though: blepharoplasty.'

'What on earth is that?'

'A surgical procedure to reshape the eyelids. The effect can be very dramatic. It's perhaps the most radical of all facial reconstructive surgeries in terms of how it can alter a person's appearance. This gentleman's lower lids are slightly hooded and the upper ones could be tightened up too.'

'What about the recovery time?'

'No longer than for the otoplasty.'

'Could the two procedures be done at the same time?'

Harman frowned again. 'I've never done the two together; I'd need to discuss it with an anaesthetist.'

***

'Say that again Edgar.'

'Six weeks.'

'Out of the question,' said Christopher Porter. 'Completely ridiculous. Frankly, I'm surprised you even thought it appropriate to bring us all here to discuss this.'

There were five of them in Porter's office. Apart from Porter himself and Edgar, Sir Roland Pearson had come over from Downing Street, and George Whitlock and Crispin Meredith had been summoned from the house near Marlow. It was the Tuesday morning, the day after Edgar had met George Harman.

'Where are we?' Porter swivelled around to glance at the calendar on the wall behind him. 'The 8th: today's the 8th February.

How long has Rolf been with you now, Crispin?'

'Just over a month.'

'And he's meant to be with you for how long… another month? Is that enough time to train him properly?'

'I'd say it's the bare minimum.'

'I thought we'd made it clear it'd have to be,' said Sir Roland. 'If this Krasotkin is already in Vienna we can't afford to let him have too much of a head start. Rolf must be there by early March at the latest. What's all this nonsense then about an operation?'

'Crispin and George have pointed out we're expecting Rolf to return to his home town, where there's a very good chance he'll be recognised,' said Edgar. 'George said he hadn't seen him for five years but thinks he's hardly changed. Rolf himself is well aware of this and it's affecting his confidence and undermining his ability to operate in Vienna.'

Meredith and Whitlock both nodded in agreement.

'This surgery would significantly alter his appearance,' continued Edgar. 'We can do other things, too, like darken his hair and give him a pair of specs. But I'd say the surgery is vital if this mission is to have a chance of success.'

'But it'll take six weeks for him to recover?' said Porter.

'Correct.'

'Which takes us into the middle of April, plus a further week to get him into Vienna. That's ridiculous.'

'Perhaps not,' said Edgar. 'I think there's a way we could have him in Vienna by the end of March, possibly even slightly earlier.'

Sir Roland looked up, interested. 'Really, how's that?'

'We operate straight away: this week. The surgeon will allow him to travel after five weeks providing there are no complications. There'll still be a few more days to get him into Vienna.'

'But what about the training?'

'It'll take him a week or so to recover from the operation, the anaesthetic and such. But, after that, we've four weeks for what we call "soft" training: briefings, handling a radio, that kind of thing – just no assault course. Not ideal, but needs must.'

No one said anything for a while. Edgar lit a cigarette, Whitlock coughed heavily and Porter studied the calendar.

'Winston's very, very concerned about the Soviets putting a top man into Vienna,' said Sir Roland. 'And this theory that they're seeking to undermine the Moscow Declaration, well he does rather see the logic of it. As much as he favours diplomacy, he has an innate distrust of communists. When he asked me what we're doing about it – actually he said "what the hell are *you* doing about it, Pearson" – I was able to tell him we've a top-class man we're preparing to send in there. Can't let him down, can we?'

'On balance then, it's probably better to send Rolf in a couple of weeks later than planned, but with a better chance of seeing his innings through, eh? Wouldn't want him bowled out in the first over.' The mention of the prime minister had evidently had an ameliorating effect on Porter.

'Very well,' said Edgar. 'I'll come back with you chaps and break it to Rolf that we're going to tinker around with his appearance.'

'I have a question,' said Sir Roland. 'How's Rolf going to get into Austria?'

'SOE have reluctantly agreed we can get him back the same

way as he came – through France into Switzerland. Basil will look after things then.'

'I see... and when he arrives in Vienna... he'll be all on his own?'

Edgar nodded.

'Money, weapons – that kind of thing? He's not going to be able to take much into Austria with him, is he?'

'I do actually have a potential source of those,' said Edgar. 'I was keeping them for a rainy day.'

'I'm sure you were. But there's no one in Vienna, is there George?'

'Not as far as we know. They've all left the country, been captured or been killed. Apart from the nun of course, but other than putting Rolf in touch with Leitner, we're not sure she's going to be of much use.'

'He won't be briefed about Leitner, will he?'

'Before he gets there? Of course not,' said Edgar. 'We can't take that risk in case he's captured. He thinks his mission is just to find Viktor and see what he's up to. You look worried?'

'I am. I'm not sure if we're asking too much of young Rolf. Is there really no one else we can send in with him?'

Edgar shook his head and started to reply then stopped himself, closing his eyes deep in thought, pressing his fingertips to his forehead. 'There could be actually,' he said. 'Let me have a word with Basil.'

***

Basil Remington-Barber had moved with what London considered an admirable degree of uncharacteristic urgency. By the time Rolf Eder arrived back in Switzerland, courtesy of the RAF and the French Resistance, MI6's Head of Station in the country had already fetched Katharina Hoch from Interlaken, where she'd been working as a nurse. He'd taken her to a safe house in Zürich, where in the four weeks or so before Rolf arrived he trained and briefed her as best he could.

While he was doing this, he sought out an old – though most reluctant – contact of his. Michael Hedinger was a senior official at Bank Leu whose past co-operation with British Intelligence was a result of blackmail rather than any conviction on his part. That blackmail – based on Hedinger's channelling of funds from Germany into his own account – still held good and he was in no position not to accede to Remington-Barber's latest request.

Rolf Eder arrived at the safe house in Zürich during the last week of March. His final briefing had taken place at RAF Tangmere, just a few hours before he was flown back to France. The normally impassive Edgar was noticeably edgy as he often was when sending an agent into the field. Rolf was doing his best to hide his own nervousness, the ubiquitous smile on his face and his eager-to-please blue eyes watching Edgar all the time.

'Two priorities then, Rolf,' said Edgar. 'Do your best to set up some kind of British operation in Vienna – you've been told how to get your hands on that trunk – then find Viktor Krasotkin and see what he's up to. You have the photograph?'

Rolf nodded and patted his coat. Edgar had persuaded the specialists in RAF Intelligence to copy the photo onto a piece of material that could be sewn into the lining of clothing.

'Basil has all the details of your cover story and your new identity: he'll brief you on that. And, remember, once you're in Vienna you'll be approached by one of our people there who'll have further instructions for you.'

'I know… Maggiore and all that stuff…'

'It's more than "stuff", Rolf. It's a vital code to ensure you know who they are and vice versa. Understand?'

Rolf nodded. Edgar noticed the Austrian's hands were shaking.

'Just one other thing. You won't be going to Vienna on your own. Basil's found someone to accompany you.'

'Who?'

'Don't worry,' said Edgar. 'You'll meet them soon enough.'

Chapter 10

Vienna, April 1944

Rolf had assumed it would be a man accompanying him to Vienna. His reaction to being told his companion was a woman was one of surprise, which turned to shock when Basil Remington-Barber told him they'd be posing as man and wife.

'You mean I'm to marry her?'

'No, no, no... don't be silly,' Remington-Barber had replied. 'You'll have all the paperwork that shows you're married. You don't need to go through some ceremony... that'd be ridiculous. Not sure the service's budget stretches to that, ha! In any case, we need to show you've been married for a few years.'

They were sitting in the lounge of the safe house in Zürich, where Rolf had arrived that afternoon. Evening was drawing in and a black cat was nosing at the French windows that led into a high-walled garden dominated by a large conifer. For as long as Remington-Barber had known him, Rolf had always been cheerful and relaxed. He now looked concerned.

'And we're to... act as man and wife?'

'Well, it'd look a bit odd if you didn't, eh?'

'No, what I mean...' Rolf hesitated, clearly uncomfortable. He looked pleadingly at Remington-Barber, hoping he'd know what he meant.

'There should be nothing in your behaviour or appearance that could lead people to suspecting you're not married. What happens in private...'

'Exactly. That's what I was getting at.'
'Well, that's up to you, isn't it…? And her, I suppose.'

***

Rolf and Katharina met later that evening. As awkward as the situation was, they felt more relaxed in each other's company than either had expected: they were close in age and both appeared to have a similar disposition and sense of humour. They were to be Gerd and Anna Schuster, a Swiss couple who'd been married for six years. Anna Schuster would be looking to work as a nurse when they'd settled in Vienna. Gerd Schuster worked for Bank Leu in Zürich and – thanks to Hedinger, Remington-Barber's reluctant contact – was being transferred to the bank's branch in Vienna, whose manager, one Herr Wolfgang Plaschke, had been surprised and delighted at the extra help. He had been asking for it for some time and it had become increasingly urgent as more of his staff had been conscripted. Zürich's answer had always been a firm 'no'. Now Hedinger in Zürich was sending out one of his staff, with a specific brief to help with transfers from Vienna to Zürich.

It was, Remington-Barber assured them, a perfect cover. 'Sending messages to Hedinger and receiving them from him will be something you'll be expected to do every day. Hedinger will pass your coded messages on to me and I get can messages out to you that way too. And Plaschke's found you somewhere to live. It's an apartment in the 3rd District. Belongs to his mother-in-law.'

Remington-Barber allowed five days for the briefing and to give Rolf and Katharina time to get to know each other. In the evenings, Michael Hedinger would come over and tutor Rolf on the work he was expected to do for the bank and, during the day, Remington-Barber would test them continuously on their story: the dates they'd met, addresses where they'd lived, their birthdays, family, friends. He held off London for as long as he could – *when on earth are they going Basil? The war will be over by the time they get to Vienna!* – before he felt he could let them go. But if anyone had asked him as he left them at Zürich station how confident he was, he'd have hesitated. Their cover story and their identities were good: they'd both been tested in the field before and Rolf had an undoubtedly cheerful and positive manner while Katharina possessed admirable poise and confidence.

Nonetheless, thought Remington-Barber, more was being asked of them than he'd ever asked of any other agents.

***

Rolf Eder believed he had a reasonable appreciation of what life was like under the Nazis. He'd lived in Zürich since 1938, where he'd heard countless first-hand accounts from the refugees, émigrés and political activists who'd flooded into the city. These accounts had a consistency to them, notwithstanding which country they emanated from: the constant fear; the rumours; the distrust of even people close to you; the uncertainty; the hunger; and the all-pervading atmosphere of menace.

Now Rolf had been in Vienna for almost a fortnight and it didn't feel to him much like the Occupied Europe he'd heard so much about and experienced himself. Certainly the city was very different from the one he'd left in 1938.

There were far more people in uniform, and much of the verve and confidence of the city seemed to have been sapped: its elegance was beginning to look faded and people were perhaps that little bit more reserved, but then Rolf would never have described Vienna as a friendly city. The cafés and restaurants were still open, though no longer packed, and even an optimist wouldn't describe supplies in the food shops and markets as being of a good quality or plentiful.

Yet, despite all this, there was nothing about Vienna that reminded him of what he'd heard about other cities under Nazi Occupation. There was little fear, if any. People would nod towards troops they encountered in the streets in a genuinely friendly manner. They queued patiently in the shops, never complaining about what was for sale or what was missing from the shelves. Not once did he or Katharina spot a resigned look or even the mildest criticism of the regime. People seemed happy to be part of the Reich and privileged to be members of a master race that was running much of Europe.

What disconcerted Rolf most about the city was how acutely he sensed the presence of Frieda in it. Being in the place where they'd spent so much time together and where he'd last been with her unsettled him. The love he had for her became almost overwhelming. He found himself looking longer than he should at any woman of a similar age or build to Frieda. He glanced too carefully into shops to see if she was there.

During their first week in Vienna, Katharina busied herself in the apartment while Rolf got used to working in the bank. The work wasn't especially onerous, but Herr Plaschke was delighted to have help and was more than happy to leave the time-consuming business of transfers to Vienna to his new clerk. Rolf had waited until the Wednesday before sending his first coded message to Hedinger, to be passed on to Remington-Barber.

Arrived safely. All in order. No problems or concerns. Waiting another week before commencing operations.

That first weekend he and Katharina had gone for a walk in the Prater Park, the former Imperial hunting grounds set between the Danube Canal and the river itself. The couple waited until they were in the park, finding security in its open spaces and the fact it was so busy. Rolf was shocked to see the Wiener Riesenrad was in a state of near-ruin. The giant Ferris wheel, he found out, had been badly damaged by Allied bombs.

'I'm not sure what to make of that,' he told Katharina as they strolled along arm in arm. 'It's such a happy memory from my childhood. I had my first proper kiss in one of those little cabins. I was just 15 and we found ourselves alone in one, high above Vienna. It seemed too good an opportunity to miss.'

Katharina laughed and briefly rested her head on his shoulder.

'Her name was Brigitte,' said Rolf. 'If the Riesenrad was working today we could've got a cabin to ourselves – it'd be the perfect place to discuss things. Who'd hear us up there?'

'I'm not sure I'd trust it. We're safer out here in the open,' said Katharina. 'You must have come here with your fiancée?'

Other than a brief conversation in which Rolf had mentioned he'd been engaged to someone in Vienna before he'd left the city, Frieda had not been mentioned. Until now.

Rolf didn't reply. He paused for a moment and slipped his arm away from Katharina's, and when he resumed walking it was some distance apart from her. When she caught up, Rolf had pulled the brim of his hat over his face and turned away from her, but even so he couldn't disguise the tears streaming down his face. A woman wrapped in a fur coat strode past, disapprovingly peering at the couple as if they were naughty children.

'Come here, Gerd, slow down. Whatever's the matter? '

'Please! I want to walk on my own,' replied Rolf, quickening his step.

'You can't, you'll be drawing attention to yourself. Look, let's go over there at least.' Katharina pointed to a bench in the shadow of a straight row of trees and guided Rolf over by his elbow. It took him a minute to stop sobbing and dry his eyes with a handkerchief she handed to him.

'When you mentioned Frieda, it was... I don't know... just too much. Being in this city and so close to where she may be, I've found it so difficult. When you asked if I'd been here with her, well I had. I know we've only be here a week but I keep being reminded of her. It's as if I constantly sense her shadow. All the feelings I had for her... have for her... they've returned. It's as if I've fallen in love again, but with a shadow. Being so long ago and moving to Zürich, I don't know, perhaps I thought I'd got over her. But I haven't. It probably makes no sense to you...'

His eyes filled with tears again and Katharina stroked his arm. 'I understand and I'm sorry I mentioned it. I'll be more sensitive in future, but you mustn't be afraid of your emotions. If you bottle them up you'll feel overwhelmed. If you feel you need to talk, just...'

'I'll be alright, Katharina.'

'You must call me Anna; you know that – I keep reminding you. If you don't get into the habit of it, you'll slip up in front of someone. Anna, remember? Are you alright now? We need to talk about what we do next.'

Rolf bit his lip and leaned forward, making an effort to compose himself. 'Basil's instructions were that we were to give ourselves a week to get settled in then start our work.'

'I know, I know… we can't wait much longer. There's so much to do.'

'We need to see if we can find out what the Soviets are up to and especially if this Viktor is in Vienna,' said Rolf. 'And we have to get hold of that strongbox from the shop in Wiedner Hauptstrasse… which isn't very far from where we're living…'

They were both quiet for a moment as they contemplated what was ahead of them. Two couples strolled past them, tall men in black SS uniforms, each with a girl on their arm. Both couples turned and smiled at the British spies as they walked past.

'If only they knew…' said Rolf. 'And of course the other thing we need to do is try to set up some kind of network. We're going to be busy.'

'And that's not all,' said Katharina. 'We're supposed to be contacted with further instructions, aren't we? Do you have any idea how – or when?'

***

In December, when Father Bartolomeo had come from Rome to

pass on a message to her, Sister Ursula insisted he pass one back to the British. She'd find another safe house for Leitner and take him to it, but that would be that. The British should then leave her alone. It was too dangerous. She'd done enough.

Father Bartolomeo returned to Vienna in April. This time there was no summons to the Archbishop's Palace, no messenger. Instead he caught up with Sister Ursula one afternoon on Liechtensteinstrasse as she returned to the convent after a long shift at the hospital, appearing silently alongside her on the pavement like a holy ghost. For a while, neither said a word as they carried on walking.

'Didn't you pass on the message, Father?'

'What message, Sister?'

'That I'd move him from Währing to another safe house and that would be that. I wasn't to be approached again. I did what I promised and I thought...'

'I'm not sure that's how the British work, Sister,' whispered Father Bartolomeo. 'I think you and I must understand that working as we do for the British is not dissimilar to giving ourselves to the church. Once we allow ourselves to enter this life then we're committed to it, whether we like it or not. They've one more task for you. Now listen, Sister, this is what you're to do...'

***

Sister Ursula waited until the Saturday, three days after her encounter with Father Bartolomeo. Since the Nazis had taken control, life had become much harder for the church. Apart from anything else, the funds it had enjoyed before 1938 had dried up. Life was especially hard at the Convent. Even though most of the nuns worked, whether as nurses or schoolteachers, Mother Superior was constantly worried about money and so she encouraged the sisters, in what little free time they had, to undertake charitable collections to keep the convent going.

So there was nothing especially remarkable about a middle-aged nun in her blue-grey habit and starched white cornette walking down Ungargasse in the 3rd District on a Saturday morning. She made a point of first stopping in two other apartment buildings on the same block as her intended destination. When she finally reached it she was tired: she'd worked until late at the hospital and the feelings of fear and self-doubt were once again overwhelming her. She'd no idea what she'd find when she reached the apartment Father Bartolomeo had given her the address of. For all she knew, it could be a trap, with the Gestapo waiting for her.

It was of little consolation that the collection had gone so well, people had been generous. Mother Superior would be delighted: *I've no idea why you decided to try Landstrasse, Sister Ursula, but I'm so delighted you did – divine inspiration!*

She visited every flat in the block until she reached the top floor. Sure enough the name *Schuster* was written on a label under the bell. She could hear movement in the apartment after she rang the bell, but it took a while for the door to open. She could feel her heart beating fast and her breathing getting heavier. A woman in her thirties opened the door.

'I'm sorry to bother you, but I'm collecting on behalf of the

Daughters of Charity of Saint Vincent de Paul. We're a poor convent and…' From inside the cloth bag she carried, she removed a small slip of flimsy paper – no larger than a matchbox – with the name of the order and the address of the convent on it. Mother Superior insisted they always hand it out. The lady took the piece of paper and held up a hand as if to say 'wait', then reached into the pocket of a coat hanging next to her. She pressed a few coins into the nun's tin.

'Would you mind if I asked to come in for a glass of water? I've been collecting for a while now and it's so warm…'

The woman seemed reluctant but the nun had already stepped into the hallway. She was shown into the lounge where a man was sitting by the window. When the woman returned with a glass of water she sat on a chair opposite the nun. The couple introduced themselves as Gerd and Anna Schuster. *Your name, sister?*

'I'm Sister Ursula. Tell me, where are you from?' the nun asked. 'You don't sound Austrian.'

'We're Swiss,' replied the woman.

'Ah – how wonderful! From which part?'

'Zürich.'

'I love Switzerland. You know, I once visited Lake Maggiore. There was a small convent in Ascona. Do you know it?'

She spotted the man shooting a glance at the woman, who was looking directly at the nun and hardly reacted, other than in the way she was supposed to.

'I don't know Ascona. I visited Locarno as a child but that was many years ago. Gerd, do you know that area at all?'

Her husband hesitated before he realised this was his cue to give his expected answer. 'No, we tended to visit Neuchâtel when I was a child.'

The nun nodded knowingly. Every reply they'd given had been correct, word-perfect. There was no phrase to indicate anything was wrong. She felt a sense of relief now. Her work was almost done. The British couldn't ask any more of her, could they? Maybe she could ask Mother Superior for a transfer – Salzburg perhaps? There was a small convent there and surely the British couldn't find her in Salzburg.

'Come closer and listen very carefully to what I have to say.'

Over the next half hour she told them about Hubert Leitner. He was, of course, well known to Rolf, though he didn't let on to the nun he was Austrian. She explained how she'd moved him from a safe house that was no longer safe in the 18th District to one in the 2nd District.

'Now I'm passing on responsibility for him to you,' said Sister Ursula. 'I'll visit the safe house to tell them you'll be visiting and you're to be trusted, then I'll have no further involvement. I'll give you the address now and all I ask is you wait at least a week before visiting. Before you go, you're to tell London and they'll pass on instructions about what they want you to do with Herr Leitner.'

***

When the nun was satisfied they fully understood what they had to do, she left – but only after giving them a warning. 'You won't see me or hear from me again, you understand? If you happen to see me in the street or elsewhere, ignore me. Resist any temptation to try and find me or contact me. It's for your safety. And mine.'

Together, Katharina and Rolf watched her as she left the apartment block and made her way back up Ungargasse towards the Innere Stadt.

'Is this man really as important as she made him out to be?'

'Perhaps more so, to be honest,' replied Rolf. 'I couldn't tell her I knew much about him, but he's easily the most important non-Nazi politician in Austria. It's remarkable he's safe and in hiding. I can quite understand why the British want him looked after. What I don't understand, though, is why we've only found out about him now. Surely they must have known about him when I was in England – or, at the very least, Basil could have told us about him.'

'Maybe it'd have been too risky for the British to tell us before we arrived,' said Katharina. 'What if we were caught and interrogated, and told the Nazis about Leitner? That would've been disastrous for the British – Leitner would've been captured. From their point of view, it was much safer for us to know nothing until we arrived. You look shocked Rolf.'

'I am. It makes us sound as if we're... I don't know... dispensable?'

Katharina patted him on the knee. 'I think it'd be a mistake to think otherwise.'

Chapter 11

Vienna, April 1944

By the time Rolf and Katharina arrived in Vienna in early April, Viktor had been in the city for almost three months. But by his own standards he'd been most unproductive: staying alive and remaining undiscovered by the Nazis preoccupied him. He'd planned to stay with Irma for just a couple of nights, but that stretched into early March.

Life in the pretty apartment just off Schulerstrasse was easy and gave him little incentive to move on. He justified his lengthy stay with Irma by the conditions in Vienna: they were far worse than he'd imagined. From what she and Paul the plumber told him, no one could be trusted. Any old comrades who were somehow still free kept their heads down. Irma knew fewer of them, but Paul said he'd occasionally pass someone in the street and they'd look terrified.

'And do you know what?' said Paul. 'So am I. I'm terrified that maybe one of these people is a V-person, a traitor, an informer. I'm terrified they'll know I was active in the party and will betray me to the Gestapo. Please don't look at me like that, Viktor, it happens. We've lost hundreds of comrades, more likely thousands. My only hope is that my party days were a long time ago and since then I've been in the Wehrmacht – and being invalided out is a real bonus, I can tell you. Thank God for that Red Army bullet! I do nothing to arouse suspicion…'

There was a long silence, during which Viktor stared at Paul, who was trembling and on the verge of tears.

'Except come here,' said the Russian.

Paul nodded. Viktor knew full well that, given half the chance, Paul the plumber would never visit the pretty apartment just off Schulerstrasse again, but he did so out of some kind of loyalty to Viktor and respect for Irma.

This conversation took place every time Paul visited ('Viktor, the neighbours will wonder what on earth is going on with my taps,' Irma would say). And each time Viktor would prevail upon him. 'Paul, please do me one favour: go to Brigittenau, no one knows you there, do they? Hang around the bars near the factories; ask if anyone needs a plumber. Buy beers for people, I'll give you the money. Then listen. Sooner or later someone will say something indiscreet or give you cause to think they could be of help. Then I can go up there.'

That went on for weeks. Paul would come back the following week and explain he'd found no joy in the bars of Brigittenau or whichever district Viktor had last sent him to. Viktor was no fool: he doubted Paul was going anywhere, it was too dangerous and he was clearly too afraid. He didn't blame him.

He knew his best course of action was to leave the apartment and move to one of the working-class suburbs in the north of the city where the KPO had been strong. At the end of February he made his first tentative moves: he visited the labour exchange in Favoriten and was relieved to find that Otto Schneider's papers were all in order. The service could still be relied upon to do some things well. Otto Schneider was a native of Vienna who'd spent much of his life in Germany, where he'd worked as an electrician.

According to his papers, his last place of employment had been a naval dockyard in Hamburg that had been destroyed in an Allied bombing raid. He'd returned to Vienna for the first time in years for a visit, he told them, even though he no longer had family here. He thought that rather than return to Hamburg, perhaps he could find work here?

Moscow had counted on the fact that they'd be so desperate for an electrician they wouldn't question his identity too much – and they were right. Otto Schneider obtained all the right papers and, at the beginning of March, moved out of Irma's apartment to a room in a boarding house in Floridsdorf, in the 21st District. One of the KPO Central Committee had said they were employing French workers at the large locomotive works there and that some of them could be communists. So Viktor had let slip in one of his interviews at the labour exchange that he'd worked as an electrician at a locomotive works in Dresden and a few days later the elderly lady whom he made a point of seeing every time he went to the exchange informed him he was going to work at the locomotive works in Floridsdorf. 'You start on Monday: be punctual and work hard. Heil Hitler!'

'Heil Hitler!' replied the Soviet agent.

***

When Viktor had arrived back in Vienna there was one person he knew he ought to contact. Uncharacteristically, he kept putting it off. It was partly because he distrusted this person and knew getting in touch with him would be fraught with risk. But there was another reason: it would mean descending into a sewer even he found distasteful.

Viktor would be the first to acknowledge that as a secret agent he inhabited a world of subterfuge, crime and deceit – one wrapped in shadows and constant menace in which none of its inhabitants could claim to be very high up any moral order. Nonetheless, this underworld did have a hierarchy. At the top were people like him, secret agents and suchlike. Bank robbers and fraudsters came fairly high up too and as for murderers – well, it depended on whom they'd murdered. But there was no doubt as to who came at the bottom: the rapists, the child sex offenders and the pimps. And Wilhelm Fuchs fitted neatly into all those categories.

But he was the kind of contact Viktor needed in every city: someone resourceful who could get their hands on whatever he needed, for whom everything had a price and who rarely asked questions. He'd first come across Fuchs in '34 or '35. He'd never actually been deceived by him, but he didn't trust him. On his last visit to Vienna in '37 he discovered that Fuchs had now developed a specialised service that was apparently doing very well. He procured children – boys and girls – for men to sleep with. *If he can do that*, Viktor had reasoned, *he can get hold of what I need.*

He'd finally found Fuchs again at the beginning of April. He spotted him in Albertina Platz, behind the opera. Tall and slightly stooped, managing to look both nervous and confident at the same time, Fuchs was sharing a cigarette with a sweet-looking boy of no more than 15. Viktor approached the pair from behind.

'Get lost,' he said to the boy. 'If I see you with him again you're in trouble.'

The boy ran away and Fuchs looked long and hard at the Russian, blowing a cloud of smoke into his face. 'What the fuck are you doing here?'

'Where are my guns?'

Fuchs shrugged. 'That was a long time ago. So much has happened since then. There's a war on, you know? Has that been reported in your papers?'

'I want them.'

'I don't have them.'

'I paid for them.'

'I can give you a refund if that's what you want, after I've deducted my costs.'

Viktor followed Fuchs as he strolled along into Augustinerstrasse. 'I insist you give me those guns,' he said. 'I paid for two semi-automatic pistols: Steyr-Hahns – and the ammunition.'

'What are you going to do – sue me? Go ahead. This city's under different ownership now. I'm amazed you had the nerve to come back, I'll give you that.'

'If you don't give me my guns, I'll…'

'… You'll do what? Go to the Gestapo? They're some of my best customers! Listen, I may be able to get my hands on the guns: give me a phone number and if you get a call saying the candlesticks have arrived then meet me outside that shop over there an hour after my call. That's the best I can promise.'

He was pointing at an ornate antiques shop that seemed to specialise in silver.

Vienna Spies

***

Walking back to Ungargasse from the Prater Park that Sunday afternoon Katharina and Rolf agreed a plan. She'd visit the church in Favoriten on her own during the week: a woman praying on her own by a religious statue would attract less attention.

'Once we have the key, you go to Café Demel to find Fuchs,' she told Rolf.

The following day Katharina waited until mid-morning before leaving the apartment and walking through the Botanical Gardens to Favoriten Strasse. She took her time, admiring the gardens and pausing by shop windows on the way, so that by the time she reached the tram stop she was certain she wasn't being followed. The tram took just 10 minutes to get to the stop nearest to the church of St Anton of Padua and the only other person to alight at that stop headed off in another direction.

Katharina had ceased to be a practising Catholic in her late teens when she'd exchanged Jesus Christ for Karl Marx, but the church had taught her well. As she entered the church, she placed a scarf over her head. A service had just finished and a few people were leaving while another dozen remained in their pews, quietly praying or waiting to take confession. Katharina knelt and crossed herself then sat down, taking a prayer book from behind the seat in front of her. Anyone watching her would see she was entirely familiar with what to do and, for a few minutes, she enjoyed the calm of the church. Gradually the numbers inside diminished. An elderly priest bustled past her and smiled, and a man in uniform sat down at the end of her row but didn't so much as glance in her direction.

175

She stood up, crossed herself again and slipped out of a side entrance, where she found herself in a peaceful if untended garden. She'd memorised the diagram carefully and knew where to find the statue of St Anton of Padua. A man and a woman in their sixties had just finished praying beside it and moved away as she approached. Looking around, she saw she was on her own and knew she needed to move fast. From her shopping bag she removed the metal spike Rolf had bought in a hardware shop. She dropped to her knees and bowed her head: anyone approaching from behind would hopefully see only a woman praying fervently. She worked out the line from the statue and swept away the leaves before poking the spike into a point that seemed to approximate the 'x' on the sketch. After three or four attempts there was an unmistakable contact with something metallic. She took out the small trowel and in less than a minute removed the metal tin. She quickly replaced the earth and swept the leaves back into position.

She was back at the apartment by lunchtime. She washed the trowel and spike, and put them in a box under the sink then sat at the kitchen table and opened the tin. Inside, wrapped in oilskin, were two keys. One was longer than the other and was clearly for the padlock. The other was the one for the safety deposit box, the same as the one drawn on the diagram: made of brass and quite chunky with the 'CA-BV' logo of the bank on the hub and the engraved numbers '49/2'.

On the Thursday morning, having already agreed with Herr Plaschke he could come in later in return for working during his lunch break, Rolf left the apartment at the normal time but walked through the Innere Stadt to Café Demel on Kohlmarkt, in sight of the Hofburg Palace. Being so close to the seat of Nazi power, the narrow streets in the area were teeming with men in uniform.

He remembered being taken to the café by his grandmother as a treat, though he suspected it was more for her than for him. As a young child the formality of the place was off-putting, the cream cakes only just making the visits worthwhile. He hadn't visited the café since he was 10: the dreadful year when both of his parents were killed in a car accident, along with his older sister. The elderly aunt with whom he was sent to live on the edge of the city in Liesing would have regarded a visit to Café Demel as an indulgence, as she did most things other than prayer and hard work.

... He never arrives before 9.00 but is always there by 9.30... they'd been told by Basil Remington-Barber in their briefing. Rolf arrived at the café at 8.55.

He sits at a small table on its own towards the back, in front of the kitchen. Rolf spotted the empty table and found one nearby, but with a good line of sight. He ordered a coffee and one of the pastries he remembered from years ago and waited. *Tall, thin, wears round spectacles, looks younger than his 35 years.* At 9.10, a man matching that description walked past him and sat at the table towards the back, in front of the kitchen. He didn't acknowledge the waitress, but nevertheless a pot of coffee appeared on his table, along with an ashtray.

Rolf waited five minutes before removing the neatly folded piece of paper he'd been given by Remington-Barber from his wallet and asked a waitress to give it to the gentleman in the corner. 'I noticed he dropped it as he came in.'

Rolf watched carefully as the waitress handed the note to

Fuchs, pointing in his direction so as to show who it was from. Fuchs read the note with as little interest as he would the bill. As far as Rolf could tell, not once did he glance in his direction. Instead, he drank another cup of coffee and smoked two further cigarettes before casually standing up, placing some change on the table and very quickly glancing in Rolf's direction: just the slightest of nods as he left the café.

Rolf followed. Fuchs strolled down Kohlmarkt, pausing to look in the window of a shop that sold antique silver, and a bit further along he showed some interest in the old maps on display in another window. At the end of Kohlmarkt, Fuchs turned left into Bognergasse and from there walked into Am Hof, the vast square where they used to hold antique markets and that Rolf had often visited with Frieda on a Saturday morning. Another memory. This morning though the square was empty of stalls and there were few people about. Those that were seemed to be hurrying in one direction or the other. At the far end of the square was an antiquarian bookshop and Fuchs stopped by it, flicking through a pile of second-hand books displayed on a trestle table, watched over by a large portrait of Hitler in the window.

Rolf stopped by the table too. Fuchs then turned to him, a broad smile on his face. 'My friend! How are you? It's so long since I've seen you! Come, let's talk.'

And with that he placed his arm around Rolf's shoulder and steered him away from the bookshop and towards the middle of the square.

'Where's Baumgartner?' His tone was threatening. He took out a cigarette and lit one, struggling to do so in the wind. He offered one to Rolf, who shook his head.

'Just take one for fuck's sake,' he said sharply. 'It looks more natural. Where the hell's Baumgartner?'

'He's not here. He asked me to come on his behalf.'

'But where is he? I've been waiting for that bastard to show up for years. Do you have the keys?'

Rolf nodded and took out his bunch of keys, showing Fuchs the chunky brass one and the longer one. Fuchs looked satisfied as he carefully inspected them.

'That's something, I suppose. I was convinced he'd conned me. Did he give you the instructions?'

Rolf nodded.

'I've been desperate for that box,' said Fuchs. 'Baumgartner said it'd be a few months at the most. I've been to that shop a few times but each time Johann refuses to help. He says he must have both keys because, without them, he's no chance of being allowed to open the safety deposit box. I still don't trust Baumgartner and I won't until that strongbox is opened. Is he alive?'

Rolf nodded.

'I wondered if he'd been in prison, the man is so untrustworthy,' said Fuchs. 'Look, I don't want to wait any longer and I'm sure Johann doesn't either. Tomorrow morning we'll meet outside the shop and go in together at 8.30, when he opens up. There are never any customers there for the first half hour or so. We should be in and out in a few minutes. You'll take your share and I'll take mine, and we never need see each other again. Just one thing though – I want more of the money because Baumgartner's waited so long. And I want the photographs and the guns. You take some of the money and the jewellery.'

'That's fine with me,' said Rolf.

***

That afternoon Viktor received the phone call he never thought he'd get. *The candlesticks have arrived.* He so distrusted Wilhelm Fuchs he assumed it was a trap, though in truth that was his approach to most contacts, so he decided to go to the antiques shop in Augustinerstrasse, where Fuchs was waiting, looking in the window with apparent interest.

'You know, I love that candelabra – I might buy it,' said Fuchs. 'Can you see the detail around the base? Quite possibly Polish. There are so many bargains to be had these days – the Jews had plenty of silver and you can pick up a piece now for half the price it was before the war, often less.'

'You sent me the message...'

'...Ah yes. I did indeed. Would you believe it, it now looks like I'll be able to get hold of your guns!'

'Fancy that, eh? After all these years and just a couple of weeks after I found you. What a happy coincidence!'

'No, no – it's true, believe me!' Fuchs looked genuinely aggrieved that the Russian doubted his integrity.

'So what happened?'

'It's so strange; I'd appreciate your opinion,' said Fuchs. 'The place where the guns are hidden, along with other items, needs a series of keys. One of these was held by an associate of mine, who I hadn't heard from in years. Then out of the blue, this morning a man turns up with a message from my associate. He has the key so we're going to go to the place where it's all hidden tomorrow. The timing's so strange that I too wondered whether it was just a coincidence.'

'You mean you think I may have something to do with this man?'

Fuchs nodded. They'd moved away from the antiques shop now and turned into Spiegelgasse. 'You can't blame me for wondering whether...'

'Don't be so bloody stupid! Do you think I've time to play games? Who was this man who turned up?'

'He didn't give a name. He had a note from my associate, with a message that let me know everything was in order and he was to be trusted. I'm desperate to get my hands on what's in that box so I'm going along with it.'

'When are you getting it?'

Fuchs hesitated: he looked as if he feared he'd told the Russian too much.

'Tomorrow.'

'And this man – did you recognise him? What did he look like?'

'Never seen him before... he'd be... I don't know, late twenties, early thirties? Light brown hair, medium build.'

'That narrows it down. Accent?'

'Bit odd: at first I couldn't place it, but then I wondered if it was Viennese. Hard to say. Look, when I give you your guns there's one thing I want from you.'

'You got the money years ago.'

'Not money, no. I want a guarantee from you. I'm not saying the war is lost, but it's not going well, is it? You hear all kinds of things, not least from some of my clients. They talk about your Red Army taking over Vienna. If that happens I want a written guarantee I'll be safe and I'll be able to carry on with my business.'

Viktor stopped suddenly and looked at Fuchs as if he'd not quite heard what he'd said. 'You want this in writing?' He sounded suitably incredulous.

Fuchs nodded.

'Very well then: give me my guns and I promise I'll give you a written guarantee.'

***

'Tomorrow morning – so soon?' Katharina sounded shocked. They were sitting at the kitchen table, leaning in close to each other and speaking barely above a whisper.

'He's desperate for what's in the strongbox: he's been waiting for years. I didn't think we could delay it.'

'It has to be done then, doesn't it?'

Rolf nodded.

'Turn on the tap,' said Katharina. 'We'll talk through the plan once more.'

Rolf couldn't recall sleeping that night. At one stage he'd got up from the sofa and strolled around the lounge, trying to compose himself. He went back to his makeshift bed, but was as restless as before. Just after 4.00 in the morning he walked through to the small kitchen. In the hallway he could see through into the bedroom, where the moonlight showed Katharina was awake too. She quietly got up and joined him in the kitchen. They both stood at the sink, sipping water.

'There's no point in fighting it,' she said. 'Who'd expect us to sleep, given…?'

'I know,' said Rolf.

'Is the sofa comfortable?'

'It's alright, I suppose.'

Katharina hesitated. 'If you ever want to sleep in the bed…'

'Pardon?'

'I meant that maybe you could sleep in the bed some nights. And I could sleep on the sofa.'

Four-and-a-half hours later Rolf was walking down Wiedner Hauptstrasse when Fuchs appeared as if from nowhere and fell into step with him. They were less than a block away from the hat shop. It was a shade before 8.30 when they reached it. Inside, they could see a short, fat man and when he spotted them he limped towards the door. When he recognised Fuchs he quickly ushered them inside.

'Are you on your own?' asked Fuchs.

'Yes. And this is…?' He was looking at Rolf.

'A friend from Gleisdorf.'

Johann Winkler looked both nervous and relieved, and spoke slightly hesitantly as he remembered the code. He appeared as anxious as Fuchs to get his hands on the money owed to him. 'And what kind of a hat would you like?' he asked Rolf.

'One that's suitable for both church and hunting.'

'Very well, but I've waited a long time. He's representing Baumgartner?'

Fuchs replied that he was.

'The keys?' Winkler was breathing heavily and leaning against the counter. Fuchs took out his brass key and held it in his palm for the other two to see. It was identical to Rolf's, brass and chunky with the 'CA-BV' logo on the hub, but with '49/1' engraved on the other side. Rolf took out his key: '49/2'. Winkler limped behind the counter and reached into cupboard, removing a box full of papers. From an envelope he produced an identical key: '49/3'.

For a moment, all three men looked at each other in an atmosphere of mutual distrust and tension. Winkler broke the silence. 'I'll take you down now. Maybe I'll put up a "closed" sign in the door first and lock it.'

'Good idea,' said Fuchs.

'No, don't do that,' said Rolf. 'If you're normally open at this time it'll look suspicious, won't it? It shouldn't take long.'

'Alright, let's move.'

They slowly made their way down to the basement, via a steep staircase that Winkler managed with some difficulty. The basement was vast, filled with deep shelves covered in boxes, some with hats poking out of them and others sealed up. Winkler led them down a narrow corridor between the racks of shelves and along an uneven floor to a small door, no more than five feet high. There were three locks on the door and, when opened, it led into a cellar with a musty atmosphere and the smell of rats. Winkler turned on the lights and there was a sound of scurrying in one corner. The room was full of rubbish, broken boxes, old hats, wrapping paper and a few empty bottles. He pointed to a cupboard on the far wall. 'Here, help me shift it.'

They moved the cupboard to reveal a large recess in the wall. Inside was a tarpaulin sheet, which Winkler pulled away, releasing a cloud of dust. And there was the strongbox, smaller than Rolf had imagined , but made out of metal and solid-looking, with two large padlocks.

'You can leave us now,' Fuchs said to Winkler.

Winkler hesitated. 'The keys? You're supposed to give me the keys at this point. That was the agreement.'

Fuchs glanced at Rolf and nodded. He handed over his key and Rolf did likewise. Winkler grasped them in his fist like a child who'd just been given a sweet.

'Be quick,' he said. 'Put the strongbox back where it was, cover it up then move the cupboard back into its space. Don't worry about the door, I'll lock it later. There are plenty of hatboxes in the basement, put whatever you're taking in those then come up. Be careful when you do. If there's anyone in the shop, just wait.'

They waited until Winkler had left before Fuchs opened one padlock with his key and Rolf did the same with his. Rolf's heart was beating so fast he was concerned Fuchs could hear it, and he shifted slightly away from him.

Do it quickly, as soon as the box is opened. Don't hesitate. He might well have the same thing in mind.

'What's that noise?' said Rolf. 'Is he coming back?'

'What?' Fuchs turned around, looking towards the door of the cellar, his back to Rolf. Then it was as if he sensed what was about to happen: his body tensed but by the time he started to turn back again, it was too late. Rolf plunged the knife into the man's neck where he'd been trained to do so, away from the spine (*'too much bone there, sir,'* the instructor had told him) but deep into the flesh, as far in as possible (*'bound to cause serious harm, very good chance of it hitting the jugular, sir... maybe try and give it a bit of twist while you're at it, sir?'*). Rolf was shocked at the noise Fuchs made, a louder cry than he'd have imagined possible and a desperate choking sound. It required some effort to pull the knife out of the neck and, as he did so, Fuchs fell to all fours, facing Rolf like a wild animal, blood dripping from his mouth and neck, his eyes swivelling around and clearly in agony. He made an effort to lunge at Rolf, but collapsed onto his front. *'Finish him off quick. One stab is very rarely enough, sir.'* Rolf straddled Fuchs, plunging the knife into his back five or six times, both sides of the spine and as deep as possible. By the time he'd finished, Fuchs had stopped moving and was silent.

Rolf wiped the blood from his hands with a handkerchief and allowed himself a few seconds to regain his breath. He wasn't finished yet.

'Are you sure?' he'd asked Basil Remington-Barber at the briefing.

'Of course I'm sure. You can't run the risk.'

He wiped the knife on Fuchs's trousers then climbed out of the cellar and through the basement. When he was near the top of the stairs and could hear no sound coming from the shop, he called out to Winkler. 'I say, could you give me a hand?'

When Rolf heard Winkler limping over he moved towards the bottom of the stairs.

'What is it?'

'We can't get the cupboard back in place, it needs three of us.'

'Are you sure? You're both younger and fitter than me. Just a moment then.'

Slowly Winkler edged his way down the stairs, clutching on to a handrail.

'Here, come and give me a hand,' he said to Rolf.

As Rolf started up the stairs, Winkler looked at him in shock. 'Hey! What's going on? You've got blood on your face – and your shirt! Hey!'

He was shouting now and starting to climb backwards, with surprising agility. Just as Rolf realised Winkler was likely to get into the shop before he could reach him, a shadow appeared across the doorway at the top and from that shadow a leg shot out, connecting with Winkler and sending him tumbling down the stairs.

Rolf had to leap out of the way as Winkler plummeted towards him, his head hitting the wall first then the floor, by which time he'd lost consciousness. Rolf knelt down beside him as Katharina hurried down the stairs.

'There's blood all over you,' she said. 'At least the door was unlocked, well done. We'd better move fast. I take it… Fuchs…?'

'Yes, he's dead. But what do we do with this one?'

'Get him into the cellar, then we can deal with him. Hurry.'

'… And the shop?'

'I put the "closed" sign up but we can't rely on that for long. Come on, let's drag him, it'll be quicker. Which way?'

It took them a couple of minutes to drag Winkler into the cellar and dump his body next to the lifeless one of Fuchs. Katharina looked at Rolf and he looked back at her. They both knew what the other was thinking.

'He's still alive,' he said.

'Give me the knife,' she replied.

'It's alright, I... I tell you what, let's drag him into that alcove first. That's where we'll hide them. It's where the strongbox was. We can cover the bodies with that tarpaulin.'

They dragged the now-groaning Winkler into the alcove, angling his body so it was pressed against the wall. Katharina held out her hand and Rolf passed the knife to her. She knelt down behind Winkler and used one hand to grab his hair and yank back his head. With the other, she cut his throat. The body went into a brief spasm then slumped. The two of them dragged Fuchs into the alcove, manoeuvring his body so it lay across Winkler's.

They turned their attention to the strongbox. Katharina had brought in a large hat box from the basement, and into it they placed the envelope containing the cash and a larger one with photographs in it, along with the two Steyr-Hahns pistols and the ammunition. Rolf started to put the jewellery in but Katharina stopped him.

'Leave it, it's too risky. What are we going to do with it? Just leave it. There's enough in here anyway. Pass me that tissue paper – and that hat.'

Once the hat box was ready they realised there was no room for the strongbox in the alcove, so they took out the large bag of jewellery and hid it under the bodies, covering them with the tarpaulin.

'What time is it?'

'Nearly 9.00,' said Katharina.

'The other staff arrive at 9.30. We need to move. Come, help me with the cupboard.'

It took all their effort and a good five minutes before the cupboard was back in position, blocking the alcove. Then they wiped themselves down with tissue paper, Katharina looking carefully to make sure there was no sign of blood on Rolf's face. Spotting some on his cheek, she licked her finger and rubbed his face, her thumb resting on his cheekbone in the same way Frieda's used to when she caressed his face.

The soiled tissue paper was stuffed into the strongbox, which was shoved into a corner, with piles of old boxes and other rubbish placed on top of it. There was a large patch of blood where Fuchs's body had been, so they covered that with a few old boxes. Then they left the cellar, turning out the light and closing the door.

'I've just realised something,' said Rolf as they made their way through the basement. 'Johann's got the three keys for the safe deposit box at the bank. We ought to take them.'

'Why?'

'The money...'

'Forget the money. We've plenty here. It'd be madness to even think of going to the bank. Come, let's go.'

The shop was silent when they re-entered it. They edged around the sides, keeping a careful eye on the doorway as they did so. Katharina took a large hat from a shelf, one that threw a shadow over her face. Rolf darted over to the door and turned the sign around: 'open'.

They left the hat shop and turned left, walking quickly but not too fast, arm in arm. As far as they could tell, no one had noticed them: a noisy group of schoolchildren were being shepherded along on the opposite pavement, but they were ahead of them, so it was unlikely the teachers would have seen them. On their side of the road there was only an old road sweeper, who didn't look up as he prodded at the pavement with an enormous brush.

They took the first left, checking all the time they'd not been followed. When they reached Neulinggasse, they began to relax and for a brief while their steps were almost sprightly.

'Look, it's 9.15,' said Katharina. 'When we get back to the apartment you'll have to hurry. You need to get washed and changed; you're going to be late for work.'

'I think we pulled that off,' said Rolf.

'Yes, but we've barely begun.'

'I know, but surely that has to be the hardest part – killing two people?'

'Maybe, who knows?'

***

By the time Rolf arrived back from work that evening the elation he and Katharina had felt after the successful outcome at the hat shop had been replaced by shock. They'd each killed a man and put themselves in extreme danger. They sat in the gloom of the kitchen, neither touching the dinner in front of them.

'Did you send the message to Switzerland?'

'Yes,' said Rolf. 'I told you that when I came in.'

'Sorry, I'm distracted. Basil ought to have it by now.'

'I hope so. You're sure the guns and everything are safely hidden?'

'As safe as can be,' said Katharina. 'But if the Gestapo tore this place apart, of course they'd find them. So, now we have to find Leitner.'

Rolf nodded, moving a potato around on his plate with his fork, allowing it to slide in the gravy. 'And then find Viktor... and set up a network...'

There was a long silence as Katharina collected the plates and placed them on the side. When they moved into the lounge they sat in the dark for a while rather than draw the curtains.

'There was no alternative, was there?'

Katharina didn't answer for a while and Rolf repeated the question.

'I don't think so,' she said eventually. 'Basil said it was too risky to do otherwise, that we'd be jeopardising the mission. You know what I realised last night, Gerd – when I couldn't sleep?'

'What?'

'You know the church where the keys were hidden? St Anton of Padua? Well, St Anton of Padua is the patron saint of lost causes.'

***

The previous afternoon, Viktor had managed to follow Wilhelm Fuchs from the antiques shop in Augustinerstrasse through the crowded Innere Stadt to a building on Schulerstrasse, behind the cathedral. If he'd been able to and if he'd had help, he'd have been outside the building early the following morning and followed Fuchs to wherever he was collecting the guns from. Apart from the fact he distrusted Fuchs, he wanted to see who the person was who'd come on behalf of his associate.

But it was impossible. Viktor had to be at the factory early that morning and he couldn't afford to attract attention by missing his shift. He hoped Fuchs would be as good as his word and contact him as promised, once he had the guns. *The candlesticks are ready for collection.*

But two weeks later the call had never come, which didn't totally surprise Viktor. He waited a couple of days more then visited the building on Schulerstrasse, which was an enormous risk but was his only way of finding Fuchs. He watched the building for two days and eventually spotted his opportunity. He saw a boy leave the building, young and blonde, not unlike the one he'd seen with Fuchs in Albertina Platz. The boy walked fast, as if he was in a hurry to leave. Viktor caught up with him in front of the cathedral.

'Are you with Fuchs?'

The boy looked terrified. 'I'm not allowed to go with you... you have to come to Schulerstrasse first. I can only see people there.' Behind long eyelashes were big blue eyes full of fear.

Viktor placed a hand on the boy's shaking shoulder and handed him a packet of cigarettes, flipping open the top. 'Here. All this is for you.'

The boy looked inside: next to half a dozen cigarettes was a bundle of Reichsmark notes. A hint of smile briefly crossed the boy's face.

'It's enough for you to leave that place, if you want,' said Viktor. The boy looked as if that could be a possibility.

'But I need you to tell me something,' said Viktor. 'Where's Fuchs, where can I find him?'

'He's dead,' said the boy. It was an odd accent. Viktor suspected he was Slovak or Czech, certainly not Austrian.

'When did this happen?'

The boy shrugged and helped himself to one of the cigarettes, making sure to put the rest of the packet carefully in the inside pocket of his jacket. 'Maybe two weeks ago, that's when he went missing. We only found out he was dead two days ago. They don't tell us much, they never do – but the rumour is he was killed. With a knife.'

His big blue eyes opened wide, incredulous that Fuchs could have been killed with a knife, of all things.

**

Rolf and Katharina's plan had been to wait a few days after the hat shop killings before seeking out Leitner. They agreed they needed to be sure there was nothing that would link them with the murders. The killings had taken place on the Friday and by the Sunday evening the shock had worn off enough for them to feel more relaxed: they appeared to have got away with it. Things were going well, so far.

That feeling would last less than 48 hours.

Chapter 12

Vienna, May 1944

On the Tuesday afternoon following the hat shop killings, Rolf had to deliver some documents to a law firm on the other side of the Innere Stadt, near the Parliament building. He was to wait for them to be signed and witnessed before returning with some others to Bank Leu – nothing especially onerous.

The business at the law firm took longer than expected: he had to wait while one document was checked; another document needed to be amended; there'd be a delay while the one of the papers from the law firm was typed up; a partner who needed to counter-sign was out, he'd be back soon.

While all this was going on, Rolf sat in the reception area. It was comfortable enough and there was a steady stream of people moving in and out, from one office to another.

It was then he spotted him.

There was no doubt in Rolf's mind it was August Unger, the nemesis from his schooldays. He and Unger had been the top two in their class for five years from the age of 13, but they couldn't have been more different: while Rolf's cleverness came naturally, for Unger it was hard-earned through work and ambition. They differed in many other ways: Rolf was good-looking with a boyish charm; Unger was thick-set, with bad acne and a gruff manner. On the football pitch Rolf was a naturally gifted winger, as quick as lightning, while Unger's contribution was as a heavy-footed defender, often resorting to fouling his opponents. Unger lived in a smart house with his large and wealthy family; Rolf was an orphan, living with an unmarried aunt in modest circumstances. While Unger clearly resented Rolf's popularity there were far more fundamental causes of resentment. In the foetid and violent atmosphere of Austrian politics in the 1920s they were on different sides: Rolf was a social democrat, Unger on the far right and it was even rumoured his father was involved with the National Socialists. For five years they were opponents, both physical and intellectual. During the 1930s, after they'd left school, they rarely encountered each other – one or two school reunions and uncomfortable fellow guests at mutual friends' weddings.

But the man who walked through reception from one part of the office to another that Tuesday afternoon was undoubtedly August Unger. He had the same awkward gait, the same demeanour about him – one that managed to be both arrogant and uncertain – and the face once covered in acne was now heavily pockmarked.

When he first walked past he glanced very briefly towards where Rolf was sitting, but there were other people there too and he didn't seem to notice him. He certainly didn't break his stride. Rolf wasn't unprepared for this, for encountering someone from his past. He recalled Edgar's warning.

Good chance of it happening. Key thing to remember is that you look very different, believe me: your ears have been pinned back and your eyelids have been operated on; you'll be dying your hair and wearing spectacles. The chances of someone recognising you and being sure it's you are slim. Be confident in your new identity.

Rolf wished he could share Edgar's confidence – that he looked so different he'd be unrecognisable to someone who knew him well. All this shot through his mind as he sat frozen in the chair in the lawyer's reception. As far as he could tell, Unger hadn't spotted him, so should he make an excuse and leave? That would probably arouse suspicion in itself. He angled the chair slightly and picked up a newspaper: if Unger came back he wouldn't have such a good view of him. But Unger did return to the reception, not once but four more times over the next hour. The first two times Rolf avoided looking at him, but as far as he could tell, Unger's step was more hesitant than before and he was sure he paused slightly when closest to Rolf.

On the third occasion he came into reception while Rolf was looking up and the two men's eyes met, briefly but enough to convince Rolf there was a flicker of recognition from Unger. Very soon after that Unger returned, this time pausing at the reception desk. Rolf could see he was speaking with the receptionist but couldn't hear what was being said, though he did notice the receptionist glancing in his direction once or twice, as if he might be the subject of whatever conversation was taking place.

When all the paperwork was in order and it was time for Rolf to leave and return to Bank Leu, he was convinced the Gestapo would be waiting for him outside. But the street was empty and no one had followed him out of the office, so he allowed himself time to study the names on the large brass plate at the entrance to the office and there, among the list of lawyers working for the firm, was that of 'August Otto Unger'.

When Rolf returned to the apartment that evening he broke the news to Katharina.

'You're certain it was him?'

'I've told you, his name was at the front of the building. Weren't you listening?'

'Don't snap at me like that. We need to be calm about this.'

'Calm! Unger's a Nazi. We had mutual acquaintances; he'd have known what I was doing. He'd have known about Frieda and he'd have known I left Vienna in '38 after the Anschluss – and you expect me to be calm!'

'It's possible he didn't recognise you.'

'I know that, but it's also very possible he did. Remember what I told you: in an hour he came through that reception area five times – five times!'

'I know, but…'

'… And on the last occasion I'm certain he was asking the receptionist about me.'

'Let's assume that's true,' said Katharina. 'What would he have asked her? Who's that man over there? And what would she have replied? His name's Gerd Schuster, he's from Bank Leu. My guess is that maybe he thought he recognised you but wasn't sure, which is why he checked. Don't forget, your appearance has changed.'

'Not that much.'

'That's not what Basil said. He said he didn't recognise you, and he'd only seen you a couple of months before.'

'Maybe he was just being nice.'

'It's not Basil's job to be nice. When would you last have seen this Unger?'

Rolf thought for a while. 'Maybe in '36, something like that: it was at a friend's wedding. We ignored each other.'

'Right then, so that was, what… eight years ago? People change a lot in eight years. Let me ask you a question, what do you think he'd have done if he really did think it was you?'

'He'd report me, that's for sure. He was always a sneak at school, he liked to get other people into trouble. He'd know full well I'm an anti-Nazi and he'd wonder what on earth I'm doing back in Vienna.'

'But he didn't, did he, Gerd? What time did you leave the lawyers' office?'

'Around 3.00, possibly a little bit later.'

'And what time did you get back to the bank?'

'Around 3.45…'

'And you left there at 5.00,' said Katharina. 'So if he really suspected you then surely something would have happened by then. The Gestapo would have turned up at Bank Leu.'

They argued for another hour, turning over all the possibilities in their minds. Maybe Unger had a meeting and would contact the Gestapo later; maybe he'd check out Rolf himself, making enquiries to see how long he'd been working; maybe he'd wait until the morning; maybe the Gestapo would come that night or in the early hours of the morning – wasn't that how they operated?

That night they retrieved the two Steyr-Hahns pistols from where they'd hidden them in the back of a wardrobe and loaded them with ammunition, convinced the noise of the magazines going into the pistols had woken up the whole block. They took it in turns to keep watch: one waiting up in the lounge, keeping an eye on the road from a crack in the curtain while the other rested on the bed.

But Vienna slept peacefully that night, even if they didn't.

Over breakfast they agreed that if Unger was going to inform the Gestapo he'd do it that day, so they agreed Katharina would leave the apartment with Rolf and stay away from it all day until he returned that evening.

But nothing happened. Fortunately there were a number of transfers to head office to be processed that kept Gerd Schuster busy, though every time the telephone rang he jumped and whenever someone came through the door he was the first to look up. By the middle of the afternoon, though, he felt confident enough to approach Herr Plaschke. *Was everything in order with the lawyers yesterday?* Herr Plaschke looked confused. Yes of course, why do you ask? *No, I was just wondering if there were any problems?* No, none at all.

***

That evening Rolf and Katharina decided to wait until the following week before approaching Leitner. They also agreed Katharina would press on with finding work as a nurse.

The Vienna General Hospital, which everyone called the AKH, was an enormous complex just to the north of the Innere Stadt in Alsergrund, the 9th district. It took Katharina the best part of an hour just to find the correct office, where a harassed-looking clerk glanced at all her papers, appearing disappointed when she could find no obvious flaw in them. *Yes, plenty of vacancies.*

'How do I apply?'

'You can either fill in a form here, leave it with us and wait to hear. We'll have to check your accreditation with the authorities in

Switzerland. In my experience that takes a long time. Or, you could go to one of the departments and see if they'll take you on straight away on a more informal basis – the pay will be slightly lower, but…' she leant conspiratorially towards Katharina, 'they're so desperate.'

Tipped off by the clerk that the orthopaedic department was among the most desperate, Katharina decided to go there first. The matron enthusiastically steered her into a side office. 'If you want to start now you'll go down as a temporary member of staff,' she said. 'It's easier and quicker, and far less paperwork. I'll need you to do a trial shift first so I can tell how capable a nurse you are.'

Katharina reported for her trial shift the following day and within an hour the matron called her into her office. 'I've seen quite enough already,' she said. 'You're very competent. Let me see your paperwork again?'

The matron flicked through it. 'How would you feel about working on the surgical ward? We've so many military personnel coming in for specialist operations that we're quite overwhelmed there. You can start tomorrow.'

***

A week later, spurred on by a series of increasingly stern messages sent by Remington-Barber via Michael Hedinger, Rolf and Katharina made their first approach to Leitner. London made it very clear what it wanted from the politician.

The nun had also been clear about to how to find him. *Listen carefully: this is the address you're to go to and this is what you need to say to this person when you get there… Memorise it very carefully, do you understand? And when you do meet Leitner, this is what you'll need to persuade him you're genuine.*

It was Katharina who went first, carefully following the nun's instructions. She'd just completed a night shift at the hospital and arrived back at the apartment at 7.00 in the morning, where she and Rolf talked through the plan once more. She'd rest for a couple of hours, get changed and set off at around 10.00. If all went well she should be back by 11.30 at the latest and would close the net curtains in the window that overlooked Ungargasse as a signal to Rolf on his return from work that it was safe.

She set off as planned at 10.00, walking as far as the Stuben Ring, from where she caught a tram across the canal to Leopoldstadt. The 2nd District was really an island, positioned in the centre of the city between the Danube Canal and the mighty River Danube itself. To the south of Leopoldstadt lay the Prater Park, where she and Rolf liked to walk and talk. To the north was the elegant Augarten Park, the city's oldest, with its stunning Baroque palace. In between the parks and around them, Leopoldstadt had been a largely Jewish area.

There were still signs of that when Katharina left the tram on Praterstrasse and headed north west. It was like visiting a ghost town that still had people living in it: signs above shops were painted over, swastikas and Nazi graffiti daubed on walls. On Leopoldgasse, she passed the ruins of what had evidently been an enormous and ornate building. The shell was burnt out and all the windows were broken. An old man shuffling by paused when he noticed her looking at it. 'The Polnische Shul,' he muttered. 'No more Jews.' He walked away, chuckling to himself.

Leopoldstadt had been a lively area, close to the centre. As the Jews had disappeared they'd been swiftly replaced, with military and Nazis families getting the pick of where to move into. One population had been swapped with another, but there was still something of the previous one hanging in the air.

Katharina felt it as she walked up Obere Augartenstrasse, with the enormous anti-aircraft tower dominating not just the park but the whole area around it. She noticed an SS officer walking behind her so she went into a tobacconist to buy some matches. When she came out, she turned left, walked around the block then carried on up Obere Augartenstrasse.

The apartment complex she spotted was far larger than she'd imagined, but slightly too run down to be described as imposing. The white walls were faded and damaged in parts, and the windows around the entrance were cracked.

The nun had been emphatic. *You must only speak to Frau Egger, you understand? She lives on the premises and is on duty in the concierge's office from six 6.00 in the morning until early evening, every day apart from Sunday.*

The concierge's office was tucked by the main staircase in the entrance hall, and had an unpleasant and slightly overpowering warmth emanating from it. Hunched up inside the entrance, occupying a vantage point from where she could watch all comings and goings, and much else besides, was a lady of an uncertain age, her face hard and lined, her eyes missing nothing. Despite the warmth she was wrapped in a thick black shawl, her fingers in mittens. She said nothing as Katharina entered, her eyes scanning her up and down, and her mouth moving as if she was chewing something unpalatable.

'Excuse me, but I'm looking for a Frau Egger?'

The old lady carried on looking at her, nodding reluctantly.

'I've a letter here, for a Frau Weber. She was an old friend of my mother's and I understand she may have moved to this block a few months ago.'

For a very brief moment Frau Egger's face registered the significance of what she was hearing. Her eyebrows shot up then down and her mouth stopped moving. Then it fell back to normal as she held out a mitten-covered hand, with chubby tobacco-stained fingers poking out. She took the envelope and studied the front carefully.

'Will you be returning to collect her reply?'

Katharina felt a mixture of relief and tension. Frau Egger's reply was the one she'd use to indicate Katharina had come to correct place and all was in order.

'If that's alright with you, yes please.'

'Come back on Saturday, around 1.00 in the afternoon.'

Katharina thanked her and explained her husband would be accompanying her. Frau Egger nodded. *I know, I know...*

Chapter 13

Vienna, May 1944

Forget about her.

That's what Edgar, George Whitlock and Crispin Meredith had all told him *ad nauseam* – and Basil Remington-Barber reminded him of it in Switzerland.

Forget about Frieda, Rolf. You're not going back to Vienna to find her. If she's in prison or worse, well then there's nothing you can do, is there? And if she's still alive and well then even making enquiries could put her life at risk and you don't want that, do you? Either way, you'll be jeopardising the mission and we can't have that.

It was all well and good for them to say that, but then they weren't engaged to her, were they? How could they expect him to return to his home town after six years and not want to find out what had happened to his fiancée? They were the ones, after all, who'd sent him back to Vienna, he hadn't volunteered for it. But now he was here, he was determined to find the answers to the questions that'd been haunting him.

The night before he'd fled Vienna in 1938 he and Frieda had had a bitter argument. He'd pleaded with her to come with him, she'd chastised him for leaving. 'How are we going to defeat the Nazis if we leave Austria?' She'd called him selfish and a typical social democrat, and he'd told her she was a typical communist, always making dramatic gestures and counting on a revolution that was never going to happen. 'You really believe your precious proletariat are going to rise up? They're the most enthusiastic Nazis!'

Vienna Spies

He'd only stayed that night at her apartment in Brigittenau because it'd have been too dangerous for him to leave it late at night. In the early hours of the morning, when he was wondering whether he should remain in Vienna with her after all, he'd leaned over to her, closing his body against hers. But instead of responding as she normally would, she'd pushed him away and moved over to the edge of the bed, pulling most of the blankets with her.

When he woke fully she was gone: no note on the table, nothing. The set of keys she'd given him for her apartment had been removed from his jacket pocket and the framed photograph of the two of them by the Danube was no longer on the mantelpiece. So he left, with no goodbye, no reconciliation – not even a grudging understanding or an agreement to disagree. Instead he was left with a feeling of guilt and regret that had haunted him every minute of every day since. It was a feeling he knew would remain with him until he'd discovered what had happened to Frieda. He'd thought returning to Vienna might give him some peace of mind, but it had made matters worse. He was unsettled, having no idea whether she dead or alive, free or in captivity, in Vienna or elsewhere.

Since the time he'd cried in the park, he'd done his best to hide his feelings from Katharina. But he was starting to doubt whether this was wise. He did wonder whether she was beginning to take their need to play the part of a married couple more literally than he was. He noticed – he couldn't fail to do otherwise – that when they were alone in the apartment she often wore a tight, white woollen sweater that showed off her breasts to their best advantage. And, though he tried to resist it, he couldn't help but be attracted to her. Katharina was one of those women whose beauty became apparent the more time was spent with her. It wasn't an obvious beauty; she wasn't pretty in that sense. But after a while he became aware of a sensuality about her that had become impossible to ignore. He found himself thinking back to the time she'd casually mentioned he perhaps didn't need to sleep on the sofa. Had she been thinking of more than just his comfort?

So Rolf had waited for a month after arriving back in Vienna before he made his first tentative enquiries about Frieda. He was well aware that, once he started to do so, he risked exposing himself to people who may remember him, but he couldn't have been more cautious. He travelled up to the 20th district, where she had lived. And on his first journey he'd remained on the tram as it went up Leipziger Strasse then back again down Pappenheim Gasse, so he'd pass both the front and rear of the block she'd lived in. There was no bomb damage and no other sign of anything out of the ordinary.

A few days later he returned to the area, this time getting off the tram at the first stop on Leipziger Strasse and walking past the apartment block. He didn't stop, but walked slowly enough to have a look at the building. Again, there was nothing unusual, though he wasn't sure what would constitute unusual. At the top of the road he turned left into Nordwestbahnhof Strasse, where he was taken aback at the extensive damage to the freight yards beyond it. Somehow a small goods train was weaving its way through the tangled metal and piles of rubble. He carried on walking, turning right into Pappenheim Gasse, from where he could see the rear of Frieda's block. He spotted her apartment on the third floor, but he couldn't make out any detail that would indicate whether she still lived there or not.

When he returned the following week he entered the apartment block, armed with what he hoped was a plausible enough cover story. Frieda had lived in apartment 3D. He had, he told the concierge, a letter for a Herr Maier in apartment 3D. *There's no Herr Maier in apartment 3D.* Are you sure? *Of course I'm sure; Frau Wallner and her daughter live in 3D. Here, let me see your letter.*

He handed over the letter. *No! This is for apartment 3D in the block across the road, Leipziger Strasse 58. We're Leipziger Strasse 53.*

Once he'd established that Frieda no longer lived in Leipziger Strasse, he was at a loss what to do. The dental surgery where she worked in the 9th District was now an opticians and he felt asking where – if anywhere – the practice had moved to would be too risky. Frieda's elderly mother lived in a village near Innsbruck in Tyrol-Vorarlberg, which was close to Switzerland, and he'd no intention of going there. He'd need to see what he could find out in Vienna, though he'd have to be careful – he couldn't risk Katharina finding out what he was up to.

Most of Frieda's group of friends had either been arrested before Rolf left the country or had fled at around the same time as him. Most had been communists, though not all members of the KPO. Some of those, because of their jobs, had kept their political affiliations very quiet and it was those he decided to seek out. There was a tight-knit and secretive group of around half a dozen that he clearly wasn't part of. He didn't even know all their names. The one he'd known best was Wolfgang Fischer, who'd been a

PhD student at the university at the same time as him, and for a while lived near him in the 18th District. One lunchtime, when he was on an errand for Bank Leu, he made a detour to the house where Fischer had rented a room.

'Why do you want Herr Fischer?' The landlady eyed him suspiciously through a half-open door.

'I'm an old friend.'

'And your name?'

A slight pause. 'Schmidt, Marcus Schmidt. Is Wolfgang here?'

'Did you know Herr Fischer well?' Her tone had switched from suspicious to hostile.

'Look, it really doesn't matter,' said Rolf. 'No, I didn't know him well. We were acquaintances more than anything else and I just happened to be passing and...'

'He's dead.'

'What?'

'Herr Fischer died two or three years ago, I don't know the circumstances – they said it was an accident or something What I do know is that when they came to search his room they ransacked it, made a terrible mess, and I received no compensation for that – not one Reichsmark!'

'Who came to search his room?' Rolf was already edging away from the entrance.

'The Gestapo, who else? What did you say your name was?'

Rolf managed to hurry away and was relieved he'd at least had the presence of mind to give a false name. But he was shocked Fischer was dead – and, by the sound of it, had been killed.

He decided to try one more friend of Frieda's. Rolf had the

impression Joachim Lang was the most important in their group; a shadowy figure who said little but to whom Frieda and the others appeared to defer. Rolf remembered Lang's father ran a small music bookshop in the 9th District and, on occasion, Frieda would ask Rolf to deliver a note there for Lang on his way to the university. *Don't get involved, none of your friendly conversations: just check it's his father you're giving it to then leave.*

The shop was still there in Berg Gasse when Rolf visited the next day. When the door opened it did so to the familiar sound of a musical chime. The shop had barely changed since his last visit: shelf after shelf of sheet music and bookcases were still groaning with dusty volumes. The shop was full of music, but conspicuously silent. Lang's father was behind the glass counter, looking slightly older. The one change to the shop as far as Rolf could make out was that on the wall behind him the portrait of Wolfgang Mozart now had a companion: Adolf Hitler. Mozart and Hitler, Vienna's ubiquitous images.

It was evident Herr Lang didn't recognise Rolf. The older man smiled kindly, pleased to see a customer and perhaps someone to talk to. How could he help, he wondered? He stubbed a cigarette out in a saucer and straightened his frayed cuffs.

'Actually, it's your son Joachim I'm after.'

The old man's face froze with fear and his leathery hands gripped the top of the counter. He stood rigid for a few moments then looked beyond Rolf in panic, trying to peer through the glass door to the street beyond. 'I've no idea where he is,' he said, his voice little more than an urgent and angry whisper. 'I've not heard from him for many years. Please go now.'

The man wiped his perspiring brow with the back of his hands, which were shaking violently. 'Go, go on,' he gestured for Rolf to leave the shop.

'Is your son alright?'

'I don't know, I told you. You must leave now.' The man shooed Rolf away and came around from behind the counter to show him out. 'Here, take this sheet music – let me put it in a bag for you. It'll look more natural if you're seen to leave the shop with something. Here you are. Now go.'

The man already had the door open with one hand and his other was on Rolf's back, pushing him out.

After the discovery that Frieda no longer lived at her apartment in Brigittenau, that Wolfgang Fischer was dead and the reaction of Lang's father, Rolf was so unnerved he decided he'd better pause in his attempts to find out what had happened to Frieda.

Maybe another opportunity would arise.

***

The Kriminalpolizei, better known as the Kripo, was one of a number of divisions of the RSHA, the Reich Central Security Office. Another division was the Gestapo. But no member of the Kripo or anyone else in the RSHA was under the illusion these divisions might in some way be equals. There was no question that the Gestapo, the secret police, outranked the Kripo and pretty much everyone else it came across, with the possible exception of the SS.

Kripo officers were well used to this. They regarded it as an annoyance and a hindrance as much as anything else, something to be lived with like the weather and rationing. Some senior officers secretly enjoyed it: the Gestapo acted in such an arrogant manner that the Kripo could be left to get on with what they regarded as proper crime on their own. One such senior officer was Kriminalrat Andreas Schwarz, a career detective with an impressive record, a cynical manner and a damaged hand that kept him safely away from military service.

Early one afternoon towards the end of May, Schwarz was sitting in a meeting room at the Gestapo headquarters on Morzinplatz, with a group of reluctant Gestapo section leaders sitting opposite him. There was Strobel from Section IVA, which looked after the communists and other enemies of the state; Grosser from IVB which was supposed to sort out the Jews and other religions; Molden from IVC, whose responsibility was Nazi Party affairs; and a nervous man called Nikolaus, who was in charge of section IVE, counter-intelligence. None of them, thought Schwarz as he surveyed the room, ranked above Kriminaldirektor. He outranked them all. And none of them would know how to handle a proper investigation even if they were eye-witness to the crime.

'Gentlemen,' said Schwarz in his most polite voice, making sure he was smiling. 'I'm very grateful for your attendance. I know how busy you are with work of such vital importance to the Reich.'

Schwarz made sure there was no hint of obvious sarcasm in his voice. 'We require your co-operation with an investigation that has many unusual aspects to it. Although there's no obvious political dimension to the crime we've hit something of a brick wall and we can't rule out the possibility of any connection with one of your departments.'

Through the cloud of cigarette smoke he could make out the blank faces of men who clearly felt their time was being wasted. 'Two weeks ago we were called to a hat shop on Wiedner Hauptstrasse,' he continued. 'Some of you may have heard about the crime. The owner of the shop had previously reported one of his employees, a Johann Winkler, as missing. Winkler appeared to have opened the shop as normal at 8.30, but when the other staff arrived an hour later there was no sign of him. Two weeks ago they had cause to enter a little-used cellar behind their basement storage area and, when they did so, there was a foul smell. They eventually worked out it came from a recess in a wall, hidden by a cupboard. Have a look at these photographs.'

Schwarz passed around a series of photographs. The Gestapo officers, no doubt against their better judgement, began to show signs of interest. 'Two bodies, as you can see,' said Schwarz. 'They'd begun to decompose, but were still in a good enough condition to reveal they'd both been murdered, stabbed with the same knife. We were able to identify one of the victims as Johann Winkler, the missing manager. The other victim, according to his identity cards and subsequently confirmed by a fingerprint check, is Wilhelm Fuchs. Fuchs has a fairly long criminal record, mostly in connection with fraud and prostitution. This is the photo from his identity card.'

He passed around another photograph.

'And there's another intriguing aspect to the case. These photographs show a large amount of jewellery, some of it very valuable. It was left with the bodies. There was also an empty strongbox that was hidden in the cellar and in the bottom of it was a single magazine of ammunition, from a Steyr-Hahns.'

'A robbery that went wrong,' said Grosser. 'What on earth makes you think it's anything we can help with? We're very busy here you know, Schwarz. Our job is to protect the Reich, not help out the Kripo when it's unable to solve a simple crime.'

Schwarz paused just long enough to let Grosser's words sink in. 'Because, Kriminaldirektor Grosser, we suspect Fuchs had political connections: he was regularly in trouble, but interestingly since 1940 he's not been convicted of any crimes. We believe he may have friends in high places. We've reason to believe he ran a brothel near the cathedral, one where the prostitutes were not only underage but included boys as well as girls. Whenever this was looked into, the investigation was shut down at an early stage.'

'Do you have any leads?'

'Very few indeed, Kriminaldirektor Molden, though we do have an eyewitness who saw a couple – a man and a woman – who left the shop at around 9.10. That'd fit with Winkler having opened the shop at 8.30 and the other members of staff arriving an hour later.'

'Who's this witness?'

'A road sweeper, something of a low-life, well known to us,' said Schwarz. 'Once he has a drink inside him he shows little respect for the law, but on that particular morning he was sober, so has proven to be uncharacteristically helpful. He was sweeping the area around the shop and saw the "open" sign in the door, then noticed it'd been replaced by a "closed" sign a few minutes later.

He was wondering what was going on when he realised it said "open" again, which he thought was odd. Soon after that, at around 9.10, as I say, he saw this couple leave the shop. He says they were walking in a hurry.'

'Can he describe them?'

'He couldn't provide a useful description of the woman; he says she was wearing a wide-brimmed hat that hid her face. But he describes the man as being in his early thirties, around six feet tall, with light-brown hair and wearing a light raincoat. One of them – he can't remember which – was carrying a large hat box.'

The meeting finished soon after that. As Schwarz gathered the photographs, one of the Gestapo officers – a fat and particularly unpleasant man called Karl Strobel who had a habit of puffing out his chest as if to compensate for his lack of height – sidled up to him. 'Schwarz, I'd like you to accompany me to my office. I may have something of mutual interest.'

Schwarz followed Strobel up to his office on the third floor and waited while the Gestapo man rooted around on his elegant desk for the file he was looking for. 'Ah, here it is,' he said. 'Now, could I ask you once again to read out that description of the man provided by the road sweeper?'

Schwarz read from his notebook. 'He described the man as being in his early thirties, around six feet tall, with light-brown hair and wearing a light raincoat.'

'Have you come across the name Frieda Brauner in your investigations, Herr Schwarz?'

Schwarz bristled at Strobel's failure to address him by his rank. 'No, I'm sure I'd have recalled that name. Why?'

Vienna Spies

'There was a communist resistance cell here in Vienna that was active for far longer than it should've been, especially during 1941 and into the early part of 1942,' said Strobel. 'We believe the cell comprised six or seven members, and it was somewhat effective, distributing defeatist leaflets and organising the sabotage of machinery in factories. Normally we deal with these groups very quickly, but not this one. We did catch two of their members in late 1941: Franz Josef Mayer and Wolfgang Fischer, but neither man revealed anything under interrogation and both died in custody. In March 1942, though, we arrested a third member of the group, Frieda Brauner. She too was interrogated and revealed very little – but, just before she died, she did pass on the code names of four other members and also of the group. The code names are of little use, they refer to the rivers of hell in Greek mythology.'

'Excuse me if I appear impatient, Herr Kriminaldirektor, but what's the connection with this case? I'm confused.'

'The landlady of the house where Wolfgang Fischer lived contacted us a couple of weeks ago to let us know a man had come to the house enquiring about Fischer,' said Strobel. 'He said his name was Schmidt, she can't remember the first name. She told him Fischer was dead and she says he left quickly. We believe this cell – which has the code name Hades, would you believe? – was led by a man called Joachim Lang. There's been no sign of Lang since sometime in 1941, but we do watch his father's shop on Berg Gasse – not all the time, of course, but most days we have a watcher there for a few hours. The day after the man calling himself Schmidt went to Fischer's house, a man turned up at this shop.

The watcher logged him, as they do every visitor. Once we connected this man with the one who visited Fischer's house we pulled Lang's father in. He eventually admitted the visitor was asking about his son. He insisted he didn't give a name and that he'd no idea who he was.'

'Description?'

'The description given by the landlady, our watcher and Lang's father were all in agreement: around six foot with dark-blond hair, wearing a light raincoat and in his late twenties or early to mid-thirties. Light-brown hair could easily be described as dark blond, so it sounds like the same man, wouldn't you say?'

Chapter 14

Vienna, June 1944

Katharina returned to the apartment block on Obere Augartenstrasse with Rolf on the morning of the first Saturday in June.

The previous night there had been bombing to the north and the west of the city, and while it hadn't been close or heavy enough to force them down to the air-raid shelter with its prying eyes and pricked ears, it had kept them awake for most of the night. According to the rumours, the Allies had captured the air base at Foggia in Italy and were launching raids on Vienna from there. They left the apartment in Ungargasse at 11.00, having planned a complicated route to Leopoldstadt to reduce the risk of their being followed.

They strolled around the Prater Park for half an hour, making sure they doubled back on themselves, crossed paths and walked through crowds of people. Just after 12.00 they split up, Rolf leaving the park through the north exit and heading along Haupt Allee, through the Praterstern square and into Augarten Park, coming out where it joined Obere Augartenstrasse at its top end. Katharina had left the Prater through another exit and walked through a series of smaller streets to enter Obere Augartenstrasse at its lower end.

It was 12.50 when they met in the middle of the street as planned – Katharina carrying her handbag in her left hand and Rolf's cap in his pocket, signalling all was safe. They chatted for a while in the street, watching each other's back. 'Well,' said Katharina. 'If anyone's followed us, they deserve the Iron Cross. Come on, let's go in.'

It was 1.00 when they entered the apartment building. Frau Egger was waiting for them in her little concierge's office. She gave each of them a brief nod by way of a greeting then shut the door, putting up a sign saying 'Closed for lunch. Open 2pm.' Beckoning them with a mittened hand, she led them to the back of the office and through another door that led into a small corridor. Her own apartment seemed to lead off it, as did another door, which she unlocked and removed two heavy bolts.

Before opening the door she paused. 'You're certain you weren't followed?' They both nodded. 'He's down here and he knows you're coming. Follow me.'

She led them down a long stone staircase into a room with a surprisingly high ceiling, its walls covered with shelves laden with cleaning supplies. 'On the other side of that wall is the storage area for the residents, each apartment has a storage cage and people are down there all the time. We had this wall built two years ago, when Sister Ursula asked Otto – that's my son – and I to prepare the basement in case we needed to hide anyone there. I never imagined it would be Herr Leitner! I managed to persuade the owners of the building that we needed this to stop the residents helping themselves to all our cleaning stuff. They were only too happy to oblige with the wall. They're devout Nazis, the owners. Can you imagine what they'd think if they found out they spent all that money on helping to protect him?'

Frau Egger walked to the far corner of the room and moved

aside a large laundry basket, revealing a trapdoor. When she pulled it open, it revealed a ladder leading down into a narrow chamber about 10 feet deep. 'Close the trapdoor behind you,' she said to Rolf. 'And, once you've done that, pull that rope. It'll drag the basket back into position over it. My son rigged that up. He also discovered this place, years ago. No one else knows about it. Be careful, you'll need to crouch when you go through this door.'

The door was little more than a hatch, which they had to stoop through. It led to a narrow corridor, at the end of which was another door, recessed into the wall. Frau Egger knocked on the door: three knocks followed by a pause then two more knocks. The door creaked open to reveal a tiny, dimly lit entrance area and the figure of an elderly man who hurried them in then locked the door. Frau Egger led them straight through into a properly lit and comfortably furnished room. The man was stooped, unshaven and unhealthily pale, but Rolf nonetheless recognised Hubert Leitner straight away: he'd been a powerful figure, charismatic and imposing, but now he stood hunched in the doorway, eyeing the two of them suspiciously.

'You've something for me?' His voice was hoarse and wary. As welcomes went, it wasn't effusive.

Rolf took out his wallet and from the lining removed a small sepia photograph, which the nun had given them. The photograph had been cut in half and at an angle, showing a man and a boy standing in a formal pose. Rolf passed it to Leitner, who grabbed it with shaking hands and took it over to a small bureau in the corner. From one of its drawers he took out an envelope and from that a similar-looking photograph. He placed the two side by side on the desktop. They were the two halves of the same photograph, matching like a jigsaw.

'This is my father and I, here on the left, and my mother and my sister on the right,' said Leitner eventually. 'I must have been seven or eight at the time. I remember the photograph was taken at a studio on Opern Ring, near the opera house. I've always kept it. When Sister Ursula told me I was being moved and would be contacted by the British I cut this photograph in half and passed the left half on to her. I'd know you were genuine when I received this.'

Leitner indicated they should sit down in the small lounge area. He asked Frau Egger to leave them and return in half an hour. The old man leaned back in his chair, coughing and spitting into a handkerchief, and observing them and the rest of the room carefully. His countenance was no less suspicious than when he'd first appeared at the door. Had his circumstances not accounted for it, both Rolf and Katharina would have described him as unfriendly. It was as if he resented their presence.

'Don't be deceived by Frau Egger's appearance,' he said eventually. 'I know she comes across as a hard and rather unsophisticated person, but that's an impression she deliberately cultivates.' Leitner spoke in a quiet voice, not soft but somewhat unsteady from lack of use. He had a habit of looking around as he spoke, rather than at them.

'She's a dedicated anti-Nazi and has been since they first raised their ugly heads in Austria in the 1920s,' he continued. 'As I understand it, her husband was killed in a street fight with Nazi thugs in 1928 or 1929. She lost her home and moved in with her mother, who was then the concierge here. A year or so later her mother died and she took over the job. She was asked from time to time to hide people on the run from the police or the Nazis and started to use this cellar. Have you met her son, Otto?'

They both shook their heads.

'Again, don't be deceived by his appearance. He comes across as – how shall I put it – as someone who's rather stupid, a simpleton if you like. In fact, he's the opposite, but it has the desired effect: it's kept him out of the army and he works here instead with his mother, acting as a handyman. He's put in a lot of work making this cellar so secure.'

'How did you end up here?'

'You'll know I disappeared after the Anschluss in March 1938,' said Leitner. 'At first, when the Germans came in, I couldn't decide what to do. I realised that because of my status and my reputation I was in a very important position, but I was torn between leaving Austria and leading the struggle for its independence from outside its borders, or remaining within. I decided to do the latter, which was a big mistake. I underestimated both the strength of the Nazis and the capacity of the Austrian people to relinquish their independence quite so enthusiastically. By then it was too late, I was trapped. I realised it'd be too risky to leave even Vienna, let alone Austria. I stayed with people I could trust, but had to keep moving.'

'There were rumours you'd been killed,' said Rolf.

'Indeed! In 1940, apparently, while trying to cross the border into Slovenia. I laughed a good deal when I heard that, as you can imagine. What was it Mark Twain is supposed to have said when he was reported to have died – that rumours of his death were exaggerated? Anyway, I had a contact at the Swiss Embassy here in Vienna, which became a consulate. He arranged for me to hide in a house in Währing… I apologise if I'm talking too much…'

'Not at all, Herr Leitner. It's important you tell us everything,' said Katharina.

'When the diplomat told me he was leaving Vienna,' continued Leitner, 'I asked if he'd try to approach the British to help me. It took a while, but Sister Ursula brought me here, where I've been since December. It's comfortable enough but the worst aspect of it by far is my lack of exposure to daylight and the fresh air that will, I imagine, will have serious consequences for my health. I've just enough food, and Frau Egger and Otto keep me in touch with the progress of the war as best they can – they occasionally listen to BBC broadcasts and pick up gossip. When I finally arrived here and began to feel safer, I got thinking. I need to do something; I can't just wait here until the war ends, which it may well do in the next year or two if what the Eggers say is true.'

It was Rolf who spoke next. 'Do something in what sense, Herr Leitner?'

The older man thought for a while, his head resting on his fingertips. He fixed his gaze on Katharina for a while then on Rolf. Just this short conversation appeared to have exhausted him.

'To try and exert my influence and – not to put too fine a point on it – set out my claim to play a significant role in this country after the war. That's why I asked for an approach to be made to the British – and I imagine that's why you're here. Tell me, what's the situation with the war in Europe?'

'It's definitely going in favour of the Allies,' said Rolf. 'Since the Red Army stopped the German advance in the Soviet Union, they've been pressing them further and further back. There's constant talk of the Allies attempting a major landing somewhere in northern Europe, most likely in France. People seem to think that's imminent. I assure you, Herr Leitner, that the British government is keen to co-operate with you, but they do need to know what it is you're seeking. Do you need money or do you want to escape from Austria?'

Leitner stood up and walked around the small room for a while, his hands behind his back. He looked like a politician on a stage, about to address an audience.

'I've already told you – to try and escape would be madness,' he said eventually. 'I'm 73 and I've been cooped up in small rooms for six years. I'd make a hopeless escapee. As for money, what would I do with it? Ask you to open an account in Switzerland for me? I'll tell you something: I already have one of those; I'm not a poor man, but the years I've spent in solitary confinement have taught me money is a much overestimated possession.'

Leitner slowly sat down on the chair opposite Rolf and Katharina. 'What I really care about is Austria. My first demand is that I want assurances from the British they'll ensure Austria becomes an independent country again after the war. I also want an assurance that once this country is rid of the Nazis, I'll be appointed head of the government and remain in that position until free elections are held, which should be within one a year. All I ask is that I'm in charge to ensure Austria's interests are paramount – not those of Britain or the Soviet Union or even the United

States. I've no interest in self-aggrandisement, nor do I have any political ambition. I shall not ally myself with any political party. My reward will be the satisfaction of knowing I've used whatever influence I have and whatever respect I've earned over the years in the interests of my country.'

'I can assure you, sir, this message will be passed on to London on Monday,' said Rolf. 'They did tell us to inform you that they hold you in the highest regard and are most keen to work with you. I don't think there'll be a problem.'

Leitner leaned forward, his head close to Rolf's and his hand on his knee.

'I'm sure they are, young man. But I want an absolute guarantee from the British government. They'll know as well as I do that the support or otherwise I give to a provisional government can make or break it. If the British are unable to help me there are always other people who can.'

***

'What did you make of that?' said Rolf. They were walking back through Leopoldstadt, arm in arm, and looking for a bridge that hadn't been bombed so they could cross the canal into the Innere Stadt and make their way home.

'He has a strength about him, doesn't he?' said Katharina. 'You'd have thought he'd be grateful we'd turned up but he didn't seem like that.'

'No, but I suppose being cooped up like that and being on the run for so long, well… it'd have an effect on anyone, wouldn't it?'

'And that cough,' said Katharina. 'He doesn't sound well. I can try and bring some medicine from the hospital, but really he needs to see a doctor.'

'Out of the question.'

'I realise that. And those demands of his...'

'He's a politician, Anna.' – Katharina squeezed his arm. She'd always had to remind him to call her that – 'That's what politicians do. He's the most influential politician in this country and...' he stopped speaking for a moment as another couple approached them then walked past. '... And he knows how much the British will need his support.'

'But that remark he made at the end, about there being other people who can help him. What do you think he meant by that?'

They'd reached a queue for a temporary footbridge across the canal and said nothing while they patiently waited their turn to cross into Innere Stadt.

'I think he meant the Russians, don't you?'

'I don't think London will be very happy about that.'

Chapter 15

London, June 1944

'And when did you say they met with Leitner?'

Christopher Porter took a deep breath before replying. 'The 3rd of June, Sir Roland. Last Saturday.'

Sir Roland Pearson looked up at Porter and Edgar for no more than a second or two then glanced pointedly at a small calendar on his desk and carried on writing in a file on his blotting pad. He frowned at one stage and the frown remained fixed on his face for longer than Porter and Major Edgar felt comfortable with. 'So let's be clear about this,' he said. 'Your chap Rolf and the German woman arrived in Vienna when – end of March, beginning of April, yes?'

Both Porter and Edgar decided it was safer to treat this as a rhetorical question. They were aware of what was coming next. It was rather how they felt themselves.

'They've been in Vienna for two whole months before making contact with Hubert Leitner – which was, after all, the primary purpose of their mission.'

'I know,' said Edgar. 'But to an extent this was out of their hands. We were relying on Whitlock's nun. They did manage to get hold of the contents of Baumgartner's strongbox, so they haven't exactly been idle. And don't forget the Soviets, Sir Roland. They were also there to see what the Soviets are up to.'

'And what have they found out on that score?'

'So far, very little but…'

'When was it I approved this mission...? December?'
'Yes, Sir Roland.'
'And I obtained Winston's permission for us to go ahead with it, notwithstanding the possible risk to our relations with the Soviets... well, that was over six months ago. Six months!' Sir Roland finally looked up from writing, eyeing them a like a headmaster faced by two particularly difficult pupils. 'Six months! We agreed this was an essential mission, yet it's taken six months for them to get around to meeting Leitner, and as far as seeing what the Soviets are up to... Well, nothing! It's not good enough, Porter, I'm sorry – and you as well, Edgar. I'm forever having to make excuses for you and dig you out of holes.'

Porter busily brushed something annoying away from the knee of his trouser leg, avoiding looking at Sir Roland. Edgar shifted his chair an inch or two forward and spoke in a quiet voice.

'Vienna is quite possibly the most hostile place in Europe for one of our agents to operate in, Sir Roland, arguably even worse than Berlin. We've very limited contact with Rolf and Katharina, we rely on coded messages he sends to Hedinger in Zürich, which are then passed on to Remington-Barber in Bern before he sends them on to us and vice versa. It's a tortuous process, but there's no alternative. So it's most difficult for us to appreciate what obstacles they've been facing in Vienna. We have to assume that, had they been able to meet with Leitner earlier, they would have done so. But the most important thing is they've met with him now – and the news he's prepared to work with us should be seen as a most positive development.'

Sir Roland gazed just beyond Edgar and slightly lowered his

head in acknowledgement that he could see Edgar's point. When he replied, it was in a much calmer voice. 'Very well then, and what are his terms for co-operating with us?'

'He wants a guarantee that Britain will ensure Austria becomes an independent country once again after the war. And he wants to be made head of the Austrian government, for at least a year – until proper elections are held.'

'Is that all? I was wondering whether he'd want money or gold or something like that,' said Sir Roland. 'It all seems straightforward enough: we have the Moscow Declaration, after all, which satisfies his first demand, and as for him being made the head of a provisional government, well we certainly can promise him that – frankly, if he wants us to resurrect the Austro-Hungarian empire and give him a crown to put on his head, we can promise that too, eh?'

'And… erm… Number 10?' Porter was fiddling with the cuffs of his shirt.

'Oh, I'll mention it to Winston and I'll make sure a note goes to Eden but, to be perfectly frank with you, everyone's attention is solely on the Normandy landings at the moment. I understand that's been keeping you rather busy, eh Edgar? Well done, I hear congratulations are in order.'

'Maybe a touch premature, Sir Roland, but let's keep our fingers crossed,' said Edgar.

During the silence that followed Sir Roland closed the file on his desk and carefully screwed the top back onto his fountain pen, clear signs the meeting had ended. Edgar made to get up but noticed Porter hadn't moved.

'Everything alright, Porter?'

'Yes, Sir Roland,' he said. 'Clearly I'm pleased we can give that response to Leitner. But… there's something troubling me, more a tiny niggle at the back of my mind.'

'Go on.'

'I suppose it surfaced when you expressed your annoyance that it had taken Rolf and Katharina so long to get around to seeing Leitner,' continued Porter. 'Edgar's right, of course, there are probably all kinds of good reasons why, but I'd been thinking myself that the failure to do anything about Viktor and the delay with Leitner didn't feel… well … quite right, I suppose. To be honest, I too would've expected them to have met with Leitner within a couple of weeks, not a couple of months.'

'Come on, Porter – no need to beat around the bush.'

'Alright then. Should we not consider the possibility, however remote and unpalatable, that perhaps Rolf deliberately delayed meeting Leitner?'

'Hang on,' said Edgar incredulously. 'What are you suggesting? That Rolf isn't to be trusted?'

'I'm merely posing the question.'

'Well,' said Sir Roland. 'That does rather set the cat amongst the pigeons, eh? What do you think Edgar?'

'I think Rolf is one of us, Sir Roland. I've never suspected him of being otherwise. Do you have any evidence, sir?'

'No of course not, Edgar, I was merely expressing my unease, that's all. You have to admit, delaying meeting up with Leitner is a bit odd, to say the least.'

'Who recruited Rolf in the first place?'

'Whitlock, Sir Roland.'

'Why don't you go and have a chat with him Edgar? Put our minds at ease.'

'I'm rather preoccupied with D-Day sir, I have an agent who...'

'... May I interrupt?' said Porter. 'Whitlock's in a pretty bad state these days. I'm not sure how long he's got. If you're going to see him then you'd better get a move on.'

***

Edgar left London early the following morning. It was time he could ill afford. The agent he was running – or trying to run – in France was his priority at the moment and, as far as he was concerned, Porter's ill-founded doubts about Rolf were a distraction. But Edgar also knew it was vital for Sir Roland to retain confidence in the Austrian mission, so clearing up any confusion with George Whitlock would ensure this wasn't a wasted journey.

He drove west out of London, a steady stream of military convoys passing in the opposite direction towards the Channel ports. He toyed with the idea of leaving the A40 early and allowing himself a nostalgic drive through the centre of Oxford and possibly even the indulgence of a few minutes wandering around his old college. But he knew he couldn't afford the time and he also knew it would unsettle him, in a way he could never admit to anyone else. It had been the one time when his life was settled and uncomplicated, with nothing to worry about, and little to fear and everything to hope for. One of his tutors had taken him aside in his last term there and asked him his plans. 'Problem with this place for chaps like you is that it's near-perfect, too much of an idyll. It won't be very long after you leave that you'll realise life will never be as good as this. Some people find that hard to deal with.'

He wondered whether it was the reason why people like Whitlock drifted back to Oxford, spending their later years in small flats or retirement homes in the north of the city, in places like Park Town and Summertown. Now Whitlock had moved from his flat just off the Banbury Road to a nursing home on the banks of the River Cherwell.

'You won't be very long with him?' said a rather stern Scottish matron. It was a statement more than a question.

'How ill is he?'

'You're not family, are you?'

'No, a friend and former colleague. Does he have long left?'

'I doubt he'll see the end of the month.'

Whitlock was propped up in an armchair by a window that looked out over a yellowing lawn with the river peeking out between rose bushes at the end of it. Despite the heat, he was swathed in blankets, his skin stretched and a strange yellow hue. A pair of bloodshot eyes swivelled around to fix on Edgar as he pulled up a chair alongside.

'Not good, eh George?'

'Apparently not, Edgar,' said the old man. 'Not long left, I fear. I can tell by the frequency with which the chaplain comes to visit me. Every day now. Looks surprised when he sees I'm still here. Probably thinks it's something to do with his prayers, eh? And my sister, she spends most of her time weeping. Suppose I've had a decent innings though. Pass me that water will you?'

Edgar lifted a glass and helped Whitlock sip slowly and painfully from it, then sat awkwardly as he coughed violently for a few minutes. 'What's the problem, Edgar?' he said after a moment.

'I've come to see how you are, George.'

'Come on, Edgar, you'll be up to your neck with D-Day. You won't have given up all this time just to pay me a social visit, eh? Out with it, Matron will come and kick you out soon.'

Edgar shifted his chair close to Whitlock, close enough to hear the other man's painful breathing. Each breath sounded as though it could be his last.

'Rolf's in Vienna. Has been for a couple of months now.'

'Is the woman with him?'

'Yes. The thing is, though, he's only just got around to meeting with Leitner and... well... Let me ask you a question, George. Did you recruit Rolf or did he recruit us?'

'Not sure I understand you, Edgar. We recruited him, of course. How on earth would he recruit us – put an advert in the *Wiener Zeitung* seeking employment from an intelligence agency?'

'What I mean,' said Edgar, 'is that sometimes it's fairly obvious when we recruit someone. We need a person working in a particular Government department, for instance, and we target specific recruits, check them out then approach them. That's us recruiting them. Then we have people who approach us, don't we?'

'The ones who turn up at the Embassy?'

'That's right, the walk-ins: you know the score. They turn up at the Embassy and ask if they can help out, offer to work for our intelligence people. Sometimes for money, sometimes not. So, in effect, they're recruiting us. We don't tend to trust those people, do we?'

'Obviously not.'

'But sometimes people are much more subtle than that. They put themselves in a position where we notice them then approach them. Sometimes takes ages to effect. They're the ones to be wary of because we think we've recruited them and therefore trust them, whereas in fact they've recruited us.'

There was another bout of coughing, this one more violent than before. A nurse hurried into the room and tended to Whitlock, looking anxiously at Edgar. 'You'll need to leave, I'm afraid. He needs to rest. He shouldn't be talking so much.'

'Five minutes,' said Edgar.

He waited until the nurse left the room. Whitlock looked worse than when he'd come in.

'And you're saying Rolf may have recruited us? Bit late to have second thoughts isn't it, Edgar, now he's working for us in Vienna?'

'No, not at all. No reason whatsoever to distrust him. I was just wondering how you'd recruited him. You said it was in '36, didn't you?'

'That's right: a long time ago now, Edgar,' said Whitlock. 'I'm sure I recruited him rather than the other way around. Remember the political situation in Vienna was pretty difficult, even then? As ever, we rather depended on a group of locals, people who could be trusted to carry messages or watch buildings – that kind of thing, low-level stuff. I ran a core of around six such people, but most of them left Austria in early '36 so I needed to recruit more. I knew a lot of social democrats in those days and one of them was a professor at the university who I trusted. Just before he got out, I asked him if any of his students could be trusted to help me with courier work and he recommended Rolf. In fact, now I think about it, what happened was that he invited me around to his apartment, where he'd arranged for a couple of likely people to turn up. Rolf was there with his fiancé, a rather forceful lady called Frieda if I remember correctly. She was a bit of a red you know. But Rolf was much more reasonable and very personable. That's how I recruited him.'

'But you see, George, what if Rolf...'

There was more coughing now and in the short gaps between the coughs Whitlock moaned. When the nurse came in she pressed a bell and the Matron entered soon after.

'You'll leave now,' she told Edgar. 'He's simply not well enough to talk.'

***

The following day they reconvened in Sir Roland's office.

'He's that bad, is he?'

'The Matron said she doesn't think he'll last the month. I don't think he'll last the week. I thought he was going to die while I was there.'

'Shame,' said Porter. 'Good chap, old school and rather traditional, but one of us. Did he have anything useful to say – about Rolf?'

'I asked him how Rolf was recruited, whether we recruited him or he recruited us. Sounded like we recruited him, as I suspected, though it wasn't clear-cut by any means.'

'Well we need to remain cautious, can't do much more than that,' said Sir Roland. 'Meanwhile, have they really not been to establish whether this Viktor is in Vienna?'

Edgar stood up and walked over to the window; a pair of pigeons were were fighting on a rooftop opposite and in the distance a squadron of Spitfires was heading south.

'If Viktor's in Vienna it doesn't surprise me in the slightest that they haven't encountered him yet.'

Chapter 16

Vienna, July 1944

It was the end of July and Viktor was experiencing an unusual range of emotions. As far as he could tell from both Radio Moscow and the BBC, the war was going well for the Allies. In the west the British, American and Canadian armies were finally breaking out of Normandy. In the east the Red Army had captured Lvov, Bialystok and Minsk, and was just a few miles from Warsaw. In his more optimistic moments he believed it was possible the war in Europe could be over by the end of the year or early in 1945.

But those optimistic moments were few and far between. He'd moved out of Irma's apartment in early March into a draughty room on the top floor of a flea-infested boarding house in Floridsdorf and had begun work at the nearby locomotive works. According to the KPO Central Committee in Moscow, there were bound to be some clandestine communists among the thousands of workers there – but if there were, Viktor couldn't find them. As an electrician he was sent to repair machinery all over the factory and he also volunteered for all the different shifts, so in the first two months at the factory he came across most of the employees. But, try as he might, he could find no comrades. Not that he'd expected it to be easy, he realised they weren't going to be wearing Lenin badges nor would they be found reading *The Communist Manifesto* during their short meal breaks; he wasn't listening out for workers whistling the *Internationale*. But he was nothing if not skilled at sniffing out likely help; after all, it was what he'd been doing throughout Europe for many years now. He was also a very good electrician, well trained by Moscow all those years ago, so he invariably finished his jobs ahead of schedule, allowing plenty of time to fall into conversation with the machine operators. These conversations would be innocent enough, but there would be concealed morsels of bait, which the right person would hopefully pick up. *I managed to get some meat at the butcher's yesterday... How long do you queue for bread...? My neighbour's son is stationed in Warsaw, I hope he's alright... One of the guys in the paint shop said they're cancelling all routine operations at the AKH, I've no idea why...*

In his experience, someone would be unlikely to respond straight away, but there might be a moment's hesitation, a slightly raised eyebrow, a barely concealed grimace or response just too carefully worded. A bolder person may pick up on one of the remarks: *I've not been able to get meat for weeks... the AKH is full of wounded soldiers... things look bad.*

But there was nothing: the Austrians, he'd come to realise, were loyal and enthusiastic Nazis. Maybe Paul the plumber had been right, there were no communists left in Vienna. There were French workers at the factory but, as he'd suspected, they were little more than slave labour. For the most part they did the more menial jobs and were closely watched. Occasionally Viktor did come into contact with them, but he felt it would be too risky to reveal he knew French. He spoke to a few in German but they were clearly as wary of him as they were of everyone else.

Viktor was a patient man: he was experienced enough to appreciate that espionage was a waiting game, one in which an agent or a contact may need to be cultivated over a period of months or even years. His job, he liked to remind Moscow, was like watching a flower grow. But for the first time in his career he was experiencing a fear of failure. It was one thing finding a potential recruit and developing that contact, but now he wasn't finding anyone at all. His one saving grace was that Vienna was so isolated Moscow had no way of contacting him: they'd be waiting to hear from him and he had no intention of doing that until he was ready.

By the end of July, Vienna was being bombed by the US Air Force on a regular basis, creating an air of unease in the city that hadn't been evident when he'd first arrived. People had developed a habit of glancing anxiously up to the sky as they walked along and, of course, it took just one person to do this for others nearby to do the same. Emboldened by this and by the good news coming from both the western and eastern fronts, Viktor decided the time had come to try one last possibility, one that had been in the back of his mind but which he knew would be so laced with danger he'd been reluctant to use it.

He had first met the agent he knew as Acheron back in 1934, at a time when looking for communists to recruit in Vienna was easy – it wasn't so much a matter of finding any, as it was now, but of being spoilt for choice. Acheron stood out from all the others: he was bright, brave and charismatic, and everyone he came into contact with respected him and was loyal to him. But Acheron had another quality, one Viktor always looked for but rarely found. It was the ability to be impressive, yet at the same time manage to remain unnoticed and be part of a crowd.

As far as Viktor was aware from what he'd picked up in

Moscow, Acheron had almost certainly been alive in early 1942. Three of the comrades from his cell had been killed, and Acheron and the remaining ones had gone to ground. That was the last anyone had heard of him. Of course, that was two years ago and in that time thousands of comrades had been captured, but Viktor knew that if anyone could survive it would be Acheron. When he last saw him, in 1937, Acheron was living in Hernals but Viktor knew he moved around every few months, so it would be pointless trying there. He decided to risk visiting the one place where there was a chance of making contact with him.

Over a period of two weeks he went to the area on half a dozen occasions. It was apparent from his first visit that the place was being watched – not very well, but watched nonetheless. As far as he could tell, there wasn't someone stationed there all the time, which was a familiar Gestapo technique; keeping an eye on somewhere, quite happy for those inside to know it and creating a degree of uncertainty.

So Viktor avoided the area for a week then returned on a Friday morning at the end of July. He'd just finished a night shift at the factory but, rather than get any rest, he went straight to the 9th District using a combination of trams and foot. He walked the last mile into Alsergrund then along Liechtensteinstrasse, managing to briefly catch a glimpse of the front of the place. It didn't look as though it was being watched, but he wasn't going to risk going through the front entrance and, in any case, a watcher could appear at any moment. He found the turning he was looking for off Liechtensteinstrasse and from there the narrow alley that backed on to the shops. He worked out which gate was the right one and the back door was simple to unlock. He silently entered, finding himself in a small room from which a door was half open into the shop. A man was standing at the counter with his back to him, a spiral of cigarette smoke drifting up. Viktor stood there for a minute, until he was absolutely certain the man at the counter was alone. He then allowed himself a small cough.

When Ernst Lang spun around he went white and his mouth dropped open, his eyes bulging with utter terror. 'No!'

He said nothing else for a minute. 'How the hell did you get in here? Please leave! Not through the front, get out the back, quickly.'

'I'm not leaving, Herr Lang. We need to talk. This is what we'll do: you'll turn around and face the door then light yourself another cigarette. I'll stay here where no one can see me, but you can listen.'

'Shall I lock the front door and put up the "closed" sign?'

'No, that'd draw attention. They weren't outside before but they're here much of the time, aren't they?'

'I don't know, I don't like to look out for them. I know they come every day, sometimes two or three times a day, and they stay for varying lengths of time. Look, this is a waste of your time, there's nothing I can do to help you. Please leave, I beg you.'

'I need to see him, Herr Lang.'

The man's shoulders slumped and he nervously took another cigarette, striking four matches before he could keep his hands still for long enough to light one.

'I've no idea where he is, I've no way of contacting him.'

'So he's alive?'

'Don't try and catch me out, I've no idea. Maybe I should be asking you that. You always seemed to know more about him than me. How the hell did you get here, anyway?'

'I need to see him,' said Viktor.

'You're not the only one.'

'What do you mean?'

'Someone else was asking for him last month: I told him I'd no idea about Joachim and sent him away with a flea in his ear. Like you, he was someone I'd not seen since before the war.'

Viktor edged closer to the door, wishing he was facing Lang's face so he could read his eyes.

'Don't mess around with me. Tell me who you're talking about.'

'I thought I recognised him at the time but couldn't place him – he looked slightly different, not just older. It was strange because I'm normally good with faces and, while he was familiar, I just couldn't put a name to him. After he left I was going over it in my mind and it was the voice that was the clue. I'm a trained musician – I have a good ear.'

'Are you going to tell me who he is?'

'He used to come here around '37 and '38, before the Anschluss, with messages for Joachim. His fiancée was an associate of Joachim's. I never asked too many questions, you understand that. The fiancée was called Frieda Brauner and he was called Rolf. I don't know if I ever knew his surname.'

'Describe him.'

'Around six foot tall, dark-blond hair, possibly early to mid-thirties. Spoke with a Viennese accent, no question of that – odd thing is, he didn't have that accent all the time, seemed to slip in and out of it. Odd.'

'Can't you be more precise than that?'

'Isn't that enough? You're as bad as they are.'

'Who's "they"?'

'The Gestapo,' said Lang. 'A few days after this Rolf visited, they pulled me in – it happens every so often. I had to admit he was asking after Joachim – and they were far more interested in him than me.'

'What do you mean?'

'I'm not sure. The man who questioned me is called Strobel; he's one of the Gestapo bosses here. I've heard plenty about him; he's a reputation for being vicious, but he's also known as something of a buffoon. He let slip something I'm sure he didn't mean to say, because the other man in the room looked surprised when he did. He told me the man who'd come to the shop – the one I think's called Rolf – had also visited the house where a Wolfgang Fischer lived. Did I know a Wolfgang Fischer, he asked?'

'And...?'

'Fischer was another associate of Joachim's. I said I hadn't heard of him.'

'Describe this Rolf to me once more.'

'I told you, around six foot tall, dark-blond hair, possibly early to mid-thirties, Viennese accent. He wore glasses, I think.'

'I have a feeling I know... When did you last speak with Joachim?'

'I told you, I have no...'

'... Tell him to meet me on Sunday afternoon, at 3.00. He'll know where.'

Vienna Spies

***

Viktor's instinct was that Acheron was still alive; his father would have been more emphatic if he wasn't. So he followed a routine he hadn't used since 1937. He started his walk on Franz-Josefs-Kai, at the point where the Danube Canal turned into the smaller Wien Fluss river. From there he walked along the banks of the canal, aware that if Acheron didn't turn up he'd run out of options. He hadn't walked very far when a tall man in an unfamiliar uniform turned as Viktor passed him. 'Do you have a light?' he said.

Before Viktor could say a word the man spoke again. 'Just give me a bloody light; it's bad enough having to meet here as it is. That building over there – it's the Gestapo headquarters!' Joachim Lang – Acheron – was smiling as he spoke, treating Viktor as if he was the old friend which in many respects he was. 'Come. Let's walk in the opposite direction, away from Morzinplatz, please.'

They walked back towards the Wien Fluss, Lang saying something about the weather. They came to a bench and both sat down. 'When my father told me you'd turned up, I didn't know whether to laugh or to cry. I couldn't believe it at first. Then I thought if anyone could find me, it'd be you Viktor. The Gestapo have been looking for me for years, but Viktor finds me: maybe I shouldn't have been surprised. How long have you been in Vienna?'

'That doesn't matter. What on earth is that uniform you're wearing, Joachim?'

'This?' He was fingering the cloth of his jacket, as if admiring its quality. 'The Wasserschutzpolizei – we're the river police. Life was becoming impossible, you know? In '41 the Gestapo arrested

Mayer and Fischer and murdered them, then in March '42 they arrested Frieda – you remember her, Frieda Brauner? I was convinced they'd break her, but as far as we can gather, they didn't get anything out of her before she died. Anyway, I laid low for six months then realised it was too risky to move around Vienna if I wasn't in uniform. I had one very good identity left and I used that to join the Wasserschutzpolizei. I rather enjoy it, to be honest. We patrol the Danube, checking the barges – that kind of thing. At least I'm safe and I'm hardly contributing to the Nazi war effort. I try to make sure of that.'

'Did your father tell you about Rolf?'

'He did, yes.'

'Have you seen him at all?'

'Of course not. I keep a very low profile these days, Viktor. When I'm out, it's almost always in uniform. How do you know him, anyway?'

'I came across him when he was working for the British in Zürich.'

'I know he went to Switzerland when he left in '38. Frieda was angry he went. So he's a British agent now?'

Viktor shrugged. 'He certainly was one in Zürich.'

Lang laughed, stretching out his long legs. 'I know you, Viktor. I wouldn't be surprised if he's also one of yours! Maybe you've chased him to Vienna!'

Viktor didn't reply at first and when he did he sounded worried. 'I'll tell you something. Did you ever meet that rat I dealt with occasionally – Fuchs, Wilhelm Fuchs?'

'Wasn't he a pimp?'

'Yes – and various other things. Nasty piece of work but resourceful, could get hold of things no one else could.'

'Yes, I remember him.'

'I caught up with him a couple of months ago, back in April. I'd paid him for some pistols years ago, before the war, and never saw them. He spun me a story that he needed a special key to get hold of the guns and promised to contact me if he could get them. I never expected to hear back from him, but I did and he told me a man had unexpectedly turned up with the key. But that was the last I heard of him. About two weeks later I found out he'd been killed. What's worrying is the description he gave me of the man who turned up with the key.'

'Go on...'

'Late twenties, early thirties he said, with light-brown hair and a medium build. He also said his accent could have been Viennese but was hard to place. That sounds odd, doesn't it?'

'An accent is either Viennese or it's not.'

'Indeed, unless you're trying to hide it. But who could that be a description of?'

Lang nodded. 'Rolf?'

'That's what I thought. If it *is* him, what's he doing in Vienna – trying to find you and Fischer then contacting Fuchs? If he's working for the British... we need to be worried. Look, I need your help, Joachim. I need to set up a unit here in Vienna. What about the others in your cell, are they around?'

Lang laughed bitterly. 'Look, after Frieda was arrested we met once more and agreed it was too dangerous to carry on, the cell would have to suspend its activities. We agreed we'd go our separate ways. Lethe, I've no idea what happened to him, he just disappeared. He was originally from Salzburg and he may have gone back there for all I know. Cocytus – the last I heard he was heading for Slovenia to try and join the partisans there, his mother was Slovenian and he spoke the language. Styx stayed in Vienna, like me. I've bumped into him once or twice; he works at the Heinkel factory.'

'Joachim, you and I need to meet up with Styx, we need to start work again. The war hasn't long to go, you must know it's only a matter of time before the Red Army reaches the Danube. I doubt your river police will be in much of a position to stop them. I keep thinking, do you have you any idea why Rolf's here in Vienna?'

'No,' said Lang. 'Maybe he came back to find Frieda, I don't know. He must be crazy to have returned here.'

'Do you think it was him?'

'Very, very few people used that method to contact me, Viktor. You did and Frieda did too, sometimes through Rolf. Wolfgang Fischer did, but he's been dead for three years now, but no one else, so the chances of it not being him are remote. And my father always recognises someone's voice; he was trained at the *conservatoire* here in Vienna. He has a bad temper, but a fine ear.'

'Coming back to Vienna to find Frieda after... what... six years doesn't make much sense, does it?'

'No. But... there's a... no... it doesn't matter. Forget it.'

'You'd better tell me what you're on about.'

'It's a rumour, that's all... a rumour and I know you want more than rumours.'

The Russian stared hard at him, his eyes unblinking. 'I'll decide that, just tell me.'

The man in the uniform looked unsettled. 'The rumour is that Hubert Leitner is alive and hiding somewhere in Vienna. The gossip is he's in contact with the British. I'm not sure how reliable this is and I've no idea where Leitner is if he's here at all, but that's what I've heard. It may be a coincidence, I don't know – but I do know I first heard this rumour just a few weeks ago.'

'I thought Leitner was dead?'

'Personally I'm certain the Gestapo never got him; we'd have heard if they had, I'm sure,' said Lang. 'If he's alive and has made contact with the British… well… is that good or bad, Viktor?'

'Get hold of Styx. We need to meet as soon as possible.'

Alex Gerlis

Chapter 17

Vienna, August and September 1944

Kriminaldirektor Karl Strobel had never taken his boss very seriously, a misjudgement he was now beginning to regret bitterly. If only he'd licked his jackboots like Molden and Nikolaus did on a daily basis or provided him with the pick of confiscated Jewish property like Grosser then he might not be in the predicament he was in now.

Police Generalmajor Franz Josef Huber was dismissed by some at Morzinplatz as just another Munich Nazi who owed his preferment to having had the good fortune to be in the right place at the right time. Since the Anschluss, he'd run the Reich Central Security Office in Vienna, which included all the Gestapo operations. Now he was bringing the full weight of that office to bear down on Strobel.

'This is an outrage!' Huber screamed so loudly that the windows overlooking the canal seemed to shake. Strobel felt himself go light-headed and the room seemed to move around. 'You absolutely promised me, Strobel, that you'd broken this cell more than two years ago and now – look – this! Come here!'

Strobel edged nervously towards the table where Huber was standing. Behind Huber was the only other person in the room, Kriminalrat Andreas Schwarz, Strobel's old adversary from the Kripo. Spread out on the table was a series of leaflets, perhaps a dozen of them, all different.

'All from the same printing machine, Strobel, you agree?'

'So it would appear, Herr Generalmajor...'

'More than appear, Strobel. Kriminalrat Schwarz's experts in the Kripo say there's no question about it – they're all printed on the same machine, using the same paper and the same ink, which means they're the same produced by that cell you promised me you'd shut down in '42. Would you care to read that leaflet out to me?'

It hadn't escaped Strobel's attention that Huber had used Schwarz's rank, but omitted his. He looked carefully at him, checking whether he was being serious about reading out loud from the leaflet. He nervously picked up the one closest to him, with an obscene and demeaning caricature of a naked Hitler on the front.

He cleared his throat. '*Citizens of Vienna and all Austria...*'

'Louder, Strobel, I can hardly hear you...'

'*... The war is lost and we shall soon be free of our German oppressors...* Is it necessary to continue, Herr Generalmajor? This is such nonsense...'

'If that leaflet's upsetting you so much, Strobel, try this one.' Huber handed him another leaflet, this one with a drawing of a hammer and sickle smashing a swastika. Strobel cleared his throat again, his hands now shaking.

'It feels wrong to read such vile sentiments out loud, Herr Generalmajor.'

'Read it, Strobel.'

'*The Red Army is moving fast towards Austria. We have nothing to fear from them. They will bring justice and freedom to the...* please sir!'

Strobel caught Schwarz's self-satisfied look: the detective was barely suppressing a smirk as he glanced down at his shoes. Huber was sorting through the leaflets and chose one more and handed it to Strobel. A series of crudely drawn Wehrmacht soldiers had bayonets sticking out of their chests.

'*Tens of thousands of young Austrian and German soldiers are being sacrificed every day in the name of Hitler...* Surely this can't be true sir?'

'Of course it's not true – I didn't expect even you to believe it, you fool. It's communist propaganda and, thanks to your incompetence, it's now being read all over Vienna! As if it's not enough that the fucking Americans seem able to bomb Vienna at will, now we've these leaflets to worry about. How many copies have been distributed?'

'I don't know for sure, sir... maybe the Americans dropped them along with their bombs?'

'Don't be so stupid, Strobel. Kriminalrat Schwarz? Maybe you can bring some sense to this.'

'You have there 10 different leaflets altogether, Herr Generalmajor,' said Schwarz. 'The first one was brought to us in the second week of August and they've been appearing regularly ever since. Of course we don't know how many copies of each leaflet have been distributed. We've managed to lay our hands on perhaps one or two dozen of each.'

'And the areas?'

'As far as we can tell, sir, mostly in Floridsdorf, Hernals, Brigittenau and Margareten. A few in Leopoldstadt and Alsergrund, and a small number in Innere Stadt.'

'This,' said Huber, thrusting a leaflet hard into Strobel's face, 'is such an utter disgrace that I should send you straight from here to the Eastern Front. Do you understand? If Berlin was to find out about this, that's what they'd order, I can assure you of that. Now, would you care to tell me about the sabotage, Strobel?'

'Fortunately, sir, there have only been two instances of this,' said Strobel meekly. 'The first was at the locomotive works in Floridsdorf on the 21st August and second was at a lorry-repair facility in Donnaustadt, just last week. In both cases, machinery was damaged by the insertion of a substance in its workings. It seems that...'

'Cut to the point, Strobel, you're rambling again.'

'The same substance was used in both cases. It's an unusual combination of acid suspended in a thick solution with sand and ground-up glass in it. It's designed to cause considerable damage to machines and is, I very much regret to report, identical to the solution the resistance cell known as Hades was using in 1941 and 1942. Our scientists were able to compare it.'

'I suppose it would be too much to expect any arrests?'

'Not as yet sir, but we remain hopeful,' said Strobel. 'With the assistance of Kriminalrat Schwarz and his colleagues we're interrogating everyone at both of the places where the sabotage took place. I'm expecting...'

'... I tell you what I'm expecting, Strobel,' Huber leant over the table and spoke softly, but with even more menace than before. 'I'm expecting you to catch the culprits and put a stop to this nonsense, otherwise you'll need to make sure you have some very warm clothing ready because where I'll be sending you, you'll most certainly need it.'

Alex Gerlis

***

Joachim Lang had promised he'd do his best to make contact with Styx and arrange a meeting. 'I'll need a few days to try and sort things. It's Sunday today... go to my father's shop next Friday. I ought to have news by then.'

When Viktor visited the shop on Berg Gasse the following Friday morning, Ernst Lang informed him of the rendezvous details. 'Do you need me to write that down?'

'Don't be ridiculous,' the Russian replied. 'Never write anything down, you should know that. You may as well compose a suicide note at the same time. Just tell me.'

Sunday afternoon: the Alte Donau.

The Alte Donau, he knew it well. A water park created from the Danube some 70 years ago, and where the Viennese would go to swim and sunbathe. Now it was August the place would be teeming with people and he wondered whether he should ask Irma to accompany him – certainly a couple would be less conspicuous than a man on his own. But he couldn't be certain this wasn't a trap and, if it was, it would be easier to get away on his own. In any case, he hadn't had a chance to warn either of them he'd have someone with him. It wouldn't do if they thought it was a trap.

He worked the Saturday night shift again and returned to his room in the boarding house for a few hours' sleep. The Alte Donau was an easy 15 minutes' walk from where he lived, but he'd no idea where he should meet them or at what time. That wasn't unusual: he'd taught them both to avoid making arrangements that were too complicated. *If you tie people down to too precise a time or location then things can go wrong more easily.*

So he left his boarding house at 2.00 and, when he got to the Alte Donau, walked along its eastern bank. He seemed to have been joined by half of Vienna: more women and children rather than families, few men and, of those that there were, many were in a uniform of one kind or another. Nor was there the same merry and relaxed atmosphere he remembered: this was where the Viennese would traditionally let their hair down in their own restrained manner, but now even that felt subdued. People were still swimming in the clear water and the rowing boats were out, but there was an air of anxiety about the place.

He stopped at a stall selling cold lemonade and climbed up a grassy bank to drink in the shade. His guess was that Acheron and Styx would have been watching him, perhaps separately. When they were as sure as they could be he hadn't been followed, one of them would approach him. Now would be a good time, he decided.

He didn't have to wait long. He'd only met Styx on two or three occasions, and the last one would have been around seven years ago, but the thin man with thick spectacles who asked him if the area next to him was free was unquestionably Styx. He was clever and committed like the entire Hades cell were – and he'd somehow survived. The two apparent strangers exchanged a few pleasantries about the weather, very gradually shifting closer to each other.

'Joachim will be watching us,' said Styx quietly. 'When he's sure it's safe he'll join us. I never thought I'd see you again.'

'The feeling's mutual. How did you manage to survive?'

'No one ever knew my true identity. My real name is Manfred Becker and, as far as far as the authorities are concerned, I'm a good citizen of the Reich and I've never been associated with the KPO. I'm a devout Roman Catholic, married with three children and a member of the Nazi Party since 1940. I'm even on the committee for our area. Once we decided to split up after Frieda and others were captured by the Gestapo I just carried on with my normal life.'

'And how have you managed to avoid conscription?'

'My eyesight...' He removed his spectacles and waved them in front of Viktor before carefully polishing them. 'Very short-sighted, I'd be useless in the armed forces, fortunately. As you can see, I fall someway short of the Aryan ideal.'

'And your job?'

'I work at the Heinkel Sud aircraft factory in Floridsdorf. I'm a specialist draughtsman, so I'm based in the research and development department. At the moment I'm working on designs for a high-altitude bomber.'

'Really? Tell me more?'

'Ha! I thought you'd be interested – you want the plans for the Soviet Air Force I suppose?'

'In due course, yes. Tell me, I seem to remember you looked after the printing for Hades, is that right?'

'It is: because of my job as a draughtsman I had access to a printer. It broke down and was thrown out because they thought it was beyond repair. I took it home, no one noticed – and repaired it. We used it for maybe three years. I still have large supplies of ink and paper. We keep it in the basement of my mother's house.'

'Does it still work?'

'I haven't tried it since early 1942, but I see no reason why not. What are you getting at…?'

'I want to reactivate the cell, Styx. We need to create a climate in Vienna that will prepare the population for the Red Army. Would it be possible to produce leaflets again – and is it safe?'

'It's a large basement, part of which is under the garden – it's more of a cellar really. The machine is well hidden and even when it's running at full speed, you can't hear it outside the house, we made sure of that. Ah, look – Joachim is joining us.'

***

So it was that on the banks of the Alte Donau on a sunny August afternoon Hades was reborn. Only two of the cell's original seven members were still involved, but now they were under the firm direction of their Russian master.

Their priority, they decided, was to produce some leaflets. Viktor dictated the theme of each leaflet; Lang wrote the text while Becker produced the drawings and printed the leaflets. Each leaflet, Viktor said, should be simple and to the point. There should be no ambiguity about what the message was.

'Remember how people will see these leaflets,' he told them. 'They pick them up and glance at them, maybe only for a few seconds. Then the most likely thing they'll do is drop them or throw them away. Very few people – if anyone – will keep them and show them to others, so we must ensure that in those few seconds they make the maximum impact: one message, short sentences – that kind of thing.'

The message of the first leaflet was that the war was lost; the people of Austria were oppressed by the Germans. Becker's drawing was a pornographic cartoon of an emasculated Hitler. Subsequent leaflets had different themes: the impending triumph of the Red Army; the appalling casualties suffered among ordinary soldiers; the deprivations being experienced by the Viennese and how this was only going to get worse; the Red Army is getting closer; the Nazi officials lining their pockets.

Becker did have someone who could help distribute the leaflets. Young Hans was 14 and lived on the same road as him. Hans's father had been killed fighting on the Eastern Front two years ago and he did odd jobs for neighbours to help his mother. Becker would pay Hans to help him with gardening and it was there one day the boy asked a question.

'We're going to lose the war, aren't we, Herr Becker?'

It was an extraordinary thing for a boy of Hans's age to say. He'd lived under Nazi rule and been subject to its indoctrination for six years; and, as he'd turned 14 a few months earlier, he'd been obliged to join the Hitler Youth. Becker decided it was a trap.

'No, no...' replied Becker. 'What makes you say that, Hans?'

'So many people are being killed. In my year at school, more than 20 of us of have lost a parent – that's 20 out of a 100, Herr Becker. In a school they can't keep things like that a secret.'

'You mustn't talk like this, Hans. We're assured our armies are repelling the attacks on both fronts and once the winter...'

'But there's never any positive news is there, Herr Becker? We used to hear about the Reich conquering this country and that country, but now all we hear is that our forces are defending this and that, and fighting bravely.'

There was such conviction in the boy's voice that Becker was inclined to believe him, but not foolish enough to show it. 'I told you, Hans, don't talk like that.'

But over the following weeks Hans continued to do so and Becker, as cautious as he was, began to believe the boy.

'Why do you confide in me like this?' Becker asked Hans one day.

'Because I trust you, Herr Becker, and because I think you agree with me.'

'What on earth makes you say that?'

'Because if you didn't, you'd have reported me, wouldn't you?'

Just the day before Lang and Becker had met with Viktor on the Alte Donau, Hans was helping Becker repair the front gate of his house. When they'd finished, he and the boy sat in the kitchen having a cold drink. 'Do you think I'll be made to fight, Herr Becker?' said Hans suddenly.

Becker's first thought was why was Hans asking *him* this? Then he realised Hans now regarded him as some kind of father figure.

'I keep telling you, Hans, call me Manfred,' he said eventually. 'In answer to your question, well – you're 14 and...'

'... Nearly 15, actually.'

'Even so, you're not due to be called up for another three years, when you're 18, and I doubt very much whether the war...' Becker stopped himself. It was the first time in weeks he'd allowed Hans a glimpse of his own views and the boy was no fool.

'Ah! So you agree with me, Manfred, the war will be over soon!'

Becker leaned across the table and clasped the boy's hand in a firm and less-than-friendly manner, leaning close to him and speaking in an urgent whisper. 'Now listen to me, Hans, you never speak like this to anyone else, understand? It can be our secret. Away from here, you'll be as loyal a member of the Hitler Youth as the next boy, you understand?'

'We have more military training these days,' said Hans. 'There are rumours that 16- and 17-year-olds may be conscripted soon and...'

'Well, just make sure you shout "Heil Hitler" the loudest – and wear your Hitler Youth uniform with pride,' said Becker. 'You remember that fairy tale – the one in which the knight had a special suit of armour that meant he could never be hurt? Well, regard your uniform as your magic suit of armour.'

***

Along with Lang, Becker and Viktor – and with the help of Irma and Paul the Plumber – there was a group of just six people to distribute the leaflets around the city. The conditions Viktor set were strict: no one should carry more than a dozen leaflets at a time and each leaflet should be distributed over one 24-hour period in as many districts of the city as possible.

'Look,' Viktor told Lang and Becker one night as they prepared the print run for another leaflet. 'Don't expect to incite some mass uprising against the Nazis, that wouldn't happen even if we were to distribute tens of thousands of leaflets. But we can unsettle them: they'll be confused and angry, and they won't be sure how many leaflets there are. The Gestapo will probably panic and worry that for every leaflet they get their hands on, there are dozens that people have read and are passing on to others.'

Hans had the perfect cover, cycling around Vienna in his Hitler Youth uniform, with its khaki top and dark shorts. He always carried with him a satchel stuffed with leaflets distributed by his and other groups, urging the good citizens of Vienna to donate warm clothes for the troops in the east. And he also had the perfect excuse to travel across the city and especially through the Innere Stadt: twice a week he volunteered to visit the AKH, helping injured soldiers there, sometimes reading to them or assisting with meals.

No one would suspect this cheerful and good-looking boy with his blond hair, blue eyes and a ready 'Heil Hitler'. Inside his satchel there was a thin compartment, in which he hid his Hades leaflets. He would leave a few at a time, on a park bench, in the stairwell of an apartment block, in an alley, through the letterbox of a closed shop. He made a point of not leaving the Hades leaflets in the same place as the Hitler Youth ones; it wouldn't do for people to put one and one together. Hans had become so prolific that Becker worried he could be too exposed, but Viktor was delighted with him and, anyway, he now had other plans. Hades needed to expand its operations.

***

'If the Nazis can link it to Hades then it'll further increase any sense of... how shall I put it...? paranoia in the Gestapo,' said Viktor.

They were in the basement of Becker's mother's house, having just completed the print run of another leaflet. The heat of the machine and the August warmth made the temperature in the basement almost unbearable. The Russian had removed his jacket and tie, but he was still dripping with sweat as he talked about their plans. 'We're not pretending that sabotaging machinery is going to bring the Nazi industrial machine grinding to a halt, any more than the leaflets are going to lead to civil insurrection. But it'll unsettle them.'

Lang explained to Viktor how Cocytus had made a solution they'd used to sabotage machinery. 'It was quite ingenious – he was an industrial chemist, so he knew what he was doing. I don't know exactly what the solution was made up of but I think it was mainly lubricating oil, the kind all machines need to keep running smoothly. But Cocytus added a highly caustic element and also sand – then tiny shards of glass and metal. The beauty of this was it took a few hours before the damage began, so it was less risky for the person applying it.'

'And you think Cocytus is in Slovenia?'

'Possibly, he's certainly not in Vienna.'

'And only he knows the formula?'

'Yes,' replied Becker 'but...'

'... So it's pointless.'

'What I was trying to say was we still have a barrel remaining.'

'Really? Where is it?'

'You're sitting on it Viktor.'

Vienna Spies

***

They decided to attempt two sabotage attacks, if only to see whether the solution still worked. Viktor agreed he'd look after one of these: he was in an ideal position to do so as he'd the run of the locomotive works, especially on night shifts when there were fewer supervisors around. His job was to repair machinery and if he or any of the other electricians had no repairs they were expected to perform routine maintenance on other machines and equipment.

The 20th August was a Sunday night, which was usually a quiet shift, and Viktor took a small bottle of the oil solution in with his snack. No opportunity presented itself that night but on the following night he found himself alone at around 3.00 in the morning, having completed the repair of one machine sooner than expected. In another part of the factory was a piece of equipment he'd had his eye on. As far as he understood, it calibrated the brakes for the locomotives, but was only used for a few hours each day. He entered the shed where the machine was located and all was quiet. He slipped under the machine and checked some of the electrical parts: if anyone came in they'd see what he was doing. He found the port where the oil went in and poured in the contents of the bottle, then slid back under the machine and checked some wires. Once he was sure no one had seen him, he hurried out. What he didn't do was sign the maintenance log to show an electrician had checked the machine. With some luck, he wouldn't be linked with the sabotage.

He was next back at work on the Wednesday, this time for a shift that began at 6.00 in the morning. When he walked past the brake calibrating shed he noticed the machine had been completely dismantled. His supervisor was in a sanguine mood. 'Everything's ground to a halt, Otto, he said. 'The brake calibrating machine broke down yesterday, it's holding up the whole production line.'

The supervisor turned conspiratorially towards Viktor, leaning close to him as he spoke quietly. 'Jürgen says they suspect sabotage and they're going to investigate. You're lucky you weren't working yesterday.'

Although the Gestapo investigated, they only seemed interested in people who'd worked on the Tuesday, the day the machine broke down. Viktor remained above suspicion.

Becker had another contact, a mechanic who worked at a military lorry repair workshop in Donnaustadt. Franz was another anti-Nazi who'd had the good fortune to keep his past concealed. One night in September he managed to slip into the workshop using a set of keys he'd stolen. He knew that in the past week or so the number of guards on duty at night had been reduced to two, the others had been conscripted. Franz managed to pour the contaminated oil into four of the workshop's five hydraulic hoists. The first of them seized at noon the next day: by 2.00 it was chaos. And when the Gestapo arrived the next day, Franz was no more a suspect than the other 100 staff at the workshop.

Chapter 18

Vienna, Bratislava and Moscow, October 1944

Paris had been liberated on the 24th August, and two days before it fell Irma's husband had somehow managed to flee the city, even though most of the German garrison remained there. With the assistance of a sympathetic doctor he'd managed to turn a badly bruised elbow into a war wound. He arrived back in Vienna without warning two days later and turned up at their apartment at 6.00 on the Thursday evening: had he arrived just two hours earlier then it would have been to the sight of Viktor and his wife in the marital bed. Viktor rarely visited Irma these days and, as always, once he left she was quick to remove any signs he'd been there: changing the bedsheets and cleaning the flat. When her husband arrived there was no sign of anything out of place. Irma did appear flustered, but he assumed that was because she feared he'd been captured in Paris. When he went in the bathroom to refresh himself, she swiftly removed the tall porcelain vase from its place on the window ledge overlooking the front of the apartment: Viktor would now know it was no longer safe to visit.

It would be another month before she met with Viktor and it wasn't an easy meeting. He needed her to deliver a message and was telling her how.

'I told you, I've no idea how long he's going to be here,' she told the Russian. 'He fears they're unhappy he left Paris in the way he did: apparently other officers who did so are being sent to the east. Please leave me for a while, Viktor: he may only be here for another week or two. If he's sent east then I'm sure I'll never see him again.'

'I don't care, Irma. I'm not interested in your feelings for this Nazi officer...'

'He's my husband, Viktor, and he's not a Nazi like...'

'... Oh, for heaven's sake, Irma! Listen to yourself! He's an officer in the Wehrmacht and a member of the Nazi Party. One can only imagine what he was up to in Paris. You're now going to tell me some of his best friends there were Jews!'

'Well, actually...'

'Look, Irma, there are far more urgent matters that need dealing with now. You have to do this one task I ask of you: it's vital. I have to get a message to Moscow. They haven't heard from me for months. They need to know how things are going and especially about Leitner and this Rolf.'

'I don't understand why you can't deliver the message?'

'Because Lang knows that area very well, he patrols it in his boat and says the security is tight. You're only allowed near the docks if you've a good reason for being there. If you were to enter the area dressed in a... certain manner...'

'You want me to become a prostitute?'

'Not become one, Irma, just dress like one for an hour or so. I don't know – lots of bright lipstick and maybe a shorter dress, perhaps some cheap perfume if you have any. It's a red light district, so you won't look suspicious. I'll give you some cash to bribe the sentries, apparently that's what the prostitutes do – it's like a tax. Lang says the barge is due to dock there a week on Monday, the 3rd October. It arrives that afternoon, unloads its coal and will sail back to Bratislava later that night. Apparently it's safer for them to travel at dark because of the bombing.'

***

The timing couldn't have been worse for Irma. On the Friday before she was due to hand over the message, her husband was summoned to Army headquarters in Vienna and subjected to a swift medical examination. He was fine, they pronounced: fit and ready for action. He was to report to Army Group A headquarters in Warsaw the following week. He'd leave on the Tuesday morning.

They both knew the Monday night could well be their last one together – certainly for a few months but, the way the war was going, probably forever. This made it all the more difficult for her to explain why she was leaving the apartment just after 4.00 that afternoon. *To get something special to eat for our dinner tonight,* she'd explained, hoping her husband was distracted by his impending departure.

She hurried to the docks around Seitenhafenstrasse at the southern end of Leopoldstadt, not bothering with Viktor's nonsense of dressing like a prostitute. She was running the risk of arriving before the boat, but she managed to find a sentry alone in a hut by the gate, sheltering from the sharp wind whipping up from the Danube. She fished out a couple of packets of Juno cigarettes and pressed them into his hand.

I've a boyfriend who sails on one of the barges... Can I dash down to see him, just for a few minutes?

The sentry must have been in his fifties and was shivering. He looked unsure, so she slipped him another packet of Junos and some Reichsmarks. *Five minutes*, he replied. *Fifteen*, she said. *Fifteen and another two packets of these when I leave.* He nodded her through and she hurried down to the dock. She soon spotted the *Jelka*, aided by a frayed Slovak flag fluttering in the wind above its little wheelhouse. A lorry was alongside, into which huge bags of coals were being loaded. She leaned over the side of the barge and shouted through the wind and the noise to one of the crew. 'I'm looking for Ján.'

'Which Ján? There are three Jáns aboard.' He turned around and carried on manoeuvring a bag of coal.

'Ján Kuchár.'

'Wait.'

He disappeared below deck and Irma stood awkwardly on the quay, praying no one would come and ask why she was there. The crewman returned and indicated for her to climb aboard, pointing to a trapdoor that led her down into a noisy engine room. A large man covered in oil and sweat beckoned her over. 'I'm Ján.'

'I've a present for your mother.' From her handbag she removed an ordinary-looking hairbrush and handed it over. The Slovak leaned towards her, a worried look on his face.

'Why have you come so early? I told them to wait until it was dark and when we'd finished unloading the coal. Too many Germans could see you.'

'This was the only time I could come. You know what to do with that?'

He nodded and slipped the hairbrush into the inside pocket of a jacket hanging on a nearby wall. 'Isn't there something else?' he said.

'Of course… I hadn't forgotten.' From her handbag she removed a roll of Reichsmarks and handed them to the Slovak, who looked at them, bounced the roll up and down in his hand as if weighing its value, then slipped it down the front of his trousers, grinning unpleasantly as he did so.

'Do you want to stay for a while?' He looked at her as if he expected her to say yes. When she explained she had to hurry, he looked surprised and dejected. Five minutes later she was handing her last two packets of Junos to the grateful guard.

She caught a tram back to the 4th District and, close to Schleifmuhlgasse, knocked at the back door of a butcher's shop. The butcher ushered her into the doorway and handed over a package. She gave him a sum of money equivalent to what she'd normally spend on food for two people in a week. She hoped any suspicions her husband might have would be offset by the black-market veal. *Your favourite meal, Wiener schnitzel. It took me so long to find it,* she'd tell him.

The only thing he was suspicious about when she arrived home a few minutes later was the coal dust all over her: on her shoes, stockings, hands and even her face. *A careless shopkeeper on Wiedner Hauptstrasse,* she said. *He dropped a bag of coal. It went everywhere. You should have seen the poor woman in front of me – she looked like she was from Africa!*

***

The *Jelka* arrived in Bratislava early the following morning, around the same time as Irma bid farewell to her husband at Ostbahn station. Once the barge docked, Ján Kuchár remained below deck long enough to allow the rest of the crew to disperse. He trudged up the steep hill to a bar in the shadow of the ruins of Bratislava Castle. He nodded at the man behind the counter and told him he'd return that lunchtime. When he did so he went straight through to the small kitchen. The messenger was waiting there, a tiny man with a weathered face and sharp green eyes. Kuchár couldn't tell if the man was dirty or just had a particularly dark complexion, but there was no doubt about his smell: it was as if he hadn't washed that year. Kuchár took the hairbrush out of his pocket and handed it over to the man, along with a roll of Reichsmarks, somewhat smaller than it had been when he was given it by the woman in Vienna. The man slipped the hairbrush into his knapsack and stuck one of his filthy fingers deep into his mouth: it was glistening with saliva when he removed it and used it to count the money; nodding to indicate he was satisfied. He proffered a sticky hand for Kuchár to shake and the Slovak reluctantly did so.

Without saying a word, the man slipped out the back. All being well the message would be in Moscow in a few days: Kuchár had no idea how and didn't really care – just so long as the Russians took care of him once they arrived in Bratislava.

***

Late that Friday night, Ilia Brodsky paced up and down his office in a corner of the Kremlin like an expectant father. There had been a telephone call that morning from the senior Red Army

Commissar in Lvov, a city not long recaptured from the Nazis. A messenger had turned up, claiming he was from Bratislava and insisting he had a message for Comrade Brodsky in Moscow. What, the Commissar wanted to know, should he do?

'You're to get on a plane now, Comrade, and personally bring that message to me.'

'I could probably come on a flight on Monday, Comrade, the situation here...'

'No, you'll go the airport immediately and commandeer an aircraft. If you encounter any problems when you arrive there, please telephone me. When you arrive in Moscow, bring the message straight to my office: you understand?'

The Commissar said he understood and would leave immediately. What, he asked, should he do with the messenger? Send him back to Slovakia?

'You say he asked for me by name?'

'Yes Comrade – Ilia Brodsky.'

'Shoot him,' he replied, his voice making it clear he was surprised the Commissar had even bothered to ask the question.

Brodsky was so angry when he read the message for the fifth or sixth time that, had the Commissar from Lvov still been in his office, he might well have shot him too. Nine months Krasotkin had been in Vienna now, nearly 10. Ten months! And this was the first message they'd received in all that time. The fact that Krasotkin was still alive was hardly any compensation. What had he achieved in all that time? Distributed a few leaflets and put a couple of machines out of action for a few days. And, even worse than that, the British seemed to have an agent in Vienna – the British of all

Alex Gerlis

people – and they may well be in touch with Hubert Leitner.

That, Brodsky decided as he made up the narrow camp bed in his office, could be a disaster and there was precious little he could do about it.

He lay awake for most of that night, wondering what would happen if Comrade Stalin found out about this. And what would be worse, him telling Stalin, or not telling him? He knew having the ear of Comrade Stalin would end up being more of a curse than a blessing: maybe there was a way he could buy himself a bit more time.

Chapter 19

Vienna, November 1944

After the sabotage at the lorry-repair garage in September, Viktor decided Hades would wait until they were in a position to carry out a more spectacular attack. The American bombing of the city had intensified as the long-range bombers from Foggia became increasingly accurate. Viktor knew any sabotage attacks on the ground would need to be spectacular to be properly noticed. The leafleting had continued though; not as frequently as before, but still enough to add to the mounting sense of paranoia at the Gestapo headquarters on Morzinplatz.

There was amazement at Morzinplatz that Kriminaldirektor Karl Strobel had somehow managed to survive for as long as he had. The gossip in the corridors and behind closed doors was that Strobel had been lucky: in addition to his job of running the Vienna Gestapo, Huber had now been put in charge of the borders with Yugoslavia, Switzerland, Italy and Hungary, and had become preoccupied with that. Hungary was especially problematic: by early November the Red Army was just 40 miles from Budapest. There was a sense of unease and even nervousness around the Vienna Gestapo, and Strobel was lucky his boss had more important things to worry about than his failure to arrest anyone from Hades.

He'd also been helped by the fact Huber had put Kriminalrat Andreas Schwarz and a team from the Kripo in charge of catching the people distributing the leaflets. They enjoyed no more luck and

271

Strobel was beginning to feel vindicated. But in the second week of November two events changed all that.

The first took place on Tuesday 7th November, but it could be traced back to a chance encounter Manfred Becker had in the middle of October. Becker's job as a draughtsman at the Heinkel aircraft factory in Floridsdorf meant he was based in the research and development offices of the factory, and rarely had cause to visit other parts of it. He usually worked during the day – increasingly long hours certainly, but he was rarely there at night. But in the middle of October there had been a problem. The workshop in the factory responsible for manufacturing ailerons had to replace some of their tools and, as a consequence, the new ailerons no longer fitted properly onto the wings. Becker was told to sort this out as a matter of urgency, which meant he spent a fair amount of his time in the ailerons workshop and on a few occasions he had to work through the night.

It was on one of these nights he met Alois, although the word 'met' would convey a somewhat formal air to their encounter. 'Bumped into' would be a better description, but even that wouldn't properly describe the drama of their meeting.

Becker had been in his office producing yet more drawings and was returning to the workshop. It was around 9.00 on a Wednesday night and winter was definitely in the air as he made his way across the complex, regretting he hadn't bothered with a coat. Before arriving at the workshop he decided to visit the toilets in a block that also contained the locker rooms where the workers got changed. It was deserted as he made his way through its narrow and dimly lit corridors. He was unsure which door led to the toilets and tried a couple that were locked and another that opened into a room containing cleaning equipment. The next door looked more promising as he could see a pool of light creeping out from under it but, when he pushed the door open, the room was dark. He felt along the wall, found the switch and when it came on found he was in a long and narrow store room, at the end of which was a man cowering in the corner, stuffing pieces of paper into a bag.

Becker shut the door behind him. 'Who are you?'

'It's nothing,' said the man, who looked terrified and fumbled as he continued to stuff papers in the bag. 'If you need the toilet, it's along the corridor. Please leave me. It's nothing, as I say. I'm just sorting things out.'

Becker walked over to the man, who was now backed against the wall, as if shielding himself from physical attack. Becker bent down and picked up one of the sheets of paper. It was a small, single sheet with stencilled writing on one side.

Our time has come
The Nazi menace will soon be at an end
The hour of our liberation approaches
Do not co-operate with the occupier
Prepare for freedom
Arise against your oppressors!

'What on earth is this?'

'If you turn me in they'll execute me – my wife and children…'
The man buried his head in his hands. 'I don't know why I did this,

I didn't intend to do anything with them, in fact I brought them here to destroy them... I found them in the street you see, and decided to destroy them...' The words spilled out, rambling and incoherent.

Becker knelt down beside the man and helped him collect the other pieces of paper and put them in the bag. 'You don't know how lucky you are it was me who came in just now,' he told the man, as he placed a reassuring hand on his shoulder. 'We need to get rid of these, don't we? What's your name?'

'Alois.'

'Well, Alois, you and I need to have a proper chat sometime, but not now and certainly not here.'

***

It took Lang and Becker a week to check out Alois. They established he lived with his wife and young children in Ottakring, the 16th District. He'd never been involved in politics, though he'd always regarded himself as being on the left. But, mostly, he just wanted a quiet life. He was grateful his job meant he wouldn't be conscripted and he'd have been happy to see out the war that way, but he'd begun to hear things: too many elderly people dying conveniently soon after they'd been taken into homes; too many young soldiers dying; too many Jews disappearing.

One day he'd been sorting out the attic at his house when he came across an old stencilling set of his children's. He came up with the idea of the leaflet. His plan was to put one in all the lockers at work. 'Including my own,' he reassured Viktor when the

Russian interrogated him. 'That way they wouldn't have suspected me.'

Viktor was in two minds about Alois. On the one hand, anyone who thought they'd be above suspicion because they'd put a leaflet in their own locker was a fool. Yet it was clear he was genuine and was a skilled engineer, often based in perhaps the most important part of the factory - the workshops where the engines were fitted.

'I've always thought that if you can take that workshop out of action,' Becker told Lang and Viktor, 'then you'd bring the whole factory to a halt. There's a sophisticated system of hoists there, to get the engines into the planes. Stop that and you stop the factory, perhaps for days.'

When they brought Alois in on the plan, he made it sound even more attractive: there was one machine on which all the hoists depended. He was sure he could access it. The machine was inside a wall and could be reached through a narrow access shaft, which meant an engineer couldn't be seen while they were working on it.

'I can either put your oil in the machine when I'm on duty in that area, or I can risk going into it when I'm meant to be elsewhere,' Alois told them.

The latter, Viktor decided. No question about it.

On the night of Monday 6th November, Alois was the duty engineer in the distributor plant. Just after 11.00 he left for his break, moving quickly through the complex, sticking to the shadows until he reached the engine-fitting workshop. Once there, the risks became very real: according to the rota on the noticeboard in their office the duty engineer should be taking his break at around the same time, but you could never be sure. Alois slipped through a side entrance and avoided anyone until he reached the shaft that led up to the hoist machinery. He used his key to unlock the door to the shaft, closed it behind him and climbed the greasy metal ladder. If he was seen in there, he'd have no excuse. But he was lucky: it took him just five minutes to access the machine and insert the contaminated oil. No one saw him when he left the shaft and he quickly made his way back to the distributor plant.

Alois left the factory at 6.00 the following morning when his shift ended. Three hours later the hoists seized up in spectacular fashion. Two engines for a He177 bomber crashed to the ground, one of them smashing into the plane and the other landing on a generator, causing a fire that destroyed two other engines which were waiting to be lifted onto aircraft. Other hoists stopped with their engines in mid-air. The machine into which Alois had inserted the oil fused and caught fire. The damage and its effect were far more severe than the Hades group could ever have imagined. Even Viktor, for whom any show of satisfaction didn't come naturally, was delighted.

The whole factory was out of action for three days and it took the engine assembly workshop another week and a half to return to normal. So serious was the incident that news of it reached Berlin. Huber returned from a visit to the Hungarian border and still had his coat on when Strobel was summoned to his office on the Tuesday afternoon.

Strobel realised that, once Huber was satisfied the sabotage had been carried out by the same group that had carried out the attacks in August and September, he'd be off to the eastern front that very night. But not for the first time, Strobel was lucky. The machine had been so badly damaged that it took another three days before the evidence came through. And, on the Friday, Strobel had an even greater piece of luck.

***

At the same time on that Friday afternoon as the Kripo scientists reached the conclusion the same contaminated oil used in the previous attacks had been used at the Heinkel factory, Hans cycled home from school and changed into his Hitler Youth uniform.

He grabbed a biscuit from a tin with a painting on the lid of a healthy-looking Hitler selflessly taking part in the harvest and jumped back on his bike. He headed to the area around Wipplinger Strasse in Innere Stadt. His plan was to distribute dozens of his Nazi Party leaflets (*'warm clothes for the troops'*) and at the same time look for somewhere to leave a few copies of the latest Hades leaflet (*'Budapest today: Vienna tomorrow!'*).

As he cycled down Wipplinger Strasse he thought he spotted the perfect place to leave the Hades leaflets; an office block apparently closed for the weekend but with a side door ajar. He'd hurry in, leave a few leaflets on the stairwells and, with luck, they'd be found when people came back to work on the Monday. Disaster struck, though, as he turned his bike across the street. His front wheel caught in the cobbles and, as he tried to free it, an army lorry clipped his back wheel, sending him flying into the gutter. When he stopped and picked himself up he was bruised but otherwise unhurt: he was more concerned about the state of his bike. A few seconds later he realised that was the least of his problems. Spread out on the cobbled street were the contents of his satchel, both the Nazi leaflets and the Hades ones. He tried to gather them up, helped by a couple of passers-by.

'What's this?' A smartly dressed older man with a swastika tie-pin and glasses perched on the end of his nose was gingerly holding the Red Army leaflet between his fingertips, as if it was contaminated. Hans snatched it and picked up another two or three from the ground.

'They're nothing to do with me! These are my leaflets, look here!' He held out the Nazi leaflets – *warm clothes for the troops*. At that moment a policeman appeared and took charge. *What on earth*, he wanted to know, *was going on?* The man explained how the boy had been knocked over then how he'd found the leaflets on the road. 'These are official ones – but look at this!' He thrust the Hades leaflet into the policeman's hand.

'Why would I be carrying that rubbish?' Hans appeared indignant.

'Why,' the man asked the policeman, 'don't you search his satchel?'

***

An hour later a terrified Hans was sitting opposite Kriminalrat Andreas Schwarz in the Kripo headquarters. Schwarz said nothing as he carefully read the leaflet, no flicker of emotion on his face. On his desk was a selection of the previous Hades leaflets. The detective held a few of them up in his right hand. 'These would appear to be from the same machine as this one, would you agree?'

In his left hand was the Red Army leaflet, one of a number the policeman had found in the compartment of his satchel. Hans was crying and said he'd no idea. He also had no idea how those terrible leaflets had got into his bag.

The detective had been quietly spoken up to now and even appeared to be understanding. He continued in the same tone. 'Look, Hans, I can well imagine the situation. Some older person or persons forced you to distribute these leaflets, maybe they gave you money, I don't know. You seem like a nice boy, I'm sure you were forced into this. I doubt if you believe this nonsense. If you tell me who they are, then I promise I'll personally ensure you'll be treated as leniently as possible.'

'I don't know anything about those leaflets,' said Hans. 'I was delivering the other ones, sir. I'm a member of the Hitler Youth. Why on earth would I have anything to do with that kind of rubbish?'

'Because, Hans, the leaflets were concealed in a compartment inside your satchel.' Schwarz had raised his voice now, enough to sound angry and impatient. 'I'm no fool, you ought to know that. I'm one of the most experienced detectives here in Vienna. I suggest you co-operate with me. If you don't, then maybe we'll have to involve the Gestapo. You're lucky you weren't handed over to them straight away.'

Over the next hour Schwarz began to make some progress. Hans had started to trust him and believe him when he said he was fortunate to be in the hands of the Kripo rather than the Gestapo.

'A man gave me the leaflets but I didn't look at them,' said Hans eventually. Schwarz didn't believe him for one moment, but it was a start. There'd be progress over the next few hours, he was sure. If not, a night in the cells would do it. Even for a grown man, a night in a police cell was a sobering experience and usually had the desired effect. Few people weren't more forthcoming the following morning. But for a 14-year-old boy – and one who was clearly frightened already – the effect would probably be dramatic.

And so it went on. *The man told him not to look at the leaflets. The man said he was a Nazi Party official. There were only a few of them. He hadn't distributed them and was going to throw them in the river. He knew nothing about any of the other leaflets. He was a good Nazi. He was counting the days until he could serve the Führer.*

Schwarz was satisfied. Hans's story was inconsistent and it was only a matter of time before he had some names. At 7.00 that evening he allowed him a break to have something to eat, then he'd question him for another hour or two before going to bed. If he didn't come up with names the following morning then they'd bring his mother in. Either way, his experience told him he'd have the names by the following lunchtime and the Kripo would chalk up a further success over the Gestapo.

But one thing Schwarz had learnt about the Gestapo was not to be surprised by anything they did. Their predilection for brutality was matched only by their stupidity, and that evening he saw both deployed in equal measure.

He was sitting at his desk, while Hans had his meal in a cell, when the door to his office burst open. In front of him appeared the stocky figure of Karl Strobel, his face red, his pointed little beard quivering and his chest heaving as he caught his breath. 'Where is he, Schwarz?'

'Where's who?'

'The boy with the leaflets, you fool! And how come I wasn't informed?'

'Because, as you know full well, it was decided the investigation into the leaflets would be handled by my team after yours failed to get anywhere.'

'Don't be so fucking insolent with me, Schwarz! I bet you sympathise with what's written on them, eh? You should be investigated. You're not even a member of the Party, are you?' Strobel was standing so close that the detective could taste the alcohol on the Gestapo man's breath.

'Sit down and I'll explain to you what's happened, as a matter of professional courtesy. I'm making some progress: the boy is frightened and is beginning to give me information. I'm confident that by late tomorrow morning he'll have provided us with the names we want.'

'And what'll you do then?'

'Give the names to you.'

'I want the boy now.'

'I told you, I'm still questioning him. Children need to be handled carefully.'

'How old is he?'

'Fourteen.'

'Fourteen! He's hardly a child! I demand to see him now. Huber said I could. Call him if you don't believe me.'

The argument went on for 15 minutes before they reached a

compromise: Schwarz would allow the man from the Gestapo to see the boy in his cell for a few minutes then Strobel would leave. If Schwarz hadn't obtained any information from him by the following lunchtime, Hans would be handed over to the Gestapo.

The moment they entered the cell, Schwarz realised he should never have trusted Strobel. 'I'm Kriminaldirektor Karl Strobel from the Vienna Gestapo!' Strobel shouted as he stood over the boy, who was picking at a meal. Hans sat frozen in fear. 'Don't you show any respect to the Gestapo, you scum?' With that he swept the plate and cup off the table and pushed the table hard into the boy's body.

'Come here, Strasser,' shouted Strobel. His assistant joined them in the cell. 'Get him up.'

'Kriminaldirektor,' said Schwarz firmly. 'I insist you leave him alone now. Our agreement was very clear; he'll remain my responsibility until tomorrow. Please... no!'

While Strasser was holding Hans upright, Strobel hit the boy hard, first in the face then in the groin. Hans squealed in pain and doubled up as far as he was able. Schwarz tried to position himself between the two, but Strobel pulled out his pistol.

'I'm taking him now, Schwarz. Call Huber if you have a problem.'

***

'Watch me,' Strobel told Strasser as they drove Hans to Morzinplatz that evening. 'I'll have those names in an hour. None of the Kripo acting like it's a kindergarten. An hour with a professional, you'll see.'

They worked on the boy for four hours, until nearly 1.00 in the morning. At first Strobel just questioned him, believing the very fact he was in the basement of the Gestapo headquarters would be enough to ensure his co-operation. But the effect was the opposite and perhaps more predictable. Hans was too terrified to utter a word. Strobel did his best to hide his embarrassment from Strasser and acted as if this was going as he expected.

'Get him on that table Strasser. Come on, quick – what's keeping you?'

Two hours later and the boy still had revealed nothing. Strasser was convinced Hans had gone into a state of shock and told Strobel this when they went into the corridor for a cigarette.

'So what are you saying, Strasser? You're as soft as the Kripo.'

'I'm simply saying he's in a state of shock and may be unable to speak. If we let him rest and start again in the morning, I think he'll be more forthcoming.'

'You think he's suffering from shock do you? I'll show you shock!'

When they returned to the cell Hans was strapped naked to a chair and electrodes were attached to his genitals. The boy was trembling violently, even before the electricity was turned on. After the first surge, he screamed so loud the stone walls seemed to shake. After the second, he sobbed and drooled then started muttering something about a man.

'What man? Can you understand what he's saying, Strasser?'

Strasser bent down in front of Hans, his ear against his mouth. 'What man? Tell me his name and we'll unplug you.'

In between noisy sobs the boy said something.

'What the hell's he saying?'

'If you're quiet for a moment, sir, then maybe I'll be able to hear what he's saying... Hang on sir, he's saying something... Go on Hans... What's that? The Russian, sir, that's what he's saying – the Russian.'

'What Russian? I want names!' Hans mouthed something but, as he did, Strobel turned on the electricity again. Hans's body arched upwards and Strasser smelt burning flesh. When Strobel finally turned off the power the boy slumped back unconscious, thick streams of blood-speckled mucus running from both nostrils and his mouth.

They had to leave him in the cell overnight. Strasser noticed that, when they went into the office, Strobel's hands were shaking as he poured them each a large measure of schnapps. 'You see what I mean, Strasser? We're almost there; you've just witnessed a professional in action. We know it's a Russian. Mark my words, he'll tell me everything in the morning. That'll show Schwarz.'

***

The following morning Strobel was summoned into the office of the head of Vienna Gestapo as soon as he arrived at Morzinplatz.

'What the hell's going on, Strobel?'

'I've arrested a suspect with the resistance leaflets and he's in the process of confessing all, sir.'

'So you have names?'

'Not yet, but I'm very close.'

Huber looked stressed as he got up from his desk. He walked

over to the window, sat down again then went to pour himself a drink before lighting a cigarette. 'I don't need this, Strobel. I thought it was clearly understood this matter was to be investigated by the Kripo. I gather you used my name to remove him from their headquarters? The boy's 14. He's a member of the Hitler Youth and you've been torturing him.'

'But he had the leaflets on him, sir?'

'And ours too! Maybe there's an explanation. All I know is that if he had something to tell us, like names, surely he'd have told us by now. Look Strobel...' Huber looked around his empty office, as if there were other people there he didn't want to overhear him. 'The Russians are in Hungary now. The way things are going they'll be here sooner than we think. I can't afford to have a matter like this taking up my time. Bring him up here.'

'Who sir?'

'The boy, you fool. Maybe if you can't get anything out of him, I can.'

Strobel and Strasser went down to the basement where Hans was being held. They met the doctor in the corridor. 'Is he still alive Rudolf?'

'Yes, sir, but don't forget he's young: he won't be as physically resilient as an adult. He was very badly hurt yesterday. And I fear if you push him too hard he won't survive... I don't want my staff or I to get the blame yet again for someone dying before you've obtained information from them.'

Strasser hauled Hans from the bench in the cell and the two of them dragged him upstairs. The boy was barely covered by a blanket, which kept slipping off.

'Leave it,' said Strobel. 'Don't bother. Humiliation is often more effective than pain.'

So Hans was dragged naked up to the top floor and into Huber's office. The bright autumn sun streamed in from large windows, which looked out over the front and side of the building. Huber looked uncertain of what to make of the sight of the naked and terrified boy in front of him.

What happened next unfolded very slowly. Strasser let go of the boy's arm and roughly pushed him towards Huber. Huber manoeuvred himself up from his chair.

At that moment Hans let out a yell and lurched towards Huber's desk. Before any of them could react he'd grabbed a large paper knife from the desk and plunged it into his neck. Blood spurted everywhere. Strasser clamped his hand over the wound and Strobel shouted for someone to fetch Doctor Rudolf.

By the time the Gestapo doctor arrived, Hans had slipped into unconsciousness, the blood still pulsing out of him. Doctor Rudolf and a nurse worked on him for a few minutes but eventually they gave up. The elderly doctor shook his head. Huber, Strobel and Strasser all looked at each other, saying nothing and not knowing who to blame.

'A boy,' said Huber eventually. 'You had a boy in your custody for 12 hours and you got nothing. Nothing. Get out of my office.'

***

Manfred Becker heard of Hans's disappearance before he heard of his death. On the Friday night the boy's mother had knocked on his door. She knew Hans often did odd jobs for him, as he did for many others in the street. *Have you seen him, Herr Becker? He came home after school and cycled off in his uniform, I've no idea where he is.*

The following morning – the Saturday – Becker's wife told him to look out into the street; there was a lot of activity around Hans's house. Becker saw it was the Gestapo going in and out of the house, taking away bags and eventually Hans's mother, younger brother and sister. He contacted Lang and they got word to Viktor. Later that afternoon they gathered in the cellar of Becker's mother's house.

'He doesn't know my real name or yours, Joachim,' said Viktor. 'If the Gestapo have got him it's just a matter of time before he speaks. But we're just speculating, aren't we? All we know is he's missing and the Gestapo are at his house.'

'But he had leaflets with him, I'm sure,' said Becker. 'The ones about the Red Army reaching Budapest. He said something about leaving some around Innere Stadt.'

'Do you have anything incriminating around your house?'

'Of course not, Viktor,' said Becker.

'Very well. I suggest we dismantle this machine now, and burn all the paper and anything else in the cellar that could get you into trouble.'

They heard about Hans's death on the Monday: the official line was he was an enemy of the state who'd killed himself after confessing to crimes against the Reich. His mother and siblings had been taken away. But as soon as they heard the news of Hans's death, they also realised that the boy had died without disclosing anything about them: had he done so, the Gestapo would have turned up long before the news did. Nevertheless, Viktor decided to put Hades activities on hold. No more leafleting or sabotage for the time being. Now the priority would be to find Rolf and Leitner.

Chapter 20

Vienna, December 1944

By the second week of December a few Christmas markets had sprung up in a half-hearted fashion around the city, mostly in the Innere Stadt, but they were miserable affairs compared to what the Viennese could remember. Most of the decorations and gifts on sale appeared to be second-hand; the food was sparse and even more expensive than in the shops; and the spiced wine was more spice than wine. The few Christmas trees on sale were little more than branches and people eyed them as if trying to estimate how long they'd last on a fire.

The American air force had done their best to add to the Christmas spirit. They'd helped light up the city by bombing the Winterhafen oil storage depot, and the fire raged for days, casting a seasonal glow over the city. The Moosbierbaum oil refinery had also been hit. As a consequence there was hardly any fuel to be found in Vienna. Virtually all non-military transport ground to a halt.

But for Rolf all this symbolised how badly things were going for the Reich: if Vienna couldn't manage even a half-decent Christmas then things must be bad. Life for him and Katharina had become somewhat routine, even ordinary since their meeting with Leitner in June. The message that had eventually come back from London had been clear enough.

Well done on locating Leitner. Tell him we agree to his terms: our intention is to ensure Austria is a free and independent state after the war and we'd like him to head up the provisional government ahead of elections. Meanwhile, keep him where he is. It sounds as if he's as safe there as anywhere else. We'll tell you when to move him. Make sure you two don't arouse any suspicion and please do let us know if you see any sign of the Russian.

That suited Rolf fine. He carried on working at the bank and Katharina at the hospital. Once a week they'd go and visit Leitner in the basement under the apartment building in Leopoldstadt. The visit would usually be on either a Saturday or a Sunday, depending on Katharina's shifts at the hospital. They always took a different route, travelling together until they crossed the canal then splitting up so that one could watch the other. They took it in turns for one of them to go into the apartment block, while the other kept watch outside. Then they'd follow the same procedure when they headed back to Ungargasse, one following the other, switching between who'd walk in front then joining up once they crossed the canal.

The main purpose of the visits was to ensure Leitner was safe and that Frau Egger and her son Otto had no problems and enough money.

To all outward appearances, Gerd and Anna Schuster were a normal married couple. Had any of them been asked, their neighbours would have described them as polite and unassuming, but then they'd no doubt have said the same about most of the people in their block. Even in the privacy of their apartment they'd assumed the life of a married couple in most respects. They chatted happily about holidays they'd been on and other innocent matters. Any conversation that strayed into more personal matters was quickly shut down. Katharina was astute enough to realise Rolf's feelings for Frieda weren't too far below the surface and she struggled to know how best to handle this. Should she gently broach the subject so he could get it off his chest, or was it best to ignore? Once or twice she did start to talk about Frieda, but soon stopped when she saw the pain in his eyes.

It was safer to discuss each other's days at work, laugh at the gossip and share titbits of information they'd heard about the war. They avoided listening to foreign broadcasts on their radio – that would be an unnecessary risk – but they enjoyed sitting together in the evenings to listen to concerts. When it came to going to bed, there'd be an awkward pause, one that lasted only a second or two but one that both were increasingly aware of. Katharina would then give Rolf a quick kiss on the cheek and go to bed, while he arranged the sofa to sleep on.

But everything changed in December.

It was Tuesday 12th December, and Katharina was on a late shift at the hospital that she wasn't due to finish until close to midnight. On such days Rolf tended not to hurry back to the apartment after work, preferring to walk through the Innere Stadt, and perhaps find a bar that had some electricity and maybe something to eat. On this particular evening he was wandering in and out of the side streets around Schelling Gasse when he found a bar at the bottom of a steep flight of steps. It was almost empty and cold so he decided to leave after one drink; but, before doing so, he went to the toilet, which was at the back, through the small kitchen. And it was in the kitchen he saw her.

***

Franzi Landauer and Frieda Brauner had enjoyed the kind of close friendship Rolf had come to realise was exclusive to women; intimate and trusting, they'd been confidantes with no secrets or ambition coming between them. They'd been friends since university, so when Rolf first met Frieda, Franzi was part of her life. For a while she and Frieda shared the same apartment and, even when Frieda moved into her own flat in Brigittenau, Franzi was always around. As with so many close friendships, the two women appeared to have little in common. Frieda was tall, with short hair and would be described as handsome rather than beautiful. She was a dentist, from a village in the west of Austria, a practising communist and a decidedly non-practising Catholic. Franzi, by contrast, was shorter than her friend, but with long dark hair and a beauty that ensured she never went unnoticed. She worked in her family's fashion business; she wasn't interested in politics and was Jewish.

But despite their differences, or possibly because of them, they were the closest of friends. The last Rolf had heard of her was that she'd fled to Paris, but the woman in the small kitchen was unquestionably Franzi. Her once long hair was now much shorter and she was wearing a pair of heavy spectacles. She stared at him in disbelief and fear.

'Franzi! What are you doing here?'

She pushed past him and shut the door leading to the bar, then checked the other door was closed too. 'Please leave Rolf. Never, ever call me Franzi. Please, I beg you. My name's Anna

Wagner.' Her voice trembled and she gripped the edge of a worktop.

'But I thought you were in Paris?'

'I never went… Look Rolf, we can't talk now. The owner will leave soon and I'll be on my own here for the last hour. Let's talk then. Hardly anyone comes in these days.'

An hour later Rolf stood at the bar with Franzi behind it. The last customer had left a few minutes before and the place was now deserted. They both spoke softly, leaning close to each other: anyone wandering in would assume he was another customer trying his luck with a barmaid.

'I never made it to Paris. I left it too late, Rolf.'

'You'll need to call me Gerd.'

'Gerd? You don't look like a Gerd – you don't look too much like Rolf either,' she said. 'We all have these different identities in this mad place, it's crazy! My parents and my younger brothers went to Paris just after the Anschluss. I was going to go later in April. The idea was I'd close down the business and arrange for my parents' house to be looked after, but the man who was going to buy the business – at a much reduced price – reneged on the deal. Of course, looking back, I should have just left and forgotten about the money, but I thought I was smart and I'd be able to sort something. But it turned into a nightmare. The man went to the authorities and said he had a deal and I'd cheated him – and you can guess who they chose to believe. Because of this trouble, I was denied an exit visa. Here Rol… Gerd… have another drink, it doesn't look good if you have an empty glass.'

She poured him a tall glass of beer and placed a schnapps alongside it.

'Even then, I could probably have got out; it was just me after all. But I'd moved back into my parents' house in Alsergrund and was trying to sort that out. It was a nice house, you know, a very smart area. But when they tried to confiscate it, I resisted and I was arrested. By the time I was released, everything had been taken from us. They even took our cats, you know? Jews aren't allowed to own pets. Sip some of your beer; it looks better if it's not a full glass.'

'So you were released?'

'Yes, but I had to report back a week later – and this time to the Gestapo in Morzinplatz. As soon as I realised we'd lost everything, I went into hiding. I decided not to risk trying to escape: what would I have done, climbed over the mountains? I thought I'd have a better chance in the city. I changed my identity and now I live here in the basement; the owner lets me in return for working for nothing. Otherwise he couldn't afford to keep this place open.'

'So you've been in Vienna all this time?'

She nodded, picking up a cloth and polishing a few glasses.

'When did you last see Frieda?'

She stopped polishing the glass and leaned back, staring long and hard at Rolf.

'Frieda?'

'Yes, you must know where she is, tell me...'

She put the glass down on the bar and placed one of her hands over his.

'Oh my God, Rolf... You mean you don't know?'

Vienna Spies

***

Franzi had no idea what to do with Rolf. He swayed slowly, looking at her as if he couldn't believe what she was saying. 'Where are you living? You must go home quickly – soon it'll be too late,' she said.

He ignored her, his only movement was the tears welling in his eyes. Franzi was now seriously worried someone would walk in and wonder what was going on. She came out from behind the bar and shepherded Rolf into the kitchen, where she sat him down and made him a strong coffee while she closed up the bar. When she returned, the coffee was untouched and Rolf was gazing into space, his face expressionless but tears streaming down his cheeks. Even if he decided to leave, he was in no fit state to go anywhere. She couldn't risk him being stopped.

He spent that night in the basement with her, a freezing cold room with a dirty mattress, a few blankets, a couple of candles, and little else beside a suitcase and a few rats. Franzi slept fitfully: every time she awoke Rolf was in the same sitting position, his eyes sometimes half-closed and once or twice the flickering light of the candle caught the beginnings of what could be a faint smile on his face. Around 6.00 in the morning she woke to see that the candle had gone out but Rolf was asleep on the mattress next to her. She covered him with her blankets and went upstairs. The owner would arrive around 11.00, in time for lunch – the only time the bar was busy these days. She'd send Rolf away before he arrived.

Franzi cleaned the bar and the kitchen, and got everything ready for opening later that morning. She went back to the basement at 10.15, but even in the gloom she could tell Rolf wasn't there. When she lit a candle there was no sign of him, no note, nothing.

Franzi allowed herself the luxury of just one minute in which to think. In the state Rolf was in the previous night he was dangerous: he could say anything to anyone, which meant she was no longer safe. She'd never regarded her situation in the bar as being ideal, but it had meant she'd survived far longer than she'd expected. She'd have to leave immediately.

As for Rolf, he'd disappeared.

Chapter 21

Vienna and London, December 1944

Katharina tried to remain calm that night and think of a plausible reason why Rolf hadn't been there when she'd arrived back at their apartment. As far as she could tell, he hadn't returned after work; everything was exactly as it had been when she left for her shift some 11 hours earlier. The sofa wasn't made up, the basins in the bathroom and the kitchen were bone-dry, and his shoes weren't in the hall. The loaf of black bread on the table was untouched, as was the cheese beside it. Those were the first things Rolf would have headed for when he returned to the apartment.

The most obvious explanation was he'd been arrested, but how come they hadn't been waiting for her? If he had been arrested, she decided, somehow they hadn't found his papers and he was refusing to reveal anything. This also seemed unlikely: there was no reason why he wouldn't have had any papers with him. But whatever had happened, she knew what she ought to do. She should leave: their instructions were very clear – if one of them was caught, they'd hold out for as long as possible, giving the other person an opportunity to disappear.

She packed a small bag with essentials but decided to wait until the morning and telephone the bank first. Maybe Herr Plaschke would have a good explanation.

Before she managed to ask Plaschke a question he had one for her. *Where's Gerd? We haven't seen him this morning.* She paused for a few seconds, just long enough to come up with what she hoped sounded like a plausible answer. 'That's why I am calling you, Herr Plaschke. He's terribly unwell, I'm afraid. He was fine last night when he went to bed, then this morning, well – would you believe it – he woke with a terrible fever and he's lost his voice completely, otherwise he'd have telephoned himself.'

Plaschke hesitated just long to make it clear he was somewhat inconvenienced, then asked her to pass on his best wishes to Gerd for a speedy recovery – with a pointed emphasis on the word 'speedy'.

Katharina was on another late shift that evening. Before she left the apartment in the afternoon she carefully arranged a few strands of dark-brown cotton thread along the width of the carpet in the hall, as Basil Remington-Barber had shown her. When she returned in the early hours of the following evening the strands were all in place: no one had been in the apartment. She did sleep a bit that night, but woke early and lay in bed thinking. It did briefly cross her mind that Rolf's disappearance could have something to do with Frieda, but she couldn't think what could have happened and realised she needed to do something. She could either leave Vienna and somehow try to get back into Switzerland or remain where she was. Either way, she'd need to get word to London.

***

'I'll get Herr Plaschke for you, Frau Schuster,' said the woman behind the counter at Bank Leu, looking Katharina up and down in a 'so this is what you look like' manner. 'Please take a seat.'

Five minutes later she was in Plaschke's office. The manager was holding the sheet of paper she'd handed to him. 'And you say this is urgent?'

'Yes, Herr Plaschke: you can see it's my husband's handwriting. He remembered last night he needed to send this urgent message to Herr Hedinger at the head office in Zürich. He'd planned to do it yesterday morning but, with his fever, he totally forgot. He asked me to give it to you personally.'

Plaschke held the sheet of paper in front of him and furrowed his brow. 'It doesn't make sense.'

'Apparently it will to Herr Hedinger. My husband says if the message could be sent as soon as possible then Herr Hedinger will no doubt appreciate it.'

For the second time, Plaschke read the message out loud.

Second transfer of last week needs to be reviewed. Please ensure proper audit and recalculation. Will advise further in due course.

Plaschke shook his head. 'As I say, it doesn't make sense to me, but if you insist... I'll have it cabled this morning. When do you expect your husband to be back at work?'

'Hopefully by the end of the week,' she replied, allowing an especially friendly smile to cross her lips before hurrying off to the hospital. The sheet of paper was one of several Rolf had prepared when they arrived in Vienna to be sent to London in the event of an emergency like this. The gist of this one was that Rolf himself had gone missing and there was no news as to where he was.

***

'I knew it,' said Christopher Porter. He was pacing around his office, red-faced and furious. Edgar was standing with his back to the window.

'Knew what, sir?'

'That Rolf couldn't be trusted. Look, this message came in over the weekend. Hedinger got it to Basil and he sent it on overnight. Read the bloody thing.'

Edgar looked at it carefully. 'It says Rolf has gone missing and Katharina has no idea where he is, but she's safe.'

'Exactly.'

'But why does it make you think Rolf isn't to be trusted?'

'Think about it, Edgar. Oh this bloody thing... my secretary...' Porter swept away a small row of paper ribbons that had been hung across the front of his desk. Christmas was just a week away.

'At this rate, Christmas will be cancelled, which'll be a merciful release in my case I can assure you,' said Porter. 'I dread the in-laws coming to stay – absolutely dread it. If I have to listen again to my father-in-law's theories on how to win the war... Christ, you know he actually brought a map along with him last year? I wouldn't mind, but he knows as much about warfare as I do about golf, which is his one other topic of conversation. Look, Edgar, it's perfectly clear: Rolf's gone missing and if Katharina's safe that means he hasn't been arrested by the Gestapo: correct?'

'So it would seem, but...'

'... No buts, he's disappeared. Absent Without Leave. Heaven knows what he's up to, but my money's on him going off with the Russians. After all, he and that woman have been in Vienna for how long, eight... nine months now? And what was he meant to be doing there? Contact Leitner and see what the bloody Soviets were up to. Well, it took them the best part of three months to contact Leitner and we've not yet heard so much as a whisper about the Soviets – not a bloody whisper, if you'll excuse my language. Sir Roland will be absolutely bloody furious and I don't even want to think what Winston…'

'Hang on, sir, you're rather jumping to conclusions aren't you? He's missing, that's all we know.'

'What about Whitlock?'

'Poor George has been dead since June, sir.'

'I know that you fool,' said Porter. 'But remind me what he said about Rolf… And be honest, Edgar. Did he say anything that could, with hindsight, point to him being a Soviet agent?'

Edgar thought carefully. What Porter was saying was a bit hasty but not completely ridiculous. The fact Katharina had managed to get the message out meant she was safe – and it did imply Rolf wasn't in the hands of the Gestapo.

'I asked George whether he recruited Rolf or whether he recruited us.'

'And…?'

'And it wasn't entirely clear, I told you as much in June,' said Edgar. 'He wasn't a walk-in, but then the Soviets are always much more sophisticated than that – the Nazis used to use that kind of ploy. But nor was it a straightforward case of us recruiting him. He could have been very, very clever and made sure he was in the right place at the right time. Plus, his fiancée was a member of the KPO, so it's not impossible. What do you want to do?'

Porter had calmed down now, probably helped by the prospect

of an in-law-free Christmas. 'There's not a lot we can do, other than contemplate that we may have been used by the Soviets,' he said. 'Rolf's most likely being feted in the Kremlin, for all we know. We can't get a message to Katharina, far too risky. If I remember correctly, isn't the plan she contacts us in another week to let us know what's going on?'

'Correct, sir. In the meantime, let's keep our fingers crossed that he's not going to lead Viktor to Leitner's lair.'

***

That very same day Katharina had some time off in Vienna, having worked two long shifts that weekend. She telephoned the bank to say that unfortunately her husband was still unwell then went shopping – or queuing, to more accurately describe it. She had some lunch, pottered around the apartment, and began to feel quite alone and frightened. For the first time since Rolf disappeared she was neither at work nor exhausted, which allowed her time to think. She was fast coming to the realisation that she couldn't carry on doing nothing for much longer. It was still possible the Gestapo would turn up – then she had to think about Leitner. Would it be safe if she went to check he was still in Leopoldstadt and, if he was, should she try and escape with him to Switzerland?

She sat on the sofa, trying to work out what to do and, at the same time, deal with another emotion, one that had struck so unexpectedly when she returned to the apartment on the Saturday night. She'd realised then she missed Rolf and not because his disappearance had jeopardised their mission and her safety. She realised she also missed his presence, his friendly chats, his mischievous smile, the way he'd help her with her coat, the way he'd insist on serving her food like an over-attentive waiter, the way he ran his fingers through his hair and the way he edged towards her when they linked arms to walk through the park.

She realised she was allowing these feelings to interfere with what should be her priority: to think clearly and come up with a plan. She knew she ought to leave Vienna, but her instinct told her the chances of making it back to Switzerland were very slim. It was simply too dangerous. She walked around the flat, pacing up and down the sitting room, walking from there into the tiny hallway, then into the bedroom and ending up in the kitchen where she leaned against the sink, staring into the hallway and at the front door. If only there was someone in Vienna who could help her, anyone…

It must have been the sight of the front door that triggered a memory of the nun. It had been nearly eight months since they'd seen her and when she had left she'd been quite adamant. *You won't see me or hear from me again… Resist any temptation to try and find me… For your safety… and mine.*

And so there hadn't had any contact with her – but now Katharina was desperate. She was alone and scared. She'd have to ask the nun for help, though for the life of her she couldn't think of how to do so. For the next hour she racked her brain in an effort to remember any details the nun had given them.

She remembered her mentioning she was from a poor convent and her giving the name of an order Katharina hadn't heard of before, but that hardly narrowed it down. The name of the nun soon came to her: her grandmother had been called Ursula, so that wasn't too hard to recall. She heated up some soup and ate it at the small table in the kitchen, allowing her mind to wander and go back over every detail of the nun's visit, from the moment the doorbell had rung. She closed her eyes, picturing the sequence of events that followed. The nun had introduced herself and said she was collecting. She was still standing in the doorway when Katharina had given her some money – she remembered that – but something else had happened between the nun introducing herself and Katharina giving her the coins. She was thinking so hard that by the time she spooned some more soup into her mouth it had turned cold.

A slip of paper. The nun had given her a small piece of paper. She remembered glancing at it and noticing it had an address on it. She'd no idea what she'd done with it. Somehow she knew she hadn't thrown it away. Rolf had said something after the nun had left about keeping it safe.

It took her two hours to find the slip of flimsy paper, inside the little letter rack on the mantelpiece in the lounge, in between other bits of paper, something from the bank, shopping lists…

The convent of the Daughters of Charity of Saint Vincent de Paul was in Alsergrund, the 9th District, not far from the hospital. She'd be able to visit that night on her way into work.

She found the convent in a small turning off Liechtensteinstrasse, not the smarter section of that road alongside the park but the part north of Alserbachstrasse. Like the turning itself – no more than a dark and narrow alley – the convent was easily missed. Dark metal doors were set into a high wall and a small brass plate bearing the name of the order had been screwed into the brickwork alongside them. Below this was a bell. When Katharina pressed it she heard nothing, she'd no idea whether it had made any sound. She waited five minutes before trying again, unsure if she was being observed from any of the windows high in the dark brick wall. Moments after she'd rung the bell for the second time a small hatch in the centre of the door opened and a bespectacled face studied her.

'What do you want?'

'I'm looking for a Sister Ursula. Is she here?'

The eyes behind the spectacles opened wide. 'Who are you?'

'I met her once and... I said I could contribute... to the... erm... charity...'

'Wait here.' The hatch closed. It started to rain and Katharina began to feel the cold wind blowing down the alley, biting into her. The delay was long enough for her to begin to feel uneasy. But just as she was wondering whether to leave, one of the metal doors opened noisily, just far enough to reveal a tall and elderly nun standing within the entrance, looking at her.

'Why do you want Sister Ursula?'

'We met her when she was collecting for your convent. She was very kind and I recently... well, I'd like to give her some money for your charitable work.'

The older nun stared at her in disbelief. She removed her hand from within her habit and held it out, as if begging. 'You can give it to me.'

Katharina fumbled in her purse and pressed a generous note into the nun's hand. 'Is Sister Ursula not here? Perhaps I could have a word with...'

'What's your name; tell me how you know her?'

'As I say, I met her in the street, months ago... she was so kind, it was a difficult time for me and she said a prayer that gave me so much comfort... Is she not here?'

The nun stared long and hard at Katharina. 'Sister Ursula is dead.'

***

Had she turned up at the convent of the Daughters of Charity of Saint Vincent de Paul just six weeks earlier Katharina would most likely have found Sister Ursula there. And it was also likely Sister Ursula would have helped her because, in the six months since she'd handed Herr Leitner over to the Schusters, Sister Ursula had regained some of her composure. She no longer felt as much self-doubt; her fear seemed to be no greater than that of so many other people and she was constantly reassured by what the priest had told her in confession. *Keep thy mind in hell and despair not.*

But then she experienced hell and realised the true meaning of despair.

Just south of the AKH hospital where Katharina worked was Saint Anna's Children's Hospital, although officially it no longer had the name. Now it was called the German Red Cross Children's Hospital and, since the spring, Sister Ursula had been working there full-time.

The hospital was now not just dealing with the routine illnesses children suffered. It was also dealing with children injured in the bombing and suffering from other deprivations of war. Sister Ursula had come to realise the despair she'd experienced was nothing compared to what she was witnessing on a daily basis on the wards.

And it was on one of those wards that Sister Ursula met a girl, who said she was eight but appeared to be older, and had been found alone and dazed in the ruins of an apartment block in Hernals after a heavy air-raid. No one knew who she was: she could only give her name as Paula. She appeared to have no connection with where she was found. But Sister Ursula had an instinct about Paula. She suspected she wasn't as confused as she seemed. Although she kept insisting her head hurt, she didn't appear to be injured or unwell.

Sister Ursula suspected Paula was Jewish. She had dark hair, coal-black eyes and a dusky complexion but, more than that, she had the aura of someone who was keeping a secret. Sister Ursula wasn't the only one to have such suspicions. There was a paediatrician at the hospital called Peter Sommer, a man whose short temper and unsympathetic manner made him singularly unsuited to his specialism. The gossip among the nurses was that he chose paediatrics because children were less able to complain about him than adults.

One day when she was in charge of the ward where Paula was, Dr Sommer approached her. 'There's nothing wrong with that girl, Paula,' he announced. 'I can see no valid medical reason for her being here. I'll tell you what I think: the girl's a liar. Someone had the idea of using the air raid as a way of getting her into hospital – and she's pretending she's has lost her memory.'

'Surely she's far too young to be able to do that,' said Sister Ursula.

Dr Sommer flicked his hand in a dismissive manner. 'And I'll tell you something else. Look at the girl: tell me she's not a Jew, eh? It's a waste of our time her being here. She should be the Gestapo's problem, not ours. They can sort her out.'

'Please Herr Doctor Sommer. I'm sure there's an innocent explanation. When the poor girl recovers she'll be able to tell us exactly who she is.'

That night Sister Ursula hatched a plan. When all was quiet around midnight she went to work. An 11-year-old girl had died from pneumonia earlier that day and Sister Ursula took her file. By the time she'd finished with it, the dead girl had Paula's identity ('surname unknown'). The body would be removed by the time Sommer returned to work on Monday. She filled in a discharge form for the girl who'd died, meaning Paula now had her identity.

At 2.00 in the morning she took Paula from the ward and explained she now had a new name and was going to be taken somewhere safe. The girl nodded. She was counting on her Mother Superior allowing the girl to stay a day or two in the convent before Sister Ursula could find somewhere for her to go. Maybe the apartment where Herr Leitner...

They left the hospital through the back entrance and were walking through the ambulance bay when she noticed the three figures in front of her. Three men, silhouetted against the moon, standing motionless in their path. She knelt down and whispered into the girl's ear. 'Can you run? Try to get away...' But at that moment a strong torchlight shone in their faces and a voice ordered them to get to their knees.

Sister Ursula and the girl were separated soon after being dragged back into the hospital, where an elated Peter Sommer told the men from the Gestapo he had an instinct the nun may do something.

'You tried to defend her, didn't you?' He was strutting around the office, looking pleased with himself. 'I thought to myself, why's that woman arguing with me? And I could tell by the look in your eye, I didn't trust you. So I came back here and found you'd swapped files. I'm no fool, you know. I can put two and two together. So I called my friends in the Gestapo and – here we are!'

The girl never revealed her true identity – she continued to insist she was called Paula. She was taken away and the Sister Ursula never discovered her fate. As for her own, that was never in doubt. Just one week after her arrest she was found guilty at the Volksgerichtshof – the People's Tribunal – of high treason and sentenced to death. In the 10 days between her death sentence being passed and her execution date, a succession of increasingly senior clergy came to visit her at the Landgericht. Their message was all the same: apologise; admit your guilt; plead for clemency. She turned them all down. In the still, dark hours before she was due to die, her Mother Superior visited her. The elderly woman knelt down beside her and whispered urgently into her ear.

'Sister, I know you were active against the Nazis. I turned a blind eye to it. But, I beg you, please give them some information, maybe the names of people less holy than us, then they will be satisfied and you will be granted clemency. That's the wish of the church.'

'What? The church wishes me to betray people?'

They came for her an hour later. She was marched into the execution chamber and made to stop by the guillotine. The Gestapo officer who stood in front of her looked almost nervous.

'Confess and give us names and you will be granted clemency. Is there anything you wish to tell us?'

Sister Ursula smiled sweetly. She felt no fear and no self-doubt. 'Keep thy mind in hell and despair not,' she replied.

***

Katharina hurried away from the convent as soon as she heard the nun was dead. She hadn't given her name and was wearing a coat over her nurse's uniform, so it would be hard for anyone to identify her. That night she made up her mind. She'd wait until the end of the week and, if there were still no sign of Rolf, she'd go to Leopoldstadt at the weekend and check on Leitner. She didn't think she could go on like this for much longer, trying to act normally. In any case, she doubted Herr Plaschke's patience would last much longer.

From Tuesday onwards she was working an early shift at the hospital, leaving the apartment at 6.00 in the morning and returning around 5.00 in the afternoon. She'd taken to leaving a note for Rolf on the kitchen table to let him know she was at work and when she'd be back, just in case. On the Wednesday, she arrived back in Ungargasse even more exhausted than usual. One of the tram routes was out of action thanks to bombing the night before and other trams were so full she'd walked most of the way in the pouring rain. It had been an especially difficult shift: a hospital train had arrived in Vienna overnight from the east and many of the soldiers were dreadfully injured. She sat with a young soldier from Mainz as his life painfully ebbed away. Not once in the four hours she was with him did he lapse into unconsciousness and there wasn't enough morphine around to make him comfortable. He remained awake until the very end, a look of terror on his face throughout. He tried to dictate a letter to his family but couldn't make it beyond the first painful sentence.

So when she entered the apartment she was too tired and distracted to notice the shoes on the carpet or the coat on a hook in the hall. She didn't see a small pool of light spilling out from under the lounge door as she went straight to the kitchen, and didn't realise the note she'd left that morning was no longer on the table. But when she went to the sink and filled a glass with water she spotted another one on the draining board, half-full. And on the other side of the sink were the remains of the loaf of black bread, half of what had been there in the morning. She leaned against the sink, a sense of fear creeping over her but one that was quickly overwhelmed by mounting excitement. She spun around to see Rolf framed in the doorway, lit from behind and in silhouette. As she took a faltering step forward she made out his features. He looked gaunt and exhausted, and had a sheepish expression on his face. They hesitated for a moment then embraced. It wasn't quite the embrace of lovers long parted but nor was it formal or awkward. It was an embrace of relief, of emotions expressing themselves and of sheer happiness.

They led each other into the lounge and sat on the sofa. Neither spoke for a long time. Rolf gazed at the carpet and occasionally at Katharina, smiling when he did so. Her presence alongside him reminded her of her vigil with the dying young soldier earlier that day: no need to speak, just to be there.

'When did you get back?' Katharina said softly, breaking the long silence.

He looked up as if he hadn't taken in her question, but he eventually replied. 'Late morning, maybe lunchtime. I saw your note, thank you.'

'Do you want to tell me what happened? I can't tell you how worried and frightened I've been. The night you didn't come back... I was waiting for the Gestapo. Please tell me: were you arrested?'

'I wasn't arrested, don't worry.' Rolf looked back at the carpet and fell silent. It was a while before he spoke again. 'The night I didn't return, I bumped into a woman who was the oldest friend of my fiancée, Frieda. She told me Frieda had been arrested by the Gestapo in 1942, in March. Apparently she was interrogated and tortured. She died after a few days...' He was speaking quietly, but almost matter-of-factly.

'I'm so sorry, did you...?'

'... She never divulged anything. I'd no idea she was dead. Frieda was such a strong woman that it somehow never occurred to me she could be dead. I thought she'd be in hiding or had escaped – maybe even in prison, but dead... no. Since I've been back here in Vienna I've assumed, for right or wrong, we'd be reunited. Don't ask me why, but I was convinced it'd happen.'

Rolf turned his head away from Katharina and looked towards

the windows, his eyes full of tears. She edged closer to him and took her hand in his.

'Tell me where you went.'

***

When Rolf was a student in Vienna the city was such an intense cauldron of politics, violence and emotions that he often felt the need to escape from it. He found his refuge in the Vienna Woods, an enormous expanse to the west of the city, where the lower foothills of the Alps dropped down towards the Danube. You can find whatever life you choose in the Vienna Woods, someone had once told him. It was part forest, part hunting grounds, part leisure area and part vineyards, and it was where Rolf could be alone and at peace. Despite having been brought up in the country – or possibly because of it – Frieda had little interest in Vienna Woods. She'd become such a city girl that she was happy to remain in its confines for ever and regarded Rolf's love for the woods as quirky behaviour.

Rolf came to know the area intimately: he'd rarely stay on the paths and found places he could go where he wouldn't see another soul for hours. In the summer months he'd sometimes camped out overnight. In winter he preferred the vineyards and he'd discovered small huts secreted among them where the workers kept their tools and rested during the harvest.

So it was to the Vienna Woods he'd fled that Wednesday morning, after Franzi had told him about Frieda. He'd waited until she was upstairs then slipped into the kitchen, where he'd taken a large sausage, some cheese and bread, and stuffed them into his bag. He'd then taken a tram to Grinzing, the small wine-producing town to the north west of Vienna that was always the starting point for his visits to the woods. From there, he'd caught a bus deeper into the forest. When it had dropped him off, he'd walked for many hours, until it was dark. He walked on instinct, heading towards a vineyard he remembered well where there was a hut hidden on its edge. When he'd arrived he was exhausted and covered in mud, but relieved the hut was as he remembered it: firmly built and dry, with a bench to sleep on and blankets in a box underneath it.

And that was where he remained. Deeper into the forest was a small stream where he could get fresh water and wash, and there were mushrooms in the woods he knew were safe to eat. There were bushes with a strange winter berry he remembered was edible, though it was quite sour. He spent most of his time sitting in the hut, though, looking out through its small window at the vineyards rolling down before him towards the Danube, with Vienna in the distance. At night, he'd watch the bombers fly in from the south – then the city would light up. The thick beams of the searchlights would pierce the sky and occasionally pick out the planes, then would come the sound of the bombs and the flash of explosions when they landed. The oil refineries and depots were often targeted, he could tell that from the ferocity of the fires. The factories of north east Vienna also seemed to be bearing the burden of the raids. He watched all this with an air of detachment, as if it was an entertainment laid on for him. And for many days he did little more than just look: he couldn't remember one thought he had during that time. It was as if he was clearing his mind of all emotions. He slept soundly at night once the air raids were over, despite the bitter cold. By what must have been the Sunday he began to think more clearly. It was then he recalled what Franzi had said to him that night, after she'd told him Frieda had been killed.

'Rolf,' she'd said. 'More than anything else she regretted you and she parted as you did. She told me you argued the night before you left for Switzerland, and that it was her fault. Yes, she wanted you to stay but she bitterly regretted not going with you. She was determined to join you in Switzerland, but it was too late. She loved you more than anything else, but you know that, don't you?'

Until Franzi had said that, he hadn't known it. Frieda had certainly never said it to him, it wasn't her way – despite their engagement. At times it was clear she was fond of him, but he'd always thought that was as far as it went. He was younger than her, not her intellectual equal, certainly not as politically committed, and sometimes he'd wondered if he was an amusement to her as much as anything else. He knew he was good-looking and had an easy-going charm, but he'd always worried she'd never seen him as more than that.

But on the Sunday in the vineyard high in the Vienna Hills, once his mind had become as clear as the air around him, he was able to take in what Franzi had said. *She loved you more than anything else...*

And, once he'd really understood that and believed it, he felt at peace. A calmness he'd never before experienced spread over him. Franzi had appeared before him with a message from Frieda and that had allowed him to live again.

***

But in the apartment on Ungargasse, Rolf simply told Katharina he was so shocked at the news of Frieda's death that he'd had wandered off into the country, where he hoped he'd find the privacy to absorb the news. He assured her he'd now come to terms with it. They continued to sit together on the sofa, now very close and each holding the other's hand. At one stage Rolf leaned forward, his head in his hands and Katharina instinctively caressed his neck. Her thumb moved up and down firmly, her fingers gently spreading out and rubbing him. It was the most extraordinary sensation for Rolf: a sense of relaxation and wellbeing spread throughout his body. And, as she continued, the feeling became quite erotic. No further words were spoken. They stood up, still holding hands, and one led the other into the bedroom.

Chapter 22

Vienna, January and February 1945

January 1945 came in the middle of a bitter Viennese winter, and the winds blowing east across the Danube and down the Alps from the north seemed to compete to see which could hurt the city most. There was such a shortage of fuel it was rare for the civilian population to be allowed any. That would be a waste of a precious commodity when it could be better put towards the war effort. As a result, the city was wrapped in an inescapable chill.

But for Viktor the third week of January brought a spring-like sense of hope and optimism after two dark months. Following the capture and death of young Hans in November, he'd brought the activities of the Hades group to a halt. At first this had been because of the strong possibility that Hans might have revealed details about the cell. But even when it was clear danger had passed, Viktor decided he should no longer risk the small group on leafleting and sabotage. His priority was to prepare for a communist takeover in the city and to find Hubert Leitner.

The sense of optimism Viktor experienced in the middle of January was first brought about by the news he heard on Soviet radio. It was, of course, illegal to listen to foreign radio broadcasts and it was often hard to receive them, but Red Army radio had begun to transmit concise, one-minute bulletins that contained news of their progress. For some reason, the authorities were having trouble blocking these and for a few weeks they were surprisingly clear. The Hades group met occasionally in the

317

basement of Manfred Becker's mother's house to listen to the broadcasts, Viktor hunched over the radio set, his ear pressed against the speaker. On Monday 15th January, Lang and Becker watched a look of disbelief then delight creep over the Russian's normally impassive face as he listened to the latest broadcast.

'It's wonderful news,' he said when the broadcast had finished and they'd hidden the radio under a pile of sacks. 'Truly wonderful news. A major offensive began last week – German forces are being attacked throughout Poland and East Prussia. In Poland it is the 1st Ukrainian and the 1st Byelorussian Fronts.'

Viktor paused, the slightest flicker of emotion in his voice covered up by a cough. 'The 2nd and the 3rd Byelorussian Fronts are advancing through East Prussia.'

'What about further south – how long before they reach here?'

'Be patient, Joachim. They're still working their way through Hungary and Slovakia. But the Red Army massively outnumbers the Nazi forces, it's only a matter of time.'

Later that week Viktor had a further cause for optimism. Since he'd carried out the devastating sabotage at the Heinkel factory in November, Alois had been under strict instructions to lay low: he was to go to work, lead a normal life and do nothing that would arouse suspicion. But one lunchtime in the middle of January, Becker was walking across the factory complex from his office towards the canteen when he heard someone hiss. When he turned around it was Alois, standing inside a doorway and gesturing for him to join him. A few moments later Becker found himself behind a large machine in the gloom of an empty workshop with Alois. 'Are you crazy? I told you: do nothing and have no contact with me. If anyone catches us… Tell me, what's going on, have you come under suspicion?'

'No, you don't need to worry. I told you, I never came under suspicion for that hoist business. No, I've something interesting to tell you that I thought maybe your friend would like to hear.'

Alois began to recount a long story, resisting Becker's urging him to get to the point. 'A few weeks ago,' he said. 'We went to visit my wife's cousin and her family out in Liesing. Before lunch I went for a drink with her cousin's husband, Walter – a nice chap, rather boring, but decent enough. He's a schoolteacher, a few years younger than me. He collects coins and stamps, that kind of person. He was very concerned about conscription, poor chap. I know that before '38 he was on the left but always kept it quiet… His job, you understand.'

'I do understand, Alois, but, really, you must get to the point.'

'At the bar there was an acquaintance of his, someone he was at school with but hadn't seen for years. Anyway, he was a bit surprised this man, Otto, appeared to be… How can I put it…? Simple. You know what I mean… Like he didn't really function normally. Walter had a chat with him and he confided it was his way of avoiding being called up. I think this Otto may have drunk too much, to be honest, but then Walter had said something about how he was worried about conscription, so maybe Otto felt able to be more indiscreet than he should have been.

'Anyway, he then said something very interesting: he told Walter he was doing his bit to help and Walter asked him what he meant. He then clammed up, as if he realised he'd said more than he intended. So I bought them both a large schnapps and asked again what he meant. Otto eventually said he was helping protect Hubert Leitner. Walter asked him where, and he said "here in Vienna" and that was it. "Forget everything I told you," he said, then hurried out of the bar.'

Becker gasped. Lang had also heard rumours about Leitner being in Vienna and possibly in contact with the British, and he knew how much importance Viktor attached to this. 'Did you find out where this Otto lives?'

'No. When I walked back with Walter after the drink he said that was the kind of conversation we need to forget very quickly. I did try and push him a bit about Otto, but all Walter would say was that he believed Otto no longer lived in Liesing. He thought he lived with his mother on the other side of the city – that was how he put it – and that possibly his mother's a concierge, but it was all unclear. Walter can't even remember Otto's surname. I didn't push him; I didn't want him to suspect anything about me.'

'When was this, Alois?'

'Just before Christmas.'

'And you waited until now to tell me?'

'I thought it'd be safer to wait until I bumped into you.'

'I know, but this is important, very important,' said Becker. 'As soon as you can, you must find a pretext to go and see this Walter and get him to find out more about Otto – his surname, where he lives now... Whatever you can find out. You have to press him on this.'

Alois looked down. 'There's a problem,' he said. 'Walter was called up a week ago. Apparently he's somewhere in Poland now.'

To Becker's surprise, Viktor chose to receive the news about Leitner in a positive manner, despite the fact Alois had failed to find out any more. 'Sure,' he told Lang and Becker when they discussed it in their basement hideout. 'It would have been wonderful to have been given the address where Leitner's living, but in my world life's rarely as easy as that, and I'd be suspicious if it was. The important thing is we now have another source confirming he's alive and here in Vienna. We need to be alert and keep our eyes open – and we could also do with a slice of luck.'

***

The following week someone was alert, kept their eyes open and had that slice of luck.

Ernst Lang found himself on Schubertring on a desperate mission. So few customers visited his music shop in the 9th District these days he was worried he'd have to close. What little money people had went on food and fuel. Even in Vienna, music was now right down the list of priorities. His lowest point had come when a man bought a large box of old sheet music – second-hand and damaged copies – and, as he paid, told Lang he was going to use it for the fire.

So Herr Lang was in Schubertring to visit his bank, pleading for yet another loan and an extension on his previous one. 'When we've won the war and business improves, I'll flourish again!' He thought that may help him, but the manager who was reluctantly dealing with his request looked at him over the top of his spectacles, his eyebrows raised just far enough to indicate that if Herr Lang really believed that he was an even worse businessman than he thought.

Come back next week, I'll look into it, he'd been told. So Lang walked dejectedly along Schubertring, looking at the various banks and wondering if any of them would help him.

Which was when he saw him.

It was unquestionably Rolf, the young man who'd turned up at the shop back in May asking about Joachim – and who Viktor was so desperate to find. He was on the other side of the road, but crossing over to Lang's side. Lang stepped back into a shop doorway and pulled up his collar. The young man paused outside the entrance to Bank Leu, spoke to a woman who was coming out then walked in. Lang waited outside the bank: he'd follow Rolf when he came out. Viktor, he hoped, would be so pleased he'd reward him. *Who needs the banks when you've got the Soviet Union!*

But Rolf didn't come out, not for five minutes, not for 10 minutes, not for 15. Herr Lang pulled his trilby as far down over his eyes as he felt he could do without arousing suspicion and entered. Rolf wasn't among any of the customers in front of the counter but he could see him quite clearly at a desk beyond it.

There was a decided spring in his step as he headed back to Berg Gasse.

***

In Paris, Viktor had as many as 12 – and a similar number in Geneva. In Zürich, he could count on 10 and even in Berlin in the mid-30s he could muster nine or 10. In cities such as Marseilles, Brussels and Madrid he'd rely on a smaller number, more like seven or eight, and the one time he'd been in London, in 1936, he'd had six. In Moscow he once trained with 15, though that was too many. But the point about these team-members was that each one of them was experienced and trained. Following someone wasn't, he'd tell them, the hardest thing in the world, but following them for day after day and in a way so they'd no idea they were being followed – well, that was quite another thing. So was following someone as part of a team.

Early in his career, when he'd been based in Moscow and apparently happily married, Viktor would occasionally take his wife to the Bolshoi and found he was able to tolerate the performances by seeing them as exercises in espionage, though that did tend to be his approach to most things in life, which hadn't made for an ideal marriage. At the Bolshoi he'd watch in admiration as the dancers moved around the stage, avoiding each other when they needed to, finding their perfect positions – all as one fluid movement. That, he'd tell his teams, was how you follow someone: to know intuitively when to fall back; to take over as lead follower; to cross a road; to follow someone from in front of them.

But in Vienna in January 1945 he had none of that. He needed to keep Irma for another task and both Lang and Becker would have to be used sparingly: neither had been trained in the art. He refused to use Alois, who he still felt was a fool, which left just him. Often having just one very skilled follower was feasible, though the fact Rolf would know what he looked like was a serious problem: it'd mean he had to be very cautious.

So many people had been called up from the locomotive works that Viktor was working far longer hours. It wasn't unusual to work six 10-hour shifts a week and there were times when he was expected to give up that one day off 'for the cause of the Reich'. There was an especially unpopular shift that began at 8.00 in the evening and ended, if they were lucky, at 6.00 in the morning. Viktor volunteered for this, which allowed him the time to wait outside the bank at around 5.00 in the afternoon when it closed – when he expected Rolf to leave.

There was a technique Viktor taught his agents, which enabled one person to follow someone in a way that would minimise suspicion. It depended on being able track the person over a period of days or even weeks. It only worked if they followed a routine, but this was an ideal opportunity.

Viktor called it the relay, the principle being that if the prey left a certain place at the same time every day and always went in the same direction, you'd pick them up at a different point each day until eventually you'd find out where they were going to.

It took Viktor a week to track Rolf from Bank Leu to the apartment block on Ungargasse. On the first day he waited among the trees on the wide island that ran along the centre of the Schubertring. He just stayed there, not attempting to follow his prey, just observing: making sure there was no other tail on Rolf or whether he was taking any special precautions. He took time to light a cigarette and generally give the annoyed appearance of waiting for someone who was late. Nearby an old lady crouched down, picking up twigs and stuffing them into what had once been an elegant handbag.

Viktor decided he could only risk following Rolf every other day. On his next trip he followed Rolf as far as the bridge over the

Wiener Fluss in the Stadt-Park. When he returned two days later he was waiting near the bridge and Rolf arrived at the time he expected him. From there he followed him as far as Am Heumarkt. It took four sessions, over the period of a week, before he finally watched Rolf enter the apartment on Ungargasse. He returned there twice over the next five days to watch him enter it after work and only then was he sure he'd found where Rolf lived.

He noticed that when Rolf entered the apartment block he checked the mailboxes on the ground floor, so a couple of days later he risked placing himself closer to the entrance as Rolf came in and managed to spot the apartment number.

Viktor returned a few days later, on a wet Wednesday afternoon in the first week of February. Working night shifts with little sleep in between was taking its toll on him, along with the reduced rations and the freezing conditions he was living in, but he knew this was a lead he couldn't let slip.

In December he'd been working on the electrical supply into the locomotive works, along with some staff from the city's Electrical Supply Authority. During that operation he'd managed to remove one of their identity cards and this provided him with perfect cover.

He watched as Rolf left the block to walk to work, then followed an elderly lady into the apartment block as she opened the front door. He climbed to the top floor, where Rolf's apartment was located. There were just three apartments on that landing. He left Rolf's apartment until last. The other two were both empty, but the final one was opened by a woman in nurse's uniform.

Is there a problem with the electricity? There've been reports that some of the apartments were having issues...

No, she assured him, everything was fine.

Perhaps I could come in and check?

It's difficult at the moment, I'm about to go to work, she told him.

So I see! Which hospital are you at? The AKH... You do a wonderful job. Anyway, I see everything's fine, so you don't need to worry.

Two days later he returned and watched the woman leave the block in her nurse's uniform just after 2.00. He entered the block, again armed with his Vienna Electrical Supply Authority identity card. It only took him just a few seconds to pick the lock to the apartment. He removed his shoes and set to work, allowing himself half an hour to find out what he could. The apartment, he discovered, was rented by Gerd and Anna Schuster, but there was nothing he could find to indicate that either of them was working for the British or had any other identity, but he knew there must be something there. He continued to search, beyond the 30 minutes he'd permitted himself. He checked the small attic but found nothing: the apartment, he felt, was a bit too sparse and devoid of clues, rather as his would have been. It was approaching an hour when he found the money under the sink, cleverly wrapped in waterproof cloth and hidden in a hollowed-out space behind the tiles.

Thousands of Reichsmarks: the amount and the fact they were hidden was proof enough they were up to something. He carefully replaced the cash, suspecting there'd be other clues in the apartment, but he'd been there too long.

He'd found enough.

Chapter 23

Vienna, Slovakia and Hungary, February and March 1945

There were occasions during that February and March when, for the first time in a long career, Viktor had to contemplate failure. The locomotive works had ground to a halt as a result of Allied bombing, and one especially heavy air raid in the middle of the month had blown to pieces a workshop that Viktor had been in just an hour before, killing everyone inside.

For a couple of days, he hung around with the other electricians in the rubble of a storeroom, unsure of what they were meant to do in a factory with no electricity supply. The Germans had a ready solution: their main barracks in Vienna, the Maria Theresien Kaserne in the 13th District, was experiencing daily power blackouts and an urgent instruction had gone out for a team of experienced electricians to be based there as the 6th SS Panzer Army had moved in and insisted on there being an uninterrupted electricity supply.

Not only was Viktor now working at the main German garrison in Vienna but he was also living close to it. He and three other electricians shared a two-bedroom apartment the army had requisitioned in Hietzing, just around the corner from the barracks. Although this meant he could move out of the filthy and freezing room in the boarding house in Floridsdorf, it was hardly the ideal place for one of the top Soviet agents in Nazi-occupied Europe to be living.

But he was able to get away from the barracks for a few hours each day. He did what he could to tail Rolf, hoping that somehow he'd lead him to where Leitner was hiding. But, despite his very best efforts, he couldn't get near him. He allowed himself various explanations. There was always the possibility that, despite what Lang and Alois had heard, Leitner wasn't in the city and Rolf had nothing to do with him. As much as that was a possibility, it was one Viktor couldn't allow himself to entertain. There were other possibilities: that he was losing his touch; that Rolf and the woman were particularly skilled or were very lucky.

If forced, he'd have guessed at a combination of the last three. On the occasions when Viktor was able to follow them, Rolf would leave the bank and head back to Ungargasse, occasionally stopping at a bar; the woman would go either to the hospital or to the local shops.

One Saturday, at the end of February, he arrived at Ungargasse just as they were both leaving. Arm in arm they strolled across the city, into the Prater then through the park. Viktor knew he was pushing his luck by following the pair for so long on his own, but it was the first time he'd managed to follow them together and his instincts were alerted by their behaviour: too many changes of directions, going back on themselves – the kind of techniques someone would use to throw off a tail.

So he carried on, until there was a quick but tender kiss and the couple separated. Had they headed in opposite directions there may have been some logic to it, but as far as he could tell, they were both heading north. He decided to stick with Rolf and followed him through Leopoldstadt, towards the Augarten Park.

It was then Viktor committed a basic error – one for which he'd have unhesitatingly sacked one of his own agents. He always instructed his agents that, when crossing a road, the follower should allow the prey to complete their crossing to the other side before beginning to cross themselves. If they didn't follow this rule there was a danger the follower could get too close to the prey or be caught out by them doubling back. Whether it was exhaustion, whether he was losing his touch or whether Rolf was being especially smart, Viktor didn't know. But when he was halfway across a busy road, Rolf hopped on to a traffic island and stood there. Unaccountably, Viktor had already begun to cross. By the time he realised he was about to stand next to Rolf it was too late: an army lorry hooted him and he couldn't turn back. Viktor knew he had to abandon the pursuit. He hurried across the road, weaving between a motorbike and a tram then turned left, walking as quickly as he could without arousing suspicion and not once glancing back.

That evening he had plenty of time to replay in his head what had happened. He was certain Rolf and the woman were heading somewhere they didn't want to be followed to. Whether Rolf had deliberately stopped suddenly on the traffic island, he didn't know. He hoped that the fact he'd gone straight across and carried on would mean Rolf suspected nothing.

But his mind was now made up. He needed help.

***

The next day Viktor went to Irma's apartment, the first time he'd done so for weeks. In the square below he paused just long enough to check the tall porcelain vase was in its place on the window ledge then went in. She wasn't expecting him and looked shocked when he arrived, but he said nothing. He pushed past her and went straight into the lounge, still wearing his heavy coat and his work boots. He loosened his black silk scarf and slumped into an armchair. He could feel himself fighting sleep. She went into the kitchen and returned with a large piece of cake on a china plate.

'I only have a few minutes,' he said, crumbs spraying out of his mouth and onto the front of his coat as he spoke.

'You look dreadful. What on earth have you been up to?'

'I wouldn't know where to begin. I need a drink,' he wiped his mouth with the black silk scarf.

Irma went to the sideboard and fussed around with various bottles. 'Would you like this Armagnac? He brought it back from France, apparently it's very good.' She poured him a large measure and sat down. 'You look like you've lost weight.'

'I've been doing a lot of walking. Look, I have to be back at work soon, so listen carefully.' He explained what he wanted her to do.

'How do you know they'll be there?'

'They're bound to be,' he said. 'Vienna is desperate for coal. If not today, then tomorrow: from what I understand they're making the journey three or four times a week at the moment, maybe more. Go there this afternoon. If he's not there, go back tomorrow. There'll be nothing in writing, just memorise what I tell you.'

'What if he refuses?'

Viktor snorted and held out his glass for a refill. 'He won't refuse, not now the Red Army's closing in. Staying alive concentrates the mind; I find it's a better incentive than money.'

Irma paused and sat quietly for a while. 'And what about me?'

Viktor raised his eyebrows, suggesting he wasn't sure what she meant.

'I mean, if the Red Army gets here. What happens to me?'

There was another pause, this one longer as Viktor thought about the question. 'Don't worry, I'll sort something.' He looked around the room and pointed at a framed photograph on the sideboard of her husband in uniform. 'Get rid of that for a start.'

Viktor stayed longer than he'd planned. The Armagnac had revitalised him so they went into the bedroom for half an hour. Irma left the apartment soon after the Russian. She went straight to the docks around Seitenhafenstrasse and bribed the same sentry with a couple of packets of Junos she'd bought on the way there.

'Is the *Jelka* in port, from Bratislava?'

He studied a list on his clipboard. 'It should be here this time tomorrow afternoon. That's a nice watch you have.'

Irma fingered the gold watch on her wrist. It had been her mother's. 'If you let me in tomorrow then it's yours on the way out.'

The following afternoon she found herself once again in the engine room of the *Jelka*. Ján Kuchár had listened carefully to her message and she asked him to repeat it. She had to lean close to hear his voice above the noise of the engines. She could feel his hot breath and smell his unwashed body as he spoke.

'Yes, yes, yes... I understand: I'm to get a message to a Political Commissar in the first Red Army unit we can find. They're to contact Department 23 in Moscow, unit six – you assure me they'll understand what that means – and tell them the blacksmith urgently needs a meeting with the cobbler. I'm to wait for the reply and I'm to deliver it to you as soon as possible: you'll be back here in four days. Sounds straightforward to me!' The big Slovak laughed sarcastically.

'What do you mean?'

'Well, assuming they don't kill this messenger like they did the last one.'

***

Irma returned to the port four days later, as arranged. Kuchár was on the quayside by the *Jelka* and pointed for her to go aboard, taking her into a cramped cabin rather than the engine room. He gestured for her to sit on the bed and she hesitated, but he remained standing against the door.

'Did you deliver the message?'

'Yes,' he replied. 'And nearly got myself killed in the process.'

'What do you mean?'

'I tell you what,' he said. 'When the Red Army is at gates of Vienna, which shouldn't be too long now, you stroll up to them and tell them you have a message for Moscow. You'll be lucky if they don't shoot you first. Fortunately I speak enough Russian to tell them I'm a comrade. The commissar wasn't sure what to make of it all and he looked like he wanted to shoot me too, but his tune soon changed when the message came back from Moscow: I was treated like a prince for the first time in my life, I could get used

to it. Your man must be very important.'
'What was their reply?'
'They want to see him, in Komárom.'
'Where's that?'
'Hungary.'
'And how's he meant to get there?'
'Looks like I'm taking him.'
'When?'
'Tonight.'

***

'I'll get shot for this,' Viktor said. 'I'm not sure which side will shoot me, but it'll be a miracle if I make it back alive.' They were in Irma's apartment and she was telling him he had to go straight to the barge.

'They'll take you to Bratislava,' she said. 'After that it may be a bit tricky, but he'll be your guide. You need to hurry though; do you need anything?'

'When work finds I've disappeared there'll be hell to pay. Look, I have an idea…'

That night Viktor managed to slip undetected into the port and board the *Jelka*. He'd brought with him most of the remaining Reichsmarks he'd stashed at Irma's apartment to buy the silence of the crew and pay for his voyage.

The next morning Irma did as Viktor had instructed. Fortunately there had been some air raids the previous night, but then it was an unusual night in Vienna if there were none. She dressed smartly and took a tram to the 9th District. In a street approaching the hospital she bought an overpriced bunch of nearly dead flowers then entered the AKH.

She was shocked by what she saw. Over the years she'd visited the hospital on a number of occasions and it had the reputation of being one of the finest hospitals in Europe, as well as one of the largest. Now it was overcrowded: there were patients left on stretchers in the corridors and dried blood and dirty bandages on the floor. She made her way to a ward on the fifth floor that seemed to be especially busy. She removed a handkerchief from her smart handbag and dabbed at her moist eyes, looking distressed.

'Are you alright… is there anything I can to do help?' asked a harassed-looking young nurse.

'I'm so sorry,' said Irma 'I can see how busy you are. I came to visit a very close friend who was injured in an air raid last week and I've just been told she died…' Irma paused, struggling to regain her composure. She was speaking in the most refined Viennese accent she could muster. 'I need to let her husband Salzburg know and I was wondering if perhaps I could use a private telephone?'

The nurse glanced around and nodded, pointing at an office behind her.

'Quick, though, if the sister sees you…'

Once in the office Irma closed the door and lifted the handset, getting connected immediately to the switchboard. Using an authoritative voice, she demanded to be connected to the Maria Theresien Kaserne barracks. She smiled as she heard the operator tell the operator at the other end it was the AKH. Could they please connect the call to the electrical workshop…? Yes, it was urgent.

Once she was connected, Irma asked to speak to Ernst, Otto Schneider's supervisor. *I'm a sister at the AKH. Unfortunately Herr Schneider was injured in an air raid last night and is likely to be away for a few days. Yes, of course she'd pass on his best wishes.*

***

They were barely an hour outside Vienna, heading east on the black mass of the Danube, when the skipper came down to the engine room and started shouting. Viktor knew enough Slovak to gather the skipper, on reflection, felt the money he'd received wasn't enough. Ján Kuchár called Viktor over: would he like to give some more?

Viktor stared at the skipper, a short, muscular man with the eyes of a bully and a nose damaged by drink and the occasional fight. 'No,' said Viktor. He was aware of the skipper bristling and Kuchár coughing.

'Tell me,' asked Viktor. 'How long do you think it'll be before the Red Army arrives in Bratislava?' The skipper shrugged and looked confused. He was unused to difficult questions. Viktor helped him out. 'A month, two months… Certainly before the summer, yes?'

The skipper nodded uncertainly and Viktor leaned close to him.

'And have you thought about what's going to happen to you and your precious barge when the Red Army finds you've been supplying the Nazis with coal, eh?'

The skipper muttered something about being forced to.

'If you shut up and behave then I'll put in a good word for you. You may even get to keep your barge.'

Kuchár and Viktor stayed in Bratislava just long enough to travel to another quay, to the boat Kuchár had arranged to take them to their destination. It was a tiny, battered vessel that looked as though it would have trouble staying afloat on a pond in a park on a windless day. The skipper was Vojtech, an elderly man with a handsome face. Kuchár assured him Vojtech was totally reliable: 'He's a good, old-fashioned red. He said it'd be an insult to offer him money.'

'I've no idea where the front line is today,' Vojtech announced as he eased the boat from the harbour into the centre of the Danube. Viktor was crouched between sacks of flour, the boat's putative cargo. 'It changes every day. I'll get you as close to it as I can.'

Viktor congratulated Kuchár on the choice of vessel: it looked and sounded so pathetic that he doubted anyone would stop it, but it performed deceptively well despite the choppy conditions. The Danube was now grey; Viktor had forgotten just how wide it was around Bratislava and, as they headed east, it became even wider, almost as if they were at sea. Kuchár told him he wasn't sure whether they were in Slovakia or Hungary. 'That's what it's going to be like from now on, the borders shift every day.'

The river began to narrow and on both banks of the river, they could see the German artillery in position. Ahead of them they could just make out the sound of gunfire. Just as a town came into

view, Vojtech swiftly turned to the south bank and expertly steered
the boat into a concealed inlet. Kuchár tied a rope to a tree while
Vojtech cut the engine and scrambled ashore, disappearing behind
a hedge. It was 20 minutes before he returned.

'We're in Hungary, at least it was two days ago,' he said. 'I'm
not going any further, I'll wait here until you return – but no more
than 24 hours, you understand? Over there, that's Gönyű. When I
last heard, the Germans had pulled out of the town but left a unit
of their Hungarian allies to hold it, part of the 3rd Army. The
Germans are probably happy to sacrifice them. Keep south of the
town and head east for about four miles, until you get to Komárom.'

'What'll we find there?'

'Your army.'

***

By the time they reached the outskirts of Komárom dusk had set
in. Kuchár suggested they hide in the woods until daybreak, but
Viktor insisted they keep going. They worked their way through
the trees, the noise of their progress masked by artillery fire and
the occasional sound of aircraft overhead. At the end of the treeline
a small grassy stretch dropped down to a lane, with ditches on
either side of it. The two men hurried down and hid in one. After
a while, a patrol of around a dozen men worked its way towards
them. Viktor watched them carefully then turned around to the
Slovak.

'They're Red Army.'

'Are you sure?'

'Of course I'm sure! They're NKVD Border regiment, I can see their green caps and shoulder boards – Beria's men. We must be further behind our lines than we thought; their job is to stop the front-line troops retreating. You wait here; one of us will look less threatening than two.' Viktor hauled his large frame out of the ditch; his hands raised high above his head.

'Comrades… Comrades! Don't be afraid, put down your guns: I've been serving the Red Army behind enemy lines! I'm here on an important mission.'

The patrol stopped when they heard his voice: some of the men dropped to the sides of the lane while an officer and the rest of his men edged forward. There was enough light for Viktor to make out the vapour of their breath hanging above them and PPS sub-machine guns pointing at him.

'Stop where you are,' the officer shouted. 'Very slowly, remove your shoes and your hat, then get down on your knees. My men will search you.' The officer muttered something and four of his men came forward. Two of them searched him while the other two kept their guns trained on him.

'He's fine sir, just this switchblade knife.'

The officer came forward. Viktor could see he was a three-star *Starshiy Leytenant*. 'What's your business?'

'I'm a senior officer in the NKVD; I need to see your most senior Commissar as a matter of urgency. If you tell him the blacksmith has come to see the cobbler he'll know all about it. Which army is it here?'

'The 3rd Ukrainian Front, Field Marshal Tolbukhin. Are you alone?'

'No, I have a Slovak comrade hiding there. Ján, come out slowly.'

An hour later they were sitting in the warmth of one of the few buildings in the centre of Komárom that was still standing. It had been taken over by the political commissars attached to the 3rd Ukrainian Front. The Slovak was being fed in the kitchen, a prince for the second time in his life. Meanwhile Viktor was upstairs in the office of the senior commissar, a Brigadier. 'We had a message... that you'd be coming,' said the Brigadier. 'You're to wait here until he arrives.'

'When will that be?'

'The morning. In the meantime, you can rest and eat. Would you like a woman?'

Viktor shook his head. The commissar looked puzzled at his refusal. 'Shame, these young Hungarian girls really are something special. You could even have two of them at the same time – have you ever tried that?'

┼○┼○┼

At 6.00 in the morning the door to Viktor's bedroom flew open and Ilia Brodsky burst in. He strode over to the window, opened the shutters and threw Viktor's clothes at him. 'Get up, we need to talk.'

An hour later Viktor had finished talking. They'd taken over the senior commissar's office and Brodsky was helping himself to a bottle of vodka he'd found on the desk. Viktor kept refusing his offer of some. Brodsky didn't look as fit or as assured as he had a year previously. He'd been fidgeting nervously as Viktor spoke, constantly running his fingers through his hair. The fact he was still trusted by Stalin was remarkable.

'I agree with you, Viktor, it sounds as if Leitner's in Vienna,' he said eventually. 'I've always thought that if he'd been killed or captured, we'd have heard about it. We've got rid of half the KPO Central Committee, but the others are always going on about Leitner: they say that if we can ensure he's on our side then we'll control Austria. If the British have him, then Austria will be theirs. You have to find him, Viktor.'

'You know me, comrade, I never fail. But this British agent is clever. If I had a few experienced agents with me, even half a dozen, I'm sure I'd track him down. But on my own… it's proving impossible.'

'Tell me again about Rolf and the woman.'

When Viktor had finished, Brodsky helped himself to a cigar from a box on the commissar's desk and walked around the room puffing on it, deep in thought, before joining Viktor on a small leather sofa. 'I've thought of a way of getting this British spy to take us to Leitner,' he said. 'Listen carefully.'

Viktor had a lifetime of subterfuge behind him and he'd readily admit he'd often been cruel and perfectly willing to resort to extreme methods if necessary. But by the time Ilia Brodsky – the rabbi's grandson – had outlined his plan, even he was shocked.

Chapter 24

Vienna, March and April 1945

By the middle of March Vienna had begun to disintegrate. Although bombing raids day and night were taking a physical toll, the disintegration manifested itself more in the atmosphere in the city and the mood of its inhabitants. The presence of the 6th SS Panzer Army created a sense of menace rather than reassurance and few other than the most ardent Nazis believed the propaganda that everything was going to be fine and the Reich would triumph. People knew the Red Army was heading towards Vienna from the east, and the British and the Americans were battling their way into Austria from all other directions. There was a tangible sense of fear, and the shortage of food and fuel meant the civilian population was now experiencing serious deprivation. The rumours about what the conquering Red Army had got up to in previously conquered cities terrified the supposedly cultured Viennese. In private and with those whom they trusted, people confided that perhaps their enthusiasm for the Nazis had been misplaced. People tried to convince each other they were victims of Nazism rather than enthusiastic proponents of it. They'd begun to quietly concoct their own version of history.

Both Rolf and Katharina were well aware of all this; their colleagues at the bank and the hospital spoke of little else in their hushed tones. But for the couple there were other priorities.

You'll need to start thinking about moving Leitner out of Vienna, London told them in the messages sent through Zürich. *The*

Russians will be there soon. Come up with a plan to head west.

Which was all very well, Rolf had replied, but when do we do this?

Wait: we'll tell you when. We need the Americans to get a bit closer.

They continued to visit Leitner once a week and told him what London had in mind. Leitner wanted to know why he couldn't remain in the safety of the cellar until the allies arrived, but they had to explain to him that it looked like the wrong kind of allies were going to be arriving first.

'I'm an old man,' he told them when they said they were going to head west. 'I've been stuck in this damn cellar for God knows how long. I'm not fit. I haven't seen sunlight for too long, I'll probably go blind. What are you going to do, steal a car?'

This conversation happened on a visit when Rolf and Katharina had gone down to the cellar together, such was the importance of the meeting.

'We're not sure, we're working something out,' said Rolf. 'Do you have any ideas, Herr Leitner?'

The old man looked at them incredulously, his arms folded tightly across his chest. 'Do I have any ideas – me? I don't remember what the world looks like any more and you want me to come up with a plan to escape from Vienna? No, that's your job and, I warn you, if you don't come up with a good plan, I'm not going: I'll take my chances with the Russians.'

So they came up with a plan, which they talked through and through, and both admitted was a good one. The idea for it came one night when Katharina was on duty in the casualty receiving area, which was a large space on the ground floor of the hospital.

The ambulances would arrive outside and be directed to different bays. And there was also an area where the ambulance drivers rested, some for a few hours at a time as most of them were working around the clock. Occasionally, when an ambulance needed to be moved and the driver was asleep, a nurse would drive it rather than disturb them.

'So we steal an ambulance?'

They were in the Prater, the safest place for them to talk. Katharina sounded excited. 'That's right! Didn't you say the simplest idea could be the best one?'

'Yes… But stealing an ambulance isn't simple.'

'Let me go through it again,' she said. 'On the night we decide to go ahead with it, you're to come to a side street near the hospital. At an agreed time, I take an ambulance, pretending I'm moving it to another part of the casualty receiving area. When I take the keys, I'll also grab a uniform for you – they usually leave dirty ones on the floor. I drive out, meet you, you drive and I sit next to you. What could look less suspicious? We then drive to Obere Augartenstrasse, collect Leitner as our patient and drive out of Vienna. I'll bandage his head so, if we're stopped, no one will be able to see his face. Oh, and one other thing I meant to mention: the other day an old man died in casualty after an air raid. I took his identity card and wallet. Leitner can have them.'

Rolf said nothing as they walked along, trying to think of flaws. 'And if we're stopped?'

'I'll create a file for him at the AKH, including a letter saying he's being transferred to somewhere in the west, like Innsbruck.'

Rolf clasped her hand, raised it to his lips and kissed it gently, then stroked his cheek with it. 'Darling, it's a clever idea, but surely an alert will go out – if an ambulance is missing?'

'Maybe, but I doubt it. Vienna's in chaos. There are armies approaching from every direction. Even at the AKH, the situation's so confused that no one knows where the ambulances are at any given time. Would they really be that concerned about one ambulance? But if you have a better idea…'

Rolf didn't have a better idea. That weekend they both went to see Leitner and explained it to him. The old man sat with a long face for a while but eventually gave a grudging nod of approval. They'd brought with them the dead man's wallet and identity card, and also decided to keep one of the Steyr-Hahns pistols and some of their cash with Leitner – it would mean they'd be there when they went to collect him, rather than having to carry them around Vienna.

The following day Rolf sent a message to London through Hedinger: we have a plan, when should we go?

Wait: we said we'll tell you when. The Russians aren't that near Vienna and the Americans aren't far enough east yet. Be patient.

It reminded Rolf of his weapons training in England. 'Always wait until you think it's too late before you fire,' the instructor had told him. 'Get the target in your sights and wait, sir: the closer they get the more chance you've got… The target can never be too close, sir, but it can be too far.'

So they waited.

And then Rolf had a visitor.

***

It was the last week in March and, like all the other banks on Schubertring and elsewhere in Vienna, Bank Leu was especially busy. Though customers didn't say so in as many words, the last place they wanted to keep their money was in the first place the Soviets would go looking for it. Rolf was inundated with transfers to Zürich: one of the many rumours swirling around the city was that the authorities were about to prohibit all money being sent abroad.

It was around 10.30 on the Wednesday morning when one of the receptionists appeared at his desk. 'A gentleman would like to see you in private,' she said. 'Here's his card.'

August Otto Unger

Rolf stared at it, as if doing so would make the name disappear. August Unger, his former schoolmate he'd seen at the law firm the previous May. Then he'd been convinced he was about to report him to the Gestapo. Unger obviously didn't like to rush.

A minute later the two men sat opposite each other in the small interview room. Unger was sweating profusely and looked nervous. Rolf did his best to appear calm but could feel his knees knocking against each other.

'I suspected it was you, Rolf, as soon as I saw you,' said Unger. 'You look a little different, I'm not sure why, but I was convinced it was you. Tell me, why do you call yourself Gerd Schuster, eh?'

Rolf was too terrified to say anything, hoping the silence would force Unger to reveal his hand. He shrugged his shoulders. 'I don't know what you're talking about. I *am* Gerd Schuster, an employee of...'

'Cut it out, Rolf, your voice is the same and you still have that smug, pretty face and that irritating look of innocence about you. I bet you're still a red aren't you...? What are you doing here – helping them and the fucking Jews, if you can find any left, that is?'

'You're mistaken...'

'Come on, come on... They'll have a file on you here, won't they – the Gestapo? They'll have all your details, maybe even your fingerprints, certainly a photograph. How long will it take them to establish that Gerd Schuster is in fact Rolf Eder...? Half an hour? Of course, if you really are Gerd Schuster, the Gestapo will understand there's been a mistake and I'll apologise, but I bet you don't want to put that to the test, do you? Then there's your girlfriend, what was her name – Frieda? Last I heard, she was entertaining the troops at Morzinplatz.'

Unger reached below the table to tie his shoelaces, peering up at Rolf with a lascivious grin. Rolf would have happily strangled Unger there and then, but he needed to stay calm.

'What do you want Unger?'

'That's better,' said Unger. 'I was going to turn you in to the authorities when I saw you last year. But you know how clever I am. I said to myself, hang on August... Rolf works for a bank, who knows when that could be of some use? So I was patient and now you can indeed help me. I want Swiss Francs, Rolf, lots of them. And the exchange rate is that I don't turn you in to the Gestapo. Seems like a brilliant deal to me.'

'It'll take me a few days, we have so much demand...'

'We don't have long, though, do we, Rolf? I'm sure you're

looking forward to it, but I don't plan to be in Vienna when your army of fucking barbarians, robbers and rapists rolls into town. I plan to be far away – and where I'm going, your Swiss Francs will be just what I need. How long before you can get hold of 10,000?'

'Ten thousand – are you mad? I won't be able to lay my hands on anything like that.'

Unger shifted uneasily in his chair. *Nine thousand – by Friday?* They negotiated for 10 minutes, like the bickering schoolboys they used to be. Eventually they settled on 5,000 Swiss Francs, by Monday.

'We're expecting a consignment in on Saturday from a special courier,' said Rolf, hoping Unger's greed would prevent him seeing through the lie. 'Come in this time on Monday and I'll have it for you. And after that, nothing – you promise?'

'Of course, Rolf, my old friend. Don't you trust me?'

***

'But if you do manage to get that money, he'll pocket it and go straight to the Gestapo,' said Katharina. They were lying in bed, a shaft of moonlight turning their bare flesh a shade of grey-blue. Katharina stroked the nape of Rolf's neck then rested her head on his naked shoulder.

'I know, I know,' he said. 'But it's all hypothetical anyway. The bank is clean out of Swiss Francs. Maybe Plaschke has a few but...'

'We need to get away from Vienna before Monday,' said Katharina.

'Obviously.'

'That's the 2nd April, isn't it?'

'Yes.'

'Damn… My next night shift isn't until that night, so we can't escape before then. Could you delay him until the Tuesday, maybe get a message to him? Tell him you can get the money on Tuesday?'

'It's too much of a risk. He wanted the money by Friday as it is.'

Half an hour later, just as she was just dozing off, Katharina was woken by Rolf leaping out of bed.

'What is it?'

'Those photographs – the ones from the strongbox…'

'What about them?'

'I need to look at them. Quick, make sure the curtains are properly closed.'

They heaved the bed to one side, lifted the carpet under it and prised up a floorboard. Rolf lay naked on the floor and stretched his arm through the small gap, emerging with a large brown envelope. They placed the bedside lamp on the floor and opened the envelope.

'What is it Rolf? Why on earth do you want to look at these disgusting photographs now?'

He ignored her, frantically leafing through the dozens of black-and-white images of men in compromising positions, mostly with girls but a few with boys. Some of the photographs were blurred, but most were surprisingly clear. Eventually he pulled one out.

'Here! I was right… You remember when we got these and we were looking through them? Well, a few minutes ago something jogged my memory. Look...'

It was a photograph taken from high up in a room, possibly from up on the ceiling. The image showed a large bed and on it a young girl, probably no more than 14, was lying on her back, a look of terror on her face. Straddling her was a naked man, his head tossed back and face looking up, contorted with effort. But still he wore a lascivious grin.

'This,' said Rolf, tapping the man's face, 'is August Otto Unger.'

***

The Vienna Offensive began that Monday, the 2nd April. The 3rd Ukrainian Front crossed the Slovakian border and the Danube south of Vienna, and quickly took the towns of Eisenstadt, Wiener Neustadt and Neunkirchen.

Though the battle was still some way south of the city it was heading inexorably towards it, and that morning the atmosphere in Vienna took on a new dimension. With the wind blowing in the right direction there was the smell of cordite in the air and the sound of artillery fire. Planes flew low overhead, mostly Luftwaffe heading for the Red Army but also Soviet planes bombing the city's defences. As he hurried to work, Rolf saw something very close to panic all around him. Lorries were dumping sandbags in the street and when he arrived at the bank he spent the first hour helping colleagues pile up the bags and cover the windows. Herr Plaschke was fussing around inside, insisting to his staff it was business as usual, that this was all just temporary while the Wehrmacht...

Rolf was glad they'd arranged to escape that night. Though the city defences were formidable, the Red Army could well be in Vienna within the week. He was almost looking forward to his meeting with Unger.

When he arrived at the bank, August Unger appeared to be both nervous and excited. 'You have the money?' He spoke even before Rolf had closed the door to the small office. 'I'm leaving tonight. I've enough fuel in my car to get well away from here. You've got all of it – all 5,000 Swiss Francs?'

Rolf had brought a number of bulging envelopes in with him, all sealed. He tapped the envelopes and Unger stared greedily at them like a child eyeing packets of sweets. 'There's some paperwork first, August,' he said.

'Don't be ridiculous, Rolf: just give me the fucking money and be thankful I'm leaving Vienna rather than going to the Gestapo. What's that? What the...?'

Rolf had removed the photograph from his pocket and turned it around to face Unger. The other man stared at it in disbelief, his mouth open and his face turning a bright red. For a second or two Rolf wondered whether Unger had stopped breathing altogether.

'What...? What...?' was all he could manage to say.

'Are you asking what this is?' said Rolf innocently. 'It's a surprisingly clear photograph taken of you in a brothel, which we understand is in Schulerstrasse, near the cathedral. We don't know the girl's name, but how old would you say she is, Unger? Thirteen...? Fourteen...? And just in case you have any ideas, there are other copies.'

Unger gaped at him.

'You're not getting any money, Unger,' said Rolf. 'But perhaps when you go to the Gestapo to inform on me, you'll be good enough to show them this – or should we wait until the Red Army arrives, eh?'

As Rolf spoke, Unger stood up, and hurriedly gathered his coat and hat, knocking over his chair in the process. And, without even pausing to put them on, fled the bank.

Chapter 25

Vienna, April 1945

Early on the morning of Monday 2nd April, Viktor was woken by one of his fellow electricians violently shaking his shoulder. Kiril was Bulgarian, but his German was poor and Viktor had to make a concerted effort to avoid speaking to him in Russian, a close sister language to Bulgarian. 'It's started Otto... listen!'

It was the unmistakable sound of artillery – a continuous, metallic, crump-like noise. As far as he could tell, it was both incoming and outgoing, and sounded as if it was to the south, which was where Brodsky had warned the attack would start. *We'll be throwing the lot at them, Viktor, don't worry: we'll have Vienna within the week; we're deploying Malinovsky's 2nd Ukrainian Front, Tolbukhin's 3rd and the 1st Bulgarian Army under Stoychev. The day it starts, that's your signal. You know what you've got to do?*

Viktor understood full well what he had to do and, though he was dreading it more than anything else he'd done before, he knew he couldn't afford to hesitate. He was due to start work at the barracks at 8.00 and he needed to be away before then. He changed into his work clothes and packed what he needed into his knapsack, telling Kiril he'd see him at the barracks.

He hurried down to Irma's apartment: the vase was in place and she was expecting him. Viktor found it hard to disguise his nervousness, which Irma wasn't used to seeing. 'Let's go through everything. You're sure she's still there?'

Irma nodded. 'There's no chance they could have found the

leaflets?' she asked.

'It's possible,' said Viktor, 'but highly unlikely. I knew they were both at work when I got in so I had enough time to do a good job. They're sealed under the sink. You'd have to know they're there to find them.'

' And they'll know...?'

'...That they're there? Yes, yes, yes... Come on, let's concentrate on this morning. I'll make the call from that café off Schubertring at 11.00. You wait outside. As soon as I've done it, I'll come out and give you the signal. You wait 40 minutes then deliver the letter: that ought to give them enough time.'

'And you?'

'I'll take up position to follow him. Once he reads the letter he won't hang around, I promise you: he'll do what Brodsky said he'd do. Why are you crying Irma?'

'Because I know what'll happen after that. You follow him and – whatever happens – you won't come back.'

Viktor put his hand on her shoulder then pulled her close to him. 'Who knows...? Who knows what'll happen?'

***

Rolf just managed to get to the toilet before he threw up. He leaned against the damp tiled wall and did his best to compose himself before once more reading the note that had been waiting for him when he'd returned to his desk after Unger had fled the bank.

To Gerd Schuster (Rolf Eder) from a friend,
By the time you read this letter, Anna will be in the custody of
the Gestapo. They don't know about you yet but will do very
soon. This is a warning for you to get away.

With violently trembling hands he tore up the letter and tried to throw the shreds of it into the toilet bowl. Who on earth knew his real name was Rolf Eder? That alone indicated the letter was to be taken seriously. He'd have to go and check on Katharina, but...

He threw up once more and felt a cold sweat break out all over his body. The receptionist had told him a smartly dressed lady had left the letter for him while he was in his meeting. That was all she could tell him.

***

Viktor's telephone call hadn't lasted long. When he'd got through to Gestapo headquarters, he'd insisted on being connected to Kriminaldirektor Karl Strobel.

Immediately? Don't you know what's going on?

'I want you to listen very carefully,' he told Strobel. 'You have a pen and paper? Take down this address.' He proceeded to give the address of the Schuster's apartment on Ungargasse then slowly repeated it. He was looking carefully at his watch: he'd allow no more than 40 seconds for this call, just short of the 55 they'd need to trace it.

'The woman who lives at this apartment is a member of the communist resistance cell that carried out the sabotage at the

Heinkel factory and has been distributing leaflets throughout the city. You'll find some of the leaflets under the sink. There's also money hidden in the wall, behind a tile under the sink.'

Strobel started to ask who he was, but Viktor spoke over him, repeating the address once more before putting down the receiver. He leaned against the wall of the telephone booth and closed his eyes. He felt ashamed and realised why there was such an enormous difference at being very good and very clever like he was, and being like Ilia Brodsky: clever enough to have the ear of Stalin.

***

Viktor was waiting opposite the bank, beneath the trees at the centre of Schubertring, when Rolf dashed out. It didn't surprise him he headed in the direction of his apartment, he fully expected him to do that – *so long as he doesn't do anything rash*. The Russian had to move faster than he was comfortable with, but Rolf was almost running. Halfway down Ungargasse, Rolf stopped dead in his tracks. The apartment block was now in view: in front of it stood a police van and two cars clearly belonging to the Gestapo. A few men in plain clothes were hanging around the front of the block and a police officer was moving people away. Another man in plain clothes came out of the building carrying a large box and was followed by two more dragging Katharina into the back of one of the waiting cars. Rolf would know now to take the note seriously if he hadn't before.

Viktor watched in horror as Rolf stayed where he was, not moving from the middle of the pavement and seemingly in shock.

If you don't move, you fool, they'll see you. Viktor edged into the doorway of a shop, worried he too could be spotted. But, just when it appeared he'd left it too late, Rolf spun around and moved back up Ungargasse, in the direction he'd come from. He looked back nervously a couple of times then seemed to compose himself, settling into a normal stride as he headed towards the canal. *That's it, Rolf,* thought Viktor as he fell in behind his prey. *Considering the circumstances, you're good. Now, do what Brodsky promised me you'd do.*

***

Katharina had been sorting out the few things she'd be able to take with her when they left Vienna that evening – as much as she could get away with in the large handbag she'd take into work with her. Laid out on the bed were a few toiletries, a change of underwear, a pullover, some cheese and the Steyr-Hahns pistol. She'd have liked to take another pair of shoes but she was already pushing it.

That was when they burst in – no knock, no warning, nothing. An almighty crash at the door, like an explosion from an artillery shell and, before she could react, there were two men in the hall pointing guns at her. She looked at her own pistol on the bed but, before she could reach for it, they'd rushed at her, forcing her to the floor. She was dragged into the lounge and pinned face down on the sofa. She tried to cry out but was silenced by a vicious kick to the ribs.

No one spoke to her as she was held down. She could hear

them searching the apartment. They found the pistol straight away and from the kitchen she heard someone say they'd found 'them' – whatever 'them' was. 'And the money?' someone asked. Some knocking and banging, then another person announced they'd found that too. Not much, they reported, but it was there. 'Like they said it'd be.'

***

In the lower basement of the Gestapo headquarters in Morzinplatz there was total chaos. Katharina was dragged from one room to another, her eyes blindfolded and her arms tied behind her back. She was pushed against a wall that seemed to be in some sort of a corridor and made to stand there with her head against the rough brick. She could hear an argument going on between two men in a room behind her – one of which was undoubtedly the man who'd been in charge of the raid on their apartment. He was demanding a cell for her to be interrogated in.

'Herr Kriminaldirektor, every room is taken up. The SS are finding resistance scum and Jews everywhere. If they put half their effort into defending the city...'

A few minutes later she was grabbed from behind and marched up a series of stairs. She was pushed so hard she kept stumbling, and by the time they reached their destination her knees were bruised and bleeding. They were in an office, quite a comfortable one, and she heard curtains being drawn as she was forced into a wooden chair. Her blindfold was removed. In front of her was a short, stocky man with a pointed beard and slightly deranged eyes.

He was sweating and breathing heavily, as if the stairs had been too much for him. There was another man in the room, taller than the stocky one and much younger. He was checking the curtains were shut and the door closed.

'Don't be misled by your surroundings,' said the stocky man. 'I assure you we can be just as effective and persuasive in my office as in one of our cells. My name is Kriminaldirektor Strobel from the Vienna Gestapo and this is my assistant Kriminaloberassistent Strasser. Your name please?'

'Anna Schuster.'

'Now let me tell you something, Anna Schuster,' said Strobel. 'We don't have much time to play with here. Normally, I could happily stretch an interrogation out over a week, even longer. But, as you may have gathered, we no longer have that luxury. So I'm not going to indulge you and let you pretend your name is Anna Schuster. I'd like your real name and also the real name of the Gerd Schuster who's shown as living with you.'

She said nothing, concentrating instead on what she needed to do, about which she was very clear. *If you're caught, hold out for 24 hours to allow the others to get away.* She and Rolf had talked about that and agreed that 24 hours seemed like a terribly long time. Rolf had said he was sure 12 hours would be enough in their case. *After all, it's just you and I, isn't it? If we're not both caught at the same time then it won't be as long as 12 hours before the other finds out, will it? More like five or six hours, eight at the most. So if you're caught, try and hold out for 12 hours. I'll be away by then and come back and rescue you!*

'You're crying already, Anna Schuster, eh? Looks like you're going to be an easy one, eh Strasser?'

But she wasn't an easy one. She was Anna Schuster, she told them; a nurse at the AKH and, what's more, a Swiss citizen. *Could the Swiss consulate please be informed?* Through a gap in the curtain she saw it was turning dark, so she'd held out for at least six of the 12 hours. So far they'd not been violent towards her, though she had little doubt it would come. When it did it gave her hope.

Strobel had been out of the room for a while and when he burst back in he leaned down in front of her, his face red and angry.

'Where the hell is he? We found out where he worked but apparently he left Bank Leu around 11.30 and didn't return. We've the manager in one of our cells downstairs to see if he can help us further. Where would he have gone, eh?'

He hit her hard across the face, a back-hander first then a punch that caught her on the chin. She rocked in the chair and, though the pain was intense, she wanted to burst out laughing. They obviously hadn't caught him. The man she loved was safe, for the time being.

The interrogation continued long into the night. At one point she was marched down to the lower basement and she thought she caught a glimpse of a clock inside an office as she was pushed along a corridor. It was either 10.00 or 11.00, close to the 12-hour point she and Rolf had agreed upon. That gave her further cause for satisfaction, but she was still determined to hold out for as long as possible.

When they arrived in the lower basement she was taken into a room where a bedraggled but vaguely familiar-looking man was slumped in a chair. She was made to stand in front of him while Strobel grabbed the man by his hair and yanked his head up.

'Now then, Plaschke, you recognise her?'

Plaschke stared at Katharina through heavily swollen eyes. He appeared to have lost most of his teeth and his nose was bleeding and misshapen. He took a while to focus on her then became animated.

'Yes! That's Gerd Schuster's wife, Anna! She'll tell you, I know nothing – I've no idea what he's supposed to be up to. As far as I'm aware, he's a clerk sent from Zürich. Please, sir, please believe me… Frau Schuster, please tell them!'

She was then dragged into a nearby cell and forced into a chair. The younger Gestapo man, the one introduced as Strasser, strapped her to it. Strobel pulled up a chair and sat in front of her, his chair at a slight angle so he had to turn to address her.

'Who else is in your group?'

'What group?'

Strobel snapped his fingers and Strasser handed him a handful of papers.

'Very well, as you wish,' said Strobel. 'So perhaps you'd care to explain these leaflets?'

He handed a selection of the Hades leaflets to her. She looked at them as best she could with her restricted movement, confusion on her face.

'I know nothing about them… Honestly, it's the first time I've seen them.'

'Don't be a fool, we found them hidden under your sink, along with Reichsmarks hidden in the wall and a pistol on the bed.'

'Yes, the Reichsmarks I know about, we had them there for safekeeping, in case anyone broke into the apartment. The pistol is to defend us from the Russians. But the leaflets, I've never seen them before...'

Strobel hesitated. She looked so confused that it occurred to him she might actually be telling the truth. 'Have a look at them again – you must know where you got them from? Loosen her hands, Strasser, she needs to read them properly.'

She looked at all the leaflets and shook her head.

'So, what do you have to say?'

'They seem to make sense.'

'What?'

'Well, they say the Red Army will liberate Vienna... Isn't that what's happening?'

They beat her up after that, badly enough for her to lose consciousness. She felt herself coming around as a doctor was checking her over, so she did her best to feign unconsciousness.

'Well, Rudolf, tell me – is she alive?'

'Yes, yes, Strobel, she's alive. But I keep warning you, if you want to get information out of them you shouldn't be so rough. I don't care what happens to them, but don't blame me if they die before they tell you anything. Leave her in here for a few hours, she'll come round soon.'

When the interrogation resumed she assumed it must be the following morning. Strasser was nowhere to be seen and Strobel appeared to be nervous.

'Things look bad for you,' he said. 'There was a pistol on your bed when we came in to your apartment, and we found money and communist leaflets under your sink. Just tell us who you are, where the man called Gerd Schuster will be and who your associates are. Think about it, a bit of information in return for your freedom…'

The cell door opened a few inches and she heard someone call Strobel out.

***

Viktor's pursuit of Rolf that Monday lunchtime was a perilous one. As his prey headed towards the canal, Luftwaffe and Soviet warplanes flew low overhead and some of the incoming artillery fire was undoubtedly getting closer. The main target for the Soviet planes seemed to be around the Danube itself, but on two occasions bombs fell on buildings nearer to them. The irony that he could be killed by his own side wasn't lost on Viktor, but he didn't permit himself to dwell on it: he needed all his concentration to ensure he didn't lose sight of his prey. Rolf crossed the canal into Leopoldstadt and worked his way north. A few times he dived for cover or had to seek shelter, which at least meant he was concentrating on what was happening around him rather than thinking about whether anyone may be following him.

Viktor allowed himself to get closer to Rolf. They passed a tram that had derailed, throwing off most of its passengers. Viktor paused long enough to help move the body of a man, taking his cloth cap as he did so. When he turned a corner, with Rolf still just in sight, he tightened his black silk scarf around the lower part of his face and swapped hats, just in case his prey had spotted a man in a trilby behind him.

Vienna Spies

When Rolf turned into Obere Augartenstrasse his pace quickened and by the time he reached a large apartment block he was almost running. Viktor had to break into a trot and move to the middle of the road to be sure of spotting which building he'd gone into.

There was another apartment block opposite so Viktor stood for an hour in its deep doorway, waiting to see if Rolf would emerge. If Brodsky was right, Hubert Leitner was in that building. After an hour he allowed himself to go down the side of the apartment block. As far as he could tell, there were no doors at the side or the rear, so he resumed his spot in the building opposite. An old lady came out of the block Rolf was in and looked in Viktor's direction two or three times, so he decided he needed a more discreet vantage point. He entered the apartment block he was standing in and climbed to the second floor: high enough to give him a good vantage point but close enough for him to make a quick exit.

He chose the apartment closest to the stairs and knocked on the door. When there was no reply it only took him a few seconds to pick the lock. He stood with his back to the door, surveying the place he had come into. It was a small flat, untidy and uncared for, with piles of dirty plates in the kitchen to his right and an unmade bed in the room to his left. Ahead of him was a small lounge, overlooking the building Rolf and Leitner were in.

That was when he noticed him, a man in his sixties, possibly a bit older, sitting rigid in the dark on an easy chair, the only one in the room. Viktor thought the man was dead but he slowly moved his heads towards Viktor, a terrified look on his face.

'Who are you?' The man spoke in a hoarse voice, as if he'd not used it for some time. 'Are you one of them?'

'Who do you mean?'

'I knew it – you're one of the Oberlanders, aren't you? I knew you'd come back! When they gave me this apartment they said none of you would ever return but I knew you would. Now the attack's started and, I said to myself, the Russians will come and bring the Jews back with them!'

Viktor said nothing, his hand searching in his pocket for the reassuring shape of his switchblade.

'Look,' said the old man 'I took care of your things. There's a case in the bedroom with some clothes in it. The SS took the silver; I promise I didn't touch it. Here, look, I have money!'

From his pocket he removed a few crumpled Reichsmarks and held them towards the Russian with a shaking hand. Viktor edged towards the window, keeping half an eye on the street below, but he needed to get closer and couldn't waste his time on this man. 'Are you here on your own?' he said.

'Yes, it's only me. I have some bread too, you can have that…'

Viktor plunged his knife into the man's side: he slumped to the floor and started to squeal so the Russian held his head down and slashed his throat. He dragged the body into the bedroom and covered it with blankets, before going into the kitchen to fetch some bread and water. He pulled the easy chair up to the window and sat on it, watching the building opposite like a hawk.

***

Kriminaldirektor Karl Strobel couldn't believe the dreadful turn in his fortune that Tuesday morning. It was the worst thing that had ever happened to him – even worse than being thrown into prison in '34. It was Rudolf Mildner's fault: he'd replaced Franz Josef Huber in December when the Bavarian had been unaccountably promoted. And while Huber had merely disliked him it was obvious Mildner couldn't stand him. Mildner turned up in the lower basement late that Tuesday morning and called Strobel out of Katharina's cell. 'What the hell's going on, Strobel?'

'I'm interrogating a suspect, Generalmajor.'

'So I understand. And what's she suspected of?'

'Resistance activities, sir. We found those Hades leaflets in her apartment along with a pistol and some money.'

'And when was that, Strobel?'

'Around 11.30 yesterday sir.'

Mildner glanced at his watch. 'Over 24 hours ago. And what has she told you?'

'Not too much yet sir, but I expect by...'

'What! You arrest a woman and, 24 hours later, you have nothing? Look Strobel, in case you haven't noticed, the Soviets are attacking Vienna: they're already approaching the southern suburbs – and you're wasting your incompetent time on a woman caught with a few leaflets...'

'... And a pistol sir...'

'Forget her Strobel,' said Mildner. 'We're sending all the political prisoners and resistance fighters we have here to Mauthausen, we can't afford to waste our time with them. They'll deal with them there. She can go with them.'

Alex Gerlis

'And what about me, Generalmajor Mildner?'
'You? You're going to help stop the Red Army, Strobel.'

***

The longest Viktor had ever stayed awake was 60 hours when he was on an especially complicated mission in Berlin in '37. But he'd been eight years younger then and had back-up. Now he was tired and on his own, but he knew he couldn't leave his vantage point. There was no movement that Monday night and none throughout the whole of the Tuesday: few people left the apartment block opposite and, of those that did, none even distantly resembled Rolf or Leitner. There was the almost constant sound of shelling and rocket fire behind him, from the direction of the Danube and also towards the south, but Obere Augartenstrasse was quiet – at times eerily so. Hunger was an even bigger problem than his exhaustion: he found some ancient cheese in the kitchen and cut away the mould with the knife he'd killed the old man with, wiping the traces of blood away with his silk scarf. He debated with himself when would be the right time to enter the apartment block opposite.

He continued his watch that Tuesday night and throughout the Wednesday. In the bedroom, where the smell of the corpse was beginning to seep through the bedclothes, he found some biscuits in a tin and that lifted his mood. He decided that if nothing happened before dark, he'd make his move then.

It was 4.00 in the afternoon when Rolf emerged into the street, accompanied by an old lady. They remained there for a minute, both nervously looking around and Rolf kicking some rubble away from the entrance to the building before going back inside. Now Viktor felt not a trace of tiredness: his instincts had been honed by 20 years or more on the streets and in the doorways of Europe. He could predict when something was going to happen.

***

He wasn't surprised when Rolf left the apartment an hour later. As he hurried down the street, Viktor had to make a quick decision: to follow him or remain where he was. His training told him to follow his prey but his instinct was that he'd return: Rolf had been in the apartment block for too long for it to be a mere resting place.

'Two hours later he began to doubt his own instincts, blunted as they were by tiredness and hunger. He'd wait until midnight then sleep. In the morning he'd enter the building: maybe the old lady could tell him something. It was 8.15 that night when an ambulance pulled up in front of the building, noisily manoeuvred into a bay at the entrance. When the ambulance driver removed his peaked cap, Viktor realised it was Rolf.

He tied his shoelaces, wrapped his black silk scarf around his face and left the apartment, stuffing the remaining piece of bread into his pocket as he did so. By the time he arrived at the entrance to his building, Rolf and another man were helping a much older man with bandages around his head into the back of the ambulance, while the old lady Viktor had seen earlier was carrying a large bag into the vehicle. On the opposite side of the road, Viktor crept along the shadow of the building to be nearer to the front of the ambulance. He moved into another doorway. The old man, he realised, was Leitner. Rolf climbed out of the back of the ambulance and walked towards the driver's door. The other man closed the rear door and went back to the building, along with the old lady.

As Rolf climbed into the ambulance Viktor sprinted across the road. He pulled open the driver's door and grabbed hold of Rolf. Though taken by surprise, the younger man had the advantage of being higher up and being able to hold on to the steering wheel. He kicked out at Viktor and missed, but did manage to get the engine started. Now Victor was standing on the running board and had produced his switchblade. He lashed out but Rolf threw himself across the seat.

The next thing Viktor remembered was a blinding flash: his hearing went and there was an overpowering ringing in his ears. He felt a sharp pain in his shoulder and a sensation of flying through the air before landing painfully on his back on the rubble-strewn road. He must have blacked out for a few seconds: when he came around the ambulance was accelerating down the street and the man who'd helped Leitner into the ambulance was running towards him.

He carried on running as Viktor picked up his knife – and he only stopped running when the Russian plunged it deep into him.

Chapter 26

London, Vienna and Lower Danube, April 1945

It was early on the morning of Monday 9th April; a week after the
Red Army had launched its assault on Vienna. Christopher Porter
and Major Edgar were sitting in the dining room of White's, the
gentlemen's club on St James's Street of which Sir Roland Pearson
was a member. 'Be there for 7.00,' he'd told them. It was now 7.30
and an arthritic waiter in a stained white jacket who'd quite
possibly been serving members since the club opened some 250
years ago was fussing around them with a pot of stewed tea.

Sir Roland appeared at the table without a word of apology or
acknowledgement of his guests, and beckoned the waiter over
with his finger. 'Kippers and brown toast please, Parsons,' he said.
'You've ordered, Porter, Edgar?'

They sat in silence while Sir Roland arranged his napkin and
ensured his tea was prepared to his taste.

'Have you been a member here long, sir?'

'It's a tradition, Porter, that one does not discuss such matters
at White's. Are you a member of a club yourself?'

'The Oxford and Cambridge, Sir Roland,' replied Porter.

'And I don't suppose you are, eh Edgar? No... Ah well. Perhaps
you ought to try The Travellers in Pall Mall, quite a few espionage
types there.' He paused. 'I say, I understand that French business
has resolved itself, Edgar... finally. All well?'

'After a fashion, Sir Roland, yes, thank you.'

'Well done. Worked out in the end.'

There was another pause as Sir Roland's kipper arrived and he carefully dissected it. Both his guests watched him, anxiously waiting for the main purpose of their visit to commence. Sir Roland slowly ate his kipper and a slice of toast before dabbing his mouth with his napkin. From an inside pocket of his jacket he removed a piece of paper and put on his spectacles.

'Liesing – is that how you pronounce it? Favoriten... Simmering...' He folded the piece of paper and replaced it in his jacket pocket. 'The southern suburbs of Vienna. According to our latest intelligence reports, they're now occupied by the Red Army, though they do acknowledge their primary source is Soviet radio. I'm sure you're aware of that.'

'Indeed sir – and it seems the two suburbs east of the Danube, Floridsdorf and Donaustadt, may now also be under Soviet control: the main battle for Vienna is being fought over the Danube. Our assessment is the whole city will be under Soviet control within the week.'

'And once they're there...' Sir Roland paused as the waiter cleared some plates from the table '... They'll try and stay, won't they?'

'That's long been the view of the Service sir, yes,' said Porter.

'Winston's aware of that,' said Sir Roland. 'But he's also rather under the impression – as am I – that when that happened we'd scupper their plan to control Austria by producing Hubert Leitner, like a magician's rabbit. But now I understand things aren't exactly going according to plan. So tell me, Porter – and you, Edgar – where is Leitner? Do Rolf and the German woman have him safe somewhere?'

Both Porter and Edgar looked at each other, each waiting for the other to speak. Porter was the first to do so. 'As far as we're aware, Sir Roland, they do have him somewhere safe, as you put it. However, the last communication from Rolf was last Monday, the 2nd April. That was the day the Soviet Offensive began. But he did send a message that morning via Zürich saying he wanted permission to move Leitner as soon as possible.'

'And?'

'Basil sent a message back telling him they should move Leitner forthwith. We understand it was sent that afternoon, just before the bank would have closed.'

Three men arrived at the table next to them and began to settle down. Sir Roland indicated for him to continue, but Porter hesitated. 'For Christ's sake, Porter, this is White's, not some grammar school common room,' said Sir Roland. 'Complete discretion is assumed of anyone here. I'd venture this is the safest place in Britain at the moment. Do carry on.'

Porter continued to speak, but leaning forward and in a lower voice. 'Hedinger heard nothing back from him,' he said. 'He waited until the Wednesday when he was able to contact the branch in Vienna. As far as he can gather, Rolf left the bank late that Monday morning and hasn't been back since. And to compound matters, the manager – a chap called Plaschke – was arrested by the Gestapo that afternoon. Hedinger can't make head or tail of what's going on there. As the Soviet offensive has intensified, communications with the branch have become increasingly tricky and are now non-existent.'

'And what have you done about it?'

'There's not an awful lot we can do at this stage, sir. I've told Basil to go to Zürich so he can be sure Hedinger is trying his hardest, but beyond that...'

Sir Roland buttered another slice of toast and spooned a generous dollop of marmalade onto it.

'We need to consider, sir,' said Edgar, 'the possibility – and I put it no higher than that – of Rolf being a Soviet double agent, which has been mentioned before. We've no evidence he is, but nor do we have any evidence he's not. I know Christopher leans towards that possibility, whereas I'm more neutral.'

'And if he is, what happens?'

'The Soviets will be the ones to produce the magic rabbit and the future of Austria under their control will be assured. Maybe Winston should at least be warned.'

'Jesus Christ,' said Sir Roland. 'Winston will be furious. When do you think this will happen?'

'Oh, as soon as they have control of Vienna.'

'Marvellous,' said Sir Roland, angrily pushing his plate of toast away. 'You know, Lady Pearson is quite a devotee of opera, absolutely adores it. I've been promising her that once this damn war is over I'll take her to the finest opera houses in Europe – make up for not being around while this war's been on. Vienna is the one she wants to go to most. I'm quite sure she has in mind something by Mozart. Judging by what you say, it's more likely to be some dreadful Soviet thing, lots of chaps in dungarees waving spanners around and singing about Socialism. She'd never forgive me.'

***

Rolf couldn't remember much about what had happened on the Monday. He did remember the encounter with Unger and a fleeting sense of satisfaction, but then there was the letter, followed by the dash to Ungargasse, the sight of Katharina being arrested by the Gestapo and the realisation he was now on his own. He'd head for Obere Augartenstrasse and hide in the cellar with Leitner then decide what to do.

The memory of the journey across the city and over the Danube Canal was a blur. It was only after he was safely in the cellar that he wondered whether he'd been followed, but he doubted it – if anyone had done, he'd have known about it.

He decided not to tell Frau Egger, Otto or Leitner about Katharina being arrested as didn't want them to panic. She'd been ordered to remain behind in Vienna, he said. He told Leitner that the Red Army was attacking the city from the south and probably the east, and they'd very soon need to head west to meet either the British or American armies – whichever they found first.

'Oh yes… And when do we do this?'

Rolf had long given up expecting Leitner to be grateful, but he could have done without his scepticism. 'I'll stay down here a day or two,' he said. 'Then see how things are.'

That night, he checked the identity card Katharina had stolen from the hospital. He oiled the pistol and ensured it was loaded and in working order. Frau Egger had ventured out on the Tuesday and Otto a couple of times on the Wednesday, and, from what they could gather, the Soviets were getting closer. On the

Wednesday afternoon Otto came back from a trip into the city centre: the talk was that very soon the Red Army would have the city encircled. Rolf knew he had to move.

He left the apartment at 5.00 and arrived at the hospital an hour and a half later. Fortunately, he'd been there a few times before to meet Katharina, so he knew his way around, but it was still light and he wanted to wait until it was darker for the next part of the operation. So he hung around for an hour, waiting in doorways with his cap pulled low over his face. It was just before 8.00 when he went into the casualty receiving area and found the room where the ambulance keys were hung on a wall while their drivers rested. On the floor by a bench someone had discarded an driver's uniform as Katharina had mentioned. There was chaos everywhere, with nurses and drivers rushing around, and no one said a word to him as he removed a key and went to find the ambulance. Ten minutes later he was driving it awkwardly out of the hospital and around the Ringstrasse towards Leopoldstadt. He was relieved it had a full fuel tank.

When he arrived at the apartment block everything went according to the plan they'd discussed, at least initially. Frau Egger had already moved Herr Leitner into her office on the ground floor and bandaged his head as best she could, then she and Otto shepherded Leitner out of the building and into the ambulance while Rolf prepared to set off. His main recollection of what happened next was a series of noises: the noise of someone trying to wrench open the door of the ambulance; the noise of the engine starting; the noise of a knife swishing through the air, then the noise of his Steyr-Hahns – which he'd grabbed from the open knapsack on the seat next to him – firing.

He drove away after that, fully expecting to be fired upon or stopped, if not pursued. He'd head west out of Vienna, hoping to find the British and American armies, even though he'd no idea how near they were. In the cellar in Obere Augartenstrasse, he'd spent time memorising a map of Austria from a school atlas and had decided he'd head in the direction of Linz. If he was stopped, his story would be he was transferring a patient there. He was counting on whoever stopped him having more to worry about than an ambulance. So he headed for the northern suburbs of Vienna then dropped south before heading west again, remembering the training he'd received in England.

Think of a journey as a series of simple stages.

Have alternative routes in case you need to change plans.

Memorise your route.

Avoid having a map open and visible in the vehicle: it'll look suspicious.

Where possible, avoid main roads.

Driving too slowly is even more likely to attract attention than driving too fast.

So driving neither too fast nor too slow, Rolf headed for St Polten, which lay on the main road from Vienna to Salzburg, about 50 miles west of the capital. He decided to ignore the advice and stay on the main road for the first part of the journey as he tried to put as much distance as possible between him and Vienna.

For the first hour he passed dozens of military vehicles hurrying towards the capital, but then the road became quiet and he decided it was time to stop for the night. He turned off the main road and drove through a network of dark country lanes before he found a place to park in a wood, where the ambulance would be well hidden.

He went into the back of the ambulance. Leitner was in a better mood than Rolf had seen him before, so he allowed him to remove his bandages. The man spent a couple of hours sitting in the open, the first time he'd done so for years.

The sky was lit up by the flashes of artillery fire. It was constant through the night. And all of it was aimed at Vienna.

Chapter 27

Vienna and Mauthausen, April 1945

Sprawled out in the rubble on Obere Augartenstrasse Viktor found he couldn't move his legs and feared he was paralysed. He raised himself as best he could, slowly realising it was the body of the man he'd stabbed lying across his legs and pinning him to the ground. He reached out to push him away but his right arm was in agony. He managed to wriggle free: the elderly woman who'd carried a bag into the ambulance was in the doorway of the apartment block, frozen with fear.

His instinct was to return to the apartment to dress his wound, but it would be too dangerous to remain in the area. A hospital was out of the question: despite the fighting going on, he'd still have to explain how he'd been shot in the centre of Vienna when the Red Army wasn't there – yet. He knew he was losing blood, his shirt was soaked, his arm and chest felt wet, and he was feeling faint. There was one place he could go but – even on a good day – it would be at least an hour's walk. And from the sounds of the battle raging around him, this wasn't one of Vienna's good days. He set out anyway, heading for the canal through a city that was part ghost town, part battlefield. One footbridge was open and he managed to cross over into Innere Stadt, the surface of the Danube lit up by low-flying artillery shells. But when he got to the other side he didn't have the energy to continue. He sat down for a few minutes and regained some kind of strength, somehow managing to fashion his black silk scarf into a sling.

He staggered across a road without looking properly, causing a lorry to brake hard. 'You fool! What the hell are you doing?' The driver had stopped to shout at him.

'I'm sorry, I was hit by shrapnel from a commie shell,' he replied.

'Do you want me to drop you near a hospital?'

'Which way are you heading?'

'South: I have to deliver these sandbags to Meidling – unless the reds have got there first.'

'Can you drop me on Wiedner Hauptstrasse?'

'Get in.'

The driver passed a flask to Viktor. It was a strong, bitter coffee laced with brandy and very quickly it had the desired effect. Viktor was not, obviously, a religious man but he'd often thought that if God existed then coffee and brandy were proof of his existence. The driver was a decent man: when they stopped on Wiedner Hauptstrasse he helped Viktor down from the lorry and he insisted he keep the flask. Five minutes later Viktor was hammering on the door of Irma's apartment. When she opened the door he just managed to step into the hall before he collapsed.

***

When Generalmajor Mildner told him he was being sent to the front, Strobel put it down to the quick temper for which the Gestapo chief was well known and feared throughout Morzinplatz. He decided not to argue about the woman being sent to Mauthausen, he'd allow Mildner that pointless victory. In any event, he had his own plans. He returned to his office on the third floor, somewhat disconcerted that so few of his staff were still around. Most of them had been sent to help shore up the city's defences. He supposed there wasn't much point in finding communists now the city was surrounded by them. But not him, he was far too important to be carrying sandbags or helping old ladies into air-raid shelters.

And, apart from anything else, Strobel had himself to think about. He'd sent Frau Strobel back to Carinthia weeks ago, promising to join her there – though he had no intention of doing so. Too many people there would know him and he didn't fancy his past catching up with him once the war was lost. Around the corner from his very pleasant house in Dobling was one belonging to an old woman and a year ago Strobel had been clever enough to rent out her garage, flashing his Gestapo card and making her promise to tell no one. He'd also been smart enough to get hold of a Mercedes Benz 170V from the garage where cars confiscated from Jews were kept, and he'd ensured he'd kept it in good condition with a full fuel tank. In the boot there was a suitcase and under the seat he'd hidden Swiss Francs, jewellery and other valuables he had plundered over the years. And, perhaps most important of all, hidden in the padded sun-visor was his new identity. He'd even had the foresight to hide a razor in the car so he could remove his beard before starting his new life. All Strobel needed to do was go back to Dobling, collect the car and make good his escape. He'd head west and there was no point in delaying matters. Strobel smiled knowingly at the thought of just how clever he was. He was looking forward to his new life.

He got down to his knees to open his safe, removing the wads of money he kept there. He'd take them with him from the office, along with his pistol, some brandy and cigars. He was still on his knees when Mildner stormed into his office.

'What the hell are you still doing here, Strobel?'

Strobel slammed the safe door shut and leapt up, spilling the money all over the carpet as he did so. Mildner looked at the desk and the brandy, pistol and cigars piled on top of it.

'I thought I told you to get to the front? Come with me... Now!'

An hour later Kriminaldirektor Karl Strobel of the Vienna Gestapo was sitting in the back of an army truck, squeezed into an ill-fitting uniform and clutching a rifle with shaking hands. They were heading south, where the Soviet advance seemed to be at its fiercest. Sending someone of his calibre to fight the Russians was a waste of a fine brain, he kept telling himself. They'd soon realise it was a mistake. He was shaking so much he had to hold his rifle with two hands. The young soldiers opposite, some no more than 14 or 15, were giggling at him and gazing in the direction of his crotch. When he looked down he was appalled to see he'd wet himself.

'Stop laughing,' he shouted at them. 'Don't you know who I am?'

'Yes,' said one of them; he was slightly older than the others and had a cigarette clasped between his teeth in a rakish manner. 'You're cannon fodder – same as the rest of us.'

***

It was the Thursday afternoon, the 5th April, when they finally came for her. That morning Katharina had been moved from her cell in the lower basement of Gestapo headquarters on Morzinplatz to a large room in the upper basement. She was blindfolded before she went in and her hands had been tied behind her back. As far as she could tell from the movement, the overpowering odour of unwashed bodies and the occasional cough, the room was crammed with people, all like her made to squat on the floor.

They had to call out the name 'Anna Schuster' three times. Her five days in captivity had confused her and for a moment she'd forgotten the name she was using. They were held in the corridor for a while then marched upstairs and into the open air, where their blindfolds were removed before they were made to climb into an army lorry. There were about 20 of them, and four or five guards. She noticed another lorry had pulled in as they came out and there were another five waiting in a line behind theirs.

A teenage boy asked if anyone knew where they were going. 'You'll find out soon enough,' said the woman next to him. 'It's somewhere worse than this.'

'Shut up!' It was the man next to her, a much older man with a bruised face that failed to conceal a distinguished countenance. 'Don't talk like that. They're moving us because the Russians are coming. Don't lose hope. It can't be long now.'

A guard shouted at them to be quiet and the lorry pulled out of Morzinplatz. The canvas at the end of the lorry had been closed so they couldn't tell where they were going. The old man muttered the name of somewhere but she couldn't make out what he was saying.

After an hour of driving through what sounded like a war zone, they arrived at a suburban station, where the prisoners from all the lorries were gathered before being herded onto a train. An hour later the train pulled out of the station but, after just a few miles, pulled into a siding where it remained overnight. They were all in goods wagons, sealed from the outside, with only room to stand. A couple of the taller men nearer the sides were able to look through the cracks but they could see nothing other than the guards patrolling the tracks and the continuous flash of artillery fire to the east.

At sunrise the train continued its journey. Two hours later they pulled into a station and half an hour after that the doors were pulled open and, to the accompaniment of barking dogs, they were ordered to leave the train and form an orderly line.

According to the signs on the platform, they were in a place called Mauthausen.

From the station they were marched first through the streets of a rural Austrian town, where women and children stood on the pavements to watch them as the guards told them to hurry up. Then they were in open countryside, though not for long. Soon, the quarries came into view and they walked through an unfamiliar landscape, where the earth had been scraped from the land and replaced by gaping holes. Dotted around the quarries were hundreds of small dots, dark against the light stone. As they got closer, they could see they were people in striped uniform, hauling stones up the steep sides.

After a three-mile walk they arrived at the camp and were marched through large wooden doors set in an imposing brick-built entrance with an enormous swastika and eagle above it.

They were made to stand in the open for what felt like another hour as they were sorted into groups. Katharina was in a state of shock: ever since they'd arrived at the camp she'd watched the prisoners returning to it from work or just moving around. They were all dressed in the same rough, striped uniform and all had a pale, skeletal look about them. Katharina found herself standing with half a dozen other women, one of the last groups to be moved.

An SS guard came up to them and, behind him a man in grey prisoner's uniform with a large inverted green triangle sewn on the breast. The prisoner walked with a pronounced limp and in a slightly bent manner, as if he was carrying something heavy over one shoulder. He had greasy hair and a face full of sores. He leered at his new charges. 'Move!'

Katharina was the only one of the group not to move quickly enough. Without warning the prisoner produced a bull whip from inside his jacket and lashed out at her, catching her across the top of her head before grabbing hold of her hair and dragging her all the way to the a large, long wooden hut. He still held onto her when they entered the hut, his filthy hands now stroking her face then running across her body, cupping her breasts as he got so close that their noses touched. She could smell alcohol on his breath as he breathed noisily.

'What's your name?' He spoke in a rough northern German accent.

She said nothing. Behind him a woman was urgently nodding at her. *Answer him.*

'Anna Schuster.'

'Speak up!'

'Anna Schuster.'

'You're nice, Anna Schuster.' He ran the bull whip down the front of her dress and rubbed it between her legs, causing the hem of the dress to rise. 'I'll see you later.'

As soon as he'd left, 10 or 12 women darted out from the shadows and descended upon them. *What news – what's happening? We hear the Russians are attacking Vienna, is that true? And the Americans – where are they? Have you brought food? Find a bed, there are plenty free these days...*

'He's a prisoner, a criminal – you can tell that from the green triangle,' one of the women confided in her as she led her to a bunk. 'They transfer them from German prisons to help look after us. They're known as *kapos* and they're worse than the SS, if you can believe that. The rumour is that one was jailed for rape, years ago. If you're lucky, he may forget about you. Here, take this bunk.'

It was a lower bunk, covered just in a thin, stained mattress with straw sticking out of it and a torn blanket. The woman who'd shown it to Katharina came and sat with her. She told her that her name was Marie and she was French, a resistance fighter. Her German was slow and accented, but Katharina could just about understand her. 'There are people here from all over Europe,' she said, turning around to check there were no guards. 'Lots of Jews early on, but now it's mainly political prisoners and Prisoners of War – and so many nationalities: French, German, Russian, Czech, even Spanish. And you know what...?' She dropped her voice and edged close to Katharina, taking her hand. 'Do you know how many people have been murdered here? The rumour is more than

100,000. Can you imagine that? Like the population of large town.'

'Why?'

'My dear, you don't know where you are, do you?'

***

Any illusions Strobel had about his importance to the Reich were dispelled within minutes of his arrival at the front line in the southern suburbs. A Panzer SS sergeant instructed him and eight other men and boys to go to an abandoned building, from where they should keep a look out for approaching Soviet troops.

'And keep your heads down when you cross that road.'

Strobel waited until the others started off then politely tapped the sergeant on the arm. 'I think there's been a misunderstanding,' he said. 'I'm a senior officer in the Vienna Gestapo.'

The sergeant looked at him as if he was mad. 'Really? And I'm Stalin's auntie – now get a move on.' And with that he kicked Strobel hard on the backside and forced him to follow the others.

Their unit retreated continuously over the next few days: some men were killed and replaced by others. By Sunday, the 7th April, they'd fallen back close to the boundary with Margareten: the Red Army was now near the city centre. Strobel's strategy for survival was a simple one: when he could, he hid. His experience as a hunter stood him in good stead; he knew when to disappear from the rest of his unit and find a room in an abandoned house to hide in or cross a roof space to a building further away from the Soviets.

For a day or two he wondered whether he could escape and

make it to Dobling, but realised that was impossible so he came up with another plan. If he surrendered before he was captured, he reckoned, the Red Army would surely look kindly upon him. He'd tell them he was a Communist and he'd been forced to fight against his will. He'd been interrogating communists for long enough to reckon he could convince the Soviets he was one too.

His opportunity came that Sunday afternoon as he was holed up in an abandoned apartment building: Soviet tanks appeared in the street below him and he heard the order to retreat again. Instead he hid under the stairs until he was sure his entire unit had gone then removed a large white handkerchief from his pocket – one he'd been keeping for this occasion. He crawled out of the building, into the street where he found a group of Russian soldiers looking down at him, broad grins on their faces. He remained awkwardly on his hands and knees while trying to hold the white cloth aloft. Out of the corner of his eye he noticed the rest of his unit being marched towards the Red Army soldiers. As they marched past him, each and every member of his unit spat on him as he knelt in the rubble and pointed at him, repeating the same word to the Red Army officer.

'Gestapo'.

Chapter 28

London, Lower Danube and Upper Danube, April and May 1945

'It's May Day,' announced Sir Roland Pearson. Christopher Porter and Major Edgar had been summoned to his office deep inside Downing Street. A narrow window covered by a dirty net curtain overlooked over an internal courtyard, allowing just a miserable amount of daylight in. This made the room unseasonably gloomy, unlike their host, who appeared – by his standards at least – in a relaxed, even jovial mood. He was in shirtsleeves, his tie loose at the collar and his feet on his desk.

'Big day for the communists, isn't it? Don't they go in for big parades and all that kind of thing, eh Edgar?'

'They certainly don't dance around maypoles waving handkerchiefs, Sir Roland,' replied Edgar. 'Their May Days tend to have more of a military aspect to them.'

'And we understand there'll be a parade in Vienna?'

'A parade of sorts we think, Sir Roland,' said Porter. 'They've been in control of the city for over two weeks now, so it's certainly a chance for them to boast about it: a victory parade, if you like.'

'And still no news of Leitner?'

'No sir, nor of Rolf or Katharina for that matter,' said Edgar. 'Let's not forget there have been tens of thousands of casualties, including many civilians. Perhaps they were in a cellar that was hit and they've been killed, perhaps they've been captured, perhaps… Who knows?'

'And if, as one has begun to suspect, Rolf had been with the Soviets all this time and had handed Leitner over to them then, well... Now would be an ideal time for them to produce him, would it not?'

Edgar looked at the man sitting next to him, hoping he'd reply, but Porter's attention seemed to be taken up by the crease in his trousers.

'It would indeed, sir,' said Edgar. 'I've slowly and most reluctantly come around to the view that we shouldn't rule out the possibility that Rolf has been working for the Soviets and has handed Leitner over to them. Now would be the ideal time for them to produce him – it'd be pointless for them to delay doing so. Having Leitner on their side will legitimise their claim to Austria.'

Sir Roland leaned back further in his chair then sprang to his feet.

'But we know where Leitner was being hidden, do we not?'

'Yes, Sir Roland,' replied Edgar. 'The address Rolf and Katharina went to was where the nun had taken him – an apartment block on Obere Augartenstrasse, in Leopoldstadt, the 2nd District.'

'Surely we could just check out that building?'

'Well...' Edgar paused, looking at Porter in the forlorn hope he might help him out. '... We could if we had anyone in Vienna. The city is under total Soviet control.'

'The nun?'

'There's no way of contacting her. Father Bartolomeo's been transferred to Madrid.'

'Whatever happens, we need to know what's going on. Agreed?'

Both men nodded. Edgar began to feel very uneasy.

'And can we get in?'

'Into Vienna? It'd be most difficult, Sir Roland...' Edgar hesitated, struggling to find the most accurate description. '... It would have to be done in a covert way.'

'Jolly good then.' Sir Roland was now behind Edgar and had slapped him on the shoulder. 'I think you'd better get out there, eh? In a "covert way", as you put it.'

There was a brief discussion as they planned Edgar's journey. 'Ought to be simple enough,' said Sir Roland. 'I'd have thought it'll a piece of cake after getting in and out of Germany while the war was on. Oh and do me a favour while you're in Vienna, Edgar.'

'What's that sir?'

'Find out about the opera, will you?'

***

When Rolf woke up it took him a while to work out where he was. It was dark as a cellar in the back of the ambulance and it was only when he opened the door that he remembered. Leitner was fast asleep, snoring loudly, and Rolf decided to let the old man rest. He strolled out into the woods: the ambulance was well concealed by the foliage and he reckoned if he manoeuvred it just a bit further into the trees then it'd be almost impossible for someone to see it until they were almost upon it.

When he returned to the ambulance Leitner was awake, shielding his eyes from the light creeping into the vehicle. Rolf checked the bags that Frau Egger had prepared for their journey.

They were stuffed with food, bought with the money Rolf had given her to buy provisions on the black market. There were sausages, cheese, a couple of cakes, two loaves of black bread and some tins of fruit.

'This'll keep us going for quite a while,' said Leitner. 'Maybe we could stay here? All we need now is something to drink.'

To Rolf's surprise, the old man smiled. Since escaping from Vienna, he'd been much more amenable. He was, it seemed, relishing his freedom, as precarious and uncertain as it was.

A few minutes later, Rolf found a small but fast-flowing stream, just yards from where they were hidden. He wandered around the woods for a while, checking there were no houses or farms nearby or footpaths that could lead people close to them. But it was clear he couldn't have chosen a better hiding place if he'd planned it. He walked around a bit longer and came up with a plan, then went to tell Austria's most eminent statesman about it.

'We're somewhere between Vienna and Linz, I don't know exactly where, possibly near St Polten.' Rolf had the school atlas of Austria open on the floor. 'The point is, the Red Army will surround Vienna in the next day or so, then I imagine they'll carry on heading west. What we do know is that the British and the Americans are also heading east. We're in this area here. It's between the two armies, but still controlled by the Nazis. I think it's too dangerous to stay here.'

'So what do we do?'

'We need to head west to reach the Allies and keep ahead of the Red Army – oh, and keep clear of the Germans...'

Vienna Spies

'In that case,' said Leitner, looking at the atlas, 'this is where we need to head for.' He was pointing at a narrow blue line marking an uncertain course north to south on the map. 'The River Enns: it's the natural border between the Lower Danube and the Upper Danube as the Nazis insist on calling it. I've spent enough time in briefings with generals to have an appreciation of how they think. The Enns has a strategic significance: my guess is the Allied and Soviet armies will regard the river as a border. Our best chance of reaching the Americans is to get to the western bank of the Enns.'

**

Rolf and Leitner remained where they were in the ambulance for the next five days. One night Rolf ventured out, walking through fields and woods for two hours until he could safely approach a small town to find out its name. Back in the ambulance he located it on the map. It was bad news: they were closer to Vienna than they thought, so they decided to head west the next day. It was around what must have been the 10th April when they resumed their journey, heading south at first then west, keeping on country roads and lanes, and seeing little other traffic. The small towns and villages they drove through seemed deserted, though Rolf could often spot eyes watching them nervously from behind drawn curtains. It was obvious the inhabitants were waiting to be occupied, but they were unsure by whom. They saw scant evidence of the army or police, though sometimes they did have to pull in to allow a convoy to pass. They encountered a few road blocks, but were always waved through. Late in the afternoons, Rolf would find somewhere to hide overnight, which wasn't difficult in an area generously dotted with woods and forests. On occasions they'd remain in their hiding place for days at a time, hoping the Americans or the British would reach them, but then they'd worry about the Russians behind them and move on.

They rationed their food but the main problem was the weather. It was bitterly cold at night, with an unforgiving wind bearing down from the mountains. Rolf began to worry about Leitner. At night the old man's breathing was heavy and he looked pale and drawn. On the few occasions he left the ambulance, he moved with difficulty. Rolf wasn't sure how long it had been since they'd fled Vienna: he estimated it was more than three weeks. It would soon be May if it wasn't already.

Despite the urgency, their progress was hampered by the fact the ambulance's fuel tank was close to empty. Once they were in the Enns river valley, Rolf knew they needed to find fuel. They found an especially good place to hide, deep in a forest where thick banks of trees shielded them from the Alpine winds.

The following day he set out to find the nearest town or village. It was an idyllic walk at first, through a pretty forest then along the edge of fields yet to be harvested. For a while, he felt as if he was the only person in the world, a sensation he used to experience in the Vienna Woods. The sun was already strong, reflecting off the peaks of the Alps, which in turn sent down a welcome breeze.

For the first time in weeks, certainly since Unger had turned up at the bank with his blackmail attempt, Rolf felt relaxed, despite worrying about Katharina. He was well aware he was still in danger, but he felt that there was a possibility they may now be nearer to the Americans or the British than the Russians. He just needed to be careful about the Germans.

This mood of optimism disappeared as he found himself approaching a small town, which he'd spotted from the top of a hill. As the houses began to build up there were no sign of life, other than dogs barking. But then he saw it, something dark and stiff swaying from a lamppost outside a small church. From a distance it looked like a scarecrow, but as he came closer he realised it was the body of a middle-aged man hanging from his neck, his head twisted at a sharp angle and his bulging eyes staring directly at Rolf. His hands and feet were bound and around his neck hung a large sign: 'This is what happens if you talk of surrender!'

Rolf looked around, sure he was being watched by many more eyes than those of the dead man. The town seemed as deserted as every other one they'd been through. All shops in the small central square were shut, some of them boarded up. Just off the square was a garage, with a petrol pump outside. The doors to the garage were shut, but inside he could hear banging. He knocked on the door and an old man in overalls emerged. Rolf explained that his ambulance had run out of fuel. The old man looked him up and down, studying the uniform carefully.

'Where have you come from?'

'Vienna.'

'I thought the Russians had Vienna now?'

'That's why I'm here,' said Rolf.

'Looking for the Americans, eh?'

'Do you know where they are?'

The old man leaned out of the doorway and looked around

before beckoning Rolf into his workshop. 'How do I know you're not Gestapo?'

'Gestapo! If I was Gestapo I wouldn't be asking you for petrol so politely, would I? Come on, where are they?'

'The rumours are they're close to Salzburg,' said the old man. 'Apparently the Americans are coming in from the north, the British from the south – from Italy. Personally I'd prefer the Americans, just so long as they don't bring any bloody Jews and blacks with them. I was told not to sell any petrol by the police last week; they said the military would need it, but I haven't seen any of that lot for a few days now. I can let you have one jerry can, that's all – and it'll cost you.'

Rolf looked at the can the man was pointing to: he reckoned it would be enough to get them over the river.

They crossed the River Enns south of Steyr as Leitner had suggested and made good progress – until they drove into the war. Rolf remembered being taught something at school about how people could smell Roman armies long before they could see them. He was driving along a long stretch of road, the window down, when he smelt it: a bitter, burning smell that went straight to his lungs. He quickly wound up the window and, soon after, clouds of thick black smoke spiralled into the air ahead of them. From the west, two fighter planes raced low overhead before banking and returning along the same path. He heard the crack of gunfire ahead and spotted a cloud speeding towards them. He swerved off the road just in time: seconds later a dozen or so German armoured vehicles sped past them, pursued by the fighter planes. The ambulance clipped a tree and skidded. Rolf heard Leitner call out from the back and only just managed to retain control of the vehicle before bringing it to a halt, the side of the ambulance scraping against another tree. On the road there was an explosion and the sound of gunfire. From where the vehicle had stopped he couldn't see the road, but after five minutes, when there had been no more noise, he quickly checked Leitner was safe then ventured out.

He crawled along the ground and surveyed the road from behind a tree. Two German armoured cars had been hit: one, further down the road was ablaze. The armoured car closer to him had rolled over on to its roof. The body of the driver was hanging out of the doors, his face a bloody mess. From inside the vehicle he could hear groaning, but what most attracted his attention was a large fuel can hanging off its side. Rolf crept to the kerb and looked up and down the road, but there was no sign of any activity, either on the ground or in the air. Cautiously, he walked over to the armoured car and removed the fuel can then carried it back to the trees and returned to the armoured car, hoping there'd be a can on the other side.

There was – and on the ground next to it, sitting in a large and spreading pool of blood, was a young officer in Waffen SS uniform. Both his legs were a pulp of blood and dirt below the knee and his head was slumped on his shoulder. As Rolf removed the fuel can, the young officer opened his eyes and looked directly at him. All the colour had drained from his face but this had the effect of accentuating his sharp, blue eyes – the only part of him that seemed to be alive.

'An ambulance? You came quickly!' He spoke in a rasping

whisper. 'It's too late, there's nothing you can do for me. Do the decent thing and finish me off... Please... I don't have the strength.' He patted a revolver holster on his side.

Rolf shook his head. Surely any time now someone would come along? The Germans or the Russians from the east or even the Americans. Whoever it was, he didn't want to be found on the road like this. He continued to unlatch the fuel can then picked a water flask that was on the road, just beyond the officer's pool of blood.

'Come on... please,' said the officer, distressed. 'I'm in agony and I could never live like this.'

'Who have you been fighting?'

'Who do you think? The Americans... Bastards. Come on... Please.'

'Where are they now?'

'Too near... Maybe five or six miles to the west, possibly a bit further but they're closing in on us all the time. You're an ambulance driver, why are you asking all these questions? Come on, I beg you... Just one bullet, please... I'll tell you what to do.'

Rolf leaned over the officer and removed the Luger from the man's holster.

'Look, remove the safety catch... There on the side...'

Rolf looked up. He thought that he could see some movement in the distance, to the west, and there was certainly the sound of artillery fire. He flung the Luger as far as he could into the field and ran back to the ambulance with the fuel can and the water flask, the desperate pleas of the SS man ringing in his ears.

The two cans of fuel meant the ambulance now had more than

half a tank: Rolf gave most of the water to Leitner, who was now coughing heavily and was obviously in some pain. Where, Rolf asked, did it hurt?

'My chest,' said Leitner. 'Maybe I have an infection. I feel weak.'

Rolf made the old man more comfortable, pulling a blanket around his shoulders and arranging a pillow behind him. Leitner patted the younger man's hand in a grateful, even affectionate manner.

'Thank you, thank you for everything... I apologise if I've not been pleasant at times but I think I might have gone slightly mad being shut away like that. Tell me, are there any medicines in this ambulance?'

'Only antiseptics and dressings,' said Rolf. 'But we've got fuel now and the Americans aren't far away. As soon as we find them they'll be able to help.'

***

They found the Americans early the following morning. Rolf had parked the ambulance overnight in a copse and he left it by foot at first light to see if he could spot anything. The countryside was deserted, with few signs of war other than pillars of smoke on the horizons, artillery fire somewhere in the distance and a dead horse lying in the road. When he returned to the ambulance he fashioned a white flag out of a towel he tied to a branch and attached to the front of the vehicle. He noticed Leitner had been sick and was now running a high temperature.

Alex Gerlis

'I'm fine,' he insisted. 'It's just an infection.'

South west of the town of Wels they came across three Tiger tanks with SS markings abandoned by the side of the road. And when they reached the main Linz to Salzburg railway line, Rolf could see more tanks parked beside it, with men moving around in the trees in the distance and the occasional crack of gunfire. He knew they needed to get to the other side of the railway line but he couldn't see a crossing point for the ambulance. He'd have risked walking across but he doubted Leitner could manage it.

He pulled up at the side of the road and turned off the engine. Within seconds, a dozen men in light brown uniforms and rounded helmets emerged from the trees and surrounded the ambulance, rifles pointing at him.

Americans: Rolf felt tears of relief welling up in his eyes. He tried to call out but couldn't manage it. One of the Americans was gesturing to put up his arms, which he did. Someone opened the passenger door of the cab and shouted 'out' in English and German.

'I'm with you,' said Rolf. 'Are you Americans?'

'We're Bobcats.' The soldier was leaning over the bonnet and chewing something, all the time training his rifle on Rolf.

'I need to find American or British soldiers.'

'Well buddy, you've found the Bobcats: the 5th Infantry Regiment of the United States Army, attached to the 71st Infantry Division. You just keep your hands up there and come down very slowly.'

When he exited the ambulance he was thoroughly searched. He told them they'd find a Steyr-Hahns revolver in the glove box. 'And I need to talk to a senior officer,' said Rolf.

'And why would that be, buddy?'

'I'm a British agent and in the back of the ambulance I've a very important passenger, Austria's most important politician.'

'So you've got Adolf Hitler in the back of your ambulance? Next thing you're going to tell me you're not a Nazi. We've been right through Germany and now we're in Austria and you know what? We've yet to meet a Nazi!'

The other men laughed then fell silent as an officer joined them and asked what was going on.

'My name is Rolf Eder, sir. I'm Austrian but I've been working for the British throughout the war. I can tell you the people in London you should contact who can vouch for me. In the meantime, I've a man called Hubert Leitner in the back of the ambulance. He's Austria's most important politician. It's essential he's looked after and is kept safe. If you have any medics with you I'd be grateful if they could have a look at him because I don't think he's very well.'

The officer nodded to some of his men and they went to the rear of the ambulance. Rolf could hear them opening the door. He and the officer stood silently watching, both smiling politely at the other.

'Captain, can you come here please?'

The captain went to the back of the ambulance and Rolf could hear some movement and some muttering. When the captain eventually returned he indicated that Rolf should follow him to the other side of the road.

'Who did you say that guy is?'

'Hubert Leitner, sir. He's a very important Austrian politician.

He was opposed to the Nazis and he's been hiding from them. I was sent to Vienna to rescue him and ensure he'd be on our side. That's the British side... And the American one, of course.'

The captain eyed Rolf carefully and took his time to open a packet of cigarettes, offering one to Rolf before lighting one himself.

'I'm afraid he's dead, pal.'

Chapter 29

Vienna, May 1945

Rolf was standing beside a pile of rubble on Franz-Josefs-Kai, his back to the Danube Canal, trying to keep a discreet eye on the large building that dominated the square in front of him.

It was Friday 4th May, a month to the day since he'd fled Vienna with Leitner and now he'd returned alone to the city. He was doing his best to appear inconspicuous: since his arrival in Vienna that morning he'd noticed how quickly Soviet troops press-ganged civilians – no matter how old or young – into clearing the roads and damaged buildings. The large building on Morzinplatz, once the home of the Vienna Gestapo, was now under new management – the new tenants either in plain clothes, not entirely unlike those worn by the Gestapo, or the distinctive dark khaki uniform and green caps of the NKVD regiment. He'd already walked around the building twice, making sure to keep a safe distance. If anywhere held the information he sought, it would be here.

Since the moment he'd been stopped by Captain Henry Steele and his unit from the 5th Infantry Regiment, Rolf had taken the view that his obligation to the British had been fulfilled: Leitner hadn't fallen into Soviet hands. The elderly Austrian had died of natural causes, the unit's doctor had assured him. He'd delivered Leitner to the Allies and if Edgar and Remington-Barber wanted to argue about it, he could always point out that no one had said anything about him being alive when he did so.

Captain Steele was a friendly man, an intellectual with an interest in 19th-century German poetry that Rolf didn't share and an innate curiosity – scepticism even – about what exactly Rolf was up to. 'Stay with us, pal, and we'll put you in touch with British Military Intelligence. They're further south now but we'll sort something out.'

Rolf realised Captain Steele didn't quite believe him, but knew the American had a war to fight and wasn't going to spend too much of his time keeping what he clearly regarded as a slightly odd Austrian ambulance driver against his will. So after they buried Leitner in a nearby wood the Americans moved on. Rolf filled up the ambulance with some US Army fuel and headed for Vienna. He had a definite purpose in heading east, a journey into uncertainty and almost certainly into danger. Just over a year ago, in a safe house in Zürich, Remington-Barber had introduced him to a German woman who, purely for the purposes of their forthcoming mission would act as his wife. To his surprise, he'd come to love her more than he thought possible and now his overriding purpose in life was to find her. He'd been devastated when he'd found out about Frieda's death. He couldn't imagine going through the same again and he was prepared to do anything to avoid that.

Rolf had his Gerd Schuster papers on him. If the Russians even suspected he was a British agent he wouldn't leave the building alive. He knew he was taking an enormous risk, but entering the building was the only way of finding out what had happened to Katharina. He strode purposefully across Morzinplatz to the main entrance, which was guarded by half a dozen NKVD troops. A one-star *Mladshiy Leytenant* asked him in German what his business was. 'I escaped from the Nazis and I've been in hiding,' Rolf told him. 'My wife was arrested by the Gestapo a month ago – we were in the resistance. I've come here to see if you've any news of her.'

The officer looked at him sceptically but took him through to a room just inside the entrance and told him to wait, which he did under the eyes of two guards with distinctive Siberian features. After half an hour, a two-star *Leytenant* appeared and Rolf repeated his story, adding more detail – how they'd lived in an apartment on Ungargasse and he'd worked at Bank Leu, and how both he and his wife had been working to undermine the Nazis... The *Leytenant* took a few notes and told him to wait. He returned an hour later and took him to a busy open office on the third floor, where a three-star NKVD *Starshiy Leytenant* asked him to repeat his story through an interpreter, a thin, sickly-looking woman with an unusual tattoo of numbers on her forearm. It was noisy and the interpreter had to raise her voice for the *Starshiy Leytenant* to hear her. 'He wants you to tell him the name of your wife again.'

'Anna Schuster.'

'Pardon? Please speak louder. Also, you should address him as comrade.'

'Anna Schuster, comrade,' he said loudly.

She repeated Anna's name, almost having to shout it. Rolf noticed the *Starshiy Leytenant* now seemed distracted, looking beyond him. At the same time Rolf became aware of a presence behind him and the NKVD officer leapt to attention.

'*Kommissar General*, Sir!'

'It's alright comrade *Starshiy Leytenant*,' Rolf heard a voice say. 'Leave him to me: we'll go into my office.'

He turned around to face a large man, his right arm in a sling. 'Come with me,' said Viktor in good German and a not altogether unfriendly voice.

***

Viktor had been minutes from death when he'd collapsed in Irma's hallway after being shot by Rolf. Irma couldn't shift him, but she could tell from the state of his shirt and the pool of blood forming beneath him how serious his injury was. He was deathly pale and his pulse very weak. She covered him with a blanket and ran down to an apartment on the second floor. She had to bang on the door for a few minutes before it opened, no more than an inch or two. 'Frau Bock, you must fetch your husband immediately! There's an emergency in my apartment.'

'My husband is asleep – and he's retired, you know that. He's an old man.'

Irma shoved the door open, pushing a startled Frau Bock into the hall. Her husband was standing in the bedroom doorway, wrapping a dressing gown around himself. 'Herr Doctor Bock, there's a man dying upstairs,' she said. 'You must come up now. You'll need to bring your medical bag with you.'

The elderly doctor worked on Viktor for two hours. With the help of Frau Bock they managed to get him on to Irma's bed and eventually the doctor stabilised him. He took Irma into the lounge. 'He's been shot you know.'

'I guessed,' said Irma.

'Who is he, Irma? Is this dangerous?'

Irma had known the Bocks for many years, long enough to doubt they'd ever been Nazis. She calculated it was worth taking the risk to trust him, a decision emboldened by the sound of approaching Soviet gunfire.

'All you need to know is that this man certainly isn't a Nazi, and nor is he German or Austrian. Saving his life could also save yours when the Soviets arrive.'

The doctor raised his eyebrows, part in interest and part in fear: he understood. 'He needs surgery to remove the bullet and a blood transfusion – he's very ill.'

'That's impossible, we can't move him.'

'He looks like a strong man.'

'He's the strongest man I know.'

'Well, he's going to need to be.'

Doctor Bock remained with Viktor day and night for the next week as he slowly recovered his health. He managed to prevent him developing a fever, though he remained very ill. The fighting outside became so intense that none of them ventured out of the apartment block. On the 12th April it sounded as if they were in the very eye of the battle: at one stage they heard the main entrance door to the apartment block crash open followed by a burst of gunfire. Irma allowed herself a peek out of the lounge window: the bodies of half a dozen German soldiers were strewn across the small square and she saw what she assumed were Red Army troops running along the side.

That night Irma lay next to Viktor on the bed: he was awake

most of the time now, though still in pain. He held her in his arms, smiling tenderly at her and leaning over to kiss her on the forehead. She was surprised the apartment block was still standing. Even though the bedroom window was covered they could still see the flashes of explosions. 'We ought to tell the Bocks to go back to their apartment, they've been wonderful,' she said.

'No, they'll be safer here, with me,' said Viktor. 'I'm afraid that some of our troops will behave very badly.'

By the following morning the fighting seemed to have abated in their area and, from what they could hear, the battle was now being fought over the Danube, to the east. That evening, the 13th, a silence descended upon the city, as if someone had flicked a switch. Viktor wrote a note in Russian that they attached to the door of the apartment and waited. For two days they heard nothing other than occasional shouting in the streets, sporadic gunfire and the odd explosion.

'I'll go out,' announced Viktor.

'Impossible,' said Doctor Bock. 'You'll collapse before you reach the bottom of the stairs.'

So they agreed Frau Bock would go out with a letter. Irma had insisted it should be her, but Viktor was adamant. 'You're too young, too attractive,' he whispered to her when the Bocks were out of the room.

'There'll be two types of troops out there,' he told Frau Bock. 'Regular Red Army and NKVD. Look for NKVD: they wear darker uniforms and the officers have dark-green caps. Give this letter to an officer.'

'What does it say?'

'It says I'm a senior Soviet officer who's been badly injured and that you're sheltering me in a nearby apartment. It also says they'll need you to take them to me.'

'Will they believe it?'

'Let's find out.'

Frau Bock only had to walk as far as Wiedner Hauptstrasse. The NKVD patrol looked amused as she handed the letter to the officer, who read it slowly. When one of the troops sidled up to Frau Bock and tried to put his hand inside her coat the officer shouted at him and the man sprang back. There were more barked instructions then Frau Bock was helped into a jeep and driven to the apartment.

They rushed Viktor to a hospital commandeered by the Red Army and two soldiers were left at Irma's apartment to guard her and the Bocks. The NKVD officer even ensured food was brought to them.

Before going under anaesthetic, Viktor had insisted on speaking confidentially to the most senior NKVD officer around and a one-star *Kommissar General* was brought to his bedside. Anyone watching the hushed conversation would have observed how it began with the General adopting a superior air. By the end, he was deferring to Viktor and nodding his head obediently.

Two days after the operation Viktor woke from a nap in his private room to find a familiar figure sitting alongside him. 'The surgeons say you're lucky to be alive,' said Ilia Brodsky.

'So are you, I'd imagine,' said Viktor, gingerly pushing himself into a sitting position, still groggy and in pain.

'I'm alright for the time being, Stalin still needs his Jews,'

Brodsky laughed. 'Apparently the bullet just missed something called the subclavian artery: if it'd hit it, I'd have been thinking about what posthumous decoration to recommend you for.'

'Hero of the Soviet Union, I hope!'

Both men laughed before Brodsky adopted a more serious tone. *Tell me everything.*

Viktor explained how, acting on Brodsky's instructions, he'd informed on Anna Schuster to the Gestapo then followed Rolf as he headed first to Ungargasse then to Obere Augartenstrasse in Leopoldstadt. *You were right, comrade; he did lead us to Leitner.* Brodsky nodded; none of this was a surprise to him. Viktor told how he'd seen Leitner being taken into the ambulance and how he'd tried to stop it, but had been shot by Rolf.

'I failed comrade, I'm sorry,' said Viktor. 'I'd no idea he had a gun.'

Brodsky waved away Viktor's apology. 'It was what – two weeks ago? If Leitner was with the British or the Americans by now then I think we'd have known about it.'

Viktor agreed. 'They drove off into the battle comrade. I doubt they'd have got very far. With some luck they'll both be dead; at least the other side won't have him.'

'Maybe, maybe… We have Vienna, so we can control Austria… But if Leitner turns up with the other side… That'll all change.' Brodsky shook his head: *a prospect too terrible to even think about.*

He stood up and patted Viktor affectionately on his left shoulder. 'The doctors say you'll be up and about in a couple of days. We've taken over the Gestapo headquarters at Morzinplatz: you go there and be my eyes and ears, alright? And congratulations by the way, comrade: you're going to be a three-star *Kommissar General*. I didn't want anyone else in the NKVD outranking you in Vienna.'

***

Rolf followed Viktor to an elegantly furnished office overlooking the Danube Canal. Two NKVD guards had come with them but Viktor dismissed them, instructing them to bring coffee. 'The Gestapo had a fine supply of real coffee: you look like you could do with some.'

Viktor said nothing as the guard served the drinks then sat behind the fine wooden desk and looked long and hard at Rolf.

'What language shall we talk in?'

Rolf shrugged: he really wasn't sure whether Viktor recognised him as the man who'd shot him.

'I assume you don't speak Russian?' said Viktor. 'Would you prefer to speak English or French maybe? My French is very good, my English less so. I have some other European languages too...'

'German is fine,' replied Rolf.

'And now you'll tell me your name and for whom you work.'

'Gerd Schuster,' said Rolf. 'I have the necessary papers with me. I'm a Swiss citizen and work for Bank Leu here in Vienna, though whether that...'

Viktor was holding out his left arm in a 'stop' gesture.

'Please, please, please... I know you work for British intelligence. I've seen you in Zürich and I know you were here in Vienna to find Hubert Leitner. I want to know everything: where

Leitner is; your real name; who you work for; who your contacts are.'

'I told you. My name's Gerd Schuster and I work for Bank Leu. I actually work for them in Zürich but was posted here last year.'

'Don't think I'm a fool!' The Russian sounded furious. He'd removed his switchblade knife from a pocket and was banging it on the desk. 'Many people have found that a costly mistake to make. A month ago, you shot me. You nearly killed me, which means you attempted to murder a senior officer in Soviet Intelligence during the military operation to defeat the Nazis. I could have you shot now, no question about it. Or I could have you put on a plane to Moscow today and put on trial there. Or...' he paused. '... You can start telling me the truth. For instance, I know full well your real name is Rolf Eder. Correct?'

Rolf remained silent but found himself nodding. He was unsure of what the current relationship was between the British and the Russians, even though they were meant to be on the same side. Certainly the Americans he'd met didn't seem to trust the Russians very much, but maybe the British would be better disposed towards then.

'Or maybe you're a German agent, some clever ruse by the Nazis to leave spies behind after they were defeated?'

'Of course not!'

'How do I know that? Maybe that's why you shot me.'

'I've been working against the Nazis.'

'Why should I believe that?'

'Because my... wife, Anna... She was arrested by the Gestapo.

It happened on the same day the Soviet Offensive began. If I was a Nazi spy I'd hardly have turned up here. I came to find out what happened to my wife.'

Viktor had flicked open his knife and was examining the tip of the blade. He continued to do so as he spoke. 'I know.'

'You know what?'

'I know Anna Schuster was arrested by the Gestapo.'

'And how would you know that?'

'Because it was me who informed on her.'

Neither man blinked, neither man stopped looking at the other, neither spoke. It was almost as if during that period of absolute silence the sun dropped and Vienna went dark and silent.

'You – you told the Gestapo about her?'

Viktor nodded, twirling the knife in his hand.

'Why on earth…?'

'… So you'd lead me to Leitner.'

'And why are you admitting all this to me?'

'I told you. Because I told the Gestapo about her.'

***

Come back tomorrow morning. You'll tell me what happened to Hubert Leitner and in return I'll try to find out what happened to Anna Schuster. The Nazis destroyed some records before they left, but not many and certainly not the most recent ones. They'll take time to track down, but I should know by tomorrow. Remember this though – I'll only tell you once you tell me the truth about Leitner.

Rolf had no choice but to agree. He walked through Innere

Stadt to Bank Leu on Schubertring, but it was now little more than a bombed-out shell. He was stopped a couple of times by Red Army troops, but Viktor had given him a letter, allowing him free passage for 24 hours.

From Schubertring he carried on to Ungargasse. He found the spare key in its hiding place, taped to the top of the landing window frame. The apartment had been ransacked, no doubt in the Gestapo raid when they came for Katharina. All the drawers and cupboards had been emptied, the bed was on its side, clothes were strewn over the floor and a few cans of food rolled about in the kitchen. He moved a few things around and found to his amazement there was some hot water. He'd have a bath, change into clean clothes, eat and rest. He sank to his knees in the kitchen and began to sort out the mess, feeling if not exactly optimistic then that he was at least getting somewhere. As he bent down, he became aware of a presence behind him, light footsteps then a long shadow cast over the kitchen.

'Is there enough food there for two of us there, eh Rolf?'

When Rolf turned around, Edgar doffed his cap, a cloud of dust rising from it as he did so.

***

Edgar had been instructed by Sir Roland Pearson to go to Vienna on 1st May. Early the following morning, a Wednesday, he took a flight from RAF Benson in Oxfordshire to Orly airport south of Paris and, from there, a lunchtime USAF flight to Neubiberg airport just outside Munich: the Bavarian capital had only been captured from the Nazis on the Monday.

A familiar figure greeted him at the aircraft's steps. 'I must say, Edgar,' said Basil Remington-Barber, 'it's rather wonderful being the occupier. Anything you want you can demand, no longer any need for all this clandestine nonsense. If it wasn't for the fact I'm English I wouldn't even need to say please or thank you! Look at this car, a beautiful Mercedes. I just asked one of the US Army liaison chaps if they could get me a car and he said take your pick. I'm rather hoping I can take it back to Bern, beautiful leather seats...'

They went straight to the US Military Intelligence offices at the airport and found a room covered in maps. Remington-Barber used the end of his pipe to indicate an arc between Linz and Vienna. 'Soviets have Vienna and everything east of it tied up. We're in the west – I say we, it's the US Army in the northern part... here... And we're further south, around here – the 8th Army coming up from Italy. So you'll have to wait until we meet up with the Soviets then ask very nicely if they'll let you into Vienna: I'd say we can get you there within a week or two.'

'No, no, no – that's fucking inconvenient, Basil,' said Edgar. 'I'm sorry to use that language, but I can't possibly wait that long. Berlin's about to fall – if it hasn't done already – yet all these godforsaken towns in the middle of Austria are still being fought over. We have to know what the hell's going on with Leitner. I don't suppose you've heard from Rolf by any chance?'

'No, Edgar, London keeps asking me. And before you ask, I've no view on whether he's a Soviet spy or not. I've certainly never had him marked down as one, but then after everything we've been through since this damned war began, nothing would surprise me. I'm not sure how you're going to get through US-controlled territory, then through Nazi-controlled territory and into Soviet-controlled Vienna and remain in one piece. I'd say your best bet is to go in as an Austrian citizen.'

'I agree, but I need to get there fast. How far east is the USAF flying?'

'I can check,' said Remington-Barber. 'But the last I heard they were still flying reasonably close to Vienna. Who controls what airspace is somewhat uncertain at the moment.'

'Come on, Basil,' said Edgar, picking up his bag and heading out. 'Let's go and find whoever's in charge of these things. They can drop me in tonight.'

Edgar lied to the deeply sceptical USAF major and assured him that of course he'd kept up with his parachute training and there was no question he was up to it. He then started to pull an impressive number of strings, including Sir Roland Pearson at number 10 Downing Street, which had the required effect on the base commander at Neubiberg. Three hours later Edgar was floating gently through the still night sky towards a field less than 10 miles north west of Vienna. It had been a perfect drop: there were no trees nearby to worry about and he was able to roll along the field as soon as his boots touched the ground. He sat still for a moment or two, catching his breath and making out as much as he could of his surroundings in the half-moon. He gathered the parachute and buried it together with all his jumping gear, and the helmet, overalls and boots. From his rucksack he removed his German clothes and the papers Remington-Barber had brought for him. Sewn into his jacket were US dollars and British identity papers. *I'm sure they'll soon count for something, Edgar, you may well need them,* Remington-Barber had said. He'd been given a cloth cap, one that bulged more at the sides than ones in England and with a deeper peak, which would help conceal his face. The cap looked a bit too pristine, so he rubbed it in the dry earth. He checked his compass and when he was satisfied which direction he should head in, buried that too.

One of the inevitable consequences of being somewhere in the immediate aftermath of a battle was the unusual movement of civilians. During the battle itself those civilians who were able to do so hid as best they could, often going without food and water for days at a time. They might be wounded or ill, or parted from loved ones or just afraid. But when the battle ended, their instinct was to move and they tended to do so in every direction; moving because they felt they ought to, rather than having any definite destination in mind.

So that Thursday morning, as soon as Edgar found the main road into Vienna, he joined a steady stream of people. More were leaving the city than going towards it but there were enough of the latter for him to not look out of place. The train of people moved slowly and silently, fearful of what they'd find in the city, clearly traumatised by whatever it was they'd left behind. They were on the outskirts of Vienna when they came across the first Soviet troops at a checkpoint just inside Penzing. Edgar shuffled along, doing his best to appear slightly lame and confused. The troops were most interested in anyone they suspected of being a German soldier and women under the age of 50. Anyone who fell into either of those categories was ushered into a nearby church. For a while the group Edgar was in was called to a halt in the road. From inside the church he could hear women squealing and, as they were moved on, he heard a volley of shots. The Red Army was clearly taking no prisoners.

'Go to Morzinplatz,' Remington-Barber had advised him. 'Assuming it's still standing, that is. Soviet Intelligence will want to base themselves there, makes sense. I'll leave it to you as to what you do when you get there, but if there's anything to find out about Leitner – it'll be there.'

Edgar arrived in Morzinplatz late that afternoon and took in as much as he could: the main thing was that it was busy and there were plenty of NKVD troops around, which was a good sign. From there he crossed the canal into Leopoldstadt and found his way to Obere Augartenstrasse. There wasn't much left of the apartment block where Leitner had been hidden, it was little more than a blackened shell. A boy told him it had caught fire.

When?

During the battle.

Did anyone survive?

What do you think? Do you have any cigarettes… or food?

Overwhelmed by exhaustion, he walked back into Innere Stadt, where a Russian soup kitchen was begrudgingly serving some lukewarm gruel. Nearby he found a bomb-damaged office block where he bedded down for the night, sharing an alcove under some stairs with a family of hungry rats.

Early the next morning, the Friday, he walked to Morzinplatz, picking up a shovel left by the side of a road. He hung around the edge of the square, watching the building and making sure to move bits of rubble around if anyone in Red Army uniform came near him.

He spotted Rolf from a distance, standing with his back to the canal on Franz-Josefs-Kai and doing a credible enough job of not making it too obvious he was monitoring the building. He moved to the other side of the square so a large tree – one of the few not to have been felled in the fighting – would help obscure him. Rolf seemed uncertain at first, then walked into the old Gestapo HQ with such a purpose that Edgar conceded he'd been wrong and Porter had been right: Rolf was a Soviet agent after all.

He was still watching the building when Rolf left it two hours later. He followed him as he walked through Innere Stadt. Twice Rolf was stopped by Soviet troops, but each time the papers he produced saw him through far quicker than any other civilians. Edgar had little doubt now that Rolf was a Soviet agent, but he needed to know why and he needed to know what had happened to Leitner. Rolf carried on walking: he paused outside Bank Leu and headed down Ungargasse. Edgar dropped back a little further and crossed to the other side of the road. He knew where Rolf was heading: at least he'd now get his chance.

***

'How long have you been working for them Rolf?'

The two men were sitting in the lounge, Rolf nervously on the edge of the sofa and Edgar on a chair he'd pulled up in front of him.

'Working for whom?'

'Come on Rolf... Come on... The Soviets. The war's all over now bar the shouting so we can be honest with each other. I can disappear from Vienna as quietly as I arrived here, I can be gone tonight – but first I'd like to know what happened.'

Rolf had a look of such hurt innocence about him that Edgar found himself in awe at how persuasive the young Austrian was. They'd all fallen for it, not least himself. Edgar regarded it as one of the most impressive performances he'd ever seen from a double agent – a breed of person in which he felt he had unequalled expertise.

'Of course I don't work for the bloody Soviets,' said Rolf. 'Don't be ridiculous.'

Edgar had to admit his indignation sounded genuine. 'So you popped into the NKVD headquarters today for what...? To report a missing dog?'

'Don't be so bloody sarcastic, Edgar. I actually risked my life going in there. I was trying to find out what happened to Katharina. I ought to tell you something, I'm not sure whether Basil realised this when he acted as matchmaker, but we're both very fond of each other and...'

'Congratulations, Rolf, but I need to know why you were there.'

'There's something else you need to know – I met Viktor there.'

Major Edgar regarded displays of emotion and temper as indulgences reserved for the English upper and working classes and he was member of neither. But he sat in a state of shock as Rolf recounted his story in such a calm and plausible manner, with the right balance of detail, emotion and occasional imprecision, that Edgar began to question his judgement of the man and wondered whether the young Austrian was telling the truth after all.

Rolf told Edgar of how, on the day the Soviet offensive began, Katharina had been arrested by the Gestapo and he'd been informed of it in a letter hand-delivered to the bank. Then he told him how he'd returned to Ungargasse and watched as she was taken by the Gestapo from the apartment block they were both now sitting in; and how he'd gone to Leitner's cellar and remained there for a couple of days before stealing the ambulance and escaping from Vienna. He told of how Viktor had appeared and he'd shot him, and of the perilous journey west to find either the British or the Americans. And, finally, he told him that Leitner had died, quite possibly just minutes before they met the Americans.

Edgar sat quietly, taking it all in.

'I'm sure you'll be wanting proof, Edgar,' said Rolf. 'Well, the American officer who can vouch for me is a Captain Henry Steele from the 5th Infantry Regiment. We buried Hubert Leitner in a wood just on the western side of the main Linz to Salzburg railway line, south west of Wels. I could show you the exact spot. He was an old, sick man. I'm sure you'll find he died of natural causes. That's certainly what the American Army doctor said.'

When he began talking about Katharina, Rolf broke down. He paused frequently to sob quietly. He told Edgar that – once he'd discovered his fiancée, Frieda, had been murdered by the Gestapo – he'd realised just how much in love he was with

Katharina and she with him. He was so desperate to find out her fate that he'd taken the enormous risk of returning to Vienna and going into the NKVD headquarters – the same building where Frieda had most probably been murdered.

'Viktor wanted to know Leitner's whereabouts, too, but when I asked about Katharina – he knows her as Anna Schuster – he admitted he was the one who'd informed on her to the Gestapo. It was a way of getting me to lead him to Leitner. I'm going back there tomorrow. Viktor's promised to find out about Katharina, and in return I promised I'd tell him about Leitner.'

***

Rolf and Edgar had talked long into the night. 'Viktor won't believe you about Leitner,' Edgar had insisted.

'But if it isn't true, why on earth would I have returned to Vienna?'

'He knows you're a British spy. Maybe he thinks we've sent you to see what they're up to.'

'Or maybe he believes I'm desperate to find out about Katharina?'

'I'm not sure Viktor's capable of that kind of empathy.'

'I'm telling you,' said Rolf. 'He seemed genuinely remorseful that he'd informed on her.'

They decided to wait and see.

***

Within minutes of Rolf's arrival back at Morzinplatz that Saturday morning he was escorted to Viktor's office. 'First, tell me who you're working for,' said the Russian.

'For the British – against the Nazis.'

Viktor looked taken aback that Rolf had been so forthcoming. 'Tell me about Leitner.'

'You promised you'd let me know about Anna…'

'… After you've told me about Leitner. I do have information for you, but I want to know about Leitner first.'

'Leitner's dead.'

The Russian nodded his head, as if it was the news he expected to hear. From an inside pocket he removed a brown leather notebook, a pencil and switchblade knife, using one to sharpen the other. As Rolf told Viktor the story, the Russian wrote laboriously in his notebook. When he'd finished, he sat motionless as he looked at Rolf, as if trying to work out whether he was telling the truth.

'If Leitner turns up alive, no matter where and no matter when, I promise you we'll kill you. Understand?'

Rolf nodded.

'Follow me.' Viktor led him down to the lower basement, along a dark, damp corridor with an uneven floor.

'According to the records we found, Anna Schuster was brought here and interrogated by a Gestapo officer named Karl Strobel. Strobel ran Section 1VA of the Gestapo, the section responsible for finding communists and other resistance groups. He'll know what happened to her. Let me do the talking.'

They stopped at a cell guarded by two NKVD soldiers. Viktor

spoke quietly to them and they unlocked the door, following him in. The cell was long, narrow and brightly lit. On the wall facing the door was a large steel frame, strapped to which was a short, stocky man with a fat, red face, a short, pointed beard and a look of fear on his face. He was suspended from the frame by chains, his arms stretched above him, his toes only just touching the floor. His shirt had been ripped open and a line of dried vomit ran down his beard onto his chest. His trousers were stained and his whole body was shaking.

Viktor arranged two chairs in front of the man, and he and Rolf sat down. The two NKVD guards stood at the back of the room. 'This is Karl Strobel,' said Viktor. 'What rank in the Gestapo were you, Strobel?'

'I have nothing to do with the Gestapo.' He spoke in a surprisingly high-pitched yet rough voice, as if the fear had taken hold in his throat. 'I was a recruit in the Wehrmacht. I surrendered to your forces as soon as I could. I keep telling your colleagues that. Look, I was wearing a Wehrmacht uniform! I'm no Nazi. In fact, I've always been something of a communist, I've even read Marx! I should be treated as a prisoner of war!'

'Strobel was in fact a Kriminaldirektor in the Gestapo, here in Morzinplatz,' said Viktor, looking first at the man then at Rolf, as if describing a work of art to a gallery visitor. 'Many people died in this basement at his hands. I'll tell you more of that soon. But, Strobel, I want to ask you about a lady called Anna Schuster. She was arrested on the 2nd April and interrogated by you here. If it helps jog your memory, that was the day the Red Army began its attack on Vienna.'

'I've no idea...'

'... I know, I know, Strobel – I've heard it so many times. You don't know anything... You're a peaceful man – a communist even, you've read Marx... Look, I'm busy and so is this gentleman. If you want to be treated as a prisoner of war, just tell me what happened to her.'

'I don't know.'

'You're sure you want to persist with this?'

Strobel said nothing. He was twisting his body around, trying to get it into a position so the tips of his toes supported him on the floor. Viktor said something in Russian and one of the NKVD guards walked up to Strobel and punched him hard: once in the face then again in the stomach. Strobel screamed, twisting violently against his chains. Viktor turned around and addressed Rolf.

'His name is all over the records we found here. He certainly interrogated Anna Schuster on at least two occasions. Now we'll start to get serious with him.'

Viktor turned back to the prisoner. 'Strobel, as an exponent of torture, are you familiar with the Chinese technique known as death by a thousand cuts?'

Strobel stared at him; his eyes wide open, nostrils flared and panicked breathing coming from his mouth. He shook his head vigorously.

'Apparently it was practised in China for hundreds of years and, as recently as the turn of this century, French travellers describe having witnessed it. The emperors and other nobility reserved it for the most serious of cases. The prisoner is stripped naked, tied to a post then cut – a thousand times. It can take up to a day for them to die.'

As he spoke Viktor removed the switchblade knife from his pocket, running a finger along the blade. 'From what I've read, if the executioner starts with the limbs then the prisoner can remain conscious for a long time. Now, tell me about Anna Schuster.'

'I saw so many people here, I can't remember any names.'

'So you did work for the Gestapo?'

'... Only in a very minor capacity, I was little more than a clerk really and a most reluctant one, I promise you.'

Viktor spoke again in Russian and a guard went over to Strobel, tore away the remains of his shirt and pulled down his trousers. 'Some accounts of a death by a thousand cuts said that, if the executioner was especially cruel or the victim's crime particularly heinous, they'd start with the genitals...'

'Mauthausen!'

'Pardon?'

'She's in Mauthausen and it wasn't my decision to send her there – I was about to release her. Ask Mildner, Rudolf Mildner – he's the man in charge of the Gestapo here. He's the man you want to question, not me! I'm just a clerk.'

'Unfortunately, Rudolf Mildner fled just before we arrived,' said Viktor, who then turned and said something to one of the guards in Russian. 'But we'll check to see if you're telling the truth.'

'What's Mauthausen?' It was the first time Rolf had spoken.

'It's a prison camp, that's all...' said Strobel. 'Whatever goes on there is nothing to do with me.'

'Shut up,' Viktor told him.

Ten minutes later the NKVD guard returned and spoke with

Viktor, handing him a sheet of paper, which looked like a long list of names.

'So it seems you were telling the truth, Strobel. According to this, Anna Schuster was indeed transported to Mauthausen on the 5th April.' Viktor stood up, straightening his jacket and moving his chair back against the wall.

'You see? I told you! You'll let me go now, yes? I'm a prisoner of war, remember that. Please let me down from here.'

'Wait a moment,' said Viktor. 'I'm not finished yet. Do either of you know a Frieda Brauner?'

Rolf looked stunned and he heard a sharp intake of breath from Strobel.

'She was you fiancée, am I right?'

Rolf nodded.

'I have to tell you this man here murdered Frieda in one of these cells in March 1942.' Viktor was pointing his knife at Strobel. The look of fear the Austrian had worn when they'd had first entered the room was nothing compared to his expression now. Rolf could see the man's heart beating hard in his chest and his face turn white as he repeated the word 'no'.

Viktor held out his knife and offered it to Rolf. 'Would you like the honour of revenge? Remember, this man murdered your fiancée.'

Rolf shook his head and tried to turn but Viktor stopped him. 'You need to watch. I'd happily do it myself, but my arm...' He beckoned one of the guards, handing the knife to him, saying just one word to him in Russian: *medlenno*. He kept on repeating the word as the guard plunged his knife into Strobel's abdomen.

***

Fifteen minutes later Rolf and Viktor were sitting in the office on the third floor, drinking brandy. Rolf was smoking his third cigarette, clutching it so tightly in his trembling hand that some of the tobacco had spilled onto his trouser leg. He was still recovering from being forced to watch Strobel's last terrible moments on earth. The NKVD guard had inserted the knife into Strobel's lower abdomen then pulled it slowly upwards towards his chest, while a desperate cry like that of a wounded animal reverberated around the cell. Rolf took another large swig of brandy, trying hard to dispel the image from his mind. 'You kept saying a word to the guard, what was it?'

'*Medlennno*,' replied Viktor. 'It means "slowly".'

It certainly been slow, thought Rolf. Strobel had been conscious for most of the minute it took him to die, not once taking his bulging and tearful eyes off Rolf.

'This was his office, you know?' Viktor was speaking in a matter-of-fact manner, sensing Rolf's discomfort and trying to change the subject. 'That's how we found out all that information; he was meticulous in keeping records. There was a file on Frieda.'

'This place he said Anna had been taken to – the prison camp?'

'Mauthausen. It's what the Nazis call a concentration camp. They've built dozens of them around occupied Europe. Hundreds of thousands of people have been murdered at some of them, mostly Jews. Recently, though, Mauthausen has been mainly for political prisoners. We know the American 3rd Army's in that area, but we don't know whether it's reached the camp yet. We'd better get you there as soon as possible.'

Viktor poured himself another large brandy and carried it to the window overlooking Morzinplatz, gazing out onto the square for a while. 'He's still there: he's very good you know, quite remarkable really. I'll tell you what – if we provide transport and an escort, he could go with you to Mauthausen. What do you think?'

'Who?'

'Your Major Edgar!' Viktor was pointing out of the window. 'At least he won't have to pretend to be a refugee any longer.'

Chapter 30

Vienna and Mauthausen, May 1945

Katharina had arrived at Mauthausen on Friday 6th April and her first few days were spent in a daze. She was slow to respond when the guards barked orders and reluctant to eat what little food there was. For some reason, the *kapo* who'd harassed her on the first day had ignored her since, but she failed to recognise her good luck. Instead she slipped into a state of depression. After a few days she was taken aside by one of the Spanish Republican prisoners in her hut, a dark-haired Catalan called Montse with jet-black eyes and a hard, thin face.

'You have to decide whether you want to live or die,' Montse told her. 'If you want to die, that's your choice. But if you want to live then I suggest you decide quickly, otherwise you'll reach the point where you won't be able to change your mind.'

'Of course I want to live,' said Katharina, though not with much conviction.

'In that case, start acting like you do,' said Montse. 'You need to eat because if you don't you'll get ill and, once that happens, you're finished. Faint from hunger and they'll put a bullet in your head. And you also need to get smart. You need to understand this place and stay one step ahead of the guards. You don't appreciate how cheap human life is here. The way you're going, you won't last the week.'

The camp was overcrowded: the rumours were that it was one of the last in Europe still under Nazi control, so in the past few weeks tens of thousands of prisoners had been force-marched there as the Allies and the Red Army had liberated camps elsewhere. As a result, disease was rife and the SS guards, sensing defeat, were even more prone than usual to kill prisoners for the slightest of excuses.

Katharina was sent to work at a quarry near the main camp, where her job was to help break up rocks that other prisoners had carried up. A Russian prisoner of war told her she was lucky it was good weather. 'In the winter, people don't last more than a week in this job, two at the most.'

'And how long do they last in this weather?'

'Three weeks – maybe four,' he replied cheerfully.

But one day, after the 6.00 morning roll call, none of the prisoners were lined up into their work details. They were made to stand in the large open areas for more than two hours before being sent back to the huts. The newer prisoners were relieved not to have been sent to work. The more experienced ones like Marie and Montse were worried. 'It's not good. We're only of any use to them if we're working,' they said.

It was the 20th April, Hitler's birthday. Until then Katharina had thought she was in hell and it couldn't get any worse – but that day it did. The rumours started later that morning: prisoners from the infirmary block were being killed, thousands of them. That afternoon all the women in her hut were ordered to the infirmary where they were forced to carry the dead patients to the crematoria. Some patients were heaped on wagons and some carried by stretcher, but there were so many of them they were forced to carry them as best they could.

Some of the prisoners were still alive. Though most were unconscious, a few were aware of what was happening. Katharina's first living victim was a Spanish man, little more than a skeleton and apparently dead, but as she hauled him over her shoulder he began to speak, in Spanish at first then in German: *let me down, carry me out of the camp, I need water...*

This continued until they reached the crematoria, where the *sonderkommando* grabbed the man from her and threw him in the ovens as he began to scream.

They carried on late into the night then lay stunned on their bunks, still having been given no food. One of the other women said she'd overheard a guard boast 3,000 people had been killed from the infirmary block that day.

Katharina had just fallen asleep when she became aware of noisy breathing next to her along with the reek of alcohol. When she opened her eyes she saw it was the *kapo*. He clamped a rough, greasy hand over her mouth as he climbed on top of her and ripped open her tunic. He was mercifully quick and almost gentle, and when he'd finished he lay over her, propped up on his elbows, his face just an inch or two from hers. He gazed down at her, his foul breath directed into her nostrils, and stroked her face with his rough hands, smiling then kissing her, on her cheek first then on the lips, his tongue forcing its way into her mouth. His kisses were almost affectionate and when he'd finished he buried his head in her hair and whispered something like 'my love' and 'tomorrow'.

And that was when she began to die. She'd become inured to the violence and the terror; that was impersonal, everyone in the camp was experiencing it. But the intimacy she couldn't cope with.

Vienna Spies

***

Rolf was so shocked the Russian had spotted Edgar from his window that he remained seated. He said nothing, hoping it was a trick. It wasn't possible, he told himself – if anyone could remain hidden, surely it'd be Edgar. Viktor turned around, smiling broadly, allowing a flash of gold teeth.

'Come here if you don't believe me – come!' Viktor waved him over to the window, like an child eager to show something to a parent. Rolf stood by the window with Viktor's arm around his shoulder and, sure enough, he could see Edgar in the distance in the square below, his cap pulled down low over his face as he shovelled bits of debris towards a pile by the canal wall. Viktor shouted out in Russian and one of his officers came in to be given a series of instructions. Viktor and Rolf waited by the window and watched as, a few minutes later, the officer and a dozen NKVD troops appeared in the square and marched towards Edgar, surrounded him and marched him to the building.

Five minutes later Major Edgar from MI6 was standing in front of Viktor Krasotkin of the GRU in the elegant third-floor office, flanked by two NKVD soldiers. The two men looked at the other with a similar countenance, one best described as a mixture of curiosity and distrust with a certain measure of respect thrown in. They stood just a foot from each other for two silent minutes, cycing each other up and down like bulls finding themselves in the same field. Viktor walked back to his desk and sat down, lit a cigarette then removed his switchblade knife from his pocket before sharpening his pencil again, allowing the shards to scatter across the desk. He spoke briefly in Russian and one of the guards pulled up a chair. The other guard pushed Edgar into it.

'Your German's obviously good enough for us to converse in.'

Edgar nodded.

'I never imagined the two of us would meet,' said Viktor, raising his eyebrows, inviting an answer.

'Well, that's the war for you, eh?'

'Indeed, but we're allies, after all, aren't we? We're on the same side, but for how much longer will that be – days, weeks? Months at the most, I'd say. And even though we're on the same side, we're also enemies at the same time, are we not?'

'I'd prefer to say rivals,' said Edgar.

The Russian laughed. 'I'm sure you would prefer to say that, Edgar. English understatement. But you're in my custody now. Of course you're not going to describe yourself as my enemy!'

The Russian smiled as he topped up his glass of brandy then poured one for Edgar, pushing it to the front of the desk towards the Englishman.

'I think we could describe the situation between us now as like a ceasefire, a very brief period…' Viktor's voice trailed off, he was thinking. 'Rolf, would you leave us please.' Then he snapped an instruction to the two guards and they left the room too.

The two spymasters were now alone. Viktor carried his chair from behind the desk and placed it alongside Edgar, positioning it so it faced in the opposite direction, their shoulders touching. 'What I'm going to say, no one should hear. You understand?'

Edgar nodded and edged his chair even closer to the Russian's.

'You'll leave Vienna today with Rolf and never return. No one need know you've been here. You understand? But you leave on two conditions. The first is that you go directly from here to Mauthausen – the Nazi concentration camp near Linz. We know Anna Schuster was sent there around a month ago. That area is either under the control of the US Army or about to be, so I expect that by the time you get there it'll have been liberated. I'll provide you with an escort.'

'Are you sure she's still alive?'

The Russian shook his head. 'No, but…'

'Why are you so keen to help?'

'Because I was responsible for her arrest. If you can rescue her, that'll ease my conscience.'

'You mean you have one?'

'I've as much or as little of a conscience as you do; we're in the same line of work after all.' Viktor turned to stare at Edgar, daring him to believe what he'd said.

'You said there were two conditions, what's the second one?'

'I'm 45,' said Viktor. 'As old as the century. You look surprised Edgar – I know I probably look much older, but then I've been in the service of my country in this capacity for more than 20 years and you'll appreciate that ages anyone. I never expected to survive this long and I've no idea how much longer I'll stay alive, but let me say I've started to think about it. One day I may need your assistance, Edgar. I may have to contact you, be it directly or indirectly. I'd like you to give me your word that, should I do so, you'll do what you can to help me.'

Edgar nodded slowly. 'And how will I know it's a genuine approach?'

Viktor looked around the room and said nothing, appearing not to have heard the question. He walked over to the desk and picked up a nearly empty bottle of brandy, a pear-shaped bottle with the words 'Baron Otard, Cognac' on the label.

'We found cases of these here, the spoils of war.' He tapped the bottle. 'Should you ever get a message that a Baron Otard is trying to contact you, you'll know it's genuine. That it's me. You understand?'

Edgar said he understood, but...

'Don't look so worried! I may never need your help. They may get me first or I may never be in danger. I could be promoted and protected, and we'll remain opponents. But remember, Baron Otard...'

***

Montse, the Spanish Republican, mentioned it first then Marie the French resistance fighter noticed it too. The eyes were the first sign – and, after the massacre at the infirmary and being raped by the *kapo*, all the life had disappeared from Anna Schuster's. She lay still on her bunk, not sleeping, not eating and barely acknowledging anyone around her. She was clearly unwell now, her body racked alternately by raging temperatures then painful chills. For a few days after the mass deaths there was an uneasy lack of activity around the camp as the SS seemed more preoccupied with themselves than the prisoners. The rumours were rife: the Americans would be here today, tomorrow – or maybe the Russians, next week. In the confusion the prisoners in their hut were left alone but they knew it wouldn't be long before the SS turned their attention back to them. Every night the *kapo* came to her bunk and, when he'd finished, he'd lie next to her, staying for as long as an hour, cuddling her, kissing her and whispering into her ear: 'We'll be so happy together.' When he left, Montse and Marie did their best to rouse Anna. *It won't be long, we'll be liberated soon. Just pull yourself together for the last few days.*

***

'You'll travel to Mauthausen on the Danube,' Viktor had announced, sounding like a travel agent discussing the itinerary with a client.

'Won't we be rather vulnerable on the river?' Edgar had replied incredulously.

'You'll be vulnerable whichever way you go. You'll be travelling from Soviet-held territory through areas still under Nazi control, then to where the Americans are: nowhere will be safe. All the time the battle lines will be shifting. The Danube may just be a safer route, who knows? Mauthausen is less than a mile from the north bank of the river, before it enters Linz.'

Viktor took them to the Floridsdorfer Bridge, one of the only ones in Vienna to have survived the battle for the city. Moored at a small quay was a battered tug, bouncing up and down in the dirty, choppy waters. The *Donau Mädchen* was long past its better days, its rusty hull pockmarked with bullet holes. It would attract little attention. Accompanying Edgar and Rolf was a young, three-star NKVD *Starshiy Leytenant* called Alexei Abelev. 'Alexei will protect you if you're stopped by our forces,' said Viktor. 'I trust him and he also speaks some German.'

'That's all very well,' said Edgar. 'But what if we run into the Germans?'

Viktor said nothing, but led them onto the boat and into the wheelhouse, where a tall man was checking the instruments. Rolf let out a gasp of recognition when he saw the man, who nodded back. The two men shook hands and slapped each on the shoulder.

'Joachim?'

'Joachim joined the Wasserschutzpolizei, the river police,' explained Viktor. 'But he's also been working for me. He knows the river well and will skipper the boat. If you come across any Nazi forces, he should be able to persuade them there's no problem.'

As dusk began to fall, the *Donau Mädchen* set sail, gently sliding along the river as it headed west towards Linz. Joachim Lang had found an old engineer whom he trusted, so there were five of them aboard. Lang remained in the wheelhouse while Edgar, Rolf and Abelev remained below deck. Lang had felt the most dangerous part of the journey would be between Vienna and Krems. 'There are more likely to be Nazi forces in that area,' he'd said. 'I'm wearing my uniform below my overalls, so if there's any problem...'

They all understood: if there was any problem even that was unlikely to be of much help. Edgar, Rolf and the young NKVD officer sat in the hold checking the PPSh-41 sub-machine guns they'd brought with them. The Russian patiently explained their workings.

'At best,' said Edgar, 'these'll buy us some time; we may be able to get away. But, with luck, anyone who spots us will have bigger things to worry about than a rusty little boat like this.' He shrugged his shoulders, not really believing his own reassurance.

Around midnight, Lang called Edgar up to the wheelhouse. They were making good progress, he said. The tug had a powerful engine and was in good condition. What little moon there was was obscured by thick cloud – and the *Donau Mädchen*, with all its lights off, would be barely visible from either bank.

An hour later they heard some noise from above and the engine quickly cut to idling speed. Lang called them up. Alongside the *Donau Mädchen* was a barge with a group of hostile-looking Red Army troops on the deck. When Abelev appeared on the deck and spoke with them, their mood changed. They were held alongside the barge for half an hour while radio messages were exchanged and, when the officer in charge of the barge was satisfied, he allowed the tug to proceed. Maybe they should all now get some sleep, Lang suggested.

The young Russian officer quickly fell asleep but Rolf stayed awake to talk with Edgar. 'When you were on your own with Viktor, did he tell you whether or not he thought she was alive?'

'He doesn't know, I promise you,' said Edgar. 'But if he knew she was dead then I doubt he'd have gone to all this trouble.'

'I don't understand why he's helping us.'

'He said it was because he was responsible for her arrest.'

'You believe that? There must be another reason he allowed us to leave…'

Edgar said nothing for a while. He glanced over at Abelev, who was asleep, but Edgar switched to English, moving closer to

Rolf. 'I'll tell you why. My turning up in Vienna was the proof he needed that we don't have Leitner. For the Soviets, Leitner being with us would've been a disaster. He knew I'd have come to Vienna to find out where he was. I think he was so relieved that he just wanted us out of the city.'

'And no other reason?'

Edgar hesitated a moment longer than he should have done before replying. 'What other reason could he have?'

***

When it became clear the arrival of the Americans at Mauthausen was imminent, the SS garrison fled and, for a few hours, the camp fell silent: most of the prisoners were too ill or exhausted to do much. Then anarchy descended.

The *kapos* who'd helped keep the camp running retreated into their huts, ones that were marginally less spartan than the others. And that's where they came for them: Red Army prisoners seeking revenge, bursting in and killing every one they found.

But a few had been smarter, Anna Schuster's *kapo* among them. As soon as the SS left the camp, he'd swapped his *kapo* uniform for one of a regular prisoner. Nor did he make the mistake of returning to his hut. Instead he hung around some of the huts towards the back of the camp, doing his best to blend in. But he was better-fed than other prisoners and feared that, despite his best efforts, he'd stand out and be recognised. He moved to the perimeter, but menacing groups of Russian and Polish prisoners were hanging around there, making sure no one left. He entered a

Vienna Spies

nearby hut but – despite the fact most of the prisoners in it could barely move – the atmosphere was too threatening. Then he realised where he should go, where he'd surely be safe. She'd protect him; she was bound to be grateful he'd shown her so much kindness. Maybe when he left the camp, she'd go with him. They'd find somewhere together in the countryside, perhaps… They could live together…

When he entered the hut it was in near-darkness and he could only sense bodies around him. He edged along the side to where her bunk was, stepping on one body and over another. A narrow beam of light pierced through the wooden shutters, picking out her still body on her bunk, and he saw her eyes were open and unblinking, staring at the bottom of the bunk above hers. He climbed alongside her, holding her tight. He'd remain there until they were free: she could protect him and he'd look after her.

He'd been next to her for no more than five minutes when she let out a piercing shriek, so loud his ears started ringing. Someone opened the shutters and quickly they were surrounded by a dozen or so inmates. The woman was screaming, trying to push him away. He propped himself up so she could see him more clearly. When she realised it was him, surely she'd stop. But now they were holding him down and the woman climbed on top of him as someone handed her what looked like a knife. There was no question she could now see it was him. She stabbed him a dozen times before they rolled his body off the bunk and she collapsed back onto it, covered in blood, her eyes still wide-open, staring at the bottom of the bunk above hers.

She continued to die.

***

They passed Krems before daybreak on Saturday and Lang decided to press on for as long as he dared. The terrain on the north bank of the Danube was harder, the trees that led into the mountains more dense, while the land on the south bank was flatter and easier. By the time the morning sun shimmered on the surface of the mighty Danube they were just west of Spitz. Lang steered the *Donau Mädchen* onto a small landing on the south bank, concealed by overhanging branches, and Abelev jumped ashore and secured the tug.

'We could press on and be in Mauthausen by nightfall,' said Lang. 'But that assumes a safe passage... Maybe we should wait here till nightfall?'

'We can't possibly wait that long,' said Rolf impatiently.

As the two men argued, Edgar and Abelev wandered off, returning after 15 minutes. 'As far as we can tell,' said Edgar, pointing to the binoculars the Russian was holding, 'there's fighting and troop movements to the south and east, a bit less to the west. It's hard to tell who's fighting who, but Alexei's sure some of the artillery is German. My sense is that the Americans are advancing towards the east. Let me have a look at your charts, Joachim.'

They spread a large map out on the deck and studied it. 'I think we can risk the Danube as far as Melk, but no further – here,' said Lang, pointing to a town on the south bank. 'Look at the terrain on the south bank – it's much flatter and, if you're right, that area ought to be under the control of either the British or the Americans.'

They set off immediately. For the next three hours the sounds of fighting were intense, though still some distance away from them. The terrain helped, both banks were heavily forested and provided a strange sense of isolation. As they passed the village of Schönbühel on the south bank, Lang steered the *Donau Mädchen* towards the centre of the river and excitedly called them up to the deck.

'Over there – can you see, on the north bank? That village is called Emmersdorf, according to this chart. Here, give me those binoculars.'

He smiled as he peered through them, handing them over to Edgar. 'Look to your left a bit – what can you see?'

Edgar fiddled with the binoculars then a grin appeared on his face. 'Good heavens… Good heavens. Well done, Joachim.'

'What is it, Edgar?'

'The Stars and Stripes. A great big bloody Stars and Stripes!'

They raised a white flag as the *Donau Mädchen* crawled towards the small stone quay at Emmersdorf. There were three or four American Army trucks by the bank of the river, as well as a couple of dozen troops and at least as many rifles watching them. Edgar perched on the bow, waving a white cloth and shouting out in English. The rifles were still trained on him as he threw a rope to one of the soldiers and the tug was pulled alongside. He spotted a young officer and called him over.

'I say, I'm a British officer,' he announced, realising how pompous he sounded. The young American nodded and told him to raise his hands, climb down slowly from the boat and allow himself to be searched. As he stood on the quay, he spoke to the officer.

'My name's Major Edgar, I'm a British Intelligence officer. I commandeered this boat and escaped from Vienna in it. I ought to tell you that on board are three Austrians who worked for the resistance in Vienna. There's also a Russian officer who came with us in case we met the Red Army. I'm on an important Allied mission and need to get to the concentration camp at Mauthausen as quickly as possible. I understand you'll need to verify who I am but, if you can get hold of whoever liaises with our chaps, I'm sure we can sort something out.'

To Edgar's amazement, they did – though it took them most of the afternoon to do so. The young officer managed to get a message through to his headquarters, who promised to speak with their British liaison officer, Edgar having given them a coded message that was meant to ensure swift action in such circumstances. By late afternoon the message came back.

'They say you're one hell of an important guy, Major, and we're to do what we can to help. In fact, as you guys have been operating under cover, it'll be an honour.'

***

She moaned throughout that night and, as dawn threatened, the moans were punctuated by increasingly frequent and longer screams. This unsettled the other prisoners, who were convinced the noise Anna Schuster was making threatened their chances of survival. So, just before first light, Montse and Marie took her from their hut and hurried her through the disappearing shadows to one of the infirmary blocks, which had begun to fill with prisoners again. They were turned away from two of the huts. 'She's even madder than the rest of us,' a Polish doctor said. 'Try that hut over there. Good luck.'

That hut was run by a Russian prisoner of war called Yulia and inside it was as if they'd entered the final gate of hell. Hundreds of prisoners were screaming, rocking and twisting violently. Montse and Marie took Anna deep into the hut, past rows and rows of bunks, each holding two or three prisoners. They found a bunk at the back, the bottom section of which had one dead body on it and another close to death. They laid the dead body on the floor and lifted Anna into its place before quickly leaving, pausing to tell Yulia her new patient was called Anna Schuster and she was to look after her.

An hour later Yulia came over to give Anna Schuster some water. To her surprise, her patient hauled herself up on the bunk and whispered something. Yulia had to bend over to hear what she was saying, and pressed her ear against her mouth. 'My name's Katharina, Katharina Hoch,' the woman said in an insistent tone. 'If anyone asks, that's my name.'

And with that, Katharina Hoch slumped back, her breathing now noisy and laboured, and all too familiar to Yulia. But she closed her eyes and appeared more at ease. She was entering the final stage of her life, but at least she'd die with her real name.

***

They'd wanted to leave Emmersdorf that evening but the Americans refused to let them. 'The Nazis are beaten but they're not finished yet,' the officer insisted. 'There are still plenty of their units around here and the SS ones in particular haven't given up. Just our luck that this godforsaken place is about the only place in Europe where there's still any fighting going on.'

They left Lang, the engineer and Abelev behind and, at first light, headed off in a US Army truck with a driver and half a dozen troops. Not far out of Emmersdorf they crossed the river, as the southern side had better roads and was under American control. The journey took nearly four hours as they paused at various points to check the way ahead was clear, and they had to negotiate their way through numerous checkpoints. When they reached Enns it was so crowded with US military vehicles that it took them the best part of an hour to pass through the town and cross the bridge over the Danube.

Half an hour later they arrived at Mauthausen. Milling around outside the camp were dozens of emaciated people, few doing little more than just sitting by the roadside. US Army troops were moving in and out of the camp. The truck stopped and they all got out, shocked at the sights around them. Hanging above an enormous stone-arch entrance was a large banner with a slogan in Spanish painted on it.

'Anyone know what that says?' asked Rolf.

The corporal who'd driven the truck read out loud: "*Los Espanoles antifascistas saludan a la fuerzas liberadas*". It means the Spanish anti-fascists salute the liberating forces, which I guess mean us. What the hell are Spaniards doing here anyway?'

It was agreed their escort would return to Emmersdorf before dark, so Edgar and Rolf walked through the arch and into the camp. There was such chaos and confusion around them that no one bothered to stop them, other than the inmates in their threadbare striped clothes, who walked silently next to them, holding out their hands for food. They eventually found an American officer who took them to a building that seemed to be acting as an office.

'This place was liberated over the weekend by the 11th Armoured Division of the United States 3rd Army, sir,' the officer told them. 'How can we help?'

Edgar asked Rolf to wait outside while he explained who they were and why they were there. 'There are thousands of prisoners here, sir,' the officer told him, 'many of them dead. People are still dying from typhus or starvation. The Nazis killed thousands over the last few days, before we got here. The chances of finding one particular person here alive are slim, but you're welcome to look around.'

'Are there any records?'

'There were some, but they aren't recent. We think the most recent records have either been destroyed or – more likely – haven't been kept at all. But we've been compiling a list of inmates who are alive. What did you say her name was again?'

'Schuster – Anna Schuster.'

'Give me an hour. I'll have my guys check it out.'

Edgar and Rolf sat in the shade of a long hut while they waited for the officer to come back to them. Edgar did his best to prepare Rolf for the worse. *Many thousands of inmates have died here in the past few weeks... It's possible Anna's still alive, but...* Rolf was impatient, pressing Edgar to go back and hurry the Americans.

'Look at these people, Edgar, they all look like they're dying. We can't afford to wait!'

When the officer came out to find them he shook his head. 'I'm sorry, there's no Anna Schuster in the lists we have... That doesn't mean she isn't alive... Remember, we're still compiling names...'

'But she'd have only been here a month,' said Rolf. 'Surely in that time...?'

The American shrugged his shoulders. 'As I say, pal, these records aren't complete yet. The best thing is for you to look around the camp and ask.'

For an hour they walked around the camp, asking every prisoner they came across whether they knew of an Anna Schuster – a woman from Vienna with dark hair. Edgar was aware Rolf was becoming agitated, short-tempered with prisoners who said they didn't know her. One of the huts they entered was larger than the others and appeared to be deserted. The two men stood in the centre of it, aware of a presence in the room but unsure of its nature. There were small sounds, muffled breathing and tiny scuttling movements. As their eyes acclimatised to the little light that found its way in, they began to realise dozens of pairs of eyes were staring at them, from behind the bunks, from beneath them and pressed against the walls. Edgar held up his arms and called out in German, 'We're British. Please don't worry.'

Gradually, a few children edged forward and within a minute they were surrounded by hundreds. Tiny eyes, all of which looked as if they belonged to old men who'd seen too much over the course of long lives, gazed up at them. Hands reached out from the ends of skeletal arms, some for food but most just for human contact. Edgar and Rolf called out Anna's name and described her in German, but no one responded.

After the children's hut they came to a clearing where a group of women were standing. *Anna Schuster, she's from Vienna, though her accent would be more German: arrived here sometime in April, dark hair?* The women shook their heads, but one of them shouted out Anna's name into a nearby hut. A dark-haired woman with black eyes and a thin face came out. 'Anna Schuster? Yes, I know her. She was in this hut.' She spoke German slowly and with a heavy accent. She'd barely finished speaking before Rolf grabbed her by the arm.

'Where is she? Tell me!'

'She went mad. We took her over to the infirmary.'

Montse led them over to the infirmary block and eventually they found the hut. Yulia, the Russian prisoner of war, was sitting outside, smoking.

'You remember we brought a woman over the other night?'

'Are you serious…? I'm meant to remember that? I didn't sleep for a week, I must have had hundreds of prisoners in there – all mad, all dead or something between the two. And you expect me to remember one prisoner? Anyway, it's nothing to do with me now. The Americans are in charge. They don't trust me.'

'You must remember her,' said Montse. 'I brought her in with another woman. Anna Schuster… think…'

Edgar handed an unopened packet of cigarettes to Yulia, who nodded and held out her hand for another one. 'Maybe if I think about it, I do remember you bringing over a woman – but her name wasn't Anna Schuster. She told me her name and it wasn't anything like that.'

'When did she tell you her name?'

'When she was dying. She had typhus when you brought her here. I gave her some water. She insisted on telling me her name and said I was to remember it if anyone asks.'

'Dying – what do you mean she was dying? That's impossible,' said Rolf.

'Hang on,' said Edgar. 'What was the name she told you to remember?'

Yulia shrugged as if she couldn't understand all the fuss. 'It wasn't anything like Anna Schuster, that's for sure. It began with a K – like Katya but different, if you know what I mean.'

'Katharina?' shouted Rolf, tears streaming down his face, his hands gripping the Russian woman by the elbows.

'Yes – that's it, Katharina something. But she'll be dead by now.' She was shouting as she said this, because Rolf had run into the hut, followed by Edgar.

They hurried from bed to bed, shouting Katharina's name and staring at the patients. All were emaciated and many appeared to be more dead than alive; it was hard to distinguish whether they were men or women. Rolf was rushing ahead, lifting patients up to get a clearer view of their face and shouting Katharina's name. Edgar caught up with him towards the back of the hut.

'Rolf, you must prepare yourself for the worse. That Russian woman said she was dying a few days ago. The chances are she's gone now. Please Rolf, this is…'

They were standing by a bunk – Rolf with his back to it, Edgar facing him. And on the bottom lay the still body of a woman curled up into the foetal position, her back to them.

Rolf was weeping inconsolably. 'I loved her more than anything, Edgar. You don't understand. What is it, Edgar? Why the hell are you smiling?'

Edgar had been watching as the body on the bottom bunk had unfurled itself and – almost as though it was being born – had straightened out and slowly turned around.

By the time Rolf turned and sank to his knees, Katharina was whispering his name. Tears caused her eyes to sparkle in the gloom.

Epilogue

Rolf Eder and Katharina Hoch were reunited at Mauthausen on Sunday 7th May, the day before the war in Europe officially ended. They returned to Zürich where Katharina received medical treatment. The couple assumed new identities and married later that year. They lived in Switzerland for the rest of their lives.

Edgar continued to work for British Intelligence until 1950. In the General Election of the following year he was returned as a Member of Parliament, a position he held until retiring in the late 1960s. A few years after that he had one further and quite unexpected encounter with Viktor Krasotkin.

Viktor was recalled to Moscow at the end of May 1945. When he arrived in Moscow, he discovered Ilia Brodsky had been summarily tried and executed as a traitor, and he assumed the same fate awaited him. But it didn't. He carried on working for Soviet intelligence for the remainder of his life.

Author's note

Vienna Spies is a work of fiction, and therefore any similarities between the characters in the book and real people should be regarded as purely coincidental. There are a couple of exceptions to this – most notably Franz Josef Huber, who was head of the Vienna Gestapo until late 1944, and his successor Rudolf Mildner. Apart from remarkably brief periods of detention after the war by the Allies, both of these men went unpunished. The leadership of the KPO (the Austrian Communist Party) was exiled in Moscow during the war and their leader was Johann Koplenig, who appears in Chapter 8.

I have endeavoured to be as accurate as possible in regards to actual events in the period covered and their historical context. In particular the Moscow Declaration of 1943 (including the Declaration on Austria) is genuine. Likewise, the details of the Red Army's advance from the east and the British and Americans from the west are as accurate as possible. I have tried to be similarly accurate in terms of locations, organisations and geography.

Austria was annexed by Nazi Germany on 13th March 1938, an event known as the Anschluss. This was endorsed with a 99.73% 'yes' vote in a plebiscite on 10th April 1938. The plebiscite was held throughout Germany and not just the Austrian part of it.

Austria thus became part of the German Reich and ceased to exist as an independent country. The area previously known as Austria was called Ostmark until 1942, after which it became the seven Danube and Alpine Gaus (or regions) of the German Reich. These regions do not exactly correspond with the regions of pre-

and post-war Austria and included parts of other countries and regions (such as Bohemia, Moravia and Yugoslavia). Some small areas of pre-1938 Austria were moved into Swabia and Upper Bavaria. For the purpose of clarity, I refer to Austria throughout the book. I have also used some of the German names of regions, such as the Upper Danube and the Lower Danube.

I refer frequently to the districts of Vienna, of which there are 23. The Nazis expanded the city limits of Vienna and, in doing so, added new districts and introduced new district numbers. However, I decided to use the district numbers that were in use before the Anschluss and again since 1945. This is partially for the sake of clarity and also because I understand that, even during the war, the Viennese tended to use the old district numbers.

Mauthausen (along with its sub camps) was the main concentration camp in Austria and the last major one to be liberated in Europe. In the period 1938-1945, an estimated 200,000 prisoners were held there, of whom around 100,000 were murdered. Most of the 50,000 Austrian Jews murdered in the Holocaust died in other camps, but some 15,000 perished at Mauthausen. Many Austrian political prisoners and members of the resistance were held there, and thousands were murdered in the final few days of the war (including those in the infirmary). The camp also held a significant number of Spanish Republican prisoners and French resistance fighters, as well as Red Army prisoners of war.

Vienna was liberated by the Soviet Red Army on 13th April 1945. After the war, Austria was occupied by the United Kingdom, the United States, the Soviet Union and France – very much like

Berlin. It had its own coalition government but it was not until 1955 that it became a fully independent state again. Much has been written about Austria's complicity in the Third Reich and its citizens' enthusiasm for it. It's only been relatively recently that there's been something of an acceptance that perhaps Austria was not quite the victim of Nazism it painted itself to be after the war and was in fact far more complicit in the Nazi regime.

However, there was resistance to the Nazis in Austria – though certainly not on the scale seen in the countries of Occupied Europe. In this respect, I am indebted the impressive work of the Documentation Centre of Austrian Resistance based in Vienna. It is well worth a visit to its museum and also its website: www.doew. at/english

I do not usually detail the books I use for reference, not least because the list would run into many dozens. However, I make an exception here and recommend *The Austrian Resistance 1938-1945* (Edition Steinbauer, Vienna 2014). This book details what resistance there was in Austria, not least from the KPO and elements of the Catholic Church. Cardinal Innitzer (Chapter 5) was the primate of the Roman Catholic Church in Austria and did indeed incur the wrath of the Nazis with his famous 'Our Fuhrer is Christ – Christ is our Fuhrer' sermon in 1938. And though the character Sister Ursula is not based directly on her, there was a Franciscan nun called Sister Maria Restitua Kafka who was executed by the Nazis in Vienna in March 1943 for her anti-Nazi activities. She also was a nurse and was betrayed by a doctor at the hospital where she worked. Some 55 years after her execution she was beatified by the Vatican. It should also be said that the role of the Vatican was complicated in regards to its opposition to the Nazis. Many individual priests did work against them though. It's also well documented that the British Diplomatic Mission to the Vatican was actively involved in espionage.

Many people have helped me with different aspects of the research that went into *Vienna Spies*. I am most grateful to all of them and most especially to the refugees from Nazi Vienna who shared their painful experiences with me along with their first-hand knowledge of the city.

Once again, my thanks and love to my wife Sonia and our daughters Amy (and her partner Phil) and Nicole, our grandson Theo and my mother.

I remain indebted to my agent Gordon Wise of Curtis Brown for his encouragement, support and expertise. I also extend my sincere thanks and admiration to Rufus Purdy of my publishers, Studio 28. His enthusiasm for *Vienna Spies* and skill in helping to get it into its final state is much appreciated.

Alex Gerlis
London, January 2017

Vienna Spies

Also available

The Swiss Spy

Alex Gerlis's thrilling second novel

'On the 20-minute drive to Lutry, the Alps rose high to his left, the lake sweeping below him to the right. That summed it up, he thought: caught between two powerful forces. Not unlike serving two masters.'

It's not unusual for spies to have secrets, but Henry Hunter has more than most and after he's stopped by British Intelligence at Croydon airport on the eve of the Second World War, he finds he has even more. From Switzerland he embarks on a series of increasingly perilous missions into Nazi Germany, all the time having to cope with different identities and two competing masters. In March 1941 in Berlin, haunted by a dark episode from his past, he makes a fateful decision, resulting in a dramatic journey to the Swiss frontier with a shocking outcome. *The Swiss Spy* is set against the true-life backdrop of the top-secret Nazi plans to invade the Soviet Union. The story paints an authentic picture of life inside wartime Europe: the menacing atmosphere, the ever-present danger and the constant intrigue of the world of espionage.

Read an excerpt now:

Chapter 1: Croydon Airport, London, August 1939

A shade after 1.30 on the afternoon of Monday 14th August, 20 people emerged from the terminal building at Croydon Airport and were shepherded across a runway still damp from heavy overnight rain.

They were a somewhat disparate group, as international travellers tend to be. Some were British, some foreign; a few women, mostly men; the majority smartly dressed. One of the passengers was a man of average height and mildly chubby build. A closer look would show bright-green eyes that darted around, eager to take everything in and a nose that was bent slightly to the left. He had a mouth that seemed fixed at the beginnings of a smile, and the overall effect was of a younger face on an older body. Despite the heavy August sun, the man was wearing a long raincoat and a trilby hat pushed back on his head. In each hand he carried a large briefcase; one black, one light tan. Perhaps because of the burden of a coat and two cases, or possibly due to his natural disposition, he walked apart from the group. At one point he absent-mindedly veered towards a KLM airliner before a man in uniform directed him back towards the others.

A minute or so later the group assembled at the steps of a Swissair plane, alongside a board indicating its destination: 'Service 1075: Basle.' A queue formed as the passengers waited for tickets and passports to be checked.

When the man with the two briefcases presented his papers, the police officer responsible for checking looked through them with extra care before nodding in the direction of a tall man who had appeared behind the passenger. He was also wearing a trilby, although his had such a wide brim it wasn't possible to make out any features of his face.

The tall man stepped forward and impatiently snatched the passport from the police officer. He glanced at it briefly, as if he knew what to expect, then turned to the passenger.

'Would you come with me please, Herr Hesse?' It was more of an instruction than an invitation.

'What's the problem? Can't we sort whatever it is out here?'

'There may not be a problem sir, but it'd be best if you came with me. It will be much easier to talk inside.'

'But what if I miss my flight? It leaves in 20 minutes.'

The taller man said nothing but gestured towards a black Austin 7 that pulled up alongside them. By now the last passenger had boarded and the steps were being wheeled away from the aircraft. The short journey back to the terminal was conducted in silence. They entered the terminal through a side door and went up to an office on the second floor.

Herr Hesse followed the tall man into the small office, which was dominated by a large window overlooking the apron and the runway beyond it. The man took a seat behind the desk in front of the window and gestured to Hesse to sit on the other side .

'Sit down? But I'm going to miss my flight! What on earth is this all about? All my papers are in order. I insist on an explanation.'

The man pointed at the chair and Hesse reluctantly sat down, his head shaking as he did so. He removed his trilby and Hesse found himself staring at one of the most unremarkable faces he'd ever seen. It had the tanned complexion of someone who spent plenty of time outdoors and dark eyes with a penetrating stare, but otherwise there was nothing about it that was memorable. Hesse could have stared at it for hours and still had difficulty picking it out of a crowd. The man could have been anything from late-thirties to mid-fifties, and when he spoke it was in grammar-school tones, with perhaps the very slightest trace of a northern accent.

'My name is Edgar. Do you smoke?'

Hesse shook his head. Edgar took his time selecting a cigarette from the silver case he'd removed from his inside pocket and lighting it. He inspected the lit end of the cigarette, turning it carefully in his hand, admiring the glow and watching the patterns made by the wisps of smoke as they hung above the desk and drifted towards the ceiling. He appeared to be in no hurry. Behind him the Swissair plane was being pulled by a tractor in the direction of the runway. A silver Imperial Airways plane was descending sharply from the south, the sun bouncing off its wings.

Edgar sat in silence, looking carefully at the man in front of him before getting up to look out of the window for a full minute, timing it on his wristwatch. During that time he avoided thinking about the other man, keeping any picture or memory out of his mind. When the minute was up, he turned around and sat down. Without looking up, he wrote in his notebook:

Complexion: pale, almost unhealthy-looking, pasty.
Eyes: bright-green.
Hair: dark and thick, needs cutting.
Nose at a slight angle (left).
Smiles.

Build: slightly overweight.
Nervous, but sure of himself.

A colleague had taught him this technique. Too many of our first impressions of someone are casual ones, so much so that they bear little relation to how someone actually looks, he had told him. As a consequence we tend to end up describing someone in such general terms that important features tend to be disregarded. *Look at them for one minute, forget about them for one minute and then write down half a dozen things about them.*

A man who at first glance was distinctly ordinary-looking, who in other circumstances Edgar might pass in the street without noticing, now had characteristics that made him easier to recall.

You'll do.

'There are a number of things that puzzle me about you, Herr Hesse. Are you happy with me calling you Herr Hesse, by the way?' As Captain Edgar spoke he was looking at the man's Swiss passport, as if reading from it.

'Why wouldn't I be?' Hesse spoke with an impeccable English accent that had a hint of upper-class drawl.

'Well,' said Edgar, tapping the desk with the passport as he did so. 'That's one of a number of things about you that puzzles me. You're travelling under this Swiss passport in the name of Henri Hesse. But do you not also have a British passport in the name of Henry Hunter?'

The man hesitated before nodding. Edgar noticed he was perspiring.

'I'm sure you'd be more comfortable if you removed your hat and coat.'

There was another pause while Hesse got up to hang his hat and coat on the back of the door.

'So you accept you're also known as Henry Hunter?'

The man nodded again.

'Passport?'

'You have it there.'

'If I were in your position Herr Hesse, I think I'd adopt a more co-operative manner altogether. I mean your British passport: the one in the name of Henry Hunter.'

'What about it?'

'I should like to see it.'

Henry Hunter hesitated.

'For the avoidance of doubt, Herr Hesse, I should tell you I have the right to search every item in your possession: the British passport please?'

Henry lifted the tan briefcase on to his lap, angled it towards him and opened it just wide enough for one hand to reach in. He retrieved a thick manila envelope, from which he removed the passport and handed it to Edgar who spent a few minutes studying it.

'Henry Richard Hunter: born Surrey, 6th November, 1909; making you 29.'

'Correct.'

Edgar held up the Swiss passport in his left hand and the British passport in his right, and moved them up and down, as if trying to work out which were the heavier.

'Bit odd, isn't it? Two passports: different names, same person?'

'Possibly, but I very legitimately have two nationalities. I cannot see...'

'We can come to that in a moment. The first thing then that puzzles me about you is you have a perfectly valid British passport in the name of Henry Hunter, which you used to enter this country on the 1st August. But, two weeks later, you're trying to leave the country using an equally valid passport, but this time it's a Swiss one in a different name.'

There was a long silence. Through the window both men could see Swissair flight 1075 edge on to the runway. Edgar walked over to the window and gazed out at the aircraft before turning back to face Henry, raising his eyebrows as he did so.

'Any explanation?'

Henry shrugged. Edgar returned to the desk and reopened his notebook. He took a fountain pen from his pocket.

'We can return to the business of flights in a moment. Let's look again at your different names. What can you tell me about that?'

'Will I be able to get on the next flight? There's one to Geneva at three o'clock I think. It would be most inconvenient if I didn't get back to Switzerland today.'

'Let's see how we get on with the explanation you're about to give me, eh? You were telling me how you manage to have two nationalities and two names.'

Henry shrugged, as though he could not understand why this would require any explanation.

'Terribly straightforward, really. I was born here in Surrey as it happens, hence Henry Hunter and the British passport. My father died when I was 14 and a year or so later my mother met a Swiss man and married him fairly soon after. We moved to Switzerland, first to Zürich and then Geneva. When I was 18, I became a Swiss national, and for the purposes of that I used my stepfather's surname. In the process, Henry became Henri. So you see, there's really no mystery. I apologise if it turns out to have been in any way irregular as far as the British Government is concerned: I'd be happy to clear matters up at the British consulate in Geneva if that helps. Do you think I'll be able to make the three o'clock Geneva flight?'

'There are a few more questions, Mr Hunter. I'm sure you understand. What is your job?'

Henry shifted in his seat, clearly uncomfortable.

'I don't have a career as such. My stepfather was very wealthy and had property all over Switzerland. I travel around to check on them – keep the tenants happy and make sure they pay their rent on time, that kind of thing: nothing onerous. I also did some work with a travel agency and a bit of translation. I've managed to keep busy enough.'

Edgar spent a few minutes flicking through his notebook and the two passports. At one stage, he made some notes, as if copying something from one of the documents. He then consulted a map he'd removed from his jacket pocket.

'You said that your stepfather was very wealthy...'

'... He died a couple of years ago.'

'And where did you live?'

'Near Nyon, by the lake.'

Edgar nodded approvingly.

'But I see you now live in the centre of Geneva, on the Rue de

Valais?'

'That's right.'

'And how would you describe that area?'

'Pleasant enough.'

'Really? From what I remember of Geneva that's rather on the wrong side of the tracks. Overlooking the railway line are you?'

'To an extent, yes.'

'Well, either one is overlooking the railway line or one is not?'

'Yes, we do overlook it.'

'Sounds rather like a fall from grace. Wish to tell me about it?'

Edgar selected another cigarette and he had smoked most of it before Henry began to answer. He appeared to be distressed, his voice now much quieter.

'After my stepfather died, it transpired he had another family, in Luzern. Of course, with hindsight that explains why he spent so much time in Zürich on business; my mother never accompanied him on those trips. The family in Luzern, it turned out, were the only legitimate family as far as Swiss law is concerned and therefore had first claim on his estate. I don't fully understand why, but my mother's lawyer assures us there is nothing whatsoever we can do about it. The property by the lake near Nyon turned out to be rented and the various bank accounts my mother had access to were more or less empty. We quickly went from being very comfortable to very hard up: hence the flat by the railway line. We've only been able to survive as we have because my mother had some funds of her own, not very much, and her jewellery: fortunately there was quite a lot of that. She's had to sell most of it. I do as much freelance translation as possible at the international organisations, but work isn't easy to find at the moment. These are difficult times on the continent.'

'As one gathers. So the purpose of your visit back to England – to get away from it all?'

'Family business, friends. That type of thing.'

Edgar stood up and removed his jacket, draping it carefully over the back of his chair before walking to the front of the desk and sitting on it. His knees were just inches from the other man's face. When he spoke it was in a very quiet voice, as if there was someone else in the room he didn't want to hear.

'*Family business, friends. That type of thing...* What you need to know Mr Hunter is that we already know an awful lot about you. We have, as they say, been keeping something of an eye on you. It would save a good deal of time if you were to be honest with me. So please could you be more specific about the family business you mentioned?'

'You said "we". Who do you mean by "we"?'

Edgar leaned back, pointedly ignoring the question.

'You were going to tell me about your family business, Mr Hunter.'

'My aunt died in July. She was my late father's elder sister. I was attending her funeral.'

'My condolences. Were you close to her?'

'Not especially, but I was her closest living relative.'

'And you are a beneficiary of the will, no doubt?'

'Yes.'

'And how much did you inherit, Mr Hunter?'

The Swissair DC-3 was now beginning to taxi down the

runway. A tanker was turning around in front of the building, filling the room with the smell of fuel. Henry shifted in his chair.

'By the sounds of it, I suspect you probably already know the answer to that.'

Edgar had returned to his chair and leaned back in it so it tilted against the window. As he did so, he crossed his arms high on his chest, staring long and hard at Henry.

'What I'm curious about, Mr Hunter, is whether my answer is going to be the same as yours. How about if I endeavour to answer my own question and you stop me if I say anything incorrect?'

'Before you do, could I ask whether you are a police officer?'

'No.'

'If you're not a police officer, what authority do you have to question me like this?'

Edgar laughed, as if he found Henry's remark to be genuinely amusing.

'Mr Hunter. When you find out on what authority I operate you will very much regret asking that question. So, shall I tell you my version of why I think you came over here?'

Henry loosened his tie and turned around in his chair, looking longingly at the door, as if he were hoping someone would come in and explain the whole business had been a terrible misunderstanding.

'Louise Alice Hunter was, as you correctly say, your late father's elder sister and you were indeed her only surviving relative.' Edgar had now opened his notebook and was referring to it as he spoke. 'She was 82 years of age and had been a resident in the Green Lawns Residential Home near Buckingham for nine years. The matron of the home informs us that you dutifully came over to visit her once a year. You visited her last November and then again in May, shortly before she died. On each of those visits you were accompanied by her solicitor. Am I correct so far?'

Henry said nothing.

'I shall assume then that you will point out if anything I say is incorrect. Your aunt died on the 24th July and you flew here on the 1st August, which was a Tuesday, if I am correct. You travelled straight to Buckinghamshire, where the funeral took place last Thursday, which would have been the 9th. So far, nothing remarkable, eh?'

Henry nodded.

'But this is where an otherwise very ordinary story does become somewhat less ordinary: sordid, perhaps. I am now relying on a statement kindly provided by a Mr Martin Hart, who, as you're aware, is your aunt's solicitor and the man who accompanied you on your last visits to your aunt. According to Mr Hart, your aunt's estate amounted to a not insubstantial eight thousand pounds, all of which was held in a deposit account administered by Mr Hart. You are indeed a beneficiary of that will; the main beneficiary most certainly, but – crucially – not the sole beneficiary. There were bequests totalling some one thousand pounds to various friends, staff and charities, but after Mr Hart had deducted fees due to him and duty was paid to Exchequer, you would expect to receive a sum of just under six thousand pounds: certainly a handsome sum. Does this sound correct to you?'

'If you say so. You do seem to know a good deal more than I do.'

'But there's a small problem, from your point of view. That money could only be passed to you once probate was granted, which could take many months, perhaps even up to a year. We've already established you and your mother have serious financial problems. Your inheritance would restore you to a position of financial security. You would once again be wealthy. However, waiting for probate is bad enough, but with the very likely – some would say imminent – possibility of war, you had a quite understandable concern that you may not be able to get that money out of England and into Switzerland for quite a long time. I...'

'... You're making a number of assumptions here, Edgar. What makes you think I've done anything improper? I...'

'Mr Hunter, who said anything about doing anything improper? I certainly didn't. But, as you raise the subject, let me tell you what the most obliging Mr Hart has told us. According to him, he was prevailed upon by you to cut a few corners, as he put it, and to ensure the entire funds of the deposit account were released straight away. This is not only improper, it is also illegal.'

Henry shifted in his chair and pulled a large handkerchief from a trouser pocket to mop his brow. Edgar had now removed a pair of reading glasses from a crocodile-skin case and, after polishing them for longer than necessary, he began to read from a document he'd extracted from the desk drawer.

'According to the best legal advice available to me, there's no question that both Mr Hart and you committed a crime, namely conspiracy to defraud. My learned friends tell me that on the evidence they've seen, a conviction would be extremely likely and a term of imprisonment would almost certainly ensue. They say there is ample *prima face* evidence to show you have conspired to defraud His Majesty's Exchequer of the duties owed to it from your great aunt's estate and you had conspired to prevent the other beneficiaries of the will from receiving the money bequeathed to them. Fraud, Mr Hunter, is a most serious criminal offence. Confronted with our evidence Mr Hart has, as I say, been most co-operative. He claims that due to a health issue, as he describes it, he allowed himself to be persuaded against his better judgement to release the funds. He admits he received a much larger fee than he would ordinarily have expected. Apparently...'

'It's not as bad as it sounds, I have to tell you.' Edgar was taken aback by how forceful Henry was sounding. 'I told Hart that if I was able to take the money to Switzerland while I could, then I'd be in a position to return the money owed to the exchequer and the other beneficiaries very soon, certainly before probate would ordinarily have been granted.'

'Really? I think you and Mr Hart cooked up a somewhat clever scheme whereby you were counting on war being declared. Mr Hart believed that, in those circumstances, he could apply to be granted a stay of probate until such a time as you were in a position to claim. In other words, Mr Hunter, he would use the war as an excuse: pretend to keep the money in the deposit account until after the war, whenever that is. Except, of course, the money would not be in the deposit account, it would be with you in Switzerland. Apparently, he – you – may well have got away with it had not the matron at the home overheard some conversation about it between yourself and Mr Hart, and contacted the police.'

'It would all have been paid back, I promise you. Once I deposited it in Switzerland, I would have transferred what I owed back. It seemed easier to send the money back from Switzerland rather than wait for probate then have it transferred from London.'

'Really? All we need to do now is find the money, eh Hunter? Do you want me to hazard a guess as to where it could be?'

Henry sat very still and stared across the airport as Edgar stood up and walked around the desk. Once in front of Henry he bent down to pick up the two leather briefcases and placed them both on the desk.

'Keys?'

Without saying anything or diverting his gaze from the runway, Henry reached into the inside pocket of his jacket and produced a set of keys, which he handed to Edgar.

It took Edgar a full 20 minutes to remove all the bundles of banknotes from the two briefcases, assembling the different denominations in separate piles. Not a word was exchanged during this process, which Henry watched with some interest, as if he had never seen so much money before. By the time Edgar had finished, there were four piles: one comprised the bundles of ten shilling notes, another the one pound notes, then five pound notes and ten pound notes. The pile of the large, white fives was by far the largest.

Edgar stepped back from the desk and stood beside Henry. The entire surface of the desk was covered in money.

'I've only of course been able to do an approximate count, but I'd say that there's seven thousand pounds there. Would that be correct, Mr Hunter?'

'More or less. I think you'll find it's more like six thousand, eight hundred pounds. Mr Hart claimed rather late in the day he needed another two hundred pounds – for expenses, apparently.'

'Two hundred pounds doesn't seem to me to be very much considering the impact this is likely to have on his professional career.'

'It's all been rather rushed, Edgar. As it was such a large sum of cash we had to withdraw it from a main branch of the Midland Bank in the city. We were only able to get hold of it this morning.'

'Yes, I'm aware of all that Mr Hunter.' Edgar was still standing next to Henry, with a hand on his shoulder. 'In a moment some colleagues of mine are going to come and take you away. I shall look after the money and all your possessions. We shall meet again in a few days.'

***

A few minutes later, Henry Hunter had been escorted from the airport in handcuffs by three uniformed police officers. In the office overlooking the runway, Edgar removed his tie, lit another cigarette and dialled a London number from the telephone nestling between the bundles of banknotes on the desk.

'It's Edgar.'

'I thought it might be you. How did it go?'

'Very much according to plan.'

'Good. We're on then?'

'Yes. Indeed. We're on, as you put it Porter.'

'And what's he like?'

'Rather as we were expecting. Not altogether the most

agreeable of types, but then that's hardly a disqualification in our line of work, is it?'

'Too true… and, um, any hint at all of… you know?'

'No, none whatsoever. He was rather impressive in that respect, I must say. Had one not been aware, one would really have had no idea at all.'

'Splendid. What now?'

'I think he needs a few days on his own. It ought to be easy enough after that.'

To buy *The Swiss Spy*, visit www.studio-28.co.uk

CPSIA information can be obtained
at www.ICGtesting.com
Printed in the USA
LVHW05s0752280918
591585LV00013BA/1012/P